VERSIONS OF BLACKNESS

Aphra Behn's short novel *Oroonoko* (1688) is one of the most widely studied works of seventeenth-century literature, because of its powerful representation of slavery and complex portrayal of ways in which differing races and cultures – European, Black African, and Native American – observe and misinterpret each other. This volume presents a new edition of *Oroonoko*, with unprecedentedly full and informative commentary, along with complete texts of three major British seventeenth-century works concerned with race and colonialism: Henry Neville's *The Isle of Pines* (1668), Behn's *Abdelazer* (1676), and Thomas Southerne's tragedy *Oroonoko* (1696). It combines these with a rich anthology of European discussions of slavery, racial difference, and colonial conquest, from the mid-sixteenth century to the time of Behn's death. Many are taken from important works that have not hitherto been easily available, and the collection offers an unrivaled resource for studying the culture which produced Britain's first major fictions of slavery.

Derek Hughes is a Professor of English at the University of Aberdeen, and formerly held a chair at the University of Warwick. He has published widely on Restoration literature in journals such as *ELH*, *Essays in Criticism*, and *Philological Quarterly*, and is internationally recognized as a leading authority on Restoration Drama. His books include *English Drama, 1660–1700* (1996), and *The Theatre of Aphra Behn* (2001). With Janet Todd, he edited the *Cambridge Companion to Aphra Behn* (2004). He is currently completing a monograph on the representation of human sacrifice in literature, which reflects extensive research into early European contacts with America.

T0381933

VERSIONS

OF

BLACKNESS

Key Texts on Slavery from the
Seventeenth Century

DEREK HUGHES

University of Aberdeen

CAMBRIDGE
UNIVERSITY PRESS

32 Avenue of the Americas, New York NY 10013-2473, USA

Cambridge University Press is part of the University of Cambridge.

It furthers the University's mission by disseminating knowledge in the pursuit of
education, learning and research at the highest international levels of excellence.

www.cambridge.org
Information on this title: www.cambridge.org/9780521689564

First published 2007

A catalogue record for this publication is available from the British Library

Library of Congress Cataloguing in Publication data
Versions of Blackness : key texts on slavery from the seventeenth century / [edited by]
Derek Hughes.
p. cm.
Includes bibliographical references and index.
ISBN-13: 978-0-521-86930-0
ISBN-10: 0-521-86930-7
ISBN-13: 978-0-521-68956-4 (pbk.)
ISBN-10: 0-521-68956-2 (pbk.)
1. English literature – 17th century. 2. Slavery – Literary collections.
I. Hughes, Derek, 1944– II. Neville, Henry, 1620–1694. Isle of pines.
III. Behn, Aphra, 1640–1689. Abdelazer. IV. Behn, Aphra, 1640–1689. Oroonoko.
V. Southerne, Thomas, 1660–1746. Oroonoko. VI. Title.
PR1127.V47 2007
820.803552 – dc22   2006028389

ISBN 978-0-521-86930-0 Hardback
ISBN 978-0-521-68956-4 Paperback

Contents

DISCUSSIONS OF COLONIALISM

Introduction

THE PRINCIPAL WORKS in this collection are Henry Neville's *The Isle of Pines* (1668); Aphra Behn's only tragedy, *Abdelazer* (1676), and her best-known work of prose fiction, *Oroonoko* (1688); and Thomas Southerne's dramatic adaptation of *Oroonoko* (1696). *The Isle of Pines* is about an Englishman, shipwrecked on an uninhabited island with four women, one of whom is black; in the final version, printed here, his multitudinous descendants – by all four women – encounter some Dutch visitors. *Abdelazer* is the story of a captive Moorish prince who gains power and high office in the Spanish court and, after many villainies – including regicide and adultery with the Queen – is eventually outsmarted and destroyed. The two versions of *Oroonoko* tell of a nobler African prince, betrayed into a worse captivity – slavery in the British colony of Surinam – and destroyed by his attempts to gain liberty. The contextual material illustrates a range of attitudes toward slavery, colonialism, black Africans, and Native Americans from the mid-sixteenth to the late seventeenth centuries. My aim has been to situate Neville, Behn, and Southerne in contexts that might have influenced them, rather than to see them as leading toward the late eighteenth century, when the mentality of imperialism was quite different and when the debate about slavery had assumed a character almost undreamed of in Behn's time.

THE ISLE OF PINES

Henry Neville (1620–94) was a republican politician and theorist, who (along with Henry Marten, who is mentioned in *Oroonoko*) opposed Cromwell's quasi-monarchical rule. His chief works are his translation of the works of Machiavelli (1675) and his republican tract *Plato Redivivus* (1681). In its first version, *The Isle of Pines* is the brief autobiographical narrative of an Englishman, George Pines. In 1589, he and four women are the sole survivors of a shipwreck and are cast away on an uninhabited island in the Indian Ocean. Pines sleeps with all four women, fathering 47 children, and by the end of an idle and otherwise unproductive life is surrounded by 1,789 descendants. Later in 1668, Neville published a sequel, set in the present, in which Pines' descendants are discovered by some Dutch visitors. In the final version, also published in 1668, the versions are merged, so that the later events frame the first, as the Dutch visitors are presented with George Pines' narrative.

This is an elusive and playful work, in which real-life parallels and applications are hinted at while remaining perhaps deliberately incomplete. As an example, we might take the four distinct peoples whom Pines sires, each with names derived from that of the founding mother. One tribe, descended from the daughter of Pines' employer, is the English. Another is the Trevors: Trevor is a distinctively Welsh name. But what of the other two tribes, the Sparks and the rebellious, trouble-making Phills (the latter descended from the black servant Philippa, who did not have a surname)? Do they correspond to the Scots and the Irish? Neither name belongs uniquely to that nation, and a genuine Irishman, Dermot Conelly, turns up at the end of the story, further spoiling any exact parallelism. Nevertheless, one cannot ignore the suggestiveness of the name "English." It seems that Neville here is suggesting an analogy, without pushing it to the point where it possesses and restricts the meaning of the work. Pines' island is a partial microcosm of some aspects of Britain.

It is perhaps best to approach the work through the intellectual traditions with which it plays. One, which figures prominently in this selection, is primitivism: a glorification of the primitive life, as being uncorrupted by the artifice and oppression of civilization, and a belief that primitive peoples, like the earliest human beings in classical myth, lived in a Golden Age where there was no violence, fraud, or need to labor. Sometimes associated with the tradition of primitivism is libertinism: the view that social and moral restrictions upon sexual freedom are artificial and repressive inventions of priests and lawgivers and that it is healthy to cast them off and recover humanity's primitive sexual freedom. Libertinism drew some nourishment from a growing sense of cultural relativism: an awareness of the immense ways in which cultures could differ in their moral and sexual values and a consequent belief that there were no absolute standards in these matters, for they were arbitrary matters of custom. Such beliefs were, of course, minority, heterodox beliefs in a predominantly Christian culture, but they had their adherents, particularly in the avant-garde milieu of the Restoration theater.

In its original form, *The Isle of Pines* portrays a return to a sexual golden age of boundless pleasure and fulfillment, in which the artificial sexual restraints of civilization are cast aside. George Pines finds that sexual inhibitions are mere conventions, created by custom and – equally – abolished by it: "custome taking away shame (there being none but us) we did it more openly, as our Lusts gave us liberty" (p. 14). He overcomes his initial reluctance to sleep with the black servant woman, though he can only ever do so in the dark; this behavior is presented as a personal and not fully explicable idiosyncrasy. Nevertheless, it is undeniable that the future trouble-makers, John and Henry Phill, are descended from the black servant.

Yet even in this version, paradise is not entirely regained: "This place," George Pines writes "(had it the culture that skilful people might bestow on it) would prove a Paradise." Paradise requires the improvement and management of nature, for which two things are necessary: symbolic systems and cutting implements. The one axe that George Pines possessed quickly became blunt and was cast aside. The palace of his descendant William Pines is therefore made of "unhewn" timber; with their "cutting instruments," however, the Dutch are able to build him a respectable palace. Cutting – the control and modification of nature with the knife – was to be one of the distinctive hallmarks of culture in *Oroonoko*, though one in which culture can easily turn against itself, as in the final dismemberment of the hero.

The Dutch also differ from the stranded British in their use of numbers. They measure the island and chart its position. For George Pines, numbering is chiefly confined to the counting of his offspring. He has been a bookkeeper – a keeper of accounts – but without blades he cannot directly manipulate the world that he regiments in his ledgers. He can only multiply. In Neville, the distinction between the mathematics and technology of the Dutch and of Pines' descendants is made clearly, but it is stated rather than developed. Later, Behn was to explore in detail the interaction between humanity's capacities for violence and for constructing symbolic systems, between cutting and counting. This interaction culminates in the quartering of Oroonoko's body.

When the Dutch arrive on the island, they are in the position of sophisticated Europeans confronting ingenuous and virtually naked primitives. They observe the natives' burial rituals – and also their Bible readings – like explorers observing the ceremonies of exotic tribes, which is, indeed, exactly what they are doing. Yet, the work also exhibits something that characterizes all the major texts in this collection: a reversal of roles between the cultured and the primitive. In part, we see the Englishman reduced to the role of the naïve primitive, but we also see familiar English cultural practices (Bible reading, monarchy) displaced into an alien context. Readers are thus distanced from the everyday values of their culture and invited to question their absolute value.

If George Pines is in a libertine's sexual paradise, he is also in the position of Adam: As the only man in the world, he is the sole progenitor of a future race. This brings us to another theoretical context. One way of defending the Stuart monarchy was to argue that Adam had exercised monarchic authority over his descendants and that kings inherit his authority: this argument was, for example, advanced by John Maxwell and Sir Robert Filmer, Filmer's work being confuted by John Locke in his *Two Treatises of Government* (excerpted in this collection). In the final version, the island community starts as a libertine sexual paradise, but turns into a realization of Stuart monarchic theory. The allusion to the Stuarts is accentuated by one of Neville's fleeting and incomplete analogies, for William Pines, the king, is rather suggestive of Charles II, who was celebrated for his ease and familiarity of manner: "though he had nothing of majesty in him, yet he had a courteous, noble and debonair spirit." The patriarchal monarchy is, however, seen through the eyes of skeptical Dutchmen, who view it as a cultural oddity. For Holland was at this time a republic.

George Pines' story starts in 1589, at the height of England's glory. This was the year after the defeat of the Spanish Armada, and it saw the publication of that great expression of the expansionist spirit, the first edition of Richard Hakluyt's *The Principall Navigations, Voiages and Discoueries of the English Nation*. The name of the Isle of Pines also evokes Elizabethan glories, for it was the name of Sir Francis Drake's base during his raids on the Spaniards in Central America (one of which is commemorated in the extract from Davenant's *The History of Sir Francis Drake*). In contrast, the year 1668, when the tale was published and where it concludes, had quite different connotations. Coincidentally, it was the year toward which Behn's *Oroonoko* gloomily points: the year after naval humiliation by the Dutch and the year in which the Dutch took possession of Surinam. George Pines sets out in the dawn of England's colonial expansion and spends his life idly copulating.

The primitive, first-generation paradise cannot be sustained. Its increasing population and resulting tensions necessitate strict government, and it may at first sight seem that the evolution into a Filmerian monarchy is inevitable. The visit of the Dutch to Calicut, however, presents us with a society whose social structure is quite different. It is different because it is derived from a differently constructed sexual morality, in which other men are permitted to sleep with the king's wives, thus making patriarchal inheritance infeasible. Patriarchy is not a universal principle; it is a local custom. Like other works in this collection, but more single-mindedly, this work uses the exotic to defamiliarize and criticize life back home.

The Isle of Pines is the island where George Pines copulates, but is the name Pines therefore – as has been suggested – a deliberate anagram of "penis"? Probably not. For one thing, seventeenth-century anagrams tend to be more elaborately blatant, as is demonstrated by the title of a 1653 pamphlet attacking the Leveller John Lilburne: *John Lilburne. Anagram. O! J. burn in hell.* There is not much rich implicitness here. More importantly, *penis* was not then the colloquially common word that psychoanalysis and school biology lessons have made it. The same goes for *anus*: Both words were Latinate rarities. In Thomas Shadwell's play *The Virtuoso* (1676), *anus* is a word used by a verbose, jargon-ridden scientist, and *penis* is used in the same sort of way in Thomas Middleton's play *Anything for a Quiet Life.*[1] *The Isle of Pines* is many things, but it is not a piece of twentieth-century schoolboy humor.

SEVENTEENTH-CENTURY CONCEPTIONS OF RACE

Aphra Behn (1640–89) was one of the most remarkable writers of the late seventeenth century. She was the first British woman to earn her living as a creative writer. One might expect that her unprecedented role made her a rather fragile and marginal figure, and she certainly encountered some prejudice against women writers – or, more specifically, against a woman writer who dared to write about sex. She also, however, enjoyed supportive friendships with a number of male writers, and during her period of literary activity (from 1670 until her death in 1689) she had significantly more new plays staged than any male playwright. In the years after 1682, when there was a serious slump in the demand for new plays, she diversified prodigally into poetry, translation, and – most fruitfully – prose fiction: *Love Letters Between a Nobleman and his Sister* (1684–87) is generally regarded as the first English novel. *Oroonoko* (1688) is the best known of a number of boldly

---

[1] Marjorie Hope Nicolson and David Rodes, eds., *The Virtuoso* (Lincoln: University of Nebraska Press, 1966), 2.3.194, 3.3.1; Thomas Middleton *Anything for a Quiet Life* (London, 1662), sig. D2.

experimental works of short realistic fiction that she produced toward the end of her life. *Abdelazer*, Behn's only tragedy, dates from an earlier period of her career, being the fourth of her plays to reach the stage. It is based on an early seventeenth-century play, *Lust's Dominion*, but it alters significantly the treatment of race in its source. It also, however, resembles a slightly earlier Restoration tragedy, Elkanah Settle's *The Empress of Morocco* (1673), which also features a monstrous, adulterous Queen Mother who arranges the murder of her own son.

Thomas Southerne (1659–1746) is less well remembered today, though his comedy *The Wives Excuse* (1691), unsuccessful in its own day, was revived with great success at Stratford in 1994. Three of his works are indebted to Behn's prose fiction, and he was like Behn an experimenter, especially in comedy: With its tenuous plot, inconsequentialities of conversation, and abrupt shifts of perspective, *The Wives Excuse* anticipates Chekhov. *Oroonoko* followed another Behn-based tragedy by Southerne, *The Fatal Marriage; or, The Innocent Adultery* (1694), which was a sentimentaliza-tion of Behn's cynical short story, *The History of the Nun* (1689), about an inadvertently bigamous ex-nun who (in the original) murders both her husbands.[2]

The principal works in this collection thus all portray black characters in conflict with – and generally destroyed by – white Europeans. All portray the alien with open-minded imaginativeness, and all treat the contrasts between alien and European as unstable, complex, and reversible; for both Behn and Southerne, moreover, the defining quality of the protagonist is his rank, not his ethnic origin. Thus, none of these works uses rigid and essentialist ideas of what came to be called "race." Although they portray the African with direct interest, however, they also use him as a means of exploring problems closer to home; the alien may be the familiar in an unfamiliar guise.

The definition of race with which we are familiar postulates hereditary differences of ability and moral character between ethnic groups of human-ity defined in quasi-scientific terms, terms that came to be influenced by Darwinian evolutionism. In the sixteenth and seventeenth centuries, the intellectual foundations of this pseudo-science had not been established, and *race* primarily meant family, genealogy, or nation[3]: When the heroine

---

[2] Southerne's other debt to Behn is in his comedy *Sir Anthony Love* (1690), which borrows from *The Lucky Mistake* (1689). In addition, the combination of comic and tragic plots in *Oroonoko* may owe something to *The Widdow Ranter* (1689), which similarly juxtaposes a male rebel with a feisty, transgressive woman.

[3] See Nicholas Hudson, "From 'Nation' to 'Race'," *Eighteenth-Century Studies*, 29 (1996), 247–66.

of Aphra Behn's *The Young King* expresses hatred for the entire "Race" of the Scythians, she is not making a racist remark, but rather is expressing hatred for the nation whose king killed her father (and whose prince she eventually marries having overcome her aversion).[4] John Ogilby's vast compilation *Africa* (1670) shows little attempt at racial generalization: It is an atomistic description of many different communities with many different characteristics. At a local level, it does show belief in tribal characteristics, but does not ascend from the characteristics of particular tribes to more general characteristics of "race": There is no hierarchical tree that rises from species, to genus, to family, and so on.

Yet, as some of the extracts in Part Two show, attempts to establish an intellectual rationale of racial inferiority began very early. In the 1540s the Spanish scholar Juan Ginés de Sepúlveda argued that the Native Americans were less than men (*homunculi*) because of their barbarous practices and their lack of courage. In 1550 Sepúlveda disputed at the University of Valladolid against Bartolomé de Las Casas, a pioneering polemicist against Spanish atrocities in the New World, and it was Las Casas who won the disputation; Sepúlveda was denied permission to publish his views. A later argument against the inferiority of alien peoples appears in the extracted passage from the Jesuit missionary from Peru, José de Acosta, who argues that seemingly innate differences of race are purely the product of education: If a black African had the education of a European nobleman, he would be his equal, and vice versa. The lot of the Native Americans under Spanish rule remained intolerable, but it was Las Casas and Acosta who influenced the outlook of King Philip II; Sepúlveda died in obscurity, despite being the king's former tutor.

The inferiority of non-white peoples was, therefore, being asserted, and belief in it certainly informed the actions of colonial conquerors and slave traders. Rabid hatred of black men informs the play that Behn was to adapt as *Abdelazer, Lust's Dominion*,[5] which shows a vigorous contempt for its black-skinned, sexually voracious, and treacherously violent protagonist. The King of Spain proposes that

> It shall be death for any Negroes hand,
> To touch the beauty of a Spanish dame.[6]

---

[4] Janet Todd, ed., *The Works of Aphra Behn*, 7 vols. (London: Pickering & Chatto, 1992–96), VII, 4.5.23. All citations to Behn's works are to this edition.

[5] *Lust's Dominion* was first published in 1657, when it was wrongly attributed to Marlowe. It is generally, though not conclusively, identified with *The Spanish Moor's Tragedy*, written in 1600 by Dekker and others, but not published at the time.

[6] Fredson Bowers, ed., *The Dramatic Works of Thomas Dekker*, 4 vols. (Cambridge: Cambridge University Press, 1953-61), IV, III.3.ii.2.48–49.

And, after the villain's just downfall, all Negroes are banished from Spain (Elizabeth I twice tried to expel black Africans from Britain). As we shall see, Behn radically altered her source.

Although a practical contempt for alien races was widespread, it had not generated an elaborate superstructure of ideology, and the qualities of the black- and brown-skinned peoples were a constant source of debate. At the other extreme from Sepúlveda is Montaigne's complex and partially idealizing view of the Native Americans and (under the influence of Las Casas) his denunciation of European barbarities in the New World. In *The Negro's & Indians Advocate* (1680), the Englishman Morgan Godwyn deplores white men's mistreatment of their slaves and their refusal to instruct them in Christianity. In the course of his argument, he describes the theoretical arguments with which English colonists justified their practical racism: that black Africans were descendants not of Adam but of an earlier man, or that they belonged to the "race" of Cain or of Cham, the son of Noah, who spied upon his father's nakedness and whose line was cursed (in perpetuity, it was argued) with servitude. Godwyn also seems aware of the dispute between Las Casas and Sepúlveda, but he reports racist theories as exotic curiosities, whose currency will barely be credible to his English readership. Nevertheless, Godwyn stops short of denouncing slavery itself. Slaves, he asserts, should be baptized and treated kindly; they will then be better slaves. In *Friendly Advice to the Gentlemen Planters of the East and West Indies* (1684), Thomas Tryon similarly denounces the mistreatment of black slaves and the belief in their inferiority, without arguing against slavery itself.

In looking at works such as Behn's *Oroonoko*, therefore, we should be aware that attitudes could be combined in ways that are impossible today. Defenders of black Africans could accept slavery (the first known condemnation of slavery is the Germantown Protest, signed in Pennsylvania by four German Quakers in 1688 – coincidentally, the year of publication of Behn's *Oroonoko* – but unpublished and unknown for nearly two centuries). Equally, race was not the primary justification for slavery; rather, it was non-Christianity. English colonists refused baptism to slaves because they feared that it would liberate them. In encouraging the baptism of slaves, therefore, North American lawgivers assured slave owners that baptism did not constitute manumission.[7] A Virginia law of 1748, however, admits that it is illegal to enslave a free man who is already a Christian.[8] It

---

[7] See, e.g., J. P., *A Complete Collection of All the Laws of Virginia now in Force* (London, 1684), 155.
[8] *The Acts of Assembly Now in Force, in the Colony of Virginia* (Williamsburg, 1752), 285.

is worth bearing this in mind, for Behn's *Oroonoko* pays far more attention to differences and prejudices of religion than it does to those of race.

Conceptually, the master-slave relationship was not yet fixed as that of white European and black African. Africans sold captives, debtors, and criminals into slavery, and until 1600 the west African export of slaves across the Sahara exceeded that across the Atlantic.[9] Native Americans used captured black Africans as slaves,[10] and white men could also be enslaved: Most of the books about slavery published in the seventeenth century relate to European enslavement in Islamic countries.[11] Royalist prisoners of war were sent from England to Barbados as forced labour in the 1650s, and British prisoners of war were sent to the galleys by the French. Behn follows common practice in referring to the white indentured servants in Surinam as "slaves." Thus, although in the seventeenth century there is a clear relationship in practice and in prejudice between slavery and racial difference, it is not the uniquely defining relationship; religious difference was the primary rationalization. Moreover, plantation owners (such as Richard Ligon, whose work is represented here) could deplore inhumanity to black slaves while coolly setting out the economics of a plantation and costing out the descending quantities and qualities of food and clothing allowable to overseers, servants, and slaves. The ambiguities of *Abdelazer* and the two *Oroonoko*s thus operate within a range of possible intellectual combinations that is not easily reproduced today.

Behn's work is also conditioned by literary conventions whose full range is not widely appreciated. This is particularly true of her treatment of sexual relations between Europeans and non-Europeans, and here there has been a tendency to read the outlook of seventeenth-century London in the light of attitudes current in other places and later periods.

Increasingly, the American provinces legislated against marriage or procreation by mixed-raced couples. A 1715 Maryland law referred to "unnatural and inordinate Copulation,"[12] but the attempt was initially to prevent

---

[9] Herbert S. Klein, *The Atlantic Slave Trade* (Cambridge: Cambridge University Press, 1999), 56.

[10] "In the Islands of S. *Vincent* and *Dominico* there are some *Caribbians* who have many *Negroes* to their Slaves, as the *Spaniards* and some other Nations have; some of them they got from the *English* Plantations, and some from *Spanish* Ships heretofore cast away on their Coasts" (Charles de Rochefort, *The History of the Caribby-Islands* [1658], trans. John Davies of Kidwelly (London, 1666), 295).

[11] For a study of white captivity, see Linda Colley, *Captives* (London: Jonathan Cape, 2002), and Abbot Emmerson Smith, *Colonists in Bondage: White Servitude and Convict Labor in America, 1607–1776* (Chapel Hill: North Carolina University Press, 1947).

[12] *A Compleat Collection of the Laws of Maryland* (Annapolis, 1727), 112. Cf. Nicholas Trott, ed., *The Laws of the Province of South-Carolina*, 2 vols. (Charles-Town, 1736), 318.

anomalous combinations of free and servile, rather than to prevent racial degeneration. An act recorded in the 1684 edition of the laws of Virginia (but not in the 1662 *The Lawes of Virginia now in Force*) makes the stipulation, usual in English territories, that all Children "shall be held Bond or Free according to the condition of the Mother" and adds that "if any Christian shall commit Fornication with a *Negro Man* or *Woman*, he or she so offending, shall pay double the Fines imposed on Fornication by the former Act."[13] This is, to be sure, discrimination, but it does not reflect horror at the contamination of the racial blood-line. Things were to get far worse:

> In 1785, the revolutionary generation defined a black person as anyone with a black parent or grandparent, thus conferring whiteness on whomever was less than one-quarter black. Virginia changed the law 125 years later to define as "Negro," as the term then was used, anyone who was at least one-sixteenth black. In 1930, Virginia adopted the notorious "one-drop" law – defining as black anyone with one drop of African blood, however that might have been determined.[14]

This is not to suggest, absurdly, that the lot of the black American was better in 1684 than in 1930. It is rather to suggest that the oppressions of the seventeenth century were driven by imperatives and anxieties that are not the same as those of more recent times and that it is a mistake to read the earlier period entirely in the light of the later one. *Abdelazer* and Southerne's *Oroonoko* both portray a sexual relationship (marriage, in both) between a black man and a white woman. Behn's *The Widdow Ranter* (not included in this volume) portrays an unconsummated romance between an Englishman and a Native American queen. Behn's Imoinda is desired by her white captors, and some scholars have (unnecessarily) postulated an unspoken relationship between Behn's Oroonoko and her female narrator. Much ink has been spilt on an assumed fear of "miscegenation" in Behn's work.

---

[13] *A Complete Collection of All the Laws of Virginia* (1684), 111. Du Tertre, who deplores the sexual abuse of slaves, records that in French territories the status of the child followed that of the father, who was obliged to maintain any illegitimate child until he or she reached the age of twelve (Jean-Baptiste Du Tertre, *Histoire générale des Antilles habitées par les François*, 4 vols. [Paris, 1667–71], I, 512–13).
[14] Gary B. Nash, "The Hidden History of Mestizo America," in *Sex, Love, Race: Crossing Boundaries in North American History*, ed. Martha Hodes, 10–32 (New York and London: New York University Press, 1999).

This is particularly inappropriate with *The Widdow Ranter*. At the height
of the legislation against mixed-race marriages, in 1920, only five states prohibited marriages between whites and Native Americans, as against thirty
prohibiting marriages between whites and African-Americans,[15] and there
was a wide spectrum of attitudes in Behn's time. It was at first French policy at the highest level to encourage intermarriage. According to Charles
de Rochefort, "Nay, there are some handsom Maids and Women amongst
the Savage *Caribbians*, witness *Madamoiselle de Rosselan*, wife to the Governour of *Saintalousia*."[16] In 1671, John Ogilby approvingly retold the story
of Pocahontas.[17] The half–Native American son of Thomas Warner, the
first British settler of Saint Kitts, was made governor of Dominica by Lord
Willoughby. In addition, racial anxieties were not a constant, but varied
according to the ratio of slaves and masters in the colonies: They were
strong in Barbados, where the slave population quickly exceeded that of
the British, and less so in Carolina. We thus cannot assume that the racial
attitudes evoked in the transient illusions of the London stage corresponded
to those of remote Barbados or the still remoter Virginia of 1785 or 1930.
Far more palpable and immediate were the attitudes of heroic romance.

HEROIC ROMANCE

The ancient Greek novel *The Ethiopian Story*, by Heliodorus (4th century CE), tells of the love of the Greek hero Theagenes and the Ethiopian
princess Chariclea. Chariclea's parents are black, but she is born white
because her mother had been looking at a portrait of Andromeda (an earlier white Ethiopian princess) at the moment of conception. Fearing her
husband's suspicion, her mother abandoned her at birth. After many separations and adventures, including capture by pirates, enslavement, and near
human sacrifice, the lovers are eventually married.

Heliodorus' novel initiates a long tradition of interracial heroic romance.
Chariclea is the model for the white Ethiopian warrior princess Clorinda
in Tasso's epic poem *Jerusalem Delivered* (1580), who is loved, mortally
wounded, and baptized at the point of death by the crusader Tancredi. It is
a symptom of the diverse constructions that different cultures can place on

---

[15] Peter M. Rinaldo, *Marrying the Natives: Love and Interracial Marriage* (DorPete Press: Briarcliff Manor, NY, 1996), 26.

[16] *The History of the Caribby-Islands* [1658], trans. John Davies of Kidwelly (London, 1666), 252. Louis de Kerengoan, sieur de Rosselan, was governor of St Lucia from 1650 until his death in 1654.

[17] *America* (London, 1671), 201–05.

interracial romance that this love has nothing whatsoever to do with miscegenation: It is an allegory of Rome's relationship with the Coptic church.[18] Chariclea is reworked yet again as the white Ethiopian princess Candace in La Calprenède's romance *Cleopatra*: She is white on this occasion because of repeated intermarriage – miscegenation – between Ethiopian kings and white women.[19] *Cleopatra* was much plundered by Restoration dramatists (Behn took one of the plots of her first play, *The Young King*, from it), and its main story reads as a simple romantic analogue to *Oroonoko*: Juba, a North African prince, becomes a slave in Rome after the defeat of his kingdom and is given a Roman name – Coriolanus – by Julius Caesar. After many separations, he is united with his true love, Cleopatra's daughter and namesake.

Indeed, Restoration drama repeatedly idealizes love between people of different races: An example is Dryden's heroic play *The Conquest of Granada*, which portrays the love of a Spanish nobleman for a Moorish princess. A minor play, William Walker's *Victorious Love* (1698), portrays the triumphant marital love of Barnagasso, king of the African state of Gualata, and a European heroine. According to Ogilby (though Thomas Browne reported otherwise), the inhabitants of Gualata are very black.[20]

It is well known that Behn's *Oroonoko* evokes and subverts the conventions of French heroic romance. During the early stages of his captivity, Oroonoko performs deeds worthy of a hero of such narratives. For example, his exploits in killing two tigresses recall the feat of Lysimachus in La Calprenède's *Cassandra* (1644–50), who kills a lion with his bare hands[21] (or of Heliodorus' Theagenes, who heroically kills a bull). The separation and surprising reunion of the lovers are the stuff of romance from the Greek novels onward in which if lovers are not abducted by British slave traders, they are abducted by pirates. The reunions in romance, however, are eventually happy, and pirates do not prosper. Although Oroonoko kills the tigers, his exploits as a romantic hero are part of a controlled exercise by his captors to keep him placid and unthreatening. Behn foregrounds a tension between what was the dominant mode of fiction in the mid-seventeenth century and the realistic fiction in which she was the British pioneer: For her, romance is a lie, generated by the imperatives of money and power.

---

[18] David Quint, *Epic and Empire: Politics and Generic Form from Virgil to Milton* (Princeton: Princeton University Press, 1992), 234–47.
[19] Gauthier de Costes, Sieur de La Calprenède, *Hymen's Praeludia* [*Cleopâtre*], trans. Robert Loveday [1652–59] (London, 1674), Part I, Book iii, 56.
[20] Ogilby, *Africa*, 315; Thomas Browne, *Pseudodoxia Epidemica* 6.10.
[21] Gauthier de Costes, Sieur de La Calprenède, *Cassandra* [1644–50], trans. Sir Charles Cotterell (London, 1661) Part II, Book ii, 126.

Surinam (Guiana), where Oroonoko is enslaved, at first seemed a land of romance. When Sir Walter Raleigh wrote his *Discoverie of the Large, Rich, and Bewtifull Empire of Guiana* (London, 1596), he was describing the imaginary empire of El Dorado, founded by the brother of Atabalipa, the last of the Incas: "whatsoeuer Prince shall possesse it, that Prince shall be Lorde of more Golde, and of a more beautifull Empire, and of more Cities and people, then eyther the king of Spaine, or the great Turke" (p. 9). American gold is the source of Spanish power, and it is by possessing the gold of El Dorado that England will rival Spain. The exoticism of romance here serves to heighten economic incentives: nations that are "marueilous rich in gold" exist to the west of nations of headless cannibals (p. 91). Raleigh is not concerned with the agricultural exploitation of the new land and indeed explicitly skips "mention of the seueral beasts birds[,] fishes, fruites, flowers, gummes, sweete woodes, and of their seuerall religions and customes" (p. 92) – all things central to Behn's account. He does, however, report that there was nothing in the Peruvian emperor's country, "whereof he had not the counterfeat in gold" (p. 12), the golden replica evidently being more important than the organic original. His two unsuccessful expeditions to Surinam, in 1594 and 1617–18, were indeed quests for gold. Robert Harcourt, who attempted to create a settlement in Surinam in 1609, does take a less purely metallurgical view of its resources, describing its fauna and its "sweet gummes" and its potential for producing sugar and tobacco.[22] Some of his crew, however, were interested only in gold, and became mutinous when reports of "Golden Mountaines" proved to be false (p. 38). "Mountains of Gold" remain a dream in Behn's *Oroonoko* (p. 174), but one that is not fulfilled.

The lasting recognition that there was no new Mexico or Peru still to be discovered, that Raleigh's "Large, Rich and Beautiful Empire of Guiana" was a fiction, transformed forever the English perception of the kind of project their Empire in America was intended to be. Confusedly at first and then with religious, and invariably self-righteous zeal, they abandoned the vision of El Dorado and Spanish-style kingdoms overseas for that of "colonies" and "plantations"; places, that is, which would be sources not of human or mineral, but of agricultural and commercial wealth.[23]

[22] Robert Harcourt, *A Relation of a Voyage to Guiana* (London, 1613), 32, 33, 36.
[23] Anthony Pagden, 'The Struggle for Legitimacy and the Image of Empire in the Atlantic to c. 1700', in Nicholas Canny and Alaine Low, eds., vol. 1 *The Oxford History of the British Empire* (Oxford: Oxford University Press, 1998–99), 36 (34–54).

In the 1620s and 1630s, the English acquired St. Christopher, Barbados, Nevis, and Montserrat and Antigua. Lord Willoughby's colony in Surinam was established in 1650. In 1655–56, Cromwell's generally unsuccessful attempt at Caribbean expansionism added Jamaica to the list. Originally, the main produce was cotton and tobacco, but in the 1640s an increase in the price of sugar inspired a switch to large-scale sugar production and led to an economic boom. It also produced a change in the labor force. The Caribbean could not provide an adequate supply of native labor, and before the "sugar revolution" the principal source of labor had been indentured white servants. The arduousness of sugar production, however, produced an increasing demand for black African labor, fueled by the high mortality rate of slaves, which necessitated constant replenishment. "By 1660 the African slave trade was the 'life line' of the Caribbean economy. In 1645, some two years after the beginning of sugar production, Barbados had only 5,680 slaves; in 1698 it had 42,000 slaves." In 1655 the ratio of whites to blacks was 23,000 to 20,000; by 1684, four years before the composition of *Oroonoko*, it was 19,568 to 46,502.[24] *Oroonoko* is thus set at a time when the Caribbean slave trade was in its infancy, but was at the same time an established and rapidly growing institution.

Slaves were bought from kingdoms on the west coast of Central Africa and sold to Europeans, Arabs, and others by kings and princelings, such as Oroonoko. Europe did not at this stage have a colonial presence in sub-Saharan Africa, but operated from trading forts such as Kormantin (which Behn transforms into the kingdom of Coromantien).[25] Slaves were traded for goods bought in Europe and brought to the New World, where they produced goods for export to Europe, though in general the slaving ships were employed only in the first two legs of the trading triangle. Neither Behn nor Southerne, however, is much interested in the economic genesis and basis of slavery. Behn mentions sugar only once, and she is far more interested in the economic value of the native flora and fauna of Surinam, such as the trees whose colored timbers are "glorious to behold; and bear a Price considerable" (p. 164). She is certainly keenly interested in varieties of social economy: Witness her juxtaposition of the militaristic patriarchy of Africa and the rule of upstart traders in Surinam. When she examines trade in *Oroonoko*, however, she is primarily interested in the cultural transpositions and dislocations that it brings about – in the fact that the

[24] Hilary McD. Beckles, "The 'Hub of Empire': The Caribbean and Britain in the Seventeenth Century," ibid., 227 (218–40).
[25] "The chief Town upon the Shore is *Kormantyn*, the principal place of Trade for the *English*:. . . Near which the *English* have a Castle fortifi'd with four Bulwarks" (Ogilby, *Africa*, 431).

feathers of exotic living birds can be transformed by the Native Americans into gorgeous artifacts and that, under her influence, these artifacts can migrate to being props in a London theatrical performance of Dryden and Howard's *The Indian Queen*, which portrays warfare between Mexico and Peru.[26] The feathers become artificial representations of another American culture, quite different from that which actually produced them. The movements of trade thus deprive the exotic feathers of any fixed significance, placing them in a changing relationship to the familiar. This change does not happen with sugar: Sugar has a fixed material character, whereas the feathers are cultural products of no fixed significance. It is the latter – cultural contingency, rather than biological essence – that Behn explores in *Oroonoko*.

ABDELAZER

Behn seems to have been actively uninterested in using the nascent racism of her time. As noted, *Lust's Dominion*, the source of *Abdelazer*, is dominated by explicit contempt for the black African. Behn omits this to the point of removing not only the polarity between Negro and white but even the words themselves. In *Lust's Dominion* there is a real, unquestionable association between the blackness of the Moor (here called Eleazer) and of the devil, as we can see in the following speech, in which an objective observer describes his conduct in battle. The diabolical, the bestial, and the black become almost synonymous:

> The *Moor*'s a Devill, never did horrid feind
> Compel'd by som Magicians mighty charm,
> Break through the prisons of the solid earth,
> With more strange horror, then this Prince of hell,
> This damned Negro Lyon-like doth rush,
> Through all, and spite of all knit opposition. (4.2.29–34)

The comparable speech in *Abdelazer*, delivered by Abdelazer's brother-in-law and erstwhile supporter, is by contrast one of subjective surprise at Abdelazer's speedy advance in battle:

> The Moor! – a Devil! – never did Fiend of Hell,
> Compell'd by some Magicians Charms,
> Break through the Prison of the folded Earth

---

[26] *The Indian Queen* is a rhymed heroic play by John Dryden and his brother-in-law Sir Robert Howard, first performed in 1664. The titular character is a villainess who has usurped the throne of Montezuma.

> With more swift horrour, then this Prince of Fate
> Breaks through our Troops, in spight of opposition. (4.i,79)

The emphasis on blackness has gone, and the devil image now refers neither to blackness nor to evil, but to speed.

Even when Abdelazer performs the ultimate black man's crime of attempting to rape a white woman, Behn handles the episode with some nuanced complexity. The intended victim is the Spanish princess Leonora, to whom Abdelazer has just surrendered the crown and who has rejected his declaration of love with disparagement of his "Person." Certainly, Abdelazer is viewed critically. He had been the lover of her mother, who has been murdered on his instructions earlier in the scene. He had knelt in hypocritical sorrow by her corpse, a gesture that is recapitulated ironically and ominously when he kneels in amorous homage to the woman whose rejection is to inspire him to rapist aggression. Yet her disparagement of his "Person" stands out as one of the very few instances of purely racial contempt for Abdelazer in the play; it gains force from the way in which her lover Alonzo has very shortly before condemned Abdelazer's affair with the Queen while stressing that his remarks have nothing to do with Abdelazer's race: "I spoke *without reflection on your Person*, / But of dishonest love" (V.i,101; italics added). In response to Leonora's rebuff, Abdelazer for the only time in the play regrets his blackness:

> And curst be Nature, that has dy'd my skin
> With this ungrateful colour! cou'd not the Gods
> Have given me equal Beauty with *Alonzo*! (V.i,104)

The attempt to rape Leonora is thus not simply presented as the kind of thing a black villain could be expected to do. It arises from a specific combination of circumstances and motives. Moreover, the prompt arrival of Osmin, the contrasting good Moor, who interrupts the rape and discloses privately to Leonora that he is on the side of virtue, confirms that Abdelazer is an individual, rather than a racial type.

Behn de-emphasizes Abdelazer's racial alienness. His ruling qualities are not ones that distinguish him from the white Spaniards, but rather those that unite him with them: warriorhood, sexual proprietorship of his wife Florella, and patriarchy (like his antagonist Philip, he wishes to avenge a slain father). In short, his ruling qualities are not those of his race but of his sex. He is an extreme embodiment of masculinity. Abdelazer's blackness makes strange that which is commonplace in any male-dominated society. His alienness is a means of defamiliarizing and scrutinizing the impulses that are common to him and the Spaniards.

BEHN'S *OROONOKO*

What of *Oroonoko*? Is this also a work that uses blackness as a means of representing something else, rather than the thing itself? Some scholars have suggested that the story is primarily about the dangers gathering about James II, his wife, and infant son in England: *Oroonoko* was published in the early summer of 1688, and James was to be ousted by William of Orange in November of that year. As Surinam fell to the Dutch in 1667, so England was to fall to the Dutch two decades later.

It is tempting to see this political situation as part of the context of the novel, but it is too simple to see it as the primary key. Parallel narratives, which use historical or foreign situations to explore contemporary English politics, were certainly common in the Restoration: Dryden's *Absalom and Achitophel* (1681) is a well-known example. Behn, however, does not use such parallelism on any other occasion, and throughout *Oroonoko* she emphasizes the mutability and deceptiveness of narrative: an emphasis that militates against the direct translation of Oroonoko's story into that of an English king. Behn repeatedly presents narrative as being second-hand or questionable in its authority. Even Oroonoko's experiences in Africa are narrated by him to the narrator, and then by her to us. Yet she feels she is not the most appropriate writer of his history: that person would have been Trefry, the man who owned him as a slave, for ownership of Oroonoko's body strangely gave him proprietorial rights over his history; Trefry, however, died before he would write this authoritative history, leaving us to the work of "a Female Pen" (p. 156). Furthermore, the narrative would have been different if written in Surinam, where "History was scarce" and where more circumstantial detail would therefore have been welcome. In London, overloaded with information, the narrator has omitted some details that would have been of interest in Surinam. Narrative thus expands or contracts to fill the available space; like the exotic feathers, it changes in significance as it moves from place to place.

Within the story, narrative is often deceptive and manipulative. During Oroonoko's captivity, the narrator attempts to pacify him by telling him the lives of the Romans; an allusion to Plutarch's parallel biographies of Greek and Roman politicians, a new translation of which had appeared in 1683. Yet the scheme misfires. Oroonoko derives an unexpected lesson from what he is told, drawing a parallel between himself and Hannibal, the North African invader of Rome, and using it to incite the slaves to rebellion. He misapplies the parallel, however, for Hannibal's invasion of Rome was unsuccessful. The narrator thus miscalculates the effect of her tale; Oroonoko misconstrues it. Narrative is, indeed, shaped by power. Behn instructs Oroonoko in Roman history at the bidding of unnamed powerful figures. Byam, the wicked deputy governor, tricks Trefry into offering Oroonoko false assurances of a pardon. Historical narrative is the exclusive property of the Europeans; it is possessed neither by the Native Americans nor the Africans. Yet the Native Americans lack not only history but also any capacity for verbal deception. In this, as in historiography, the Europeans' abilities are unrivaled.

The capacities for history and mendacity seem to develop in tandem and in close interrelationship, and this is typical of Behn's portrayal of culture and cultural progress. Culture is contradictory: The primitive paradise of the Native Americans and the conceptual sophistication of the Europeans both coexist with horrifying violence, and the contrasts among the three cultures portrayed in the novel are counterbalanced by deeper affinities. The dismemberment of Oroonoko parallels and outdoes the rituals in which the Indian military leaders compete for supreme command, by vying to see which of them can cut the most parts off himself; and it foreshadows their future brutality in cutting some Dutch settlers to pieces.

The relationship between cultures is particularly slippery in the sphere of religion. Behn narrates the bogus, sleight-of-hand cures with which the Indian priests bemuse their gullible followers. Whereas some clerical writers saw such impostures as inspired by the devil,[27] Behn implicitly sees them as paralleling the impostures of Christianity; in the same year as the publication of *Oroonoko*, she published her translation of Fontenelle's *L'Histoire des Oracles* (1687), *The History of Oracles, and the Cheats of the Pagan Priests*. This translation implicitly uses the absurdity of pagan practices to suggest the absurdity of Christianity itself. Conversely, the advanced free-thinking of Oroonoko's French tutor inculcates in him an anti-Christian skepticism that is at once a symptom of the most avant-garde European thought and a reconstitution of the non-Christianity of the "primitive"; it is the very feature that, in European eyes, renders him liable to enslavement. The savage and the civilized, the exotic and the familiar constantly change places, in ways that are quite incompatible with fixed notions of racial character.

---

[27] Du Tertre, I, 368–69.

SOUTHERNE'S *OROONOKO*

If Behn's *Oroonoko* is only tangentially about the future misfortunes of
James II, Southerne – writing eight years after James's deposition – may be
more influenced by them. He had been a supporter of James and perhaps
had spent the immediate aftermath of the Revolution in exile on the Continent. He accommodated himself to the new regime, however, and his next
tragedy after *Oroonoko*, *The Fate of Capua*, may reflect on Ireland's impru-
dent support in 1689–91 for James's military campaign to regain his crown,
for it concerns Capua's disastrous support of Hannibal during his invasion
of Italy (this is the sort of neat historical parallel that Behn avoided). The
possible relevance of the Revolution to *Oroonoko* lies in the play's portrayal
of a cultural shift: the failure of values based on faith and the vow, and their
replacement by commerce and self-interest. In this respect, it resembles
Southerne's previous play, *The Fatal Marriage*, which was based on Behn's
story, *The History of the Nun*. Here, the heroine is driven by poverty to betray
her vows to her first husband, whom she believes to be dead, and to remarry
for security and survival. Her first husband promptly returns. Neither play
is an allegory of the deposition of James, but both portray a movement
away from the rule of the oath to a more materialistic mode of life, and
both subliminally reflect the political changes that had gripped Britain.

Behn was fascinated by the occupied territory. It also occurs in *The Rover*
(Naples is ruled by the Spanish) and *The Widdow Ranter*. She supported
colonization (which in theory involved coexistence with native peoples
rather than Spanish-style subjugation of them), yet at the same time she
saw the colonized land as imaging the condition of the woman in a world
ruled by men. Southerne addresses this topic more directly in the parallel between Oroonoko and Charlot Welldon: Both are dislocated figures,
confronting a new world in new roles (as a slave and in male disguise), and
both illustrate that the universal principle of human intercourse is the sale
of the body, whether in the marriage market or the slave market. Yet, in
portraying the transition from a world of bonds and oaths to one of naked
commerce, Southerne clearly does not deplore the institution of slavery,
but rather the inhumanity with which slaves are treated, and the treacherous enslavement of a prince. Southerne was, indeed, already courting
the patronage of Christopher Codrington, a literary enthusiast who was
also one of the greatest (if also one of the more humane) slave owners in
the Caribbean.[28] When Oroonoko denounces the cowardice of the quickly

---

[28] Codrington College in Barbados was founded with a bequest in Codrington's will. One
of his purposes was to provide slaves with a Christian education, though this was initially
frustrated by the Barbados government. His desire for legislation against cruelty to slaves

cowed rebel slaves, his words express the contempt not only of the nobleman for the mob but also of the white man for the average black African,
undignified by princely rank or aristocratic values:

> I wou'd not live on the same Earth with Creatures,
> That only have the Faces of their Kind:
> Why shou'd they look like Men, who are not so?
> When they put off their Noble Natures, for
> The groveling qualities of down-cast Beasts,
> I wish they had their Tails. (4.2,253)

This is the only approach to racism in any of the three principal texts in
this volume, and even here the theme is the loss of humanity, not its innate
absence.

Neither version of *Oroonoko* is a covert representation of events in
England, yet both link the uprooting of the slave-prince to changes and
upheavals in the authors' own societies. Behn was the daughter of a barber,
yet in *Oroonoko* transformed her father into an aristocratic colonial admin-
istrator. As the university-educated son of a successful Dublin brewer,
Southerne was of more substantial bourgeois origin and was more overtly
critical of the gentry and aristocracy. The slaver captain who in Behn's version kidnaps Oroonoko has a veneer of gentility which belies his amoral and
predatory commercialism; the principles of Southerne's captain, as Stanmore observes, are those through which most great aristocratic estates are
brought into being (I.i.ooo). If Behn's captain points to a post-aristocratic
world, Southerne's is a proto-aristocrat. Two of Southerne's comedies, *The
Wives Excuse* and *The Maid's Last Prayer*, satirize a fashionable upper-class
consumerism that hungers for exotic imports. Yet for him, as for Behn,
humane values are aristocratic values, of honor and trust. The slaver is
monstrous not because he kidnaps a brother human being, but because he
kidnaps a prince. If neither writer condemns the slave trade, both view with
suspicion the moral blindness of trade itself.

Other writers in the collection are more forward looking. Henry Neville
was a serious thinker, who in *Plato Redivivus* (1681) argued that there was a
severe tension between the traditional constitutional power of the aristocracy and the new economic power of the commons. In his *Two Treatises of
Government*, John Locke argued trenchantly against the monarchic system

---

was also thwarted. Behn's comedy *The Younger Brother*, to which she alludes in *Oroonoko*,
was after her death dedicated to Codrington by Charles Gildon, who brought the play
to the stage.

that Behn throughout her career defended, albeit with great reservations. He developed a theory of property rights grounded upon labor. Such rights entitled the technologically and economically advanced to settle and exploit land that was under-exploited by less advanced natives; the failure to protect such rights deprived rulers of their authority to govern.

The foregrounding of property rights did nothing to benefit slaves, who were themselves considered to be property. In setting out the constitution of Carolina, Locke had given "Every *Freeman* of *Carolina*. . . absolute Power and Authority over his *Negro Slaves*."[29] Paradoxically, it was writers longing for the glamor of older, feudal values who entered imaginatively into the horrors of enslavement. Locke's attack on political absolutism in Britain is an important moment in intellectual and political history, but the European imagination had to develop a long way before his hatred of tyranny could be applied to the condition of black Africans. This anthology presents us with the fragments of the future, but they were not yet combined as the future was to combine them. Of the works represented here, perhaps only the Germantown Protest speaks to us in entirely familiar terms.

Yet Oroonoko's character was so powerful that later authors were able to transplant him to a more advanced moral atmosphere. Three revisions of Southerne's play appeared in the years 1759–60, all omitting the comic plot. The most successful, which displaced Southerne's play, was commissioned by David Garrick from John Hawkesworth. The others were by Francis Gentleman and by an anonymous author. All add to the pathos of the main characters and criticism of the ignoble elements in the planters, though only the anonymous version condemns the slave trade directly. A fully abolitionist version was provided in John Ferriar's *The Prince of Angola* (1788). In 1745, Pierre-Antoine La Place had brought out a French adaptation of Behn's novel, in which Oroonoko and Imoinda (white, as in Southerne) are freed and return to reign in Africa, and an adaptation of Southerne's play by Schiller's friend Wolfgang von Dalberg (1789) concludes with the abolition of slavery, after the death of the hero and heroine. In 1999, the Royal Shakespeare Company staged an adaptation of Behn's *Oroonoko* by the Nigerian writer 'Biyi Bandele. Bandele's principal contribution was in the first part, which is a greatly modified version of the Coromantien section (not previously dramatized), one of whose innovations is to increase African complicity in the slave trade (Oroonoko is betrayed by one of his own people). The second part is, silently, taken from Hawkesworth's version

[29] *The Fundamental Constitutions of Carolina* [London, 1670], 25.

of Southerne's version of Behn.[30] Yet newspaper reviewers had no difficulty in accepting as the work of a contemporary Nigerian that of an eighteenth-century gentleman, who was to become a director of the East India Company. One critic indeed praised Bandele for the historical fidelity of sentiment in the line "[They] bought us in an honest way of trade,"[31] which was in fact penned by Southerne, the slave owner's client: This is clear testimony that texts can resonate beyond the contexts that produced them.

Behn and Southerne wrote when opposition to slavery was being voiced, for the first time, in far-away Pennsylvania, by four German immigrants of whom they could not have heard; when even a Morgan Godwyn could commend benevolence to slaves on the grounds that it would make them more docile. They deplored the excesses of the institution, rather than the institution itself. Yet their moral indignation at the excesses of the institution was the precondition for indignation at the institution itself, and the figure of heroic suffering that Behn created proved a potent imaginative symbol, whose meaning evolved as the abolitionist cause advanced.

---

[30] *Aphra Behn's "Oroonoko": In a New Adaptation by 'Biyi Bandele-Thomas* (Charlbury: Amber Lane Press: 1999). See Jessica Munns, "Reviving *Oroonoko* 'in the scene': From Thomas Southerne to 'Biyi Bandele," in *Troping "Oroonoko" from Behn to Bandele*, ed. Susan B. Iwanisziw (Aldershot and Burlington: Ashgate, 2004), 174–97.

[31] Benedict Nightingale in *The Times*, December, 22 1999, 32. Bandele, 92. Southerne 3.2,236.

A Note on the Texts

THE TEXT OF *The Isle of Pines* is taken from the final 1668 edition, which combines the original narrative (also published in 1668) with its sequel, *A New and Further Discovery of the Islle* [sic] *of Pines*. *Abdelazer* is taken from the first edition of 1677, the only text to be published in Behn's lifetime. The text of Southerne's *Oroonoko* is that of the first edition of 1696.

Oroonoko was first published separately in 1688. It was reissued the same year in a collection of novels by Behn entitled *Three Histories*, the other two stories being *The Fair Jilt* and *Agnes de Castro*. This printing is not strictly a new edition, but in the seventeenth century sheets were corrected while publication was in progress, and the text in *Three Histories* is in general more accurate than in the earlier printing. A copy in the Bodleian Library, Oxford, however, uniquely preserves something from very early in the printing history of *Oroonoko*: a passage in the dedication praising the Roman Catholic religion, which was excised, doubtless because of its political sensitivity. The text in *Three Histories* has been used as the basis for this edition.

Original spellings have been retained, but obvious misprints, including some eccentric spellings not sanctioned by seventeenth-century usage, have been corrected. *The Isle of Pines* is more carelessly printed than the other texts, and here some eccentricities of punctuation have been rectified. In the two plays, speech prefixes have been expanded and regularized. The original numbering of scenes has been retained, though not every change of scene is numbered.

Chronology

1620	Henry Neville born.
1625	Death of James I. Accession of Charles I.
1640	Aphra Johnson, the daughter of the barber Bartholomew Johnson, born in Canterbury. She is probably Aphra Behn.
1642	Start of the Civil War. Theaters closed.
1649	Charles I executed. England proclaimed a Commonwealth.
1650	Lord Willoughby's colony in Surinam established.
1653	Cromwell becomes Lord Protector.
1655	Cromwell's "Western Design," an attempt at colonial expansion in the Caribbean, is largely unsuccessful, but results in the acquisition of Jamaica.
1658	Death of Cromwell.
1659	Birth of Thomas Southerne.
1660	Restoration of the monarchy. The theaters reopen.
1663–64	Aphra Behn probably visited Surinam.
1665	Second Dutch War begins. Great Plague of London.
1666	Behn sent as spy to Antwerp to obtain information about Dutch. Great Fire of London.
1667	The Dutch humiliate the British by sailing up the Medway to Chatham and destroying and capturing a number of ships, including "The Royal Charles," which had brought Charles II back to England in 1660. The Treaty of Breda cedes Surinam to the Dutch.
1668	Publication of *The Isle of Pines*.

1670	Behn's first play, *The Forc'd Marriage*, staged by the Duke's Company.
1672–74	Third Dutch War.
1673	James Duke of York (Charles II's brother) acknowledges his Catholicism publicly and marries the Catholic princess, Mary of Modena.
1675	Neville's translation of Machiavelli published.
1676	*Abdelazer* performed.
1677	*The Rover*, Behn's most successful play, performed. From then until the first performance of *The City-Heiress* (1682) Behn had at least eight new plays performed.
	The Duke of York's daughter Mary marries William of Orange.
1678–81	In September 1678 Titus Oates reveals details of an alleged Roman Catholic plot to massacre Protestants and put the Duke of York on the throne. This leads to a campaign to exclude the Duke of York from the succession (the Exclusion Crisis), defeated in March 1681.
1681	Neville's *Plato Redivivus*.
1682	Thomas Southerne's first play, *The Loyal Brother*, performed. One of many plays (including *The City-Heiress*) celebrating the defeat of the Exclusion movement.
	Poor management of the King's Company led to a merger of the two rival theater companies in London. The absence of competition greatly reduced the demand for new plays. Behn diversified into prose fiction, poetry, and translation.
1683	Rye House Plot to murder Charles II and Duke of York is discovered.
1684	First part of Behn's novel, *Love-Letters Between a Nobleman and His Sister*, published anonymously. The second and third parts follow in 1685 and 1687.
1685	Death of Charles II. The Duke of York succeeds as James II. Charles's illegitimate son, the Duke of Monmouth, leads an unsuccessful rebellion and is executed.
1686	*The Luckey Chance*. First performance of a new Behn play since 1682.
1688	Publication of *Oroonoko*.

Invited by seven noblemen to intervene, William of Orange invades Britain on November 5. James flees to France and the protection of Louis XIV.

1689   Behn dies on April 16, five days after the coronation of William and Mary.

The War of the League of Augsburg (against Louis XIV's France) begins.

Behn's *The Widdow Ranter* posthumously performed. It is a failure.

1690   The Battle of the Boyne thwarts James's attempts to use Ireland as a base from which to recover his throne.

Southerne's *Sir Anthony Love* (partially based on Behn's *The Lucky Mistake*) performed.

1694   Death of Henry Neville. Death of Queen Mary.

First performance of Southerne's *The Fatal Marriage*, based on Behn's *The History of the Nun*.

1695   Group of aggrieved actors, led by Thomas Betterton, sets up a breakaway company. The resumption of theatrical competition increases the demand for new plays, and a second generation of women dramatists emerges.

1696   First performances of Southerne's *Oroonoko* and of Behn's *The Younger Brother* (to which she alludes in *Oroonoko*). The latter play is unsuccessful.

1697   The Treaty of Ryswick ends the War of the League of Augsburg.

1698–1700   Previously unpublished fiction by Behn appears in *The Histories and Novels* (1698) and *Histories, Novels and Translations* (1700). The authenticity of the new pieces is uncertain.

1701   War of the Spanish Succession (against Louis XIV's France) begins, ending in 1713.

1703   Death of William III. Accession of Queen Anne.

1746   Death of Thomas Southerne.

PART ONE

THE MAJOR
TEXTS

HENRY NEVILLE

The Isle of Pines (1668)

The ISLE of
PINES,

OR,

A late Discovery of a fourth ISLAND near
Terra Australis, Incognita[1]

BY

Henry Cornelius Van Sloetten.

Wherein is contained.

A True Relation of certain *English* persons, who in Queen *Elizabeths* time, making a Voyage to the *East Indies* were cast away, and wracked near to the Coast of *Terra Australis, Incognita*, and all drowned, except one Man and four Women. And now lately *Anno Dom.* 1667. a *Dutch* Ship making a Voyage to the *East Indies*, driven by foul weather there, by chance have found their Posterity, (speaking good *English*) to amount (as they suppose) to ten or twelve thousand persons. The whole Relation (written, and left by the Man himself a little before his death, and delivered to the *Dutch* by his Grandchild) Is here annexed with the Longitude and Latitude of the Island, the scituation and felicity thereof, with other matter observable.

Licensed *July* 27. 1668.

LONDON, Printed for *Allen Banks* and *Charles Harper* next door to the three Squerrills in *Fleet-street*, over against *St. Dunstans* Church, 1 6 6 8 .

[1] The unknown southern land (*australis* means 'southern'). An undiscovered southern continent had been postulated by ancient geographers, and the idea was revived after the voyages of Vasco da Gama and Magellan in the southern seas. Europeans were driven off course to Australia in the seventeenth century, but it was not formally discovered until 1770.

Two Letters concerning the Island of *Pines* to a Credible person in *Covent Garden*

Amsterdam, *June* the 29ᵗʰ 1668.

I T is written by the last post from Rochel, *to a Merchant in this City, that there was a* French *ship arrived, the Master and Company of which reports, that about 2 or 300 Leagues Northwest from* Cape Finis Terre,[2] *they fell in with an Island, where they went on shore, and found about 2000* English *people without cloathes, only some small coverings about their middle, and that they related to them, that at their first coming to this Island (which was in Queen* Elizabeths *time) they were but five in number men and women, being cast on shore by distress or otherwise, and had there remained ever since, without having any correspondence with any other people, or any ship coming to them. This story seems very fabulous, yet the Letter is come to a known Merchant, and from a good hand in* France, *so that I thought fit to mention it. It may be that there may be some mistake in the number of the Leagues, as also of the exact point of the Compass, from* Cape Finis Terre; *I shall enquire more particularly about it. Some* English *here suppose it may be the Island of* Brasile[3] *which have been so oft sought for, Southwest from* Ireland: *if true, we shall hear further about it; Your friend and Brother,*

Abraham Keek.

Amsterdam, *July* the 6ᵗʰ, 1668.

I T is said that the ship that discovered the Island, of which I hinted to you in my *last, is departed from* Rochel,[4] *on her way to* Zealand. *Several persons here have writ thither to enquire for the said Vessel, to know the truth of this business. I was promised a Copy of the Letter that came from* France, *advising the discovery of the Island abovesaid, but it's not yet come to my hand; when it cometh, or any further news about this Island, I shall acquaint you with it,*

Your Friend and Brother,
A. Keek.

---

[2] A peninsula in northwest Spain.
[3] Hy-Brasil (variously spelled). A mythical island in Irish legend. *O-Brazile*, a satirical pamphlet of 1675, narrates the discovery of an enchanted island off the coast of Ireland.
[4] Rochelle, a port on the Atlantic coast of France.

The Isle of Pines,

DISCOVERED

Near to the Coast of *Terra Australis Incognita*, by *Henry Cornelius Van Sloetten*, in a Letter to a friend in *London*, declaring the truth of his Voyage to the East *Indies*.

SIR,

I Received your Letter of this second instant, wherein you desire me to give you a further account concerning the Land of *Pines*, on which we were driven by distress of Weather the last Summer. I also perused the Printed Book thereof you sent me, the Copy of which was surreptiously taken out of my hands, else should I have given you a more fuller account upon what occasion we came thither, how we were entertained, with some other circumstances of note wherein that relation is defective. To satisfie therefore your desires, I shall briefly yet fully give you a particular account thereof, with a true Copy of the Relation it self; desiring you to bear with my blunt Phrases, as being more a Seaman then a Scholler.

April the *26th 1667*. We set sail from *Amsterdam*, intending for the *East-Indies*; our ship had to name the place from whence we came, the *Amsterdam*, burthen 350. Tun, and having a fair gale of Wind, on the 27 of *May* following we had a sight of the high Peak of *Tenriffe* belonging to the *Canaries*. We have touched at the Island *Palma*,[5] but having endeavoured it twice, and finding the winds contrary, we steered on our course by the Isles of *Cape Verd*, or *Insulæ Capitis Viridis*,[6] where at St. *James*'s we took in fresh water, with some few Goats, and Hens, where with that Island doth plentifully abound.

June the 14. we had a sight of *Madagascar*, or the Island of St. *Laurence*,[7] an Island of 4000 miles in compass, and scituate under the Southern Tropick;

---

[5] Tenerife and Palma, islands in the Canary Islands.
[6] Cape Verde ("green cape"), a group of islands in the North Atlantic Ocean, west of Senegal.
[7] A common name for Madagascar.

thither we steered our course, and trafficked with the inhabitants for Knives, Beads, Glasses and the like, having in exchange thereof Cloves and Silver. Departing from thence, we were incountred with a violent storm, and the winds holding contrary, for the space of a fortnight, brought us back almost as far as the Isle *Del Principe*;[8] during which time many of our men fell sick, and some dyed, but at the end of that time it pleased God the wind favoured us again, and we steered on our course merrily, for the space of ten days: when on a sudden we were encountered with such a violent storm, as if all the four winds together had conspired for our destruction, so that the stoutest spirit of us all quailed, expecting every hour to be devoured by that merciless element of water. Sixteen dayes together did this storm continue, though not with such violence as at the first, the Weather being so dark all the while, and the Sea so rough, that we knew not in what place we were. At length all on a sudden the Wind ceased, and the Air cleared, the Clouds were all dispersed, and a very serene Sky followed, for which we gave hearty thanks to the Almighty, it being beyond our expectation that we should have escaped the violence of that storm.

At length one of our men mounting the Main-mast espyed fire, an evident sign of some Countrey near adjoyning, which presently after we apparently discovered, and steering our course more nigher, we saw several persons promiscuously° running about the shore, as it were wondering and admiring° at what they saw: Being now near to the Land, we manned out our long Boat with ten persons, who approaching the shore, asked them in our *Dutch* Tongue 𝔚𝔞𝔱 𝔈𝔶𝔩𝔞𝔫𝔱 𝔦𝔰 𝔡𝔦𝔱?[9] to which they returned this Answer in English, *That they knew not what we said.* One of our Company named *Jeremiah Hanzen* who understood *English* very well, hearing their words, discourst to them in their own Language; so that in fine we were very kindly invited on shore, great numbers of them flocking about us, admiring at our Cloaths which we did wear, as we on the other side did to find in such a strange place, so many that could speak *English*, and yet to go naked.

Four of our men returning back in the long Boat to our Ships company, could hardly make them believe the truth of what they had seen and heard, but when we had brought our ship into harbour, you would have blest your

---

promiscuously: confusedly   **admiring:** wondering

[8] An island off West Africa.
[9] According to Bruce, the Dutch would be "Welk Eiland is dat?" (Susan Bruce, ed. *Three Early Modern Utopias: Thomas More, "Utopia", Francis Bacon, "New Atlantis", Henry Neville, "The Isle of Pines"* [Oxford. Oxford University Press, 1999], 241).

self to see how the naked Islanders flocked unto us, so wondering at our ship, as if it had been the greatest miracle of Nature in whole World.

We were very courteously entertained by them, presenting us with such food as that Countrey afforded, which indeed was not to be despised; we eat of the Flesh both of Beasts, and Fowls, which they had cleanly drest, though with no great curiosity°, as wanting materials, wherewithal to do it; and for bread we had the inside or Kernel of a great Nut as big as an Apple, which was very wholsome, and sound for the body, and tasted to the Pallat very delicious.

Having refreshed our selves, they invited us to the Pallace of their Prince or chief Ruler, some two miles distant off from the place where we landed; which we found to be about the bigness of one of our ordinary village houses. It was supported with rough unhewn pieces of Timber, and covered very artificially with boughs, so that it would keep out the greatest showers of Rain; the sides thereof were adorned with several sorts of Flowers, which the fragrant fields there do yield in great variety. The Prince himself (whose name was *William Pine* the Grandchild of *George Pine* that was first on shore in this Island) came to his Pallace door and saluted us very courteously, for though he had nothing of Majesty in him, yet had he a courteous noble and deboneyre spirit, wherewith your English Nation (especially those of the Gentry) are very much indued.

Scarce had he done saluting us when his Lady or Wife, came likewise forth of their House or Pallace. Attended on by two Maid-servants, she was a woman of an exquisite beauty, and had on her head as it were a Chaplet of Flowers, which being intermixt with several variety of colours became her admirably. Her privities were hid with some pieces of old Garments, the Relicts of those Cloaths (I suppose) of them which first came hither, and yet being adorned with Flowers those very rags seemed beautiful; and indeed modesty so far prevaileth over all the Female Sex of that Island, that with grass and flowers interwoven and made strong by the peelings of young Elms (which grow there in great plenty) they do plant together so many of them as serve to cover those parts which nature would have hidden.

We carried him as a present some few Knives, of which we thought they had great need, an Ax or Hatchet to fell Wood, which was very acceptable unto him, the Old one which was cast on shore at the first, and the only one that they ever had, being now so quite blunt and dulled, that it would not cut at all. Some few other things we also gave him, which he very thankfully accepted, inviting us into his House or Pallace, and causing us

curiosity: elegance

to sit down with him, where we refreshed our selves again, with some more Countrey viands which were no other then such we tasted of before; Prince and peasant here faring alike, nor is there any difference betwixt their drink, being only fresh sweet water, which the rivers yield them in great abundance.

After some little pause, our Companion (who could speak *English*) by our request desired to know of him something concerning their Original and how that people speaking the Language of such a remote Countrey should come to inhabit there, having not, as we could see, any ships or Boats amongst them the means to bring them thither, and which was more, altogether ignorant and meer strangers to ships, or shipping, the main thing conducible to that means, to which request of ours, the courteous Prince thus replyed.

Friends (for so your actions declare you to be, and shall by ours find no less) know that we are inhabitants of this Island of no great standing, my Grandfather, being the first that ever set foot on this shore, whose native Countrey was a place called *England*, far distant from this our Land, as he let us to understand; He came from that place upon the Waters, in a thing called a Ship, of which no question but you may have heard; several other persons were in his company, not intending to have come hither (as he said) but to a place called *India*, when tempestuous weather brought him and his company upon this Coast, where falling among the Rocks his ship split all in pieces; the whole company perishing in the Waters, saving only him and four women, which by means of a broken piece of that Ship, by Divine assistance got on Land.

What after passed (said he) during my Grandfathers life, I shall show you in a Relation thereof written by his own hand, which he delivered to my Father, being his eldest Son, charging him to have a special care thereof, and assuring him that time would bring some people or other thither to whom he would have him to impart it, that the truth of our first planting here might not be quite lost, which his commands my Father dutifully obeyed; but no one coming he at his death delivered the same with the like charge to me, and you being the first people, which (besides our selves) ever set footing in this Island, I shall therefore in obedience to my Grandfathers and Fathers commands, willingly impart the same unto you.

Then stepping into a kind of inner room, which as we conceived was his lodging Chamber, he brought forth two sheets of paper fairly written in *English*, (being the same Relation which you had Printed with you at *London*) and very distinctly read the same over unto us, which we hearkened unto with great delight and admiration, freely proffering us a Copy of the same, which we afterward took and brought away along with us; which Copy hereafter followeth.

A Way to the East *India's* being lately discovered by Sea, to the South of *Affrick* by certain *Portugals*,° far more safe and profitable then had been heretofore;[10] certain *English* Merchants encouraged by the great advantages arising from the Eastern Commodities, to settle a Factory° there for the advantage of Trade. And having to that purpose obtained the Queens Royal Licence *Anno Dom.* 1569. 11. or 12. *Eliz.*[11] furnisht out for those parts four ships, my Master being sent as Factor to deal and Negotiate for them, and to settle there, took with him his whole Family, (that is to say) his Wife, and one Son of about twelve years of age, and one Daughter of about fourteen years, two Maidservants, one *Negro* female slave, and my Self, who went under him as his Book-keeper, with this company on Monday the third of *April* next following, (having all necessaries for House-keeping when we should come there, we Embarqued our selves in the good ship called the *India Merchant*, of about four hundred and fifty Tuns burthen, and having a good wind, we on the fourteenth day of *May* had sight of the *Canaries*, and not long after of the Isles of *Cape Vert*, or *Verd*, where taking in such things as were necessary for our Voyage, and some fresh Provisions, we stearing our course South, and a point East, about the first of *August* came within sight of the Island of St. *Hellen*,° where we took in some fresh water. We then set our faces for the Cape of Good hope, where [we arrived] by Gods blessing after some sickness, whereof some of our company died, though none of our family; and hitherto we had met with none but calm weather, yet so it pleased God, when we were almost in sight of St. *Laurence*, an Island so called, one of the greatest in the world, as Marriners say, we were overtaken and dispersed by a great storm of Wind, which continued with such violence many days, that losing all hope of safety, being out of our own knowledge, and whether we should fall on Flats or Rocks, uncertain in the nights, not having the least benefit of the light, we feared most, alwayes wishing for day, and then for Land, but it came too soon for our good; for about the first of *October*, our fears having made us forget how the time passed to a certainty; we about the break of day discerned Land (but what

---

Portugals: Portuguese   **Factory:** trading station
St. Hellen: St. Helena

---

[10] Vasco da Gama had rounded the Cape of Good Hope in 1497, and the Portuguese had discovered the Moluccas in 1512.

[11] Referring to an act passed in the eleventh or twelth year of the reign of Elizabeth I, who became queen in 1558.

we knew not). The Land seemed high and Rockey, and the Sea continued still very stormy and tempestuous, insomuch as there seemed no hope of safety, but looked suddenly to perish. As we grew near Land, perceiving no safety in the ship, which we looked would suddenly be beat in pieces: The Captain, my Master, and some others got into the long Boat, thinking by that means to save their lives, and presently after all the Seamen cast themselves overboard, thinking to save their lives by swimming. Only my self, my Masters Daughters, the two Maids, and the *Negro* were left on board, for we could not swim, but those that left us, might as well have tarried with us, for we saw them, or most of them perish, our selves now ready after to follow their fortune, but God was pleased to spare our lives, as it were by miracle, though to further sorrow. For when we came against the Rocks, our ship having endured two or three blows against the Rocks, (being now broken and quite foundred in the Waters), we having with much ado gotten our selves on the Bowspright, which being broken off, was driven by the Waves into a small Creek, wherein fell a little River, which being encompassed by the Rocks, was sheltered from the Wind, so what we had opportunity to land our selves, (though almost drowned) in all four persons, besides the *Negro*. When we were got upon the Rock, we could perceive the miserable Wrack to our great terrour. I had in my pocket a little Tinder-box and Steel, and Flint to strike fire at any time upon occasion, which served now to good Purpose, for its being so close, preserved the Tinder dry. With this, and the help of some old rotten Wood which we got together, we kindled a fire and dryed our selves, which done, I left my female company, and went to see, if I could find any of our Ships company, that were escaped, but could hear of none, though I hooted and made all the noise I could; neither could I perceive the footsteps of any living Creature (save a few Birds, and other Fowls. At length it drawing towards the Evening, I went back to my company, who were very much troubled for want of me. I being now all their stay in this lost condition, we were at first affraid that the wild people of the Countrey might find us out, although we saw no footsteps of any not so much as a Path; the Woods round about being full of Briers and Brambles, we also stood in fear of wild Beasts. Of such also we saw none, nor sign of any. But above all, and that we had greatest reason to fear, was to be starved to death for want of Food, but God had otherwise provided for us as you shall know hereafter; this done, we spent our time in getting some broken pieces of Boards, and Planks, and some of the Sails and Rigging on shore for shelter. I set up two or three Poles, and drew two or three of the Cords and Lines from Tree to Tree, over which throwing some Sailcloathes and having gotten Wood by us, and three or four Sea-gowns, which we had dryed, we took up our Lodging for that night altogether (the *Blackmoor* being less sensible then the rest we made our Centry). We slept soundly that night, as having not slept in three or four nights before (our fears of what happened preventing us), neither could our hard lodging, fear, and danger hinder us we were so overwatcht.°

On the morrow, being well refresht with sleep, the winde ceased, and the weather was very warm; we went down the Rocks on the sands at low water, where we found great part of our lading, either on shore or floating near it. I by the help of my company, dragged most of it on shore; what was too heavy for us [we] broke, and we unbound the Casks and Chests, and, taking out the goods, secured all; so that we wanted no clothes, nor any other provision necessary for Housekeeping, to furnish a better house than any we were like to have; but no victuals (the last water having spoiled all) only one Cask of bisket,° being lighter than the rest was dry. This served for bread a while, and we found on Land a sort of fowl about the bigness of a Swan, very heavie and fat, that by reason of their weight could not fly. Of these we found little difficulty to kill, so that was our present food; we carried out of *England* certain Hens and Cocks to eat by the way; some of these when the ship was broken, by some means got to land, & bred exceedingly, so that in the future they were a great help unto us. We found also, by a little River, in the flags, store of eggs, of a sort of foul much like our Ducks, which were very good meat, so that we wanted nothing to keep us alive.

On the morrow, which was the third day, as soon as it was morning, seeing nothing to disturb us, I lookt out a convenient place to dwell in, that we might build us a Hut to shelter us from the weather, and from any other danger of annoyance, from wild beasts (if any should finde us out): So close by a large spring which rose out of a high hill over-looking the Sea, on the side of a wood, having a prospect towards the Sea, by the help of an Ax and some other implements (for we had all necessaries, the working of the Sea, having cast up most of our goods) I cut down all the straightest poles I could find, and which were enough for my purpose. By the help of my company (necessity being our Master) I digged holes in the earth setting my poles at an equal distance, and nailing the broken boards of the Caskes, Chests, and Cabins, and such like to them, making my door to the Seaward, and having covered the top, with sailclothes strain'd, and nail'd, I in the space of a week had made a large Cabbin big enough to hold all our goods and our selves in it. I also placed our Hamocks for lodging, purposing (if it pleased God to send any Ship that way) we might be transported home, but it never came to pass, the place, wherein we were (as I conceived) being much out of the way.

---

overwatcht: wearied with lack of sleep   **bisket:** a dry, unleavened bread

We having now lived in this manner full four months, and not so much as seeing or hearing of any wild people, or of any of our own company, more then our selves (they being found now by experience to be all drowned) and the place as we after found, being a large Island, and disjoyned, and out of sight of any other Land, was wholly uninhabited by any people, neither was there any hurtful beast to annoy us. But on the contrary the countrey so very pleasant, being always clothed with green, and full of pleasant fruits, and variety of birds, ever warm, and never colder then in *England* in *September*: So that this place (had it the culture, that skilful people might bestow on it) would prove a *Paradise*.

The Woods afforded us a sort of Nuts, as big as a large Apple, whose kernel being pleasant and dry, we made use of instead of bread, that fowl before mentioned, and a sort of water-fowl like Ducks, and their eggs, and a beast about the size of a Goat, and almost such a like creature, which brought two young ones at a time, and that twice a year, of which the Low Lands and Woods, were very full, being a very harmless creature and tame, so that we could easily take and kill them: Fish, also, especially Shell-fish (which we could best come by) we had great store of, so that in effect as to Food we wanted nothing; and thus, and by such like helps, we continued six moneths, without any disturbance or want.

Idleness and Fulness of every thing begot in me a desire of enjoying the women. Beginning now to grow more familiar, I had perswaded the two Maids to let me lie with them, which I did at first in private, but after, custome taking away shame (there being none but us) we did it more openly, as our Lusts gave us liberty; afterwards my Masters Daughter was content also to do as we did. The truth is, they were all handsome Women when they had Cloathes, and well shaped, feeding well. For we wanted no Food, and living idlely, and seeing us at Liberty to do our wills, without hope of ever returning home made us thus bold: One of the first of my Consorts with whom I first accompanied (the tallest and handsomest) proved presently with child, the second was my Masters Daughter, and the other also not long after fell into the same condition: none now remaining but my *Negro*, who seeing what we did, longed also for her share; one Night, I being asleep, my *Negro*, (with the consent of the others) got close to me, thinking it being dark, to beguile me, but I awaking and feeling her, and perceiving who it was, yet willing to try the difference, satisfied my self with her, as well as with one of the rest: that night, although the first time, she proved also with child, so that in the year of our being here, all my women were with child by me, and they all coming at different seasons, were a great help to one another.

The first brought me a brave Boy. My Masters Daughter was the youngest, she brought me a Girl, so did the other Maid, who being something fat sped worse at her labour. The *Negro* had no pain at all, brought me a fine white Girl, so I had one Boy and three Girls. The Women were soon well again, and the two first with child again before the two last were brought to bed, my custome being not to lie with any of them after they were with child, till others were so likewise, and not with the black at all after she was with child, which commonly was at the first time I lay with her, which was in the night and not else, my stomach would not serve me, although she was one of the handsomest Blacks I had seen, and her children as comly as any of the rest; we had no clothes for them, and therefore when they had suckt, we laid them in Mosse to sleep, and took no further care of them, for we knew, when they were gone more would come, the Women never failing once a year at least, and none of the Children (for all the hardship we put them to) were ever sick; so that wanting now nothing but Cloathes, not them much neither, other then for decency, the warmth of the Countrey and Custome supplying that Defect, we were now well satisfied with our condition. Our Family beginning to grow large, there being nothing to hurt us, we many times lay abroad on Mossey Banks, under the shelter of some Trees, or such like, for having nothing else to do, I had made me several Arbors to sleep in with my Women in the heat of the day. In these I and my women passed the time away, they being never willing to be out of my company.

And having now no thought of ever returning home, as having resolved and sworn each to other, never to part or leave one another, or the place; having by my several wives, forty seven Children, Boys and Girls, but most Girls, and growing up apace, we were all of us very fleshly, the Country so well agreeing with us, that we never ailed any thing; my *Negro* having had twelve, was the first that left bearing, so I never medled with her more; My Masters Daughter (by whom I had most children, being the youngest and handsomest) was most fond of me, and I of her. Thus we lived for sixteen years, till perceiving my eldest Boy to mind the ordinary work of Nature, by seeing what we did, I gave him a Mate, and so I did to all the rest, as fast as they grew up, and were capable: My Wives having left bearing, my children began to breed apace, so we were like to be a multitude; My first Wife brought me thirteen children, my second seven, my Masters Daughter fifteen, and the *Negro* twelve, in all forty seven.

After we had lived there twenty two years, my *Negro* died suddenly, but I could not perceive any thing that ailed her; most of my children being grown, as fast as we married them, I sent them and placed them over the

River by themselves severally, because we would not pester one another; and now they being all grown up, and gone, and married after our manner (except some two or three of the youngest) for (growing my self into years) I liked not the wanton annoyance of young company.

Thus having lived to the sixtieth year of my age, and the fortieth of my coming thither, at which time I sent for all of them to bring their children, and there were in number descended from me by these four Women, of my Children, Grand-children, and great Grand-children, five hundred sixty five of both sorts. I took off the Males of one Family, and married them to the Females of another, not letting any to marry their sisters, as we did formerly out of necessity. So blessing God for his Providence and goodness, I dismist them, I having taught some of my children to read formerly. For I had left still the Bible. I charged it should be read once a moneth at a general meeting. At last one of my Wives died being sixty eight years of age, which I buried in a place, set out on purpose, and within a year after another, so I had none now left but my Masters Daughter, and we lived together twelve years longer. At length she died also, so I buried her also next the place where I purposed to be buried my self, and the tall Maid my first Wife next me on the other side, the *Negro* next without her, and the other Maid next my Masters Daughter. I had now nothing to mind, but the place whether I was to go, being very old, almost eighty years. I gave my Cabin and Furniture that was left to my eldest son after my decease, who had married my eldest Daughter by my beloved Wife, whom I made King and Governour of all the rest: I informed them of the Manners of *Europe*, and charged them to remember the Christian Religion, after the manner of them that spake the same Language, and to admit no other, if hereafter any should come and find them out.

And now once for all, I summoned them to come to me, that I might number them, which I did, and found the estimate to contain in or about the eightieth year of my age, and the fifty ninth of my coming there; in all, of all sorts, one thousand seven hundred eighty and nine. Thus praying God to multiply them, and send them the true light of the Gospel, I last of all dismist them: For, being now very old, and my sight decayed, I could not expect to live long. I gave this Narration (written with my own hand) to my eldest Son, who now lived with me, commanding him to keep it, and if any strangers should come hither by chance: to let them see it, and take a Copy of it if they would, that our name be not lost from off the earth. I gave this people (descended from me) the name of the *ENGLISH PINES*, *George Pine* being my name, and my Masters Daughters name *Sarah English*, my two other Wives were *Mary Sparkes*, and *Elizabeth Trevor*, so their severall Descendants are called the *ENGLISH*, the *SPARKS*, and the *TREVORS*, and the *PHILLS*, from the Christian Name of the Negro, which was *Philippa*, she having no surname: And the general name of the whole the *ENGLISH PINES*; whom God bless with the dew of Heaven, and the fat of the Earth, AMEN.

Ater the reading and delivering unto us a Coppy of this Relation, then proceeded he on in his discourse.

My Grandfather when he wrote this, was as you hear eighty yeares of age, there proceeding from his Loyns one thousand seven hundred eighty nine children, which he had by the four women aforesaid. My Father was his eldest son, and was named *Henry*, begotten of his wife *Mary Sparkes*, whom he appointed chief Governour and Ruler over the rest; and having given him a charge not to exercise tyranny over them, seeing they were his fellow brethren by Fathers side (of which there could be no doubt made of double dealing therein) exhorting him to use justice and sincerity amongst them and not to let Religion die with him, but to observe and keep those Precepts which he had taught them, he quietly surrendred up his soul, and was buried with great lamentation of all his children.

My father coming to rule, and the people growing more populous, made them to range further in the discovery of the Countrey, which they found answerable to their desires, full both of Fowls and Beasts, and those too not hurtful to mankinde, as if this Country (on which we were by providence cast without arms or other weapons to defend our selves, or offend others,) should by the same providence be so inhabited as not to have any need of such like weapons of destruction wherewith to preserve our lives.

But as it is impossible, but that in multitudes disorders will grow, the stronger seeking to oppress the weaker; no tye of Religion being strong enough to chain up the depraved nature of mankinde, even so amongst them mischiefs began to rise, and they soon fell from those good orders prescribed them by my Grandfather. The source from whence those mischiefs spring, was at first, I conceive, the neglect of hearing the Bible read, which (according to my Grandfathers prescription) was once a moneth at a general meeting. But now many of them wandring far up into the Country, they quite neglected the coming to it, with all other means of Christian instruction, whereby the sence of sin being quite lost in them, they fell to whoredoms, incests, and adulteries; so that what my Grand-father was forced to do for necessity, they did for wantonness; nay not confining themselves within the bound of any modesty, but brother and sister lay openly together. Those who would not yeild to their lewd embraces, were by force ravished, yea many times endangered of their lives. To redress those enormities, my father assembled all the Company near unto him, to whom he declared the wickedness of those their brethren; who all with one consent agreed that they should be severely punished; and so arming themselves with boughs, stones, and such like weapons, they marched against them, who having notice of their coming, and fearing their deserved punishment, some of them fled into woods, others passed over a great River, which runneth through the heart of our Countrey, hazarding drowning to escape punishment; But the grandest offender of them all was taken, whose name was *John Phill*, the second son of the *Negro-woman* that came with my Grandfather into this Island. He being proved guilty of divers ravishings & tyrannies committed by him, was adjudged guilty of death, and accordingly was thrown down from a high Rock into the Sea, where he perished in the waters. Execution being done upon him, the rest were pardoned for what was past, which being notified abroad, they returned from those Desart and Obscure places, wherein they were hidden.

Now as Seed being cast into stinking Dung produceth good and wholesome Corn for the sustentation of mans life, so bad manners produceth good and wholesome Laws for the Preservation of Humane Society. Soon after my Father with the advice of some few others of his Counsel, ordained and set forth these Laws to be observed by them.

1. That whosoever should blaspheme or talk irreverently of the name of God should be put to death.

2. That who should be absent from the monethly assembly to hear the Bible read, without sufficient cause shown to the contrary, should for the first default be kept without any victuals or drink, for the space of four days, and if he offend therein again, then to suffer death.

3. That who should force or ravish any Maid or Woman should be burnt to death, the party so ravished putting fire to the wood that should burn him.

4. Whosoever shall commit adultery, for the first crime the Male shall lose his Privities, and the Woman have her right eye bored out, if after that she was again taken in the act, she should die without mercy.

5. That who so injured his Neighbour, by laming of his Limbs, or taking any thing away which he possesseth, shall suffer in the same kind himself by loss of Limb; and for defrauding his Neighbour, to become servant to him, whil'st he had made him double satisfaction.

6. That who should defame or speak evil of the Governour, or refuse to come before him upon Summons, should receive a punishment by whipping

with Rods, and afterwards be exploded° from the society of all the rest of the inhabitants.

Having set forth these Laws, he chose four several persons under him to see them put in Execution, whereof one was of the *Englishes*, the Off-spring of *Sarah English*; another of his own Tribe, the *Sparks*; a third of the *Trevors*, and the fourth of the *Phills*; appointing them every year at a certain time to appear before him, and give an account of what they had done in the prosecution of those Laws.

The Countrey being thus settled, my Father lived quiet and peaceable till he attained to the age of ninety and four years, when dying, I succeeded in his place, in which I have continued peaceably and quietly till this very present time.

He having ended his Speech, we gave him very heartily thanks for our information, assuring him we should not be wanting to him in any thing which lay in our powers, wherewith we could pleasure him in what he should desire; and thereupon proferred to depart, but before our going away, he would needs engage us to see him, the next day, when was to be their great assembly or monethly meeting for the celebration of their Religious Exercises.

Accordingly the next day we came thither again, and were courteously entertained as before. In a short space there was gathered such a multitude of people together as made us to admire; and first there was several Weddings celebrated, the manner whereof was thus. The Bridegroom and Bride appeared before him who was their Priest or Reader of the Bible, together with the Parents of each party, or if any of their Parents were dead, then the next relation unto them, without whose consent as well as the parties to be married, the Priest will not joyn them together: but being satisfied in those particulars, after some short Oraizons, and joyning of hands together, he pronounces them to be man and wife: and with exhortations to them to live lovingly towards each other, and quietly towards their neighbors, he concludes with some prayers, and so dismisses them.

The Weddings being finished, all the people took their places to hear the Word read, the new married persons having the honour to be next unto the Priest that day. After he had read three or four Chapters he fell to expounding the most difficult places therein, the people being very attentive all that while. This exercise continued for two or three hours, which being done, with some few prayers he concluded, but all the rest of that day was

exploded: driven away

by the people kept very strictly, abstaining from all manner of playing or pastimes, with which on other dayes they use to pass their time away, as having need of nothing but victuals, and that they have in such plenty as almost provided to their hands.

Their exercises of Religion being over, we returned again to our Ship, and the next day, taking with us two or three Fowling-pieces, leaving half our Company to guard the Ship, the rest of us resolved to go up higher into the Country for a further discovery: All the way as we passed the first morning, we saw abundance of little Cabbins or Huts of these inhabitants, made under Trees, and fashioned up with boughs, grass, and such like stuffe to defend them from the Sun and Rain; and as we went along, they came out of them much wondering at our Attire, and standing aloof off from us as if they were afraid. But our companion that spake English, calling to them in their own Tongue, and giving them good words, they drew nigher, some of them freely proffering to go along with us, which we willingly accepted; but having passed some few miles, one of our company espying a Beast like unto a Goat come gazing on him, he discharged his Peece, sending a brace of Bullets into his belly, which brought him dead upon the ground; these poor naked unarmed people hearing the noise of the Peece, and seeing the Beast lie tumbling in his gore, without speaking any words betook them to their heels, running back again as fast as they could drive. Nor could the perswasions of our Company, assuring them they should have no hurt, prevail any thing at all with them, so that we were forced to pass along without their company: all the way that we went we heard the delightful harmony of singing Birds, the ground very fertile in Trees, Grass, and such flowers, as grow by the production of Nature, without the help of Art. Many and several sorts of Beasts we saw, who were not so much wild as in other Countries; whether it were as having enough to satiate themselves without ravening upon others, or that they never before saw the sight of man, nor heard the report of murdering Guns, I leave it to others to determine. Some Trees bearing wild Fruits we also saw, and of those some whereof we tasted, which were neither unwholsome nor distastful to the Pallate. And no question had but Nature here the benefit of Art added unto it, it would equal, if not exceed many of our *European* Countries. The Vallyes were every where intermixt with running streams, and no question but the earth hath in it rich veins of Minerals, enough to satisfie the desires of the most covetous.

It was very strange to us, to see that in such a fertile Countrey which was as yet never inhabited, there should be notwithstanding such a free and clear passage to us, without the hinderance of Bushes, Thorns, and such like stuff, wherewith most Islands of the like nature are pestered: the length of the Grass (which yet was very much intermixt with flowers) being the only impediment that we found.

Six dayes together did we thus travel, setting several marks in our way as we went for our better return, not knowing whether we should have the benefit of the Stars for our guidance in our going back, which we made use of in our passage: at last we came to the vast Ocean on the other side of the Island, and by our coasting it, conceive it to be of an oval form, only here and there shooting forth with some Promontories. I conceive it hath but few good Harbours belonging to it, the Rocks in most places making it inaccessible. The length of it may be about two hundred, and breadth one hundred miles, the whole in circumference about five hundred miles.

It lyeth about seventy six degrees of Longitude, and twenty of Latitude, being scituate under the third Climate,° the longest day being about thirteen hours and fourty five minutes. The weather as in all Southern Countries, is far more hot than with us in *Europe*; but what is by the Sun parched in the day, the night again refreshes with cool pearly dews. The Air is found to be very healthful by the long lives of the present inhabitants, few dying there till such time as they come to good years of maturity, many of them arriving to the extremity of old age.

And now speaking concerning the length of their Lives, I think it will not be amisse in this place to speak something of their Burials, which they used to do thus.

When the party was dead, they stuck his Carkass all over with flowers, and after carried him to the place appointed for Burial, where setting him down, (the Priest having given some godly Exhortations concerning the frailty of life) then do they take stones (a heap being provided there for that purpose) and the nearest of the kin begins to lay the first stone upon him, afterwards the rest follows, they never leaving till they have covered the body deep in stones, so that no Beast can possibly come to him, and this shift were they forced to make, having no Spades or Shovels wherewith to dig them Graves; which want of their we espying, bestowed a Pick-ax and two Shovels upon them.

Here might I add their way of Christening Children, but that being little different from your in *ENGLAND*, and taught them by *GEORGE*

climate: "A belt of the earth's surface contained between two given parallels of latitude" (OED).

PINES at first which they have since continued, I shall therefore forbear to speak thereof.

After our return back from the discovery of the Countrey, the Wind not being fit for our purpose, and our men also willing thereto, we got all our cutting Instruments on Land, and fell to hewing down of Trees, with which, in a little time, (many hands making light work) we built up a Pallace for this *William Pines* the Lord of that Countrey; which, though much inferiour to the houses of your Gentry in *England*, yet to them which never had seen better, it appeared a very Lordly Place. This deed of ours was beyond expression acceptable unto him, loading us with thanks for so great a benefit, of which he said he should never be able to make a requital.

And now acquainting him, that upon the first opportunity we were resolved to leave the Island, as also how that we were near Neighbours to the Countrey of *England*, from whence his Ancestors came; he seemed upon the news to be much discontented that we would leave him, desiring, if it might stand with our commodity to continue still with him, but seeing he could not prevail, he invited us to dine with him the next day, which we promised to do, against which time he provided, very sumptuously (according to his estate) for us, and now was he attended after a more Royal manner then ever we saw him before, both for number of Servants, and multiplicity of Meat, on which we fed very heartily; but he having no other Beverage for us to drink, then water, we fetched from our Ship a Case of Brandy, presenting some of it to him to drink, but when he had tasted of it, he would by no means be perswaded to touch there of again, preferring (as he said) his own Countrey Water before all such Liquors whatsoever.

After we had Dined, we were invited out into the Fields to behold their Country Dauncing, which they did with great agility of body; and though they had no other then only Vocal Musick (several of them singing all that while) yet did they trip it very nearly, giving sufficient satisfaction to all that beheld them.

The next day we invited the Prince *William Pines* aboard our Ship, where was nothing wanting in what we could to entertain him. He had about a dozen of Servants to attend on him. He much admired at the Tacklings of our Ship, but when we came to discharge a piece or two of Ordance, it struck him into a wonder and amazement to behold the strange effects of Powder. He was very sparing in his Diet, neither could he, or any of his followers be induced to drink any thing but Water. We there presented him with several things, as much as we could spare, which we thought would any wayes conduce to their benefit, all which he very gratefully received, assuring us of his real love and good will, whensoever we should come thither again.

And now we intended the next day to take our leaves, the Wind standing fair, blowing with a gentle Gale *South* and by *East*, but as we were hoising of our Sails, and weighing Anchor, we were suddenly Allarm'd with a noise from the shore, the Prince, *W. Pines* imploring our assistance in an Insurrection which had happened amongst them, of which this was the cause.

Henry Phil, the chief Ruler of the Tribe or Family of the *Phils*, being the Off-spring of *George Pines* which he had by the *Negro*-woman; this man had ravished the Wife of one of the principal of the Family of the *Trevors*, which act being made known, the *Trevors* assembled themselves all together to bring the offender unto Justice: But he knowing his crime to be so great, as extended to the loss of life: sought to defend that by force, which he had as unlawfully committed, whereupon the whole Island was in a great hurly burly, they being two great Potent Factions, the bandying of which against each other, threatned a general ruin to the whole State.

The Governour *William Pines* had interposed in the matter, but found his Authority too weak to repress such Disorders; for where the Hedge of Government is once broken down, the most vile bear the greatest rule, whereupon he desir'd our assistance, to which we readily condescended, and arming out twelve of us went on Shore, rather as to a surprize then fight, for what could nakedness do to encounter with Arms. Being conducted by him to the force of our Enemy, we first entered into parley, seeking to gain them rather by fair means then force, but that not prevailing, we were necessitated to use violence, for this *Henry Phill* being of an undaunted resolution, and having armed his fellows with Clubs and Stones, they sent such a Peal amongst us, as made us at the first to give back, which encouraged them to follow us on with great violence. But we discharging off three or four Guns, when they saw some of themselves wounded, and heard the terrible reports which they gave, they ran away with greater speed then they came. The Band of the *Trevors* [12] who were joyned with us, hotly pursued them, and having taken their Captain, returned with great triumph to their Governour, who sitting in Judgment upon him, he was adjudged to

---

[12] Bruce (241) points out the similarities between this legislation and laws enunciated in Exodus 20–22. But what is the point of these similarities? Is reinvention of the Law of Moses a cultural advance or part of the general regression to the primitive?

death, and thrown off a steep Rock into the Sea, the only way they have of punishing any by death, except burning.

And now at last we took our solemn leaves of the Governour, and departed from thence, having been there in all, the space of three weeks and two dayes. We took with us good store of the flesh of a Beast which they call there *Reval*, being in tast different either from Beef or Swines-flesh, yet very delightful to the Pallate, and exceeding nutrimental. We took also with us alive, divers Fowls which they call *Marde*, about the bigness of a Pullet, and not different in taste. They are very swift of flight, and yet so fearless of danger, that they will stand still till such time as you catch them: We had also sent us in by the Governour about two bushels of eggs, which as I conjecture were the *Mards* eggs, very lusscious in taste, and strengthening to the body.

June 8. We had a sight of *Cambaia*,[13] a part of the *East Indies*, but under the Government of the great *Cham*° of *Tartary*; here our Vessel springing a leak, we were forced to put to shore, receiving much damage in some of our Commodities; we were forced to ply the Pump for eighteen hours together, which, had that miscarried, we had inevitably have perished; here we stai'd five days mending our Ship, and drying some of our Goods, and then hoising Sail, in four days time more we came to *Calecute*.[14]

This *Calecute* is the chief Mart Town and Staple of all the *Indian* Traffique. It is very populous, and frequented by Merchants of all Nations. Here we unladed a great part of our Goods, and taking in others, which caused us to stay there a full Moneth, during which space, at leisure time I went abroad to take a survey of the City, which I found to be large and populous, lying for three miles together upon the Sea-Shore. Here is a great many of those persons whom they call *Brachmans*,° being their Priests or Teachers whom they much reverence. It is a custome here for the King to give to some of those *Brachmain*, the hanselling° of his Nuptial Bed; for which cause, not the Kings, but the Kings sisters sons succeed in the Kingdom, as being more certainly known to be of the true Royal blood: And these sisters of his choose what Gentleman they please, on whom to bestow their Virginities; and if they prove not in a certain time to be with child, they betake themselves to these *Brachman Stallions*, who never fail of doing their work.

Cham: Khan   **Brachmans:** Brahmins
hanselling: inaugurating; consummating

---

[13] A kingdom in India, whose capital was Cambay.
[14] Calicut, an important trading centre for spices in Malabar, on the west coast of India.

The people are indifferently civil and ingenious. Both men and women imitate a Majesty in their Train and Apparel, which they sweeten with Oyles and Perfumes: adorning themselves with Jewels and other Ornaments besitting each Rank and Quality of them.

They have many old Customs amongst them which they observe very strictly; as first, not knowing their Wives after they have born them two children: Secondly, not accompanying them, if after five years cohabitation they can raise no issue by them, but taking others in their rooms. Thirdly, never being rewarded for any Military exploit unless they bring with them an enemies Head in their Hand. But that which is strangest, and indeed most barbarous, is that when any of their friends falls sick, they will rather chuse to kill him, then that he should be withered by sickness.

Thus you see there is little employment there for Doctors, when to be sick, is the next way for to be slain, or perhaps the people may be of the mind rather to kill themselves, then to let the Doctors do it.

Having dispatched our business, and fraighted again our Ship, we left *Calecute*, and put forth to Sea, and coasted along several of the Islands belonging to *India*. At *Camboia* I met with our old friend Mr. *David Prire*, who was overjoyed to see me, to whom I related our Discovery of the Island of *Pines*, in the same manner as I have related it to you; he was then but newly recovered of a Feaver, the Air of that place not being agreeable to him. Here we took in good store of Aloes, and some other Commodities, and victualled our Ship for our return home.

After four dayes sailing, we met with two *Portugal* Ships which came from *Lisbon*, one whereof had in a storm lost its Top-mast, and was forced in part to be towed by the other. We had no bad weather in eleven dayes space, but then a sudden storm of Wind did us much harm in our Tacklings, and swept away one of our Sailors off from the Fore-Castle. *November* the sixth had like to have been a fatal day unto us, our Ship striking twice upon a Rock, and at night was in danger of being fired by the negligence of a Boy, leaving a Candle carelesly in the Gun-room; the next day we were chased by a Pyrate of *Argiere*,[15] but by the swiftness of our Sails we out ran him. *December* the first we came again to *Madagascar*, where we put in for a fresh recruit° of Victuals and Water.

During our abode here, there hapned a very great Earthquake, which tumbled down many Houses. The people of themselves are very Unhospitable and Treacherous, hardly to be drawn to Traffique with any people; and now, this calamitie happening upon them, so enraged them against the

recruit: supply

---

[15] Algiers. Europeans were frequently captured and enslaved by North Africans.

Christians, imputing all such calamities to the cause of them, that they fell upon some *Portugals* and wounded them, and we seeing their mischievous Actions, with all the speed we could put forth to Sea again, and sailed to the Island of St. *Hellens.*

Here we stayed all the *Christmas Holy-dayes*, which was very much celebrated by the Governour there under the King of *Spain*: Here we furnished our selves with all necessaries which we wanted; but upon our departure, our old acquaintance Mr. *Petrus Ramazina*, coming in a Skiff out of the Isle *del Principe*, or the Princes Island, retarded our going for the space of two dayes, for both my self and our Purser had Emergent business with him, he being concerned in those Affairs of which I wrote to you in *April* last. Indeed we cannot but acknowledge his Courtesies unto us, of which you know he is never sparing. *January* the first, we again hoised Sail. Having a fair and prosperous gail of Wind, we touched at the *Canaries*, but made no tarriance, desirous now to see our Native Countrey; but the Winds was very cross unto us for the space of a week. At last we were favoured with a gentle Gale, which brought us on merrily; though we were on a sudden stricken again into a dump; a Sailor from the main Mast discovering five Ships, which put us all in a great fear, we being Richly Laden, and not very well provided for Defence; but they bearing up to us, we found them to be *Zealanders* and our Friends; after many other passages concerning us not so much worthy of Note, we at last safely arrived at home, *May 26*, 1668.

Thus Sir, have I given you a brief, but true Relation of our Voyage, Which I was the more willing to do, to prevent false Copies which might be spread of this nature: As for the Island of *Pines* it self, which caused me to Write this Relation, I suppose it is thing so strange as will hardly be credited by some, although perhaps knowing persons, especially considering our last age being so full of Discoveries, that this Place should lie Dormant for so long a space of time; Others I know, such Nullifidians° as will believe nothing but what they see, applying that Proverb unto us, *That Travelors may lye by authority.* But Sir, in writing to you, I question not but to give Credence, you knowing my disposition so hateful to divulge Falsities; I shall request you to impart this my Relation to Mr. *W. W.* and Mr. *P. L.* remembring me very kindly unto them, not forgetting my old acquaintance Mr. *J. P.* and Mr. *J. B.* No more at present, but only my best respects to you and your second self, I rest

Yours in the best of friendship,
Henry Cornelius Van Sloetten.

July 22, 1668.

Nullifidians: disbelievers

POST-SCRIPT.

One thing concerning the Isle of *Pines*, I had almost quite forgot, we had with us an *Irish* man named *Dermot Conelly* who had formerly been in *England*, and had learned there to play on the Bag-pipes; which he carried to Sea with him; yet so un-Englished he was, that he had quite forgotten your Language, but still retained his Art of Bagpipe-playing, in which he took extraordinary delight; being one day on Land in the Isle of *Pines*, he played on them, but to see the admiration of those naked people concerning them, would have striken you into admiration; long time it was before we could perswade them that it was not a living creature, although they were permitted to touch and feel it, and yet are the people very intelligible, retaining a great part of the Ingenuity and Gallantry of the *English* Nation, though they have not that happy means to express themselves; in this respect we may account them fortunate, in that possessing little, they enjoy all things, as being contented with what they have, wanting those alurements to mischief, which our *European* Countries are enriched with. I shall not dilate any further. No question but time will make this Island known better to the world; all that I shall ever say of it is, that it is a place enriched with Natures abundance, deficient in nothing conducible to the sustentation of mans life, which were it Manured by Agri-culture and Gardening, as other of our *European* Countries are, no question but it would equal, if not exceed many which now pass for praiseworthy.

FINIS.

Abdelazer (1676)

Abdelazer was first performed by the Duke's Company in the summer of 1676 and published the following year. Later in the century, Henry Purcell provided his still famous incidental music for the play. In 1695, when theatrical competition resumed in London after thirteen years in which only a single company had operated, *Abdelazer* was chosen by the established company to compete with the opening night of its new rival, which saw the première of Congreve's great comedy, *Love for Love*. The revival was not a success, and *Abdelazer* disappeared from the repertory.

The principal actors in the first performance were as follow:

- Thomas Betterton (1635–1710), Abdelazer. The leading actor of the period, he took a leading role in theater management after the death in 1668 of Sir William Davenant, the founder of the Duke's Company. He had an enormous range. Behn chiefly exploits his talent for portraying dangerous glamor (also exemplified in his portrayal of the icy seducer Dorimant in Etherege's *The Man of Mode* [1676]).
- Henry Harris (c. 1634–1704), Ferdinand. Along with Betterton and Smith, he was one of the chief Duke's Company actors in the 1660s and 1670s. He retired in 1682.
- William Smith (d. 1695), Philip. After Betterton, Smith was the leading Duke's Company actor and for some years was co-manager of the company with Betterton. He not only played many heroic tragic characters but also more ambiguous or intemperate roles, such as Philip in this play. In comedy, he generally took one of the two male leads, but he also created the vacuous Sir Fopling Flutter in Etherege's *The Man of Mode*.

Aphra Behn, *Abdelazer, or The Moor's Revenge* (London, 1677).

- Elizabeth Barry (c. 1658–1713), Leonora. One of the leading actresses of the late seventeeth century, she was here at the beginning of her career. She was to create the part of the lively Hellena in *The Rover* (1677) and excelled in roles of passionate sensuality, such as Lady Galliard in Behn's *The Luckey Chance* (1682). At some stage, perhaps very early, she took over the part of Angellica Bianca in *The Rover*.
- Mary Betterton (c. 1637–1712), Florella. She was the wife of Thomas Betterton. She often took vulnerable roles (such as Ophelia), and Behn always used her in them. Her greatest role, however, was Lady Macbeth. In Elkanah Settle's *The Empress of Morocco* (1673), which resembles *Abdelazer* in a number of ways, she played the lustful queen, and Mary Lee (here the Queen Mother) played the virtuous heroine.
- Mary Lee (née Aldridge, later Lady Slingsby) (d. 1694), Queen Mother. She was an actress who excelled in passionate or lustful roles, but was not typecast in them.

The Actors Names.

Mr. *Harris,*	Ferdinand	A young King of *Spain*, in Love with *Florella.*
Mr. *Smith,*	Philip	His Brother.
Mr. *Betterton,*	Abdelazer	The Moor.
Mr. *Medburne,*	Mendozo	Prince Cardinal, in Love with the Queen.
Mr. *Crosbie,*	Alonzo	A young Nobleman of *Spain,* contracted to *Leonora.*
Mr. *Norris,*	Roderigo	A Creature to the Moor.
Mr. *John Lee,*	Antonio Sebastian	Two Officers of *Philips.*
Mr. *Percivall,* Mr. *Richards,*	Osmin Zarrack	Moors, and Officers to *Abdelazer.*

Officers, Pages, and Attendants.

Mrs. *Lee,*	Isabella	Queen of *Spain*, Mother to *Ferdinand* and *Philip*, in Love with *Abdelazer.*
Mrs. *Barrer,*	Leonora	Her Daughter, Sister to *Ferdinand* and *Philip.*
Mrs. *Betterton,*	Florella	Wife to *Abdelazer*, and Sister to *Alonzo.*
Mrs. *Osborne,*	Elvira	Woman to the Queen.

Other Women, Attendants.

SCENE *Spain*, and in the Camp.

ABDELAZER,

OR THE

MOOR'S REVENGE.

ACT I.

SCENE I. *A Rich Chamber.*

A Table with Lights, Abdelazer *sullenly leaning his head on his hands; – after a little while, still*° *Musick plays.*

SONG.

Ove in Phantastique Triumph sat,
Whilst Bleeding hearts about him flow'd,
For whom fresh payns he did create,
And strange Tyrannick pow'r he shew'd;
From thy bright Eyes he took his fires,
Which round about in sport he hurl'd;
But 'twas from mine he took desires,
Enough t' undoe the Amorous world.

From me he took his sighs and tears,
From thee his pride and cruelty;
From me his languishments and fears,
And ev'ry killing Dart from thee:
Thus thou, and I, the God have arm'd,
And set him up a Deity,
But my poor heart alone is harm'd,
Whilst thine the Victor is, and free.

After which he rouzes, and gazes.

still: soft

— 33 —

Abdelazer. On me this Musick lost? – this found on me
     That hates all softness? – What ho, my Slaves!

                         Enter Osmin, Zarrack.

Osmin. My gracious Lord –   *Enter Queen,* Elvira.
Queen. My dearest *Abdelazer* –
Abdelazer. Oh, are you there? – Ye Dogs, how came she in?
     Did I not charge you on your lives to watch,
     That none disturb my privacy?   [*Exeunt* Osmin; Zarrack]
Queen. My gentle *Abdelazer,* 'tis thy Queen,
     Who 'as laid aside the bus'ness of her State,
     To wanton in the kinder joys of Love. –
     Play all your sweetest Notes, such as inspire   *To the Musick;*
     The active Soul with new and soft desire,   *they play softly.*
     Whilst we from Eyes – thus – dying, fan the fire.   *she sits down by him.*
Abdelazer. Cease that ungrateful noise – –   *Musick ceases.*
Queen. Can ought that I command displease my Moor?
Abdelazer. Away, fond° woman –
Queen. Nay, prithee be more kind. –
Abdelazer. Nay, prithee good Queen, leave me, – I am dull,
     Unfit for dalliance now. –
Queen. Why dost thou frown? – to whom was that Curse sent?
Abdelazer. To thee. –
Queen. To me! – it cannot be; – to me, sweet Moor! –
     No, no, it cannot; – prithee smile upon me; –
     Smile whilst a thousand *Cupids* shall descend
     And call thee *Jove,*° and wait upon thy smiles,
     Deck thy smooth brow with flowers;
     Whilst in my Eyes, needing no other Glass,
     Thou shalt behold and wonder at thy beauty.
Abdelazer. Away, away, be gone. –
Queen. Where hast thou learnt this language, that can say
     But those rude words, – Away, away, be gone?
     Am I grown ugly now?
Abdelazer. Ugly as Hell. –
Queen. Didst thou not love me once, and swore that Heav'n
     Dwelt in my face and eyes?

fond: foolish   **Jove:** Jupiter

Abdelazer. Thy face and eyes! – Bawd, fetch me here a Glass,   *To* Elvira.
 And thou shalt see the balls of both those eyes
 Burning with fire of Lust. –
 That bloud that dances in thy Cheeks so hot,
 That have not I to cool it
 Made an extraction ev'n of my Soul,
 Decay'd my Youth, only to feed thy Lust!
 And wou'dst thou still pursue me to my Grave?
Queen. All this to me, my *Abdelazer*!
Abdelazer. I cannot ride through the *Castilian* Streets,
 But thousand eyes
 Throw killing looks at me; –
 And cry, – That's he that does abuse our King; –
 There goes the Minion° of the *Spanish* Queen,
 Who, on the lazie pleasures of his Love,
 Spends the Revenues of the King of *Spain:* –
 This many-headed-beast your Lust has arm'd. –
Queen. How dare you, Sir, upbraid me with my Love?
Abdelazer. I will not answer thee, nor hear thee speak.
Queen. Not hear me speak! – Yes, and in thunder too;
 Since all my passion, all my soft intreaties
 Can do no good upon thee,
 I'le see (since thou hast banisht all thy Love,
 That Love, to which I've sacrific'd my Honour)
 If thou hast any sence of Gratitude,
 For all the mighty graces I have done thee.
Abdelazer. Doe; – and in thy story too, do not leave out
 How dear those mighty graces I have purchas'd!
 My blooming Youth, my healthful vigorous Youth,
 Which Nature gave me for more Noble Actions
 Then to lie fawning at a womans feet,
 And pass my hours in idleness and Love. –
 If I cou'd blush, I shou'd through all this Cloud
 Send forth my sence of shame into my Cheeks.
Queen. Ingrate!°
 Have I for this abus'd the best of men?
 My noble Husband!

---

minion: paramour   **ingrate:** ungrateful

Depriving him of all the joys of Love,
To bring them all intirely to thy bed;
Neglected all my vows, and sworn 'em here a-new,
Here, on thy lips; –
Exhausted Treasures that wou'd purchase Crowns,
To buy thy smiles, – to buy a gentle look; –
And when thou didst repay me, – blest the Giver! –
Oh *Abdelazer*, more then this I've done. –
This very hour, the last the King can live,
Urg'd by thy witchcraft I his life betray'd:
And is it thus – my bounties are repaid?
What e're a crime so great deserves from Heav'n,
By *Abdelazer* might have been forgiv'n. –   *Weeps.*
But I will be reveng'd by penitence,
And e're the King dies, own my black offence. –
And yet that's not enough – *Elvira* –   *Pauses.*
Cry murder, murder, help, help. –   *She and her woman*
Elvira. Help, murder, murder. –   *cry aloud, he is*
Abdelazer. Hell, what's this! – peace Bawd, – 'sdeath,   *surpriz'd, the Queen*
   They'le raise the Court upon me, and then I'me lost. –   *falls, he draws a*
   My Queen, – my Goddess, – Oh raise your lovely eyes,   *Dagger at Elvira.*
   I have dissembled coldness all this while;
   And that deceit was but to try thy Faith. –
   Look up, – by Heav'n't was Jealousie,   *Takes her up,*
   Pardon your Slave, – pardon your poor Adorer.   *sets her in a Chair,*
Queen. Thou didst upbraid me with my shamefull passion.   *then kneels.*
Abdelazer. I'le tear my tongue out for its profanation.
Queen. And when I woo'd thee, but to smile upon me,
   Thou crydst, – Away, I'me dull, unfit for dalliance.
Abdelazer. Call back the frighted bloud into thy Cheeks,
   And I'le obey the dictates of my Love,
   And smile, and kiss, and dwell for ever here. –

             Enter Osmin *hastily.*

How now! – why star'st thou so? –
Osmin. My Lord, – the King is dead.
Abdelazer. The King dead! – 'twas time then to dissemble.   *Aside.*
   What means this rudeness? –   *One knocks.*

Enter Zarrack.

Zarrack. My Lord, – the Cardinal enquiring for the Queen,
   The Court is in an uproar, none can find her.
Abdelazer. Not find the Queen! and wou'd they search her here!
Queen. What shall I do? I must not here be found.
Abdelazer. Oh, do not fear, – no Cardinal enters here;
   No King, – no God, that means to be secure. –
   Slaves, guard the doors, and suffer none to enter,
   Whilst I, my charming Queen, provide for your security: –
   You know there is a Vault deep under ground,
   Into the which the busie Sun ne're entred,
   But all is dark, as are the shades of Hell;
   Through which in dead of night I oft have pass'd,
   Guided by Love, to your Apartment, Madam. –
   They knock agen; – thither, my lovely Mistress,   *Knock.*
   Suffer your self to be conducted. –
   Osmin, attend the Queen, – descend in haste, *Queen*, Osmin *and* Elvira
   My Lodgings are beset.   *descend the Vault.*
Zarrack. I cannot guard the Lodgings longer,
   Don *Ordonio*, Sir, to seek the Queen.
Abdelazer. How dare they seek her here?
Zarrack. My Lord, the King has swounded° twice,
   And being recover'd, calls for her Majesty.
Abdelazer. The King not dead! – go *Zarrack*, and aloud
   Tell Don *Ordonio* and the Cardinal,
   He that dares enter here to seek the Queen,   *Puts his hand*
   Had better snatch the She from the fierce side   *to his Sword.*
   Of a young Amorous Lion, and 'twere safer. –
   Again, more knocking! –   *Knocking.*
Zarrack. My gracious Lord, it is your Brother,° Don *Alonzo.*
Abdelazer. I will not have him enter, – I am disorder'd. –
Zarrack. My Lord, 'tis now too late.

Enter Alonzo.

Alonzo. Saw you not the Queen, my Lord?
Abdelazer. My Lord?

---

swounded: swooned   **Brother:** brother-in-law

Alonzo. Was not the Queen here with you?

Abdelazer. The Queen with me!

   Because, Sir, I am married to your Sister,

   You, like your Sister, must be jealous too:

   The Queen with me! with me! a Moor! a Devil!

   A Slave of *Barbary*! for so

   Your gay young Courtiers christen me: – but Don,

   Although my skin be black, within my veins

   Runs bloud as red, and Royal as the best. –

   My Father, Great *Abdela*, with his Life

   Lost too his Crown: both most unjustly ravisht

   By Tyrant *Philip*; your old King I mean.

   How many wounds his valiant breast receiv'd,

   Ere he wou'd yield to part with Life and Empire:

   Methinks I see him cover'd o're with bloud,

   Fainting amidst those numbers he had conquer'd;

   I was but young, yet old enough to grieve,

   Though not revenge, or to defie my Fetters;

   For then began my Slavery: and e're since

   Have seen that Diadem° by this Tyrant worn,

   Which Crown'd the Sacred Temples of my Father,

   And shou'd adorn mine now; – shou'd! nay and must; –

   Go tell him what I say, – 'twill be but death: –

   Go Sir, – the Queen's not here. –

Alonzo. Do not mistake me, Sir; – or if, I wou'd,

   I've no old King to tell, – the King is dead; –

   And I am answer'd, Sir, to what I came for,

   And so good night. –   *Exit.*

Abdelazer. Now all that's brave and Villain° seize my soul,

   Reform each faculty that is not Ill,

   And make it fit for Vengeance; noble Vengeance!

   Oh glorious word! fit only for the Gods,

   For which they form'd their Thunder,

   Till man usurpt their Power, and by Revenge

   Swayed Destiny as well as they,

   And took their trade of killing. –

   And thou, almighty Love!

Diadem: crown   **villain:** villainous

Dance in a thousand forms about my Person,
That this same Queen, this easie *Spanish* Dame
May be bewitcht and dote upon me still:
Whilst I make use of the Insatiate flame
To set all *Spain* on fire: –
Mischief, erect thy Throne,
And sit on high; here, here upon my head;
Let Fools fear Fate, thus I my Stars defie,   *Points to his*
The influence of this – must raise my glory high.   *Sword.*

Exit.

[ACT I] SCENE II.

Enter Ferdinand *weeping,* Ordonio *bearing the Crown, followed by* Alonzo *leading* Leonora *weeping;* Florella, Roderigo, Cardinal, *met by the Queen weeping;* Elvira, *and women.*

Queen. What dolefull cry was that, which like the voice
    Of angry Heav'n struck through my trembling soul!
    Nothing but horrid shrieks, nothing but death;
    Whilst I, bowing my knees to the cold Earth,
    Drowning my Cheeks in Rivulets of tears,
    Sending up prayers in sighs t'implore from Heav'n
    Health for the Royal Majesty of *Spain,* –
    All, cry'd the Majesty of *Spain* is dead.
    Whilst the sad sound flew through the ecchoing Air,
    And reacht my frighted soul – Inform my fears,
    Oh my *Fernando,* oh my gentle Son. –   *Weeps.*
King. Madam, read here the truth, if looks can shew
    That which I cannot speak, and you wou'd know:
    The common Fate, in ev'ry face appears;
    A Kings great loss, the publique grief declares,
    But 'tis a Fathers death that claims my tears.   *Cardinal leads in the*
Leonora. Ah Sir!   *Queen attended.*
    If you thus grieve, who ascend by what y'ave lost
    To all the greatness that a King can boast;
    What tributes from my eyes and heart are due,
    Who've lost at once a King and Father too?

King. My *Leonora* cannot think my grief
   Can from those empty Glories find relief;
   Nature within my soul has equal share,
   And that and Love surmount my glory there.
   Had Heav'n continu'd Royal *Philips* life,
   And giv'n me bright *Florella* for a wife,   *Bows to* Florella
   To Crowns and Scepters I had made no claim,
   But ow'd my blessings only to my flame.
   But Heav'n well knew in giving thee away,   *To* Florella.
   I had no bus'ness for another joy. –   *weeps.*
   The King, *Alonzo*, with his dying breath,   *Turns to* Alonzo
   To you my beauteous Sister did bequeath;   *and* Leonora
   And I his generosity approve,
   And think you worthy *Leonora*'s love.

          Enter Cardinal and *Queen weeping.*

Alonzo. Too gloriously my services are paid,
   In the possession of this Royal Maid,
   To whom my guilty heart durst ne're aspire,
   But rather chose to languish in its fire.

      Enter Philip *in a Rage*, Antonio *and* Sebastian.

Philip. I know he is not dead; what envious powers
   Durst snatch him hence? he was all great and good,
   As fit to be ador'd as they above.
   Where is the body of my Royal Father?
   That body which inspir'd by's sacred soul,
   Aw'd all the Universe with ev'ry frown,
   And taught'em all obedience with his smiles.
   Why stand you thus distracted? – Mother – Brother –
   My Lords – Prince Cardinal –
   Has sorrow struck you dumb?
   Is this my welcome from the toyls of War?
   When in his bosome I shou'd find repose,
   To meet it cold and pale! – Oh guide me to him,
   And with my sighs I'le breath new life into't.
King. There's all that's left of Royal *Philip* now,   Philip *goes out.*
   Pay all thy sorrow there; – whilst mine alone
   Are swoln too high t' admit of lookers on.

           Exit King weeping.

Philip *returns weeping.*

Philip. His soul is flew to all Eternity:
   And yet methought it did inform his body
   That I, his darling *Philip* was arriv'd
   With Conquest on my Sword; and even in death
   Sent me his Joy in smiles.
Queen. If souls can after death have any sense
   Of humane things, his will be proud to know
   That *Philip* is a Conquerour. –   *Enter* Abdelazer.
   But do not drown thy Lawrels thus in tears,
   Such tributes leave to us, thou art a Souldier.
Philip. Gods! this shou'd be my Mother. –
Cardinal. It is, Great Sir, the Queen.
Philip. Oh she's too foul for one or t'other title.
Queen. How Sir, do you not know me?
Philip. When you were just, I did, –
   And with a reverence such as we pay Heav'n,
   I paid my awfull° duty, –
   But as you have abus'd my Royal Father,
   For such a sin the basest of your Slaves
   Wou'd blush to call you Mother.
Queen. What means my Son?
Philip. Son! by Heav'n I scorn the title.
Queen. Oh insolence! – out of my sight, rude Boy.
Philip. We must not part so, Madam;
   I first must let you know your sin and shame: –
   Nay hear me calmly, – for by Heav'n you shall. –
   My Father whilst he liv'd, tir'd his strong Arm
   With numerous Battels 'gainst the Enemy,
   Wasting his brains in Warlike stratagems,
   To bring confusion on the faithless Moors,
   Whilst you, lull'd in soft peace at home, – betray'd
   His name to everlasting Infamy;
   Suffer'd his Bed to be defil'd with Lust,
   Gave up your self, your honour, and your vows,
   To wanton in yon Sooty Leacher's arms.   *Points to* Abdelazer.

awfull: reverent

Abdelazer. Me dost thou mean!

Philip. Yes, Villain, thee, thou Hell-begotten Fiend,
   'Tis thee I mean.

Queen. Oh most unnatural to dishonour me!

Philip. That Dog you mean, that has dishonour'd you,
   Dishonour'd me, these Lords, nay and all *Spain*;
   This Devil's he, that –

Abdelazer. That – what? – Oh pardon me if I throw off
   All tyes of Duty: – wert thou ten Kings Sons,
   And I as many souls as I have sins,
   Thus – I wou'd hazard all –   *Draws, they all*

Philip. Stand off, – or I'le make way upon they   *run between.*
   Bosome. –

Abdelazer. How got you, Sir, this daring? –

Philip. From injur'd *Philips* death,
   Who, whilst he liv'd, unjustly cherisht thee,
   And set thee up beyond the reach of Fate;
   Blind with thy brutal valour, deaf with thy flatteries,
   Discover'd not the Treasons thou didst act,
   Nor none durst let him know 'em: – but did he live,
   I wou'd aloud proclaim them in his ears.

Abdelazer. You durst as well been damn'd. –

Philip. Hell seize me if I want revenge for this, –
   Not dare!
   Arise thou injur'd Ghost of my dead King,
   And through thy dreadfull paleness dart a horrour,
   May fright this pair of Vipers from their sins.

Abdelazer. Oh insupportable! dost hear me Boy!

Queen. Are ye all mute, and hear me thus upbraided?   *To the Lords.*

Philip. Dare ye detain me, whilst the Traytor braves me?

Cardinal. Forbear, my Prince, keep in that noble heat,
   That shou'd be better us'd then on a Slave.

Abdelazer. You politick° Cheat –

Cardinal. Abdelazer, –
   By the Authority of my Government,
   Which yet I hold over the King of *Spain*,
   By warrant from a Councel of the Peers,
   And (as an Unbeliever) from the Church,

politick: scheming

I utterly deprive thee of that Greatness, —
Thofe Offices and Trusts you hold in *Spain*.
Abdelazer. Cardinal, — who lent thee this Commission?
Grandees of *Spain*, do you consent to this?
All. We doe. —
Alonzo. What reason for it? let his Faith be try'd.
Cardinal. It needs no tryal, the proofs are evident,
And his Religion was his veil for Treason.
Alonzo. Why should you question his Religion, Sir?
He does profess Christianity.
Cardinal. Yes, witness his habit, which he still retains
In scorn to ours. —
His Principles too are as unalterable.
Abdelazer. Is that the only Argument you bring? —
I tell thee, Cardinal, not thy Holy Gown
Covers a soul more sanctify'd
Than this Moorish Robe.
Philip. Damn his Religion, — he has a thousand crimes
That will yet better justifie your sentence.
Cardinal. Come not within the Court, for if you do,
Worse mischief shall ensue: — you have your sentence.   *Exeunt*
Alonzo. My Brother banisht! 'tis very sudden;   (Philip & *Cardinal*)
For thy sake, Sister, this must be recall'd.   *To* Florella
Queen. Alonzo, joyn with me, I'le to the King,
And check the pride of this insulting Cardinal.   *Exeunt all, except*

Manent° Abdelazer, Florella.

Abdelazer. Banisht! if I digest this gall,
May Cowards pluck the wreath from off my brow,
Which I have purchas'd with so many wounds,
And all for *Spain*; for *Spain*! ingrateful *Spain*! —
Oh my *Florella*, all my Glory's vanisht,
The Cardinal (Oh damn him!) wou'd have me banisht.
Florella. But Sir, I hope you will not tamely go.
Abdelazer. Tamely! — ha, ha, ha, — yes by all means;
A very honest and Religious Cardinal!
Florella. I wou'd not for the world you shou'd be banisht.

manent: remain

Abdelazer. Not *Spain* you mean; – for then she leaves the King.   *aside.*
    What if I be? – Fools! not to know – All parts oth' world
    Allow enough for Villanie, – for I'le be brave no more.
    It is a crime, – and then I can live any where. –
    But say I go from hence; – I leave behind me
    A Cardinal that will laugh; – I leave behind me
    A *Philip* that will clap his hands in sport: –
    But the worst wound is this, – I leave my wrongs,
    Dishonours, and my Discontents, all unreveng'd. –
    Leave me, *Florella*, – prithee do not weep;
    I love thee, – love thee wondrously; – go, leave me, –
    I am not now at leisure to be fond;[1] –
    Go to your Chamber, – go. –
Florella. No, to the King I'le fly,
    And beg him to revenge thy Infamy.   *Exit* Florella.

                    To him Alonzo.

Alonzo. The Cardinal's mad° to have thee banisht *Spain*;
    I've left the Queen in angry contradiction,
    But yet I fear the Cardinal's reasoning:
Abdelazer. This Prince's hate proceeds from Love, ⎫
    He's jealous of the Queen, and fears my power. ⎭   *Aside.*
Alonzo. Come, rouze thy wonted spirits, awake thy soul,
    And arm thy Justice with a brave Revenge.
Abdelazer. I'le arm no Justice with a brave Revenge.   *Sullenly.*
Alonzo. Shall they then triumph o're thee, who were once
    Proud to attend thy Conqu'ring Chariot wheels?
Abdelazer. I care not; – I am a Dog, and can bear wrongs.
Alonzo. But Sir, my Honour is concern'd with yours,
    Since my lov'd Sister did become your Wife;
    And if yours suffer, mine too is unsafe.
Abdelazer. I cannot help it. –

---

mad furiously eager

---

[1] An echo of a famous boast by Almanzor, the hero of Dryden's *The Conquest of Granada*:
    "I have not leisure yet to dye" (Part I, 1.i.233, in Edward Niles Hooker et al., eds., *The
    Works of John Dryden*, 20 vols. [Berkeley: University of California Press, 1956–2000], XI).
    It is also echoed by Willmore in *The Rover*: "I am not now at leisure to be kill'd" (1.211,
    in Janet Todd, ed., *The Works of Aphra Behn*, 7 vols. [London: Pickering & Chatto,
    1992–96], V).

Alonzo. What Ice has chil'd thy bloud?
   This patience was not wont to dwell with thee.
Abdelazer. 'Tis true, but now the world is chang'd you see;
   Thou art too brave to know what I resolve: –   *Aside.*
   No more, – here comes the King with my *Florella*,
   He loves her, and she swears to me she's chast; ⎫
   'Tis well, if true; – well too, if it be false: ⎬   *Aside.*
   I care not, 'tis Revenge –   ⎟
   That I must sacrifice my love and pleasure to. ⎭

                        Alonzo *and* Abdelazer *stand aside.*

      Enter King, Lords, Guard *passing over the Stage,*
        Florella *in a suppliant posture weeping.*

King. Thou woo'st me to reverse thy Husbands doom,
   And I wooe thee, for mercy on my self;
   Why shou'dst thou sue to him for life and liberty
   For any other, who himself lies dying,
   Imploring from thy eyes a little pity.
Florella. Oh mighty King! in whose sole power, like Heav'n,
   The lives and safeties of your Slaves remain,
   Hear and redress my *Abdelazer*'s wrongs.
King. All lives and safeties in my power remain!
   Mistaken charming creature, if my power
   Be such, who kneel and bow to thee,
   What must thine be,
   Who hast the Soveraign command o're me and it!
   Wou'dst thou give life? turn but thy lovely eyes
   Upon the wretched thing that wants it,
   And he will surely live, and live for ever.
   Canst thou do this, and com'st to beg of me?
Florella. Alas Sir, what I beg's what you alone can give,
   My *Abdelazer*'s pardon.
King. Pardon! can any thing ally'd to thee offend?
   Thou art so sacred and so innocent,
   That but to know thee, and to look on thee,
   Must change even vice to virtue.
   Oh my *Florella*!
   So perfectly thou dost possess my soul,
   That ev'ry wish of thine shall be obey'd:

Say, wou'dst thou have thy Husband share my Crown?
Do but submit to love me, and I yield it.
Florella. Such love as humble Subjects owe their King,   *Kneels, he takes*
And such as I dare pay, I offer here.   *her up.*
King. I must confess it is a price too glorious:
But my *Florella* –
Abdelazer. I'le interrupt your amorous discourse.   (*Aside.*   Abdelazer
Florella. Sir, – *Abdelazer*'s here –   *comes up to them.*
King. His presence never was less welcome to me; –   *Aside.*
But Madam, durst the Cardinal use this insolence?
Where is your Noble Husband?
Abdelazer. He sees me, yet enquires for me.   *Aside.*
Florella. Sir, my Lord is here –
King. Abdelazer, I have heard with much surprize
O th' injuries y'ave receiv'd, and mean to right you:
My Father lov'd you well, made you his General,
I think you worthy of that Honour still.
Abdelazer. True, – for my Wifes sake –   *Aside.*
King. When my Coronation is solemnized,
Be present there, and reassume your wonted State and place;
And see how I will check the Insolent Cardinal.
Abdelazer. I humbly thank my Soveraign –   (*Aside.*   *Kneels and kisses*
That he loves my Wife so well. –   *the Kings hand*
                                                                        Exeunt.

Manent Abdelazer, Florella.

Florella. Wilt thou not pay my service with one smile?
Have I not acted well the Suppliants part?
Abdelazer. Oh wonderfully! y'ave learnt the art to move;
Go, leave me. –
Florella. Still out of humour, thoughtful, and displeas'd!
And why at me, my *Abdelazer,* what have I done?
Abdelazer. Rarely! you cannot do amiss you are so beautiful,
So very fair! – Go, get you in, I say. –   *Turns her in ruffly.*
She has the art of dallying with my soul,
Teaching it lazie softness from her looks. –
But now a nobler passion's enter'd there.
And blows it thus, – to Air. – Idol Ambition,
Florella must to thee a Victim fall:
Revenge, – to thee – a Cardinal and Prince:
And to my Love and Jealousie, a King. –

More yet, my mighty Deities, I'le do,
None that you e're inspir'd like me shall act;
That fawning servile crew shall follow next,
Who with the Cardinal cry'd banish *Abdelazer*:
Like Eastern Monarchs I'le adorn thy Fate,
And to the shades thou shalt descend in state.   *Exit.*

ACT II.

SCENE I.

Enter the King Crown'd, Philip, *Cardinal, Queen,* Leonora, Florella, Elvira, Alonzo, Roderigo, Ordonio, Sebastian, Antonio, *Officers and Guards; met by* Abdelazer, *follow'd by* Osmin, Zarrack, *and Moors attending. He comes in with Pride, staring on* Philip *and Cardinal, and takes his stand next the King.*

Philip. Why stares the Devil thus, as if he meant
    From his infectious eyes to scatter Plagues,
    And poison all the world; was he not banisht? –
    How dares the Traytor venture into th' Presence? –
    Guards, spurn the Villain forth.
Abdelazer. Who spurns° the Moor
    Were better set his foot upon the Devil! –
    Do, spurn me; and this hand thus justly arm'd,
    Shall like a Thunder-bolt, breaking the Clouds
    Divide his body from his soul; – stand back!–   *To the Guards.*
    Spurn *Abdelazer*! –
Philip. Death, shall we bear this Insolence!
Alonzo. Great Sir, I think his Sentence was unjust.   *To the King.*
Cardinal. Sir, you're too partial to be Judge in this,
    And shall not give your Voice.
Abdelazer. Proud Cardinal, – but he shall, – and give it loud,
    And who shall hinder him? –
Philip. This, – and cut his Wind-pipe too,   *Offers to draw.*
    To spoil his whisp'ring.   Abdelazer *offers to draw,*
King. What means this violence?   *his Attendants do the same.*
    Forbear to draw your Swords, – 'tis we command.

spurns: kicks

Abdelazer. Sir, do me Justice, I demand no more,   *Kneels, and offers*
 And at your feet we lay our weapons down.   *his Sword.*
Cardinal. Sir, *Abdelazer* has had Justice done,
 And stands by me banisht the Court of *Spain.*
King. How, Prince Cardinal!
 From whence do you derive Authority
 To banish him the Court without our leave?
Cardinal. Sir, from my care unto your Royal Person,
 As I'me your Governour; – then, for the Kingdoms safety.
King. Because I was a Boy, must I be still so?
 Time, Sir, has given me in that formal Ceremony,
 And I am of an age to Rule alone;
 And from henceforth, discharge you – of your care.
 We know your near relation to this Crown,
 And wanting Heirs, that you must fill the Throne,
 Till when, Sir, I am absolute Monarch here, –
 And you must learn obedience.
Cardinal. Pardon my zealous duty, which I hope
 You will approve, and not recall his Banishment.
King. Sir, but I will; and who dares contradict it, is a Traytor.
Philip. I dare the first, yet do defie the last.
King. My hot-brain'd Sir, I'le talk to you anon.
Cardinal. Sir, I am wrong'd, and will Appeal to *Rome.*
Philip. By Heav'n I'le to the Camp; – Brother, farewell,
 When next I meet thee, it shall be in Arms;
 If thou can't get loose from thy Mistress Chains,
 Where thou ly'st drown'd in idle wanton Love.
Abdelazer. Hah! – his Mistress! – who is't Prince *Philip* means?
Philip. Thy wife! thy wife! proud Moor, whom thou'rt content
 To sell (for Honour) to eternal Infamy. –
 Does't make thee snarle! – bite on, whilst thou shalt see,
 I go for Vengeance, and 'twill come with me.
         Going out, turns and draws.
Abdelazer. Stay! for 'tis here already; – turn, proud Boy. Abdelazer *draws.*
King. What mean you, *Philip*? –   *Talks to him aside:*
Queen. Cease! cease your most impolitick Rage! –   *to* Abdelazer
 Is this a time to shew't? – Dear Son, you are a King,
 And may allay this Tempest.
King. How dare you disobey my will and pleasure?   *To* Abdelazer.
Abdelazer. Shall I be calm, and hear my wife call'd Whore?

Were he great *Jove*, and arm'd with all his Lightning,
By Heav'n I could not hold my just Resentment.
Queen. 'Twas in his passion, noble *Abdelazer:* –   *King talking*
　Imprudently thou dost disarm thy Rage,   *to* Philip *aside.*
　And giv'st the Foe a warning, e're thou strik'st;
　When with thy smiles thou might'st securely kill. –
　You know the Passion that the Cardinal bears me,
　His power too o're *Philip*, which well manag'd
　Will serve to ruine both; – put up your Sword, –
　When next you draw it, teach it how to act.
Abdelazer. You shame me, and command me.
Queen. Why all this Rage? – does it become, you, Sir?   *To Cardinal*
　What is't you mean to do?   *aside.*
Cardinal. You need not care, whilst *Abdelazer*'s safe.
Queen. Jealousie upon my life; – how gay it looks.
Cardinal. Madam, you want that pitying regard
　To value what I do, or what I am;
　I'le therefore lay my Cardinals Hat aside,
　And in bright Arms, demand my Honour back.
Queen. Is't thus, my Lord, you give me proofs of Love?
　Have then my eyes lost all their wonted power?
　And can you quit the hope of gaining me,
　To follow your Revenge? – go, – go to fight,
　Bear Arms against your Country, and your King,
　All for a little worthless Honour lost.
Cardinal. What is it, Madam, you would have me do?
Queen. Not side with *Philip*, as you hope my Grace. –
　Now Sir, you know my pleasure think on't well.
Cardinal. Madam, you know your Power o're your Slave,
　And use it too tyrannically; – but dispose
　The Fate of him, whose Honour, and whose Life,
　Lies at your mercy; –
　I'le stay and dye, since 'tis your gracious pleasure.
King. *Philip*, upon your life,
　Upon your strict Allegiance, I conjure you
　To remain at Court, till I have reconcil'd you.
Philip. Never Sir, –
　Nor can you bend my temper to that tameness.
King. 'Tis is my power to charge you as a Prisoner;
　But you're my Brother; – yet remember too

I am your King. – No more. –

Philip. I will obey.

King. Abdelazer,

    I beg you will forget your cause of hate

    Against my Brother *Philip,* and the Cardinal;

    He's young, and rash, but will be better temper'd,

Abdelazer. Sir, I have done, and beg your Royal pardon.

King. Come *Philip,* give him your hand.

Philip. I can forgive without a Ceremony.

King. And to confirm ye Friends,

    I invite you all to Night to Banquet with me,

    Pray see you give Attendance: – Come Brother,

    You must along with us.

                Exeunt all but Abdelazer, Queen, and Women.

Queen. Leave me. –   *To the Women, who Exeunt*

    Now my dear Moor –

Abdelazer. Madam. –

Queen. Why dost thou answer with that cold Reserve? –

    Is that a look, – an action for a Lover?

Abdelazer. Ah Madam. –

Queen. Have I not taken off thy Banishment?

    Restor'd thee to thy former state and honours?

    Nay, and heapt new ones too, too mighty for thy hopes;

    And still to raise thee equal to this heart,

    Where thou must ever Reign.

Abdelazer. 'Tis true, my bounteous Mistress, all this you've done, –

    But –

Queen. But what, my *Abdelazer.*

Abdelazer. I will not call it to your memory.

Queen. What canst thou mean?

Abdelazer. Why was the King remov'd?

Queen. To make thy way more easie to my arms.

Abdelazer. Was that all?

Queen. All! –

Abdelazer. Not but it is a blessing, Gods would languish for; –

    But as you've made it free, so make it just.

Queen. Thou meanst, and marry thee.

Abdelazer. No, by the Gods! –   *(Aside.*

    Not marry me, unless I were a King.

Queen. What signifies the Name, to him that Rules one?

Abdelazer. What use has he of life, that cannot live
    Without a Ruler?
Queen. Thou wouldst not have me kill him.
Abdelazer. Oh by no means, not for my wretched life!
    What, kill a King! – forbid it Heav'n!
    Angels stand like his Guards, about his Person.
    The King!
    Not for so many Worlds as there be Stars
    Twinkling upon the embroider'd Firmament!
    The King!
    He loves my wife *Florella*, shoul'd he dye –
    I know none else durst love her.
Queen. And that's the reason you wou'd send him hence.
Abdelazer. I must confess, I wou'd not bear a wrong,
    But do not take me for a Villain, Madam;
    He is my King, and may do what he pleases.
Queen. 'Tis well, Sir.
Abdelazer. Again that frown, it renders thee more charming,
    Than any other Dress thou cou'dst put on.
Queen. Away, you do not love me.
Abdelazer. Now mayst thou hate me, if this be not pretty.
Queen. Oh you can flatter finely –
Abdelazer. Not I, by Heav'n!
    Oh that this head were circled in a Crown,
    And I were King, by Fortune, as by Birth!
    And that I was, till by thy Husband's power
    I was divested in my Infancy. –
    Then you shou'd see, I do not flatter ye.
    But I, instead of that, must see my Crown
    Bandy'd from head to head, and tamely see it;
    And in this wretched state I live, 'tis true,
    But with what joy, you, if you lov'd, might, guess.
Queen. We need no Crowns; Love best contented is
    In shadie Groves, and humble Cottages,
    Where when 'twou'd sport, it safely may Retreat,
    Free from the noise, and danger of the Great;
    Where Victors are ambitious of no Bays,°
    But what their Nymphs bestow on Holy-days;

Bays: laurels

Nor Envy, can the amorous Shepherd move,
Unless against a Rival in his love.
Abdelazer. Love and Ambition, are the same to me,
In either, I'le no Rivals brook.
Queen. Nor I;
And when the King you urge me to remove,
It may be from Ambition, not from Love.
Abdelazer. Those scruples did not in your bosom dwell,
When you a King, did in a Husband kill.
Queen. How Sir! dare you upbraid me with that sin,
To which your Perjuries first drew me in?
Abdelazer. You interrupt my sense, I only meant
A sacrifice, to Love, so well begun,
Shou'd not Devotion want to finish it;
And if that stop to all our joys were gon,
The envying world wou'd to our Power submit:
But Kings are Sacred, and the Gods alone
Their Crimes must judge, and punish too, or none, –
Yet he alone destroys our happiness.
Queen. There's yet one more –
Abdelazer. One more! give me his name,
And I will turn it to a Magick Spell,
To bind him ever fast.
Queen. Florella.
Abdelazer. Florella! Oh I cou'd gnaw my Chains,   *Aside.*
That humble me so low as to adore her:
But the fond blaze must out, – while I erect
A nobler fire more fit for my Ambition.
– *Florella*, dies, – a Victim to your will.
I will not let you lose one single wish,
For a poor life, or two;
Though I must see my Glories made a prey,
And not demand 'em from the Ravisher,
Nor yet complain, – because he is my King!
But *Philip*'s brow, no Sacred Oyntment Deifies,
If he do wrong, stands fair for the Revenger.
Queen. Philip! instruct me how t' undoe that Boy I hate;
The publick Infamy I have receiv'd,
I will Revenge, with nothing less than death.
Abdelazer. 'Tis well we can agree in our Resentments,

For I have vow'd he shall not live a day,
He has an art to pry into our secrets:
To all besides, our love is either hid,
Or else they dare not see; – but this Prince
Has a most dangerous spirit must be calm'd.
Queen. I have resolv'd his death,
And now have waiting in my Cabinet
Engines to carry on this mighty work of my Revenge.
Abdelazer. Leave that to me, who equally am injur'd;
You, like the Gods! need only but command,
And I will execute your sacred will. –
That done, there's none dare whisper what we do.
Queen. Nature be gone, I chase thee from my soul,
Who Love's Almighty Empire does controul;
And she that will to thy dull Laws submit,
In spight of thee, betrays the Hypocrite.
No rigid Virtue shall my soul possess,
Let Gown-men preach against the wickedness;
Pleasures were made by Gods! and meant for us,
And not t' enjoy 'em, were ridiculous.
Abdelazer. Oh perfect, great and glorious of thy Sex!
Like thy great self 'twas spoke, resolv'd and brave! –
I must attend the King; – where I will watch
All *Philip*'s motions –
Queen. And – after that – if you will beg admittance,
I'le give you leave to visit me to night.
Abdelazer. Madam, that blessing now must be deferr'd;   *Leads her to*
My wrongs and I will be retir'd to Night,   *the door.*
And bring forth Vengeance, with the Mornings light.

Enter Osmin, Zarrack.

Osmin. My gracious Lord –
Abdelazer. Come near – and take a secret from my lips;
And he who keeps not silence, hears his death. –
This night the Prince, and Cardinal – do you mark me –
Are murder'd!
Osmin. Where Sir! –
Abdelazer. Here in the Court.
Osmin. By whom, Great Sir!

Abdelazer. By thee! – I know thou dar'st. –
Osmin. Whatever you command.
Abdelazer. Good! – then see it be perform'd.
   – *Osmin*, how goes the Night?
Osmin. About the hour of Eight,
   And you're expected at the Banquet, Sir:
   Prince *Philip* storms, and swears you're with the Queen.
Abdelazer. Let him storm on! the Tempest will be laid;° –
   Where's my Wife? –
Osmin. In the Presence, Sir, with the Princess and other Ladies.
Abdelazer. She's wondrous forward! – what – the King –
   (I am not jealous tho') – but he makes Court to her;
   – hah, *Osmin!*
   He throws but love from Eyes all languishing; –
   Come tell me, – he does sigh to her; – no matter if he do: –
   And fawns upon her hand, – and – kneels; – tell me, Slave!
Osmin. Sir, I saw nothing like to Love; he only treats her
   Equal to her Quality.
Abdelazer. Oh damn her Quality!
Zarrack. I came just now.
   From waiting on his Person to the Banquet.
   And heard him ask, if he might visit her to night,
   Having something to impart to her, that concern'd his life.
Abdelazer. And so it shall, by Heav'n!   (*Aside.*
Zarrack. But she deny'd, and he the more intreated, –
   But all in vain, Sir.
Abdelazer. Go *Osmin*, (you the Captain of my Guard of Moors)
   Chuse out the best affected Officers,
   To keep the Watch to night: –
   Let every Guard be doubled; – you may be liberal too, –
   And when I give the word, be ready all. –
Osmin. What shall the word be?   *Exit* Zarrack.
Abdelazer. Why – Treason: – mean time make it your bus'ness,
   To watch the Prince's coming from the Banquet;
   Heated with Wine, and fearless of his Person,
   You'l find him easily to be attaqu'd.
Osmin. Sir, do not doubt my management nor success.   *Exit* Osmin.
Abdelazer. So, I thank thee Nature, that in making me

laid: calmed

Thou didst design me Villain!
Fitting each faculty for Active mischief: –
Thou skilful Artist, thank thee for my face,
It will discover nought that's hid within. –
Thus arm'd for ills,
Darkness! and Horrour! I invoke your aid;
And thou, dread Night! shade all your busie Stars[2]
In blackest Clouds,
And let my Daggers brightness only serve
To guide me to the mark, – and guide it so,
It may undoe a Kingdom at one blow.   *Exit.*

[ACT II]

SCENE II.

A Banquet; under a Canopy the King, Leonora, Florella, *Ladies waiting;* Philip,
Cardinal, Alonzo, Ordonio, Antonio, Sebastian, *Lords and Attendants: as
soon as the Scene draws off, they all rise, and come forward.*

King. My Lords you're sad to night; give us loud Musick, –
    I have a double cause to mourn;
    And grief has taken up its dwelling here, –
    Beyond the art of Love, or Wine to conquer. –
    'Tis true, my Father's dead, – and possibly
    'Tis not so decent to appear thus gay;
    But life, and death, are equal to the wretched, –
    And whilst *Florella* frowns, – 'tis in that number   *To* Florella.
    I must account her Slave. – *Alonzo,*
    How came thy Father so bewitch'd to Valour,
    (For *Abdelazer* has no other Virtue)
    To recompence it with so fair a Creature?
    Was this – a Treasure t' inrich the Devil with?
Alonzo. Sir, he has many Virtues, more than Courage,

---

[2] An echo of Lady Macbeth:

> Come thick night,
> And pall thee in the dunnest smoke of hell,
> That my keen knife see not the wound it makes

(1.5.48–50, in Stephen Greenblatt et al., eds., *The Norton Shakespeare* [New York: Norton,
1997]). Abdelazer, however, *wants* his weapon to be visible.

   Royally born, serv'd well this King, and Country;
   My Father brought him up to Martial toyls,
   And taught him to be Brave; I hope, and Good; –
   Beside, he was your Royal Father's Favourite,
King. No, *Alonzo,* 'twas not his love to Virtue,
   But nice obedience to his King, and Master,
   Who seeing my increase of Passion for her,
   To Kill my hopes, he gave her to this Moor.
Alonzo. She's now a virtuous woman, Sir.
King. Politique Sir, who would have made her other? –
   Against her will, he forc'd her to his arms,
   Whilst all the world was wondring at his madness.
Alonzo. He did it with her Approbation, Sir.
King. With thine, *Florella*! cou'dst thou be so criminal!
Florella. Sir, I was ever taught Obedience;
   My humble thoughts durst ne're aspire to you,
   And next to that – death, or the Moor, or any thing.
King. Oh God! had I then told my tale
   So feebly, it could not gain belief!
   Oh my *Florella*! this little faith of thine
   Has quite undone thy King! – *Alonzo,*
   Why didst not thou forbid this fatal Marriage,
   She being thy only Sister?
Alonzo. Great Sir, I did oppose it, with what violence
   My duty would permit; and wou'd have dy'd
   In a just quarrel, of her dear defence:
   And Sir, though I submitted to my Father,
   The Moor, and I, stand on unequal terms.
Philip. Come, who dares drink Confusion to this Moor?
Antonio. That, Sir, will I.
Sebastian. And I.
Philip. Page, fill my Glass, I will begin the Round;
   Ye all shall pledge it; – *Alonzo,* first to thee.   *Drinks.*
Alonzo. To me, Sir!
Philip. Why yes; thou loves him, – therefore –
   Nay you shall drink it, though 'twere oth' Stygian Lake:° –
   Take it, – by Heav'n thou'dst Pimp for him to my Mother, –
   Nay and after that, give him another Sister.
Alonzo. 'Tis well you are my Prince.

Stygian Lake: the Styx, a river in Hades

Philip. I'de rather be a Prince of Curs; – come, pledge me –
Alonzo. Well Sir, I'le give you way – *Drinks.*
Philip. So wou'dst thou any, – though they trod on thee.
   So – nay Prince Cardinal, though it be not decent
   For one so sanctify'd to drink a Health;
   Yet 'tis your Office, both to damn and bless: –
   Come, drink and damn the Moor.
Cardinal. Sir, I'm for no carousing.
Philip. I'm in an humour now to be obey'd,
   And must not be deny'd: – but see, the Moor
                              Enter Abdelazer, *gazes on them.*
   Just come to pledge at last, – Page, fill again –
Abdelazer. I'le do you reason,° Prince, whate're it be.   *Gives him the Glass.*
Philip. 'Twas kindly said; – Confusion to the Moor.
Abdelazer. Confusion to the Moor – if this vain Boy,
   See the next rising Sun.
Philip. Well done my Lad. – *[Aside.]*
King. Abdelazer, you have been missing long,
   The Publique good takes up your whole concern,
   But we shall shortly ease you of that load. –
   Come, let's have some Musick; –
   Ordonio, did I not call for Musick?
Ordonio. You did, Sir.
Abdelazer. Roderigo. –
Roderigo. My gracious Lord. – Roderigo *whispers to* Abdelazer.
Abdelazer. No more, – the Prince observes us.
Philip. There's no good towards when you are whisp'ring.
Ordonio. The Musick you commanded, Sir, is ready.

[Enter Nymph]

SONG.

M̱ake haste Amintas, *come away,*
   The Sun is up and will not stay,
And oh how very short's a Lovers day.
   Make haste, Amintas, *to this Grove,*
   Beneath whose shade so oft I've sat,
   And heard my dear lov'd Swain repeat,

do you reason: drink your health

How much he Galatea *lov'd,*
Whilst all the listening Birds around,
Sung to the Musick of the blessed sound.
Make haste Amintas *come away,*
The Sun is up and will not stay,
And oh how very short's a Lovers day.

Swain enters, with Shepherds and Shepherdesses, and Pipes.

I hear thy charming voice, my Fair,
And see bright Nymph, thy Swain is here,
Who his devotions had much earlier paid,
But that a Lamb of thine was stray'd:
And I the little wanderer have brought,
That with one angry look from thy fair eyes,
Thou mayst the little Fugitive chastise,
Too great a punishment for any fault.
Come Galatea, *haste away,*
The Sun is up and will not stay,
And oh how very short's Lovers day.

Dance.

King. How likes *Florella* this?
Florella. Sir, all delight's so banisht from my soul,
　I've lost the taste of every single joy.
Abdelazer. Gods! this is fine! give me your Art of flattery,
　Or something more of this, will ruine me. –
　Though I've resolv'd her death, yet whilst she's mine,
　I would not have her blown by Summer Flyes.
Philip. Mark how he snarles upon the King!
　The Cur will bite anon. 　　　　　　　　　　　　　*[Aside.]*
Abdelazer. Come my *Florella,* is't not Bed-time, Love?
Florella. I'le wait upon you, Sir. 　　　　　　　　　*Going out.*
Philip. The Moor has ta'en away, we may depart.
Abdelazer. What has he ta'en away? 　　　　　　　*Turns about.*
Philip. The fine gay play-thing, that made us all so merry.
Abdelazer. Was this your sport? 　　　　　　　　　*To his Wife.*
King. *Abdelazer,* keep your way: – Good night, fair Creature!
Abdelazer. I will obey, for once. 　　　　*Exit* Abdelazer *and* Florella.
King. Why this Resentment, Brother, and in publick?

Philip. Because he gives me cause, and that in publick.
  And Sir, I was not born to bear with Insolence;
  I saw him dart Revenge, from both his Eyes,
  And bite his angry Lip between his teeth,
  To keep his Jealousie from breaking forth;
  Which when it does, – stand fast my King.
King. But *Philip*, we will find a way to check him;
  Till when we must dissemble; – take my counsel, – Good night.
Philip. I cannot, nor I will not; – yet Good night.   *Exit King,*
  Well Friends, I see the King will sleep away his anger,   *and all but*
  And tamely see us murder'd by this Moor;   Philip's *Party.*
  But I'le be Active, Boys. –
  Therefore *Antonio*, you Command the Horse;
  Get what more numbers to our Cause you can:
  'Tis a good Cause, and will advance our credit.
  We will awake this King, out of his Lethargy of Love,
  And make him absolute: – Go to your Charge,
  And early in the morning I'le be with you, –   *Exeunt all but* Philip.
  If all fail, *Portugal* shall be my Refuge,
  Those whom so late I Conquer'd shall Protect me. –
  But this *Alonzo*, I shou'd make an Interest in;
  Cou'd I but flatter, – 'tis a Youth that's Brave.

Enter Cardinal in haste.

Cardinal. Fly, fly, my Prince, we are betray'd and lost else.
Philip. Betray'd and lost! Dreams, idle Coward dreams.
Cardinal. Sir, by my Holy Order, I'm in earnest,
  And you must either quickly fly, or dye;
  'Tis so ordain'd: – nor have I time to tell
  By what strange miracle I learnt our Fate.
Philip. Nor care I, I will stay, and Brave it,
Cardinal. That Sir you shall not, there's no safety here,
  And 'tis the Army only can secure us.
Philip. Where had you this Intelligence?
Cardinal. I'le tell you as we go to my Apartment;
  Where we must put our selves in Holy dress,
  For so the Guards are set in every place,
  (And those all Moors, the Slaves of *Abdelazer*)
  That 'tis impossible in any other Habit to escape.
  Come, haste with me, and let us put 'em on.

Philip. I'de rather stay and kill, till I am weary; –
    Let's to the Queens Apartment, and seize this Moor;
    I am sure there the Mongrel's Kennell'd.
Cardinal. Sir, we lose time in talking, – come with me.
Philip. Where be these Lowsie Gaberdines?[3]
Cardinal. I will conduct you to 'em.
    Mother, – and Moor – Farewell, –
    I'le visit you again, and if I do,
    My black Infernal, I will Conjure you.   *Exeunt.*

ACT III.

SCENE I.

Enter Abdelazer, *and* Zarrack.

Zarrack. *Osmin* (my Lord) by this has done his task,
    And *Philip* is no more among the living. –
    Will you not rest to Night?
Abdelazer. Is this a time for sleep and idleness? – dull Slaves. –
Zarrack. The bus'ness we have order, Sir, to doe,
    We can without your aid.

Enter Osmin.

Abdelazer. *Osmin!*
    Thy ominous looks presage an ill success;
    Thy Eyes no joyful news of Murders tell:
    I thought I should have seen thee drest in bloud; –
    Speak! Speak thy News! –
    Say that he lives, and let it be thy last. –
Osmin. Yes Sir, he lives –
Abdelazer. Lives! thou ly'st, bafe Coward, – lives! – renounce thy Gods!
    It were a sin less dangerous! – speak again.
Osmin. Sir, *Philip* lives.
Abdelazer. Oh treacherous Slave!
Osmin. Not by my fault, by Heav'n!
Abdelazer. By what curst chance,
    If not from thee, could he evade his Fate?

---

[3] "A loose upper garment of coarse material" (OED).

Osmin. By some intelligence from his good Angel.
Abdelazer. From his good Devil!
  Gods! must the Earth another day at once
  Bear him and me alive!
Osmin. Another day! – an Age for ought I know;
  For Sir, the Prince is fled, the Cardinal too.
Abdelazer. Fled! Fled! – sayst thou?
  Oh I cou'd curse the Stars, that rule this Night:
  'Tis to the Camp they're fled; the only refuge
  That Gods, or men cou'd give 'em. –
  Where got you this intelligence?
Osmin. My Lord, enquiring for the Prince
  At the Apartment of the Cardinal, (whither he went)
  His Pages answer'd me, he was at his Devotions:
  A lucky time (I thought) to do the deed;
  And breaking in, found only their empty Habits,
  And a poor sleeping Groom, who with much threatning,
  Confess'd that they were fled, in Holy Robes.
Abdelazer. That case of Sanctity was first ordain'd,
  To cheat the honest world:
  'Twas an unlucky chance; – but we are idle. –
  Let's see, how from this ill, we may advance a good: –   *Pawses:*
  'Tis now dead time of Night, when Rapes, and Murders,
  Are hid beneath the horrid Veil of darkness; –
  I'le ring through all the Court, with doleful sound,
  The sad alarms of Murder, – Murder. – *Zarrack*,
  Take up thy standing yonder; – *Osmin*, thou
  At the Queens Apartment; – cry out, Murder!
  Whilst I, like his ill Genius, do awake the King.
  Perhaps in this disorder I may kill him.   *Aside.*
  – Treason – Murder – Murder – Treason.

Enter Alonzo, *and Courtiers.*

Alonzo. What dismal crys are these? –
Abdelazer. Where is the king? – Treason! – Murder! –
  Where is the sleeping Queen? – arise! – arise!
Osmin. The Devil taught him all his arts of falshood.   *Aside.*

Enter King in a Night-Gown, with Lights.

Who frights our quiet slumbers with this noise?

Enter Queen and Women, with Lights.

Queen. Was it a dream, or did I hear the sound
    Of Treason, call me from my silent griefs?
King. Who rais'd this rumour, *Abdelazer*, you?
Abdelazer. I did, Great Sir.
King. Your Reasons.
Abdelazer. Oh Sir, your Brother *Philip*, and the Cardinal,
    Both animated by a sense of wrongs,
    (And envying, Sir, the fortune of your Slave)
    Had laid a Plot, this Night, to murder you;
    And 'cause they knew it was my waiting Night,
    They would have laid the Treason, Sir, on me.
King. The Cardinal, and my Brother! bring them forth,
    Their lives shall answer it.
Abdelazer. Sir, 'tis impossible;
    For when they found their Villany discover'd,
    They in two Friers Habits made escape.
King. That Cardinal is subtle, as Ambitious,
    And from him *Philip* learnt his dangerous Principles.
Queen. The Ambition of the one, infects the other,
    And they are both too dangerous to live. –
    But might a Mothers counsel be obey'd,
    I wou'd advise you, send the valiant Moor
    To fetch 'em back, e're they can reach the Camp:
    For thither they are fled, – where they will find
    A welcome fatal to us all.
King. Madam, you counsel well; and *Abdelazer*,
    Make it your care to fetch these Traytors back,
    Not only for my safety, and the Kingdoms,
    But for they are your Enemies; and th' envious world
    Will say, you made this story to undoe'em.
Abdelazer. Sir, I'le obey; nor will I know repose,
    Till I have justify'd this fatal truth.

                              Abdelazer *goes to the Queen, and talks to her.*
King. Mean time I will to my *Florella's* Lodging,
    Silence, and Night, are the best Advocates
    To plead a Lover's cause. – *Abdelazer*, – haste.   *Aside.*
    Madam, I'le wait on you to your Chamber.
Abdelazer. Sir, that's my duty.

King. Madam, good night; – *Alonzo*, to your rest.

Ex. all but Queen, and Abdelazer.

Queen. Philip escap'd!
  Oh that I were upon some Desart shore,
  Where I might only to the waves and winds
  Breath out my sense of Rage for this defeat.

Abdelazer. Oh 'tis no time for Rage, but Action, Madam.

Queen. Give me but any hopes of blest Revenge,
  And I will be as calm, as happy Lovers.

Abdelazer. There is a way! and is but – that alone;
  But such a way, as never must be nam'd.

Queen. How! not be nam'd! Oh swear thou hat'st me rather,
  It were a torment equal to thy silence.

Abdelazer. I'le shew my passion rather in that silence.

Queen. Kind Torturer, what mean'st thou?

Abdelazer. To shew you, Madam, I had rather live
  Wrong'd and contemn'd by *Philip*,
  Than have your dearer Name made Infamous.

Queen. Heav'ns! dost thou mock my Rage! can any sin
  I cou'd commit, undoe my Honour more
  Than his late Insolence!
  Oh name me something may revenge that shame!
  I wou'd encounter killing Plagues, or fire
  To meet it. – Come, oh quickly give me ease.

Abdelazer. I dare no more reveal the guilty secret,
  Then you dare execute it when 'tis told.

Queen. How little I am understood by thee: –
  Come, tell me instantly, for I grow impatient;
  You shall obey me, – nay I do command you.

Abdelazer. Durst you proclaim – *Philip* a Bastard, Madam.

Queen. Hah proclaim my self – what he wou'd have me thought!
  What mean'st thou? –

Abdelazer. Instruct you in the way to your Revenge.

Queen. Upon my self, thou mean'st. –

Abdelazer. No; –
  He's now fled to th' Camp, where he'l be fortify'd
  Beyond our power to hurt, but by this means;
  Which takes away his hopes of being a King,
  (For he'd no other aim in taking Arms)
  And leaves him open to the Peoples scorn;

Whom own'd as King, numbers would assist him,
And then our lives he may dispose,
As he has done our Honours.
Queen. There's reason in thy words, but oh my Fame!
Abdelazer. Which, I, by Heav'n, am much more tender of,
	Then my own life or Honour; and I've a way
	To save that too, which I'le at leisure tell you.
	In the mean time, send for your Confessor,
	And with a borrow'd penitence confess,
	Their Idol *Philip* is a Bastard;
	And zealously pretend you're urg'd by Conscience:
	A cheap pretence to cozen fools withall.
Queen. Revenge, although I court thee with my fatal ruine,
	I must enjoy thee! there's no other way,
	And I'm resolv'd upon the mighty pleasure;
	He has prophan'd my purer flame for thee,
	And merits to partake the Infamy. – *He leads her out.*
Abdelazer. Now have at my young King: –
	I know he means to Cuckold me to night,
	Whilst he believes, I'le tamely step aside; –
	No, let *Philip* and the Cardinal gain the Camp,
	I will not hinder 'em; –
	I have a nobler Sacrifice to make
	To my declining Honour; shall redeem it,
	And pay it back with Interest: – well then in order to't,
	I'le watch about the Lodgings of *Florella*,
	And if I see this hot young Lover enter,
	I'le save my Wife the trouble of allaying°
	The Amorous heat: – this – will more nimbly do't, *Snatches out*
	And do it once for all. – *his Dagger.*

				Enter Florella *in her Night-cloaths.*

Florella. My *Abdelazer*, – why in that fierce posture,
	As if thy thoughts were always bent on Death: –
	Why is that Dagger out? – against whom drawn?
Abdelazer. Or stay, – suppose I let him see *Florella*,
	And when he's high with the expected bliss,
	Then take him thus, – Oh 'twere a fine surprize! *[Aside.]*

allaying: calming

Florella. My Lord, – dear *Abdelazer* –

Abdelazer. Or say – I made her kill him, – that were yet

    An action much more worthy of my vengence.   [*Aside.*]

Florella. Will you not speak to me? what have I done?

Abdelazer. By Heaven it shall be so. –   [*Aside.*]

Florella. What shall be so? –

Abdelazer. Hah! –

Florella. Why dost thou dress thy Eyes in such unusual wonder?

    There's nothing here that is a stranger to thee;

    Or what is not intirely thine own.

Abdelazer. Mine!

Florella. Thou canst not doubt it.

Abdelazer. No, – and for a proof thou art so, – take this Dagger.

Florella. Alas, Sir! – what to do?

Abdelazer. To stab a heart, *Florella*, a heart that loves thee. –

Florella. Heaven forbid!

Abdelazer. No matter what Haven will, I say it must –

Florella. What must –

Abdelazer. That Dagger must enter the heart of him

    That loves thee best, *Florella* – guess the man.

Florella. What means my Moor? –

    Would't thou have me kill thy self?

Abdelazer. Yes, – when I love thee better then the King.

Florella. Ah Sir! what mean you?

Abdelazer. To have you kill this King,

    When next he does pursue thee with his love; –

    What do you weep? –

    By Heav'n they shall be bloudy tears then. –

Florella. I shall deserve them, – when I suffer love

    That is not fit to hear; – but for the King,

    That which he pays me, is so innocent –

Abdelazer. So innocent! – damn thy dissembling tongue;

    Did I not see, with what fierce wishing Eyes

    He gaz'd upon thy face, whilst yours as wantonly

    Return'd, and understood the Amorous language.

Florella. Admit it true, that such his Passions were,

    As (Heaven's my witness) I've no cause to fear,

    Have not I Virtue to resist his flame,

    Without a pointed Steel?

Abdelazer. Your Virtue! – Curse on the weak defence;

Your Virtue's equal to his Innocence. –
Here, – take this Dagger, and if this Night he visit thee,
When he least thinks on't, – send it to his heart.
Florella. If you suspect me, do not leave me, Sir.
Abdelazer. Oh – I'm dispatch'd away, – to leave you free, –
   About a wonderful affair: – mean time,
   I know you will be visited; – but as you wish to live,
   At my Return, let me behold him dead, –
   Be sure you do't. – 'tis for thy Honours safety. –
   I love thee so, that I can take no rest,
   Till thou hast kill'd thy Image in his breast.
   – Adieu, my dear *Florella* –   *Exit.*
Florella. Murder my King! – the man that loves me too! –
   What Fiend, what Fury such an act wou'd do?
   My trembling hand, wou'd not the weapon bear,
   And I shou'd sooner strike it here, – than there. –

                                  Pointing to her breast.

   No! though of all I am, this hand alone
   Is what thou canst command, as being thy own;
   Yet this has plighted no such cruel vow:
   No Duty binds me to obey thee now.
   To save my King's, my life I will expose,
   No Martyr dies in a more Glorious Cause.   *Exit.*

[ACT III]

SCENE II.

Enter the Queen in an undress alone, with a Light.

Queen. Thou grateful Night, to whom all happy Lovers
   Make their devout and humble Invocations;
   Thou Court of Silence, where the God of Love,
   Lays by the awfull terrour of a Deity,
   And every harmfull Dart, and deals around
   His kind desires; whilst thou, blest Friend to joys,
   Draw'st all thy Curtains made of gloomy shades,
   To veil the blushes of soft yielding Maids;
   Beneath thy covert grant the Love-sick King,
   May find admittance to *Florella*'s arms,

And being there, keep back the busie day;
Maintain thy Empire till my Moor returns;
Where in her Lodgings he shall find his Wife.
Amidst her Amorous dalliance with my Son. –
My watchful Spyes are waiting for the knowledge;
Which when to me imparted, I'le improve,
Till my Revenge be equal to my Love.

Enter Elvira.

– *Elvira*, in thy looks I read success; –
What hast thou learnt?
Elvira. Madam; the King is gone as you imagin'd,
   To fair *Florella's* Lodgings.
Queen. But art thou sure he gain'd Admittance?
Elvira. Yes, Madam;
   But what welcome he has found, to me's unknown,
   But I believe it must be great, and kind.
Queen. But now, *Elvira*, for a well-laid Plot,
   To ruine this *Florella*; – though she be innocent,
   Yet she must dye; so hard a Destiny
   My passion for her Husband does decree:
   But 'tis the way, I stop at. –
   His Jealousie already I have rais'd;
   That's not enough, his Honour must be toucht:
   This meeting 'twixt the King, and fair *Florella*,
   Must then be render'd Publick;
   'Tis the disgrace, not Action, must incense him. –
   Go you to Don *Alonzo's* Lodging strait,   *Exit* Elvira.
   Whilst I prepare my story for his Ear. –
   Assist me all that's ill in Woman-kind,
   And furnish me with sighs, and feigned tears,
   That may express a grief, for this discovery. –
   My Son, be like thy Mother, hot and bold,
   And like the Noble Ravisher of *Rome*,[4]
   Court her with Daggers, when thy Tongue grows faint,
   Till thou hast made a Conquest o're her Virtue.

[4] According to Roman legend, Lucretia, a virtuous married woman, was raped by Sextus
Tarquinius, son of the seventh king of Rome. Her rape and subsequent suicide caused
the overthrow of the monarchy and establishment of a republic.

Enter Alonzo, Elvira.

– Oh *Alonzo*, I have strange News to tell thee!
Alonzo. It must be strange indeed, that makes my Queen
    Dress her fair eyes in sorrow.
Queen. It is a Dress that thou wilt be in love with,
    When thou shalt hear my story. –
    You had a Sister once.
Alonzo. Had!
Queen. Yes, had – whilst she was like thy self, all Virtue;
    Till her bewitching Eyes kindled such flames,
    As will undoe us all.
Alonzo. My Sister, Madam! sure it cannot be:
    What eyes? what flames? – inform me strait.
Queen. *Alonzo*, thou art honest, just, and brave,
    And should I tell thee more –
    (Knowing thy Loyalty's above all Nature)
    It would oblige thee to commit an outrage,
    Which baser Spirits will call cruelty.
Alonzo. Gods, Madam! do not praise my Virtue thus,
    Which is so poor, it scarce affords me patience
    To attend the end of what you wou'd deliver –
    Come Madam, say my Sister – is a Whore;
    I know 'tis so you mean: and being so,
    Where shall I kneel for Justice?
    Since he that shou'd it me,
    Has made her Criminal. –
    Pardon me, Madam, 'tis the King I mean.
Queen. I grieve to own, all thy Prophetick fears
    Are true, *Alonzo*, 'tis indeed the King.
Alonzo. Then I'm disarm'd,
    For Heaven can only punish him.
Queen. But *Alonzo*,
    Whilst that Religious patience dwels about thee,
    All *Spain* must suffer, nay Ages that shall ensue,
    Shall curse thy Name, and Family;
    From whom a Race of Bastards shall proceed,
    To wear that Crown.
Alonzo. No, Madam, not from mine,
    My Sister's in my power, her Honour's mine;

I can command her life, though not my Kings.
Her Mother is a Saint, and shou'd she now
Look down from Heaven upon a deed so foul,
I think even there, she wou'd invent a Curse,
To thunder on her head. –
But Madam, whence was this intelligence?
Queen. *Elvira* saw the King enter her Lodgings,
With Lovers haste, and joy.
Alonzo. Her Lodgings! – when?
Queen. Now, not an hour ago, –
Now, since the Moor departed.
Alonzo. Damnation on her! can she be thus false? –
Come, lead me to the Lodgings of this Strumpet,
And make me see this truth,
Or I will leave thee dead, for thus abusing me.   *to* Elvira.
Queen. Nay dear *Alonzo*, do not go inrag'd,
Stay till your temper wear a calmer look;
That if, by chance, you shou'd behold the Wantons,
In little harmless Dalliance, such as Lovers
(Aided with silence, and the shades of Night)
May possibly commit,
You may not do, that which you may repent of.
Alonzo. Gods! should I play the Pander!
And with my patience, aid the Am'rous sin? –
No, I shall scarce have so much tameness left,
To mind me of my Duty to my King.
Ye Gods! behold the Sacrifice I make
To my lost Honour: behold, and aid my justice.   *Exit* Alonzo.
Queen. It will concern me too, to see this wonder,
For yet I scarce can credit it.   *Exeunt.*

[ACT III] SCENE III. Florella's *Lodgings.*

Enter the King, leading in Florella *all in fear.*

Florella. Ah Sir, the Gods and you would be more merciful,
If by a death less cruel than my fears,
You would preserve my Honour; begin it quickly,
And after that I will retain my Duty,
And at your feet breathe thanks in dying sighs.

King. Where learnt you, Fairest, so much cruelty,
    To charge me with the Pow'r of injuring thee?
    Not from my Eyes, where Love and languishment
    Too sensibly inform thee of my heart.
Florella. Call it not injury, Sir, to free my soul
    From fears which such a Visit must create,
    In dead of Night, when nought but frightful Ghosts
    Of restless souls departed walk the Round.
King. That fleeting thing am I, whom all repose,
    All joys, and every good of life abandon'd,
    That fatal hour thou gavest thy self away;
    And I was doom'd to endless desperation:
    Yet whilst I liv'd, all glorious with my hopes,
    Some sacred Treasures in thy breast I hid,
    And near thee still my greedy soul will hover.
Florella. Ah rather like a Ravisher you come,
    With love and fierceness in your dangerous Eyes;
    And both will equally be fatal to me.
King. Ah do not fear me, as the fair *Lucretia*
    Did the fierce *Roman* Youth;[5] I mean no Rapes,
    Thou can't not think that I wou'd force those joys,
    Which cease to be so, when compell'd, *Florella*: −
    No, I wou'd sooner pierce this faithful heart,
    Whose flame appears too Criminal for your mercy.
Florella. Why do you fright me, Sir? methinks your looks
    All pale; your eyes thus fixt, and trembling hands,
    The awfull horrour of the dark and silent night,
    Strikes a cold terrour round my fainting heart,
    That does presage some fatal Accident.
King. 'Tis in your cruel Eyes the danger lies: −
    Wou'd you receive me with that usual tenderness
    Which did express it self in every smile,
    I should dismiss this horrour from my face,
    And place again its Native calmness there;
    And all my Veins shall re-assume their heat,
    And with a new, and grateful Ardour beat.
Florella. Sir, all my soul is taken up with fear,
    And you advance your Fate, by staying here: −

[5] See n. 4.

Fly, fly, this place of death; – if *Abdelazer*
Shou'd find you here, – all the Divinity
About your Sacred Person, could not Guard you.
King. Ah my *Florella*, cease thy needless fear,
And in thy soul let nothing reign but Love!
Love! that with soft desires may fill thy Eyes,
And save thy Tongue the pain t'instruct my heart;
In the most grateful knowledge Heav'n can give me.
Florella. That knowledge, Sir, wou'd make us both more wretched,
Since you, I know, wou'd still be wishing on,
And I shou'd grant, till we were both undone.
And Sir, how little she were worth your care,
Cou'd part with all her honourable fame,
For an inglorious life, – short and despis'd. –
King. Can't thou believe a flame thy Eyes have kindled,
Can urge me to an infamous pursuit? –
No, my *Florella*, I adore thy Virtue,
And none prophane those Shrines, to whom they offer;
– Say but thou lov'st, – and I thus low will bow, –   *Kneels.*
And sue to thee, to be my Soveraign Queen;
I'le circle thy bright Forehead with the Crowns
Of *Castile*, *Portugal*, and *Aragon*;
And all those petty Kingdoms, which do bow
Their Tributary knees to thy Adorer.
Florella. Ah Sir! have you forgot by Sacred vow
All that I am, is *Abdelazers* now.
King. By Heav'n it was Sacrilegious theft!
But I the Treasure from his breast will tear,
And reach his heart, though thou art seated there.
Florella. A deed like that, my Virtue wou'd undoe,
And leave a stain upon your Glories too;
A sin, that wou'd my hate not passion move,
I owe a Duty, where I cannot love.
King. Thou think'st it then no sin to kill thy King;
For I must dye, without thy love, *Florella*.
Florella. How tamely, Sir, you with the Serpent play,
Whose fatal Poison must your life betray;
And though a King, cannot Divine your Fate;
Kings only differ from the Gods in that.
See, Sir, with this – I am your Murderer made;   *Holds up a Dagger.*

By those we love, we soonest are betray'd.

King. How! can that fair hand acquaint it self with death?

– What wilt thou do, *Florella*?

Florella. Your Destiny divert,

And give my heart those wounds design'd for yours.

– If you advance, I'le give the deadly blow.

King. Hold! – I command thee hold thy impious hand,

My heart dwels there, and if you strike – I dye.

Enter Queen, Alonzo, *and* Elvira.

Queen. Florella! arm'd against the King! –   *Snatches the Dagger and*
    Oh Traitress!   *stabs her; the King rises.*

King. Hold! – hold, inhuman Murdress;

What hast thou done, most barbarous of thy Sex!

                                               Takes Florella *in his arms.*

Queen. Destroy'd thy Murdress, – and my too fair Rival.   *Aside.*

King. My Murdress – what Devil did inspire thee

With thoughts so black and sinfull? cou'd this fair Saint

Be guilty of a Murder! – No, no, too cruel Mother,

With her Eyes, her charming lovely Eyes,

She might have kill'd; and her too virtuous cruelty.

– Oh my *Florella*! Sacred lovely Creature!

Florella. My death was kind, since it prevented yours!

And by that hand, which sav'd mine from a guilt: *Points to the Queen.*

– That Dagger, I receiv'd of *Abdelazer*,

To stab that heart – he said, that lov'd me best,

But I design'd to overcome your Passion,

And then to have vanquisht *Abdelazer*'s Jealousie;

But finding you too faithfull to be happy,

I did resolve to dye, – and have my wish.

– Farewell – my King, – my soul begins it[s] flight,

– And now – is hovering – in eternal – Night.   *Dyes.*

King. She's gon, – she's gone, – her sacred soul is fled

To that Divinity, of which it is a part;

Too excellent to inhabit Earthly bodies.

Alonzo. Oh Sir, you grieve too much, for one so foul

King. What prophane breath was that pronounc'd her foul!

Thy Mothers soul, though turn'd into a Cherubin,

Was black to hers: – Oh she was all Divine.

– *Alonzo*, – was it thou? – her Brother!

Alonzo. When she was good, I own'd that title, Sir.

King. Good! – by all the Gods she was as chaste as Vestals![6]

As Saints translated[7] to Divine abodes.

– I offer'd her to be my Queen, *Alonzo*!

To share the growing Glories of my Youth;

But uncorrupted she my Crown contemn'd

And on her Vertues Guard stood thus defended.   Alonzo *weeps.*

Oh my *Florella*! let me here lie fix'd   *Kneels.*

And never rise, till I am cold and pale,

As thou fair Saint art now: – but sure

She cou'd not dye; – that noble generous heart,

That arm'd with love and honour, did rebate

All the fierce sieges of my Amorous flame,

Might sure defend it self against those wounds

Given by a Womans hand, – or rather 'twas a Devils.   *Rises.*

– What dost thou merit for this Treachery?

Thou vilest of thy Sex –

But thou'rt a thing I have miscall'd a Mother,

And therefore will not touch thee, – live to suffer

By a more shamefull way; – but here she lyes;

Whom I, though dead, must still adore as living.

Alonzo. Sir, pray retire, there's danger in your stay;

When I reflect upon this Nights disorder,

And the Queens Art to raise my Jealousie;

And after that my Sisters being murder'd,

I must believe there is some deeper Plot,

Something design'd against your Sacred Person.

King. Alonzo! raise the Court, I'le find it   *Exit* Alonzo.

Though 'twere hid within my Mothers soul,

Queen. My gentle Son, pardon my kind mistake,

I did believe her arm'd against thy life.

King. Peace Fury! Not ill-boding Raven shrieks,

Nor Midnight cries of murder'd Ghosts, are more,

Ungratefull, than thy faint and dull excuses.

– Be gone! and trouble not the silent griefs

Which will insensibly decay my life,

---

[6] In ancient Rome, virgin priestesses who guarded the sacred flame in the temple of the goddess Vesta.

[7] Removed from earth to heaven without undergoing death.

Till like a Marble Statue I am fixt,   *Kneels, and weeps*
Dropping continual tears upon her Tomb.   *at* Florella's *feet.*
Abdelazer within. Guard all the Chamber doors! – fire and confusion
 Consume these *Spanish* Dogs! – was I for this
 Sent to fetch back a *Philip*, and a Cardinal,
 To have my Wife abus'd?

Enter Abdelazer.

Queen. Patience! dear *Abdelazer*!
Abdelazer. Patience and I am Foes! where's my *Florella*? –
 The King! and in *Florella*'s Bed-Chamber!
 – *Florella*! dead too! –
 Rise! thou Eternal Author of my shame;
 Gay thing – to you I speak!   *King rises.*
 And thus throw off Allegiance.
Queen. Oh stay your fury, generous *Abdelazer*!
Abdelazer. Away! fond woman.   *Throws her from him.*
King. Villain! to me this language!
Abdelazer. To thee, young Amorous King!
 How at this dead and silent time of Night,
 Durst you approach the Lodgings of my Wife?
King. I scorn to answer thee.
Abdelazer. I'le search it in thy heart then. *They fight,* Queen *and* Elvira
King. The Devil's not yet ready for his soul, *run out crying Treason.*
 And will not claim his due: – Oh I am wounded! *Falls.*
Abdelazer. No doubt on't, Sir these are no wounds of Love.
King. Whate're they be, you might have spar'd 'em now,
 Since those *Florella* gave me were sufficient:
 – And yet a little longer – fixing thus –
 Thou'dst seen me turn to Earth, without thy aid.
 – *Florella*! – *Florella*! – is thy soul fled so far
 It cannot answer me, and call me on? –
 And yet like dying Ecchoes in my Ears,
 I hear thee cry, my Love! – I come – I come, fair Soul!
 – Thus at thy feet – my heart shall – bleeding – lye,
 Who since it liv'd for thee, – for thee – will – dye. *Dyes.*
Abdelazer. So – thou art gone; – there was a King but now,
 And now a senseless, dull, and breathless nothing.
A noise of fighting without.

Enter Queen *running.*

Queen. Oh Heav'ns! my Son – the King! the King is kill'd! –
　Yet I must save his Murderer: – Fly, my Moor;
　Alonzo, Sir, assisted by some Friends,
　Has set upon your Guards,
　And with resistless fury is making hither.
Abdelazer. Let him come on.

Enter Alonzo *and others led in by* Osmin,
Zarrack, *and Moors.*

　– Oh are you fast? –　　　　　　　　　　*Takes away their Swords.*
Alonzo. What mean'st thou, Villain!
Abdelazer. To put your Swords to better uses, Sir,
　Then to defend the cause of Ravishers.
Alonzo. Oh Heavens! the King is murder'd!
Abdelazer. Look on that Object, –
　Thy Sister! and my Wife! who's doubly murder'd,
　First in her spotless Honour; then her life.
Alonzo. Heaven is more guilty then the King in this!
Queen. My Lords, be calm; and since your King is murder'd,
　Think of your own dear safeties, chuse a new King
　That may defend you from the Tyrants Rage.
Alonzo. Who shou'd we chuse? Prince *Philip* is our King.
Abdelazer. By Heaven but *Philip* shall not be my King!
　Philip's a Bastard, and Traytor to his Country:
　He braves us with an Army at our Walls,
　Threatning the Kingdom with a fatal ruine.
　And who shall lead you forth to Conquest now,
　But *Abdelazer*, whose Sword reapt Victory,
　As oft as 'twas unsheath'd, – and all for *Spain*!
　– How many Lawrels has this Head adorn'd?
　Witness the many Battels I have won,
　In which I've emptied all my Youthfull Veins,
　And all for *Spain*! – ungratefull of my favours!
　– I do not boast my Birth,
　Nor will not urge to you my Kingdoms ruine;
　But loss of bloud, and numerous wounds receiv'd,
　And still for *Spain*! –
　And can you think, that after all my Toyls

I wou'd be still a Slave! – to Bastard *Philip* too!
That dangerous Foe! who with the Cardinal
Threatens with Fire and Sword. – I'le quench those flames,
Such an esteem I still preserve for *Spain*. –
Alonzo. What means this long Harangue! what does it aim at?
Abdelazer. To be Protector of the Crown of *Spain*,
Till we agree about a lawful Successor.
Alonzo. Oh Devil! –
Queen. We are betray'd, and round beset with horrours;
If we deny him this, – the Power being his,
We're all undone, and Slaves unto his mercy. –
Besides, – Oh give me leave to blush when I declare,
That *Philip* is – as he has rendred him. –
But I in love to you, love to my *Spain*,
Chose rather to proclaim my Infamy,
Than an Ambitious Bastard should be Crown'd.
Alonzo. Here's a fine Plot, –
What Devil reigns in Woman, when she doats!   *Aside.*
Roderigo. My Lords, I see no remedy but he must be Protector.
Alonzo. Oh treachery! – have you so soon forgot
The noble *Philip*, and his glorious Heir
The murder'd *Ferdinand*! –
– And Madam, you so soon forgot a Mothers name,
That you wou'd give him Power that kill'd your Son!
Abdelazer. The modesty wherewith I'le use that Power,
Shall let you see, I have no other Interest
But what's intirely *Spains*. – Restore their Swords,
And he amongst you all who is dissatisfy'd, –
I set him free this minute.
Alonzo. I take thee at thy word, –
And instantly to *Philips* Camp will fly.   *Exit.*
Abdelazer. By all the Gods my Ancestors ador'd,
But that I scorn the envying World shou'd think
I took delight in bloud, – I wou'd not part so with you,
– But you, my Lords, who value *Spains* Repose,
Must for it instantly with me take Arms: –
Prince *Philip*, and the Cardinal, now ride
Like *Jove* in Thunder; we in Storms must meet them.
To Arms! to Arms! and then to Victory,
Resolv'd to Conquer, or resolv'd to dye.   *Exeunt.*

ACT IV.

Enter Abdelazer, Osmin *bearing his Helmet of Feathers,* Zarrack
with his Sword and Truncheon.[8]

Abdelazer. Come *Osmin,* Arm me quickly, for the day
   Comes on apace; and the fierce Enemy
   Will take advantages, by our delay.

Enter Queen and Elvira.

Queen. Oh my dear Moor!
   The rude, exclaiming, ill-affected Multitude,
   (Tempestuous as the Sea) run up and down,
   Some crying, kill the Bastard, – some the Moor;
   These for King *Philip,* – those for *Abdelazer.*
Abdelazer. Your fears are idle, – blow 'em into air.
   I rusht amongst the thickest of their Crowds,
   And with the awfull° splendour of my Eyes,
   Like the Imperious Sun, dispers'd the Clouds.
   But I must Combate now a fiercer Foe,
   The hot-brain'd *Philip,* and a jealous Cardinal.
   And must you go, before I make you mine?
   That's my misfortune; – when I return with Victory,
   And lay my wreaths of Lawrel at your feet,
   You shall exchange them, for your glorious Fetters.
Queen. How canst thou hope for Victory, when their numbers
   So far exceed thy Powers?
Abdelazer. What's wanting there, we must supply with Conduct.
   I know you will not stop at any thing
   That may advance our Interest, and enjoyment.
Queen. Look back on what I have already done,
   And after that, look forward with Assurance.
Abdelazer. You then (with only Women in your Train)
   Must to the Camp, and to the Cardinal's Tent; –
   Tell him, your Love to him hath drawn you thither:
   Then undermine his Soul, – you know the way on't.

---

awfull: inspiring reverence

[8] "A staff carried as a symbol of office" (*OED*).

And sooth him into a belief, that the best way to gain your heart, is
to leave *Philip's* Interest; urge 'tis the Kingdoms safety, and your
own; and use your fiercest threats, to draw him to a Peace with me:
not that you Love me, but for the Kingdoms good: then in a Tent
which I will pitch on purpose, get him to meet me: he being drawn
off, thousands of Bigots (who think to cheat the world into an
opinion, that fighting for the Cardinal is a pious work) will (when he
leaves the Camp) desert it too.

Queen. I understand you, and more then I have time to be
  Instructed in, I will perform, and possibly
  Before you can begin, I'le end my Conquests.

Abdelazer. 'Twill be a Victory worthy of your Beauty.
  – I must to Horse, farewell my generous Mistress.

Queen. Farewell! and may thy Arms as happy prove,
  As shall my Art, when it dissembles Love.   *Exeunt.*

SCENE, Philip's *Tent*

Enter Philip, Alonzo, *and Guards.*

Philip. 'Tis a sad story thou hast told, *Alonzo*;
  Yet 'twill not make me shed one single tear:
  They must be all of bloud, that I will offer,
  To my dear Brothers Ghost! –
  But gallant Friend, this good his ills have done,
  To turn thee over to our juster Interest,
  For thou dids't love him once.

Alonzo. Whilst I believ'd him honest, and for my Sisters sake;
  But since, his Crimes have made a Convert of me.

Philip. Gods! is it possible the Queen should countenance
  His horrid Villanies!

Alonzo. Nay worse then so, 'tis thought she'l marry him!

Philip. Marry him! then here upon my knees I vow,   *Kneels.*
  To shake all Duty from my soul,
  And all that reverence Children owe a Parent,
  Shall henceforth be converted into hate.   *rises*
  – Damnation! marry him! Oh I cou'd curse my Birth! –
  This will confirm the world in their opinion,
  That she's the worst of women;
  That I am basely born too, (as she gives it out)

That thought alone, does a just Rage inspire,
And kindles round my heart an active fire.
Alonzo. A disobedience, Sir, to such a Parent,
Heaven must forgive the sin, if this be one:
– Yet do not, Sir, in words abate that fire,
Which will assist you a more effectual way.
Philip. Death! I cou'd talk of it an Age;
And like a Woman, fret my anger high,
Till like my Rage, I have advanc'd a Courage
Able to fight the World against my Mother!
Alonzo. Our wrongs without a Rage, will make us fight,
Wrongs that wou'd make a Coward resolute.
Philip. Come, Noble Youth,
Let us joyn both our several wrongs in one,
And from them make a solemn resolution,
Never to part our Interest, till this Moor,
This worse then Devil Moor be sent to Hell.
Alonzo. I do.
Philip. Hark, – hark, – the Charge is sounded, let's to Horse,
St. *Jaques*[9] for the right of *Spain* and me.   *Exeunt.*

SCENE, *a Grove.*

Drums and Trumpets a far off, with noise of fighting at a distance:
after a little while, enter Philip *in Rage.*

Philip. Oh unjust powers! why d'ye protect this Monster; –
And this damn'd Cardinal, that comes not up
With the *Castilian* Troops; curse on his formal Politiques; –

Enter Alonzo.

– *Alonzo*, where's the Moor?
Alonzo. The Moor! – a Devil! – never did Fiend of Hell,
Compell'd by some Magicians Charms,
Break through the Prison of the folded Earth
With more swift horrour, then this Prince of Fate
Breaks through our Troops, in spight of opposition.

---

[9] St James, the patron saint of Spain.

Philip. Death! 'tis not his single arm that works these wonders,
But our Cowardice; – Oh this Dog Cardinal! –

Enter Antonio.

Antonio. Sound a Retreat, or else the day is lost.
Philip. I'le beat that Cur to death that sounds Retreat.

Enter Sebastian.

Sebastian. Sound a Retreat.
Philip. Who is't that tempts my Sword? – continue the Alarm,
Fight on Pell mell, – fight – kill – be damn'd – do any thing
But sound Retreat: – Oh this damn'd Coward Cardinal! –   *Exeunt.*

The noise of fighting near, after a little while
Enter Philip *again.*

Philip. Not yet, ye Gods! Oh this eternal Coward –

Enter Alonzo.

Alonzo. Sir, bring up your Reserves, or all is lost;
Ambition plumes the Moor, and makes him act
Deeds of such wonder, that even you wou'd envy them.
Philip. 'Tis well; – I'le raise my Glories to that dazling height
Shall darken his, or set in endless Night.   *Exeunt.*

SCENE, *a Grove.*

Enter Cardinal and Queen; the noise of a Battel continuing
a far off all the Scene.

Queen. By all thy Love, by all thy languishments,
By all those sighs and tears paid to my Cruelty,
By all thy vows, thy passionate Letters sent,
I do conjure thee, go not forth to fight:
Command your Troops not to engage with *Philip,*
Who aims at nothing but the Kingdoms ruine.
– *Fernando*'s kill'd, – the Moor has gain'd the power,
A power that you nor *Philip* can withstand,
And is't not better he were lost, then *Spain?*
Since one must be a Sacrifice. –
Besides, – if I durst tell it,

There's something I cou'd whisper to thy soul,
Wou'd make thee blush at ev'ry single good
Thou'ast done that insolent Boy: – but 'tis not now
A time for stories of so strange a nature, –
Which when you know, you will conclude with me,
That every man that Arms for *Philip*'s Cause,
Merits the name of Traytor. –
Be wise in time, and leave his shamefull Interest,
An Interest thou wilt curse thy self for taking;
Be wise, and make Alliance with the Moor.
Cardinal. And Madam, shou'd I lay aside my wrongs,
Those publick injuries I have receiv'd,
And make a mean and humble Peace with him?
– No, let *Spain* be ruin'd by our Civil Swords,
Ere for its safety I forgo mine Honour. –

Enter an Officer.

Officer. Advance Sir, with your Troops, or we are lost.
Cardinal. Give order –
Queen. That they stir not on their lives;
Is this the Duty that you owe your Country?
Is this your Sanctity, – and Love to me?
Is't thus you treat the Glory I have offer'd
To raise you to my Bed?
To rule a Kingdom, be a Nations safety,
To advance in Hostile manner to their Walls,
Walls that confine your Countrymen, and Friends,
And Queen, to whom you've vow'd eternal Peace,
Eternal Love; and will you Court in Arms?
Such rude Addresses wou'd but ill become you.
No, – from this hour renounce all claims to me,
Or *Philip*'s Interest; – for let me tell you, – Cardinal,
This Love – and that Revenge – are inconsistent.
Cardinal. But Madam –
Queen. No more; – disband your Rebel Troops,
And straight with me to *Abdelazer*'s Tent,
Where all his Claims he shall resign to you
Both in my self, the Kingdom, and the Crown:
You being departed, thousands more will leave him,
And you're alone the Prop to his Rebellion.

Enter Sebastian.

Sebastian. Advance, advance, my Lord, with all your Force,
    Or else the Prince and Victory is lost,
    Which now depends upon his single Valour;
    Who like some Ancient *Hero*, or some God,
    Thunders amongst the thickest of his Enemies,
    Destroying all before him in such numbers,
    That Piles of dead obstruct his passage to the living. –
    Relieve him straight, my Lord, with our last Cavalry and hopes.
Cardinal. I'le follow instantly –   *Exit* Sebastian.
Queen. Sir, but you shall not, unless it be to death: –
    Shall you preserve the only man I hate,
    And hate with so much reason? – let him fall
    A Victim to an injur'd Mothers Honour.
    – Come, I will be obey'd, – indeed I must. –   *Fawns on him.*
Cardinal. When you're thus soft, can I retain my anger? –
    Oh look but ever thus – in spight of injuries –
    I shall become as tame and peaceable,
    As are your charming Eyes, when dress'd in Love,
    Which melting down my Rage, leave me defenceless.
    – Ah Madam, have a generous care of me,
    For I have now resign'd my power to you.   *Shout within.*
Queen. What shouts are these?

Enter Sebastian.

Sebastian. My Lord, the Enemy is giving ground,
    And *Philip*'s arm alone sustains the day;
    Advance Sir, and compleat the Victory. –   *Exit.*
Queen. Give order straight that a Retreat be sounded;
    And whilst they do so, by me conducted
    We'l instantly to *Abdelazer*'s Tent: –
    Hast, – hast, my Lord, whilst I attend you here.   *Exeunt severally.*

Cardinal going out, is met by Philip.

Philip. Oh damn your lazie Order, where have you been, Sir?
    – But 'tis no time for questions,
    Move forward with your Reserves.
Cardinal. I will not, Sir.

Philip. How, will not!

Cardinal. Now to advance would be impolitique;
   Already by your desperate attempts,
   You've lost the best part of our hopes.

Philip. Death! you lye.

Cardinal. Lye, Sir!

Philip. Yes, lye Sir: – therefore come on,
   Follow the desperate Reer-Guard, which is mine,
   And where I'le dye or Conquer; – follow my Sword
   The bloudy way it leads, or else by Heaven
   I'le give the Moor the Victory in spight,
   And turn my force on thee; –
   Plague of your Cowardice, – Come, follow me.   *Exit Cardinal.*

SCENE, *the Grove.*

As Philip *is going off, he is overtook by* Alonzo, Antonio, Sebastian, *and other*
   Officers: At the other side some Moor[s], and others of Abdelazer's *Party, enter*
   and fall on Philip *and the rest; – the Moors are beaten off; – one left dead on the*
   Stage. – Enter Abdelazer, *with* Roderigo *and some others.*

Abdelazer. Oh for more work, – more souls to send to Hell!
   – Ha ha ha, here's one going thither, – Sirrah – Slave –
   Moore – who kill'd thee? – how he grins: – this breast,
   Had it been temper'd and made proof like mine,
   It never wou'd have been a mark for Fools.

Abdelazer *going out: Enter* Philip, Alonzo, Sebastian, Antonio,
and Officers, as passing over the Stage.

Philip. I'le wear my Sword to th'Hilt, but I will find
   The subject of my Vengeance. –
   Moor, 'tis for thee I seek, where art thou Slave? –

Abdelazer. Here, *Philip* –   Abdelazer *turns.*

Philip. Fate and Revenge, I thank thee! –

Abdelazer. Why – thou art brave, whoe're begot thee.

Philip. Villain, a King begot me.

Abdelazer. I know not that,
   But I'le be sworn thy Mother was a Queen;
   And I will kill thee handsomely for her sake.   *Offer to fight, their*

Alonzo. Hold – hold, my Prince.   *Parties hinder them.*

Osmin. Great Sir, what mean you? *To* Abdelazer.
   The Victory being yours, to give your life away
   On one so mad and desperate. *Their Parties draw.*
Philip. Alonzo, hold,
   We two will be the Fate of this great day.
Abdelazer. And I'le forgoe all I've already won,
   And claim no Conquest; though whole heaps of Bodies,
   Which this right hand has slain, declare me Victor.
Philip. No matter who's the Victor; I have thee in my view
   And will not leave thee,
   Till thou hast Crown'd those heaps, and made 'em all
   The glorious Trophies of my Victory. – Come on Sir –
Alonzo. You shall not fight thus single;
   If you begin, by Heaven we'l all fall on:
Philip. Dost thou suspect my power!
   Oh I am arm'd with more then compleat Steel,
   The justice of my Quarrel; when I look
   Upon my Fathers wrongs, my Brothers wounds,
   My Mothers infamy, *Spains* misery,
   I am all fire, and yet I am too cold
   To let out bloud enough for my Revenge:
   – Therefore stir not a Sword on my side.
Abdelazer. Nor on mine.

They fight, both their Parties engage on either side; the Scene draws off and discovers
   both the Armies, which all fall on and make the main Battel: Philip *prevails, the*
   Moors give ground: then the Scene closes to the Grove. Enter some Moors flying
   in disorder. [Exeunt]

SCENE *changes to a Tent.*

Enter Abdelazer, Roderigo, Osmin, Zarrack, *and some*
others of his Party.

Roderigo. Oh fly, my Lord, fly, for the day is lost.
Abdelazer. There are three hundred and odd days ith' year,
   And cannot we lose one? – dismiss thy fears,
   They'l make a Coward of thee.
Osmin. Sir, all the Noble *Spaniards* have forsook you;
   Your Souldiers faint are round beset with Enemies,
   Nor can you shun your Fate, but by your flight.

Abdelazer. I can, – and must, – in spight of Fate:
    The wheel of War shall turn about again,
    And dash the Current of his Victories. –
    This is the Tent I've pitch'd, at distance from the Armies,
    To meet the Queen and Cardinal:
    Charm'd with the Magick of Dissimulation,
    I know by this h'as furl'd his Ensigns up,
    And is become a tame and coward Ass.   *A Retreat is*
    – Hark – hark – 'tis done; Oh my inchanting Engine!   *sounded.*
    – Dost thou not hear Retreat sounded?
Roderigo. Sure 'tis impossible!
Abdelazer. She has prevail'd, – a womans tongue and eyes,
    Are Forces stronger then Artilleries.

        Enter Queen, Cardinal, Women, and Souldiers.

    – We are betray'd –
Queen. What means this jealousie? lay by your weapons
    And embrace; – the sight of these begets suspicion:
    – *Abdelazer*, by my Birth he comes in Peace,
    Lord Cardinal, on my Honour so comes he.
Abdelazer. Let him withdraw his Troops then.
Queen. They're Guards for all our safeties:
    Give me your hand, Prince Cardinal; – thine, *Abdelazer*; –
               She brings them together, they embrace.
    This blest Accord I do behold with joy.
Cardinal. Abdelazer,
    I at the Queens command have met you here,
    To know what 'tis you will propose to us.
Abdelazer. Peace and eternal Friendship 'twixt us two:
    How much against my will I took up Arms,
    Be witness Heav'n nor was it in Revenge to you,
    But to let out th'infected bloud of *Philip*,
    Whose sole aim
    Is to be King, – which *Spain* will never suffer;
    Spain gave me Education, though not Birth,
    Which has intitl'd it my Native home,
    To which such reverence and esteem I bear,
    I will preserve it from the Tyrants rage. –
    The People who once lov'd him, now abhor him,
    And 'tis your power alone that buoys him up;

And when you've lifted him into a Throne,
'Tis time to shake you off.
Cardinal. Whilst I behold him as my Native Prince,
My Honour and Religion bids me serve him;
Yet not when I'm convinc'd that whilst I do so,
I injure *Spain.*
Abdelazer. If he were so, the Powers above forbid
We shou'd not serve, adore, and fight for him;
But *Philip* is a Bastard: – nay 'twill surprize ye,
But that 'tis truth, the Queen will satisfie you.
Queen. With one bold word he has undone my Honour: *Weeps.*
Too bluntly, *Abdelazer*, you repeat,
That which by slow degrees you shou'd have utter'd.
Abdelazer. Pardon my roughness, Madam, I meant well.
Cardinal. Philip a Bastard!
If by such Arts you wou'd divide me from him,
I shall suspect you wou'd betray us both.
Queen. Sir, he informs you truth; and I blush less
To own him so, then that he is a Traytor.
Cardinal. Philip a Bastard! Oh it cannot be: –
Madam, take heed you do not for Revenge,
Barter your dearer Honour, and lose both.
Queen. I know what's due to Honour, and Revenge,
But better what I owe to *Spain*, and you. –
You are a Prince oth' Bloud, and may put off
The Cardinal when you please, and be a Monarch.
Cardinal. Though my Ambition's equal to my Passion,
Neither shall make me act against those Principles
My Honour ever taught me to obey.
– And Madam –
'Tis a less sin, not to believe you here,
Then 'tis to doubt your Virtue.
Queen. I wish it were untold, if it must forfeit
The least of your Esteems, – but that 'tis truth,
Be witness Heav'n, my shame, my sighs, and tears.   *Weeps.*
Cardinal. Why Madam was't so long conceal'd from me?
Queen. The Circumstances I shall at leisure tell you:
And for the present,
Let it suffice, he cannot rule in *Spain*,
Nor can you side with him, without being made

As much incapable to reign as he.

Cardinal. Though Love and Honour I have always made
  The business of my life;
  My soul retains too, so much of Ambition,
  As puts me still in mind of what I am,
  A Prince! and Heir to *Spain*!
  Nor shall my blinded zeal to Loyalty,
  Make me that glorious Interest resign,
  Since *Philip's* claims are not so great as mine.
  – Madam, though I'm convinc'd I've done amiss
  In taking Arms for *Philip*,
  Yet 'twill be difficult to dis-ingage my self.

Abdelazer. Most easily; –
  Proclaim it in the head of all your Troops,
  The justice of your Cause for leaving him;
  And tell 'em, 'tis a work of Piety
  To follow your example:
  The giddy Rout are guided by Religion,
  More then by Justice, Reason, or Allegiance.
  – The Crown which I as a good Husband keep,
  I will lay down upon the empty Throne;
  Marry you the Queen, and fill it; – and for me,
  I'le ever pay you duty as a Subject.   *Bows low.*

Cardinal. On these Conditions all I am is yours;
  Philip we cannot fear, all he can do
  Is to retire for refuge into *Portugal*.

Abdelazer. That wou'd be dangerous; –
  Is there no arts to get him in our power?

Cardinal. Perhaps by Policy, and seeming Friendship,
  For we have reason yet to fear his Force;
  And since I'm satisfy'd he's not my lawful Prince,
  I cannot think it an impiety
  To sacrifice him to the Peace of *Spain*,
  And every Spirit that loves Liberty;
  First we'l our Forces joyn, and make 'em yours,
  Then give me your Authority to Arrest him;
  If so we can surprize him, we'l spare the hazard
  Of a second Battel.

Abdelazer. My Lord, retire into my inner Tent,
  And all things shall be instantly perform'd.   *Exeunt all.*

SCENE, *the Grove.*

Enter some of Philip's *Party running over the Stage, pursu'd by*
Philip: Alonzo, Sebastian, Antonio, *and some few Officers more.*

Alonzo. Do not pursue 'em, Sir, such Coward Slaves
  Deserve not death from that illustriate[10] hand.
Philip. Eternal Plagues consume 'em in their flight:
  Oh this damn'd Coward Cardinal has betray'd us!
  When all our Swords were nobly dy'd in bloud,
  When with red sweat that trickled from our wounds
  We'ad dearly earn'd the long-disputed Victory,
  Then to lose all! then to sound base Retreat!
  It swells my anger up to perfect madness.
Alonzo. Indeed 'twas wondrous strange.
Sebastian. I'm glad Sir –
Philip. Art glad of it? art glad we are abandon'd?
  That I, and thou have lost the hopefull'st day –
Sebastian. Great Sir, I'm glad that you came off alive.
Philip. Thou hast a lean face – and a carrion heart –
  A Plague upon the Moor and thee; – Oh *Alonzo,*
  To run away! – follow'd by all the Army!
  Oh I cou'd tear my hair, and curse my soul to Air!
  – Cardinal – thou Traytor *Judas,* that wou'dst sell
  Thy God again, as thou hast done thy Prince.
  – But come – we're yet a few,
  And we wil fight till there be left but one; –
  If I prove him, I'le dye a glorious death.
Antonio. Yes, but the Cardinal has took pious care
  It shall be in our beds.
Sebastian. We are as bad as one already, Sir, for all our Fellows are craul'd
  home, some with ne're a Leg, others with ne're an Arm, some with their
  Brains beat out, and glad they escap'd so.
Philip. But my dear Countrymen, you'l stick to me,
1st Souldier. Aye, wou'd I were well off. –   *Asides.*
Philip. Speak stout *Sceva,*[11] wilt thou not?

---

[10] Illustrious (though not in *OED*, and not properly derived from Latin).
[11] Cassius Scaeva was a centurion who fought on Julius Caesar's side in the civil war against
  Pompey: "with one eye struck out, pierced through his thigh and shoulder, and his shield
  penetrated in a hundred and twenty places, he continued to guard the gate of the fortress
  that had been put in his charge" (Suetonius, *Caesar* 46). His exploits are described at
  length in Lucan, *Pharsalia* 6.144–262.

1st Souldier. *Sceva* Sir, who's that?

Philip. A gallant *Roman*, that fought by *Cæsar's* side,
Till all his Body cover'd o're with Arrows,
Shew'd like a monstrous Porcupine.

1st Souldier. And did he dye, Sir?

Philip. He wou'd not but have dy'd for *Cæsar's* Empire.

1st Souldier. Hah, – why Sir I'm none of *Sceva*, but honest *Diego*, yet would as willingly dye as he, but that I have a Wife and Children; and if I dye, they beg.

Philip. For every drop of bloud which thou shalt lose,
I'le give thy Wife – a Diadem.

1st Souldier. Stark mad, as I'm valiant. –

    Enter Cardinal, Officers and Souldiers: Philip *offers to run on him,*
    is held by Alonzo.

Philip. Oh Heaven! is not that the Cardinal?
Traytor, how dar'st thou tempt my rage and justice?

Cardinal. Your Pardon, Sir, I come in humble love
To offer happy Peace.

Philip. Was that thy aim when base Retreat was sounded?
Oh thou false Cardinal! – let me go, *Alonzo*, –
Death! offer happy Peace! – no offer War,
Bring Fire and Sword; – Hell and damnation – Peace!
Oh damn your musty Peace: – No, will you fight, and cry,
Down with the Moor! and then I'le dye in peace.
I have a heart, two arms, a soul, a head,
I'le hazard these, – I can but hazard all. –
Come – I will kneel to thee, – and be thy Slave, –   *Kneels.*
I'le let thee tread on me, do any thing,
So this damn'd Moor may fall.

Cardinal. Yes Sir, he shall –

Philip. Gods! shall he! – thy Noble hand upon't,
And for this promise, take my gratefull heart.   *Embraces him.*
– Shall *Abdelazer* fall!

Cardinal. Yes, upon thee –
Like the tall ruines of a falling Tower,   *As they embrace, the Guards*
To crush thee into dust: –   *seize him and the rest.*
Traytor, and Bastard, I arrest thee of High Treason.

Philip. Hoh! – Traytor! – and Bastard! – and from thee!   *They hold*

Cardinal. Guards, to your hands the Prisoner is committed,   Philip's
    hands.

There's your warrant: – *Alonzo,* you are free.   *Exit Cardinal.*
Philip. Prithee lend me one hand – to wipe my eyes,
    And see who 'tis dares Authorize this Warrant:
    – The Devil and his Dam! the Moor! – and Queen!
    Their Warrant! – Gods! *Alonzo,* must we obey it?
    Villains, you cannot be my Jaylors; there's no Prison,
    No Dungeon deep enough; no Gate so strong,
    To keep a man confin'd – so mad with wrong.
    – Oh dost thou weep, *Alonzo!*
Alonzo. I wou'd fain shed a tear,
    But from my eyes so many showrs are gone,
    They are too poor to pay your sorrows Tribute;
    There's now no remedy, we must to Prison.
Philip. Yes, and from thence to death: –
    I thought I should have had a Tomb hung round
    With tatter'd Ensigns, broken Spears and Javelins;
    And that my body with a thousand wounds,
    Shou'd have been borne on some Triumphant Chariot,
    With solemn Mourning Drums and Trumpets sounding;
    Whilst all the wondring World with grief and envy,
    Had wish'd my Glorious Destiny their own:
    But now, *Alonzo,* – like a Beast I fall,
    And hardly Pity waits my Funeral.   *Exeunt.*

ACT V.

SCENE I. *A Presence Chamber, with a*
Throne and Canopy.

Enter Abdelazer, *Cardinal,* Alonzo, Ordonio, Roderigo, *and other Lords, one*
    bearing the Crown, which is laid on the Table on a Cushion; the Queen, Leonora,
    and Ladies. They all seat themselves, leaving the Throne and Chair of State empty.
    Abdelazer *rises and bows,* Roderigo *kneeling presents him with the Crown.*

Abdelazer. Grandees of *Spain,* if in this Royal Presence
    There breaths a man, who having laid his hold
    So fast on such a Jewel, and dares wear it
    In the contempt of Envy, as I dare;
    Yet uncompell'd (as freely as the Gods

Bestow their blessings) wou'd give such Wealth away,
Let such a man stand forth – Are ye all fixt?
No wonder, since a King's a Deity!
And who'd not be a God! –
This glorious Prospect when I first saw the Light,
Met with my Infant hopes; nor have those Fetters
(Which e're I grew towards man, *Spain* taught me how to wear)
Made me forget what's due to that Illustrious Birth:
– Yet thus – I cast aside the Rays of Majesty, –

Kneels, and lays the Crown on the Table.

And on my knee, do humbly offer up
This splendid Powerful thing, and ease your fears
Of usurpation and of Tyranny.

Alonzo. What new device is this?   *Aside.*

Cardinal. This is an Action generous and just; –
Let us proceed to new Election.

Abdelazer. Stay, Peers of *Spain*, –
If young Prince *Philip* be King *Philip*'s Son;
Then is he Heir to *Philip*, and his Crown;
But if a Bastard, then he is a Rebel,
And as a Traytor to the Crown shou'd bleed:
That dangerous Popular Spirit must be laid,
Or *Spain* must languish under Civil Swords;
And *Portugal* taking advantages in these disorders,
(Assisted by the Male-contents° within,
If *Philip* live) will bring Confusion home.
– Our remedy for this, is first to prove,
And then proclaim him Bastard.

Alonzo. That project wou'd be worth your Politiques.   *Aside.*
– How shou'd we prove him Bastard?

Abdelazer. Her Majesty being lately urg'd by Conscience,
And much above her Honour prizing *Spain*,
Declar'd this Secret, but has not nam'd the Man;
If he be Noble, and a *Spaniard* born,
He shall repair her fame, by marrying her.

Cardinal. No, *Spaniard*, or Moor, the daring Slave shall dye.

Queen. Wou'd I were cover'd with a Veil of Night,   *Weeps.*
That I might hide the blushes on my Cheeks;

Male-contents: malcontents

But when your safety comes into dispute.
My Honour, nor my Life, must come in competition.
– I'le therefore hide my eyes, and blushing own,
That *Philip*'s Father is ith' Presence now.
Alonzo. Ith' Presence! name him.
Queen. The Cardinal –   *All rise in amazement.*
Cardinal. How's this, Madam!
Abdelazer. How! the Cardinal!
Cardinal. I *Philip*'s Father, Madam!
Queen. Dull Lover – is not all this done for thee!
   Dost thou not see a Kingdom and my self,
   By this Confession, thrown into thy arms?
Cardinal. On terms so infamous I must despise it.
Queen. Have I thrown by all sense of modesty,
   To render you the Master of my Bed,
   To be refus'd? – was there another way? –
Cardinal. I cannot yield; this cruelty transcends
   All you have ever done me: – Heavens! what a contest
   Of Love, and Honour, swells my rising heart.
Queen. By all my Love, if you refuse me now,
   Now when I have remov'd all difficulties,
   I'le be Reveng'd a thousand killing ways.
Cardinal. Madam, I cannot own so false a thing,
   My Conscience, and Religion will not suffer me.
Queen. Away with all this canting; Conscience, and Religion!
   No, take advice from nothing but from Love.
Cardinal. 'Tis certain I'm bewitch'd, – she has a Spell
   Hid in those charming Lips.
Alonzo. Prince Cardinal, what say you to this?
Cardinal. I cannot bring it forth –
Queen. Do't, or thou'rt lost for ever.
Cardinal. Death! what's a womans power!
   And yet I can resist it.
Queen. And dare you disobey me?
Cardinal. Is't not enough I've given you up my power,
   Nay and resign'd my life into your hands,
   But you wou'd damn me too? – I will not yield. –
   Oh now I find a very Hell within me:
   How am I misguided by my passion!
Alonzo. Sir, we attend your Answer.

Queen. 'Tis now near twenty years, when newly married,
    (And 'tis the Custom here to marry young)
    King *Philip* made a War in *Barbary*,[12]
    Won *Tunis*, Conquer'd *Fez*, and hand to hand
    Slew great *Abdela*, King of *Fez*,[13] and Father
    To this *Barbarian* Prince.
Abdelazer. I was but young, and yet I well remember
    My Fathers wounds, – poor *Barbary*; – but no more.
Queen. In absence of my King, I liv'd retir'd,
    Shut up in my Apartment with my Women,
    Suffering no Visits, but the Cardinals,
    To whom the king had left me as his Charge;
    But he unworthy of that Trust repos'd,
    Soon turn'd his business into Love.
Cardinal. Heavens! how will this story end?
Queen. A tale, alas! unpleasant to my Ear,
    And for the which I banisht him my Presence:
    But oh the power of Gold! he bribes my Women,
    That they should tell me (as a secret too)
    The King (whose Wars were finish'd) would return
    Without acquainting any with the time;
    He being as Jealous, as I was fair and young.
    Meant to surprize me in the dead of Night:
    This pass'd upon my Youth, which ne're knew Art.
Cardinal. Gods! is there any Hell but Womans falshood!   *Aside.*
Queen. The following Night, I hasted to my Bed,
    To wait my expected Bliss;– nor was it long
    Before his gentle steps approach'd my Ears:
    Undress'd he came, and with a Vigorous haste
    Flew to my yielding Arms, I call'd him King!
    My dear lov'd Lord! and in return he breath'd
    Into my bosom in soft gentle whispers –
    My Queen! my Angel! my lov'd *Isabella*!
    And at that word – I need not tell the rest.
Alonzo. What's all this, Madam, to the Cardinal?

---

[12] "Barbary" originally referred to the Berbers, but was conveniently suggestive of "barbarian." The British used it "as a blanket term for the entire North African region (excluding Egypt)" (Linda Colley, *Captives*, 44).
[13] The former capital of Morocco.

Queen. Ah Sir, the night too short for his Caresses,
  Made room for day, day that betray'd my shame,
  For in my guilty Arms, I found the Cardinal!
Alonzo. Madam, why did not you complain of this?
Queen. Alas, I was but young, and full of fears;
  Bashfull, and doubtfull of a just belief,
  Knowing King *Philips* rash and jealous temper,
  But from your Justice I expect Revenge.
Roderigo. His crime, my Lords, is death, by all our Laws.
Cardinal. Have you betray'd me by my too much Faith?
  Oh shameless Creature, am I disarm'd for this?
  Had I but so much ease to be inrag'd,
  Sure I shou'd kill thee for this Treachery;
  But I'm all shame, and grief. – By all that's Holy,
  My Lords, I never did commit this Crime.
Abdelazer. 'Tis but in vain, Prince Cardinal, to deny it.
Queen. Do not believe him, Lords; –
  Revenge – let Sentence pass upon the Traytor.
Cardinal. I own that name with horrour, which you drew me to,
  When I betray'd the best of Men, and Princes;
  And 'tis but just you fit me for despairs,
  That may instruct me how to follow him in death:
  Yet as I'm Prince oth' Bloud, and Cardinal too,
  You cannot be my Judges.
Abdelazer. You shall be try'd, Sir, as becomes your Quality.
  Osmin, we commit the Cardinal to your Charge.
Cardinal. Heaven! shou'd I live to that! no,
  I have within me a Private shame,
  That shall secure me from the Publick one.
Alonzo. A pretty turn of State, – we shall all follow, Sir.
Cardinal. The Powers above are just, –
  Thus I my Prince a Sacrifice first made,
  And now my self am on the Altar laid.   *Exit Cardinal Guarded.*
Abdelazer. Madam, retire, you've acted so Divinely,
  You've fill'd my soul with new admiring Passion; –
  I'le wait on you in your Apartment instantly,
  And at your feet pay all my thanks, and Love.
Queen. Make haste, my deares Moor, whilst I retire,
  And fit my soul, to meet thy kind desire.

Exeunt Queen and her Train, Leonora *advancing to follow is staid*
                    by Abdelazer

Abdelazer. Stay, beauteous Maid, stay and receive that Crown,

Leads her back.

    Which as your due Heav'n and all *Spain* present you with.
Alonzo. But granting *Philip* is – that thing you call him,
    If we must grant him so, who then shall Reign?
    Not that we do not know who ought to Reign,
    But ask who 'tis you will permit to do so.   *to Abdelazer.*
Abdelazer. Who but bright *Leonora*! the Royal Off-spring
    Of Noble *Philip*, whose Innocence and Beauty,
    Without th'advantage of her Glorious Birth,
    Merits all Adoration.
All. With joy we do salute her Queen.
Abdelazer. Live *Leonora*! beauteous Queen of *Spain*!   *Shout[s].*
Alonzo. From *Abdelazer* this! it cannot be,
    At least not real.   *Aside.*
Abdelazer. My Lords,
    Be it now your care magnificently to provide
    Both for the Coronation, and the Marriage
    Of the fair Queen;
    Let nothing be omitted that may shew,
    How we can pay, where we so vastly owe.   *Bows.*
Alonzo. I am much bound to *Spain*, and you, my Lords,
    For this great Condescention.
Leonora. My Lords, I thank ye all,
    And most the gallant Moor: – I am not well –   *Turns to* Alonzo.
    Something surrounds my heart so full of death,
    I must retire to give my sorrow breath.

Exit Leonora *follow'd by all but* Abdelazer *and*
Roderigo, *who looks on* Abdelazer.

Roderigo. Sir, – what have you done?
Abdelazer. What every man that loves like me shou'd do,
    Undone my self forever, to beget
    One moments thought in her, that I adore her;
    That she may know, none ever lov'd like me,
    I've thrown away the Diadem of *Spain:* –
    – 'Tis gone! and there's no more to set but this –

(My heart) at all, and at this one last cast
　　Sweep up my former losses, or be undone.
Roderigo. You Court at a vast rate, Sir.
Abdelazer. Oh she's a Goddess! a Creature made by Heaven!
　　To make my prosperous Toyls, all sweet and charming!
　　She must be Queen, I, and the Gods decree it.
Roderigo. Sir, is she not design'd *Alonzo*'s Bride?
Abdelazer. Yes, so her self, and he have ill agreed;
　　But Heaven and I, am of another mind,
　　And must be first obey'd.
Roderigo. Alonzo will not yield his Interest easily.
Abdelazer. Wou'd that were all my stop to happiness; –
　　But *Roderigo*, this fond Amorous Queen
　　Sits heavy on my heart.
Roderigo. She's but a woman, nor has more lives than one.
Abdelazer. True, *Roderigo*, and thou hast dealt in Murders,
　　And know'st the safest way to –
Roderigo. How Sir! –
Abdelazer. Thou dar'st not sure pretend to any Virtue;
　　Had Hell inspir'd thee with less Excellency
　　Than Arts of Killing Kings! thou'dst ne're been rais'd
　　To that exalted height t' have known my secrets.
Roderigo. But Sir –
Abdelazer. Slave, look back upon the wretchedness I took thee from,
　　What merits hadst thou to deserve my bounty?
　　But Vice, brave prosperous Vice!
　　Thou'rt neither Wise, nor Valiant.
Roderigo. I own my self that Creature rais'd by you,
　　And live but to repay you, name the way.
Abdelazer. My business is – to have the Queen remov'd;
　　She does expect my coming this very hour,
　　And when she does so, 'tis her custom to be retir'd,
　　Dismissing all Attendance, but *Elvira.*
Roderigo. The rest, I need not be instructed in.　　　　*Exit* Roderigo.

Enter Osmin.

Osmin. The Cardinal, Sir, is close confin'd with *Philip.*
Abdelazer. 'Tis well.
Osmin. And do you think it fit, Sir, they shou'd live?

Abdelazer. No, this day they both must dye, some sort of death
  That may be thought was given them by themselves:
  I'm sure I give them cause. – *Osmin*, view well this Ring,
  Whoever brings this Token to your hands,
  Without considering Sex, or Quality,
  Let 'em be kill'd.
Osmin. Your will shall be obey'd in every thing.   *Exeunt severally.*

SCENE, *a fine Chamber.*

A Table and Chair.

Enter Queen and Elvira.

Queen. Elvira, hast thou drest my Lodgings up
  Fit to receive my Moor?
  Are they all gay, as Altars, when some Monarch
  Is there to offer up rich Sacrifices?
  Hast thou strew'd all the Floor his feet must press,
  With the soft new-born Beauties of the Spring?
Elvira. Madam, I've done as you commanded me.
Queen. Let all the Chambers too be fill'd with Lights;
  There's a Solemnity methinks in Night,
  That does insinuate Love into the soul!
  And makes the bashfull Lover more assur'd.
Elvira. Madam,
  You speak as if this were your first Enjoyment.
Queen. My first! Oh *Elvira*, his Power, like his Charms,
  His Wit, or Bravery! every hour renews:
  Love gathers sweets like Flow'rs, which grow more fragrant
  The nearer they approach maturity.   *Knock.*
  – Hark! 'tis my Moor, – give him Admittance straight.
  The thought comes o're me like a gentle Gale,
  Raising my bloud into a thousand Curls.
Elvira. Madam, it is a Priest –
Queen. A Priest! oh send him quickly hence;
  I wou'd not have so cold, and dull an Object,
  Meet with my Nobler sense, 'tis mortifying.
Elvira. Perhaps 'tis some Petition from the Cardinal.
Queen. Why what have I to do with Priest or Cardinal?
  Let him not enter. –   *Elvira goes out, and returns with*

Elvira. From *Abdelazer;* Madam.   Roderigo, *drest like a Fryer.*

Queen. H'as nam'd a word will make all places free.

Roderigo. Madam, be pleas'd to send your Woman hence,
　　I've something to deliver from the Moor,
　　Which you alone must be acquainted with.

Queen. Well, your Formality shall be allow'd;– retire –   *To* Elvira.
　　What have you to deliver to me now?

Roderigo. This –   *Shews a Dagger, and takes*

Queen. Hah –   *her roughly by the hands.*

Roderigo. You must not call for help, unless to Heaven.

Queen. What daring thing art thou?

Roderigo. One that has now no time to answer thee. *Stabs her, she struggles,*

Queen. Oh hold thy killing hand! I am thy Queen.   *her arm bleeds.*

Roderigo. Thou mayst be Devil too, for ought I know;
　　I'le try thy substance thus –   *Stabs again.*

Queen. Oh *Abdelazer* –
　　Thou hast well reveng'd me – on my sins of Love; –   *He seats her in*
　　But shall I die thus tamely unreveng'd? –   *the Chair.*
　　– Help – murder – help –   *He offers to stab again.*

Enter Elvira, *and other Women.*

Elvira. Oh Heavens! the Queen is murder'd! – help the Queen!
                                              Roderigo *offers to stab Elvira.*

Enter Abdelazer.

Abdelazer. Hah! the Queen! what Sacrilegious hand,
　　Or heart so Brutal –
　　Durst thus prophane the Shrine ador'd by me!
　　Guard well the Passages. –

Queen. Thou art that Sacrilegious –Brutal thing, –
　　And false as are the Deities thou worship'st.

Abdelazer. Gods! let me not understand that killing language!
　　– Inform me quickly how you came thus wounded,
　　Lest looking on that Sacred stream of bloud,
　　I dye e're I've reveng'd you, on your Murderer.

Queen. Haste then, and kill thy self; thou art my Murderer.
　　Nor had his hand, if not by thee instructed,
　　Aim'd at a sin so dangerous. –

Abdelazer. – Surely she'l live.– (*aside*) – This! –
　　Can mischief dwell beneath this Reverend shape?

Confess who taught thee so much cruelty!
Confess! or I will Kill thee. –
Roderigo. The Cardinal.
Queen. The Cardinal!
Abdelazer. The Cardinal! – Oh impious Traytor! –
How came I mention'd then?
Roderigo. To get Admittance.
Abdelazer. But why do I delay thy Punishment   *Aside.*
Dye, – and be damn'd together. –   *Stabs him.*
– But oh my Queen! – *Elvira*, – call for help!
Have I remov'd all that oppos'd our flame,   *Kneels.*
To have it thus blown out? thus in a minute!
When I, all full of Youthfull fire! all Love!
Had rais'd my soul with hopes of near delights,
– To meet thee cold, – and pale; – to find those Eyes,
Those Charming Eyes thus dying; – Oh ye Powers! –
Take all the prospect of my future joys,
And turn it to despair, – since thou art gone.–
Queen. Cease – cease – your kind complaints, – my struggling soul,
'Twixt Death – and Love – holds an uneasie contest;
This will not let it stay, – nor that depart; –
And whilst I hear thy voice – thus breathing Love,
It hovers still – about – the gratefull – sound.
– My Eyes – have took – an everlasting leave –
Of all that blest their sight, and now a gloomy darkness
Benights the wishing sense, – that vainly strives –
To take another view, – but 'tis too late, –
And life – and Love – must yield – to death – and – Fate.   *Dyes.*
Abdelazer. Farewell my greatest Plague –   *He rises with joy.*
Thou wert a most impolitique° loving thing,
And having done my bus'ness which thou wert born for,
'T was time thou shou'dst retire,
And leave me free to Love, and Reign alone.

Enter Leonora, Alonzo, Ordonio,
and other men and women.

– Come all the world, and pay your sorrows here,
Since all the world has Interest in this loss.

impolitique: injudicious

Alonzo. The Moor in tears! nay then the sin was his.
Leonora. The Queen my Mother dead!
    How many sorrows will my heart let in,
    Ere it will break in pieces!   *Weeps over her.*
Alonzo. I know the source of all this Villany,
    And need not ask you how the Queen came murder'd.
Elvira. My Lord, that Frier, from the Cardinal did it.
Alonzo. The Cardinal! –
    'Tis possible, – for the injuries she did him.   *Aside.*
    Cou'd be repaid with nothing less than death.
    – My Fair, your griefs have been so just of late,
    I dare not beg that you would weep no more;
    Though every tear those lovely Eyes let fall,
    Give me a killing wound:– remove the Body,   *Guards remove the body.*
    Such objects suit not souls so soft as thine.
                            Exeunt all but Alonzo *&* Leonora.
Leonora. With horrours I am grown of late familiar;
    I saw my Father dye, and liv'd the while,
    I saw my beauteous Friend, and thy lov'd Sister,
    Florella, whilst her breast was bleeding fresh;
    Nay and my Brothers too, all full of wounds!
    The best and kindest Brother, that ever Maid was blest with,
    Poor *Philip* bound, and led like Victims for a Sacrifice:
    All this I saw, and liv'd –
    And canst thou hope for pity from that heart,
    Whose hardned sense is proof gainst all these miseries?
    – This Moor, *Alonzo,* is a subtle Villain,
    Yet of such Power, we scarce dare think him such.
Alonzo. 'Tis true, my charming Fair, he is that Villain,
    As ill, and powerful too, yet he has a heart
    That may be reacht with this, – but 'tis not time,   *Points to his Sword.*
    We must dissemble yet, which is an Art
    Too foul for souls so Innocent as thine.

                    Enter Abdelazer.

    – The Moor!
    Hell! will he not allow us sorrowing time.
Abdelazer. Madam, I come to pay my humblest duty,
    And know what service you command your Slave.

Leonora. Alas, I've no Commands, or if I had,
    I am too wretched now to be obey'd.
Abdelazer. Can one so fair, and great, ask any thing
    Of Men, or Heaven, they wou'd not grant with joy?
Leonora. Heav'ns will I'm not permitted to dispute,
    And may implore in vain; but 'tis in you
    To grant me what may yet preserve my life.
Abdelazer. In me! in me! the humblest of your Creatures!
    By yon bright Sun, or your more splendid Eyes;
    I wou'd divest my soul of every hope,
    To gratifie one single wish of yours;
    – Name but the way. –
Leonora. I'm so unhappy, that the only thing
    I have to ask, is what you must deny;
    – The liberty of *Philip.* –
Abdelazer. How! *Philips* liberty! – and must I grant it!
    I (in whose hands Fortune had put the Crown)
    Had I not lov'd the good and Peace of *Spain,*
    Might have dispos'd it to my own advantage;
    And shall that Peace,
    Which I've preferr'd above my proper Glories,
    Be lost again in him, in him a Bastard!
Alonzo. That he's a Bastard, is not Sir believ'd;
    And she that cou'd love you, might after that
    Do any other sin, and 'twas the least
    Of all the number to declare him Bastard.
Abdelazer. How Sir! that cou'd love me! what is there here –
    Or in my soul, or Person, may not be belov'd?
Alonzo. I spoke without reflection on your Person,
    But of dishonest love, which was too plain,
    From whence came all the Ills we have endur'd;
    And now being warm in mischiefs,
    Thou dost pursue the Game, till all be thine.
Abdelazer. Mine!
Alonzo. Yes, thine; –
    The little humble Mask which you put on
    Upon the face of Falshood, and Ambition,
    Is easily seen through; you gave a Crown!
    But you'l command the Kingly power still,
    Arm, and disband, destroy or save at pleasure.

Abdelazer. Vain Boy, (whose highest fame,
  Is that thou art the great *Alvaro*'s Son)
  Where learnt you so much daring, to upbraid
  My generous Power thus falsly? – do you know me?
Alonzo. Yes, Prince, and 'tis that knowledge makes me dare;
  I know thy fame in Arms; I know in Battels
  Thou hast perform'd deeds much above thy years:
  My Infant courage too,
  (By the same Master taught) grew up to thine,
  When thou in Age out didst me, not in Bravery.
  – I know thou'st greater Power too, – thank thy Treachery!
Abdelazer. Dost thou not fear that Power?
Alonzo. By Heaven not I,
  Whilst I can this – command.   *Lays his hand on his Sword.*
Abdelazer. I too command a Sword,   Abdelazer *Lays his hand on his,*
  But not to draw on thee, *Alonzo*;   *and comes close up to him;*
  Since I can prove thy Accusations false
  By ways more gratefull: – take this Ring, *Alonzo,*
  The sight of it will break down Prison Gates,
  And set all free, as was the first born man.
Alonzo. What means this turn?
Abdelazer. To enlarge *Philip*; but on such Conditions,
  As you think fit to make for my security:
  And as thou'rt Brave, deal with me as I merit.
Alonzo. Art thou in earnest? –
Abdelazer. I am, by all that's Sacred.
Leonora. Oh let me fall before you, and ne're rise,
  Till I have made you know what Gratitude
  Is fit for such a Bounty! –
  Haste, my *Alonzo*, – haste – and treat with *Philip*;
  Nor do I wish his freedom, but on such terms
  As may be advantageous to the Moor.
Alonzo. Nor I, by Heaven! I know the Prince's soul,
  Though it be fierce, 't has Gratitude and Honour!
  And for a deed like this, will make returns,
  Such as are worthy of the brave Obliger.   *Exit* Alonzo.
Abdelazer. Yes, if he be not gone to Heaven before you come.   *Aside.*
  – What will become of *Abdelazer* now?
  Who with his Power, has thrown away his Liberty.

Leonora. Your Liberty! Oh Heaven forbid that you,
  Who can so generously give Liberty,
  Should be depriv'd of it!
  It must not be whilst *Leonora* lives.
Abdelazer. 'Tis she that takes it from me.
Leonora. I! Alas, I wou'd not for the world
  Give you one minutes pain.
Abdelazer. You cannot help it, 'tis against your will!
  Your Eyes insensibly do wound and kill!
Leonora. What can you mean? and yet I fear to know.
Abdelazer. Most charming of your Sex! had Nature made
  This clouded face, like to my heart, all Love,
  It might have spar'd that language which you dread;
  Whose rough harsh sound, unfit for tender Ears,
  Will ill express the business of my life.
Leonora. Forbear it, if that business, Sir, be Love.
Abdelazer. Gods!
  Because I want the Art to tell my story
  In that soft way, which those can do whose business
  Is to be still so idly employ'd,
  I must be silent, and endure my pain;
  Which Heaven ne're gave me so much tameness for.
  Love in my soul! is not that gentle thing
  It is in other breasts; instead of Calms,
  It ruffles mine into uneasie Storms.
  – I wou'd not Love, if I cou'd help it, Madam;
  But since 'tis not to be resisted here –
  You must permit it to approach your Ear.
Leonora. Not when I cannot hear it, Sir, with Honour.
Abdelazer. With Honour!
  Nay I can talk in the defence of that:
  By all that's Sacred, 'tis a flame as virtuous,
  As every thought inhabits your fair soul,
  And it shall learn to be as gentle too;
  – For I must merit you –
Leonora. I will not hear this language! merit me!
Abdelazer. Yes, – why not?
  You're but the Daughter of the King of *Spain*,
  And I am Heir to Great *Abdela*, Madam.

I can command this Kingdom you possess,
(Of which my Passion only made you Queen)
And re-assume that which your Father took
From mine, – a Crown as bright as that of *Spain*.
Leonora. You said you wou'd be gentle –
Abdelazer. I will! this sullen heart shall learn to bow,
And keep it self within the bounds of Love,
Its language I'le deliver out in sighs,
Soft as the whispers of a yielding Virgin.
I cou'd transform my soul to any shape;
Nay I could even teach my Eyes the Art
To change their natural fierceness into smiles.
– What is't I wou'd not do to gain that heart!
Leonora. Which never can be yours! that and my vows,
Are to *Alonzo* given; which he lays claim to
By the most Sacred tyes, Love and Obedience;
All *Spain* esteems him worthy of that Love.
Abdelazer. More worthy it than I! it was a Woman,
A nice, vain, peevish Creature that pronounc'd it,
Had it been Man, 't had been his last transgression!
– His Birth! his glorious Actions! are they like mine?
Leonora. Perhaps his Birth wants those advantages,
Which Nature has laid out in Beauty on his Person.
Abdelazer. Aye! there's your cause of hate! Curst be my Birth,
And curst be Nature, that has dy'd my skin
With this ungrateful colour! cou'd not the Gods
Have given me equal Beauty with *Alonzo*!
– Yet as I am, I've been in vain Ador'd,
And Beauties great as thine have languish'd for me.
The Lights put out! thou in my naked arms
Wilt find me soft and smooth as polisht Ebony,
And all my kisses on my balmy lips as sweet,
As are the Breezes, breath'd amidst the Groves,
Of ripening Spices in the height of day:
As vigorous too,
As if each Night were the first happy moment
I laid thy panting body to my bosom.
Oh that transporting thought! –
See, – I can bend as low, and sigh as often,   *Kneels.*

And sue for blessings only you can grant,
As any fair and soft *Alonzo* can; –
If you could pity me as well. –
But you are deaf, and in your Eyes I read   *Rises with anger.*
A scorn which animates my Love and Anger;
Nor know I which I shou'd dismiss or cherish.

Leonora. The last is much more welcome than the first;
Your Anger can but kill, but Sir your Love –
Will make me ever wretched, since 'tis impossible
I ever can return it.

Abdelazer. Why kill me then! you must do one or t'other,   *Kneels.*
For thus – I cannot live: – why dost thou weep?
Thy every tear's enough to drown my soul! –
How tame Love renders every feeble sense!   *Rises.*
– Gods! I shall turn Woman, and my Eyes inform me
The Transformation's near: – death! I'le not endure it,
I'le fly before sh'as quite undone my soul. –   *Offers to go.*
But 'tis not in my power, – she holds it fast, –
And I can now command no single part. –   *Returns.*
Tell me, bright Maid, – if I were amiable,
And you were uningag'd, cou'd you then love me?

Leonora. No! I cou'd dye first.

Abdelazer. Hah! – awake my soul from out this drowsie fit,
And with thy wonted Bravery, scorn thy Fetters.
– By Heaven'tis gone! and I am now my self: –
Be gone, my dull submission! my lazie flame
Grows sensible! and knows for what 't was kindled.
– Coy Mistress, you must yield, and quickly too:
Were you devout as Vestals, pure as their Fire,
Yet I wou'd wanton in the rifled spoils
Of all that sacred Innocence and Beauty.
– Oh my desires grow high!
Raging as Midnight flames let loose in Cities,
And like that too, will ruine where it lights.
– Come, – this Apartment was design'd for pleasure,
And made thus silent, and thus gay for me;
There I'le convince that errour, that vainly made thee think
I was not meant for Love. –

Leonora. Am I betray'd! are all my Women gone!

And have I nought but Heaven for my defence!
Abdelazer. None else, and that's too distant to befriend you.
Leonora. Oh take my life, and spare my dearer Honour!
   – Help! help! – ye Powers that favour innocence.

Enter Women.

Just as the Moor is going to force in Leonora,

Enters to him Osmin *in haste.*

Osmin. My Lord, *Alonzo* –
Abdelazer. What of him, you Slave, – is he not secur'd?
   Speak, dull Intruder, that know'st not times and seasons,
   or get thee hence.
Osmin. Not till I've done the business which I came for.
Abdelazer. Slave! – that – thou cam'st for.   *Stabs him in the arm.*
Osmin. No, 'twas to tell you, that *Alonzo,*
   Finding himself betray'd, made brave resistance;
   Some of your Slaves h'as kill'd, and some h'as wounded,
Abdelazer. 'Tis time he were secur'd;
   I must assist my Guards, or all is lost.   *Exit.*
Leonora. Sure *Osmin* from the Gods thou cam'st,
   To hinder my undoing; and if thou dy'st,
   Heaven will almost forgive thy other sins,
   For this one pious deed! –
   But yet I hope thy wound's not mortal.
Osmin. 'Tis only in my arm; – and Madam for this pity,
   I'le live to do you service.
Leonora. What service can the Favourite of the Moor,
   Train'd up in bloud and mischiefs, render me?
Osmin. Why Madam, I command the Guard of Moors,
   Who will all dye, when e're I give the word.
   – Madam, 'twas I caus'd *Philip* and the Cardinal
   To fly to th' Camp,
   And gave'em warning of approaching death.
Leonora. Heaven bless thee for thy goodness.
Osmin. And I am weary now of being a Tyrants Slave,
   And bearing blows too; the rest I cou'd have suffer'd.
   – Madam, I'le free the Prince!
   But see, the Moor returns. –

Leonora. That Monsters presence I must fly, as from a killing Plague.

Exit with her Women.

Enter Abdelazer, *with* Zarrack *and a Train of Moors.*

Abdelazer. It is Prodigious, that a single man
 Should with such Bravery defend his life,
 Amongst so many Swords; – but he is safe.
 Osmin, I am not us'd to sue for Pardon,
 And when I do, you ought to grant it me.
Osmin. I did not merit, Sir, so harsh a usage.
Abdelazer. No more, I am asham'd to be upbraided,
 And will repair the injury I did thee.
Osmin. Acknowledgment from you is pay sufficient.
Abdelazer. Yet *Osmin*, I shou'd chide your negligence,
 Since by it *Philip* lives still, and the Cardinal.
Osmin. I had design'd it, Sir, this Evenings Sacrifice.
Abdelazer. *Zarrack* shall now perform it, – and instantly:
 Alonzo too must bear 'em company.
Zarrack. I'le shew my Duty in my haste, my Lord.   *Exit* Zarrack.
Osmin. Death! I'm undone; – I'le after him, and kill him.   *Offers to go.*
Abdelazer. *Osmin*, I've business with you –   Osmin *comes back bowing.*

As they are going off, Enter Leonora, Ordonio, *other Lords,*
and Women.

Leonora. Oh Prince! for pity hear and grant my suit,   *Kneels.*
Abdelazer. When so much Beauty's prostrate at my feet,
 What is't I can deny? – rise, thou brightest Virgin
 That ever Nature made;
 Rise, and command my life, my soul, my honour!
Leonora. No, let me hang for ever on your knees,
 Unless you'l grant *Alonzo* liberty.
Abdelazer. Rise, I will grant it; though *Alonzo*, Madam,
 Betray'd that Trust I had repos'd in him.
Leonora. I know there's some mistake; let me negotiate
 Between my Brother, and the gallant Moor.
 I cannot force your Guards,
 There is no danger in a Womans arm.
Abdelazer. In your bright Eyes there is, that may corrupt 'em more,
 Than all the Treasures of the Eastern Kings.

Yet Madam, here I do resign my Power,
Act as you please, dismiss *Alonzo's* Chains.
And since you are so generous, to despise
This Crown, which I have given you,
Philip shall owe his Greatness to your Bounty,
And whilst he makes me safe, shall Rule in *Spain*.   *Whispers.*
– *Osmin* –
Ordonio. And will you trust him, Madam!
Leonora. If he deceive me, 'tis more happy far
    To dye with them, than live where he inhabits.
Osmin. It shall be done. –
Abdelazer. Go *Osmin*, wait upon the Queen: –
    And when she is confin'd, I'le visit her,   *Aside.*
    Where if she yield, she reigns; if not, she dyes.

        Exit Abdelazer *one way,* Leonora, Osmin *and the rest another.*

SCENE, *a Prison.*

Discovers[14] Philip *chain'd to a Post, and over against him the*
Cardinal *and* Alonzo *in Chains.*

Philip. Oh all ye cruel Powers! is't not enough
    I am depriv'd of Empire, and of Honour!
    Have my bright Name stoln from me, with my Crown!
    Divested of all Power! all Liberty!
    And here am Chain'd, like the sad Andromede,[15]
    To wait destruction from the dreadfull Monster!
    Is not all this enough without being damn'd,
    To have thee, Cardinal, in my full view!
    If I cou'd reach my Eyes, I'de be reveng'd
    On the officious and accursed Lights,

---

[14] Restoration theaters had two sets of scenic shutters, probably in groups of three. Most acting was done on a large forestage in front of the proscenium arch, but shutters could be drawn to reveal action in progress in the area behind them. Behn was particularly fond of such "discovery scenes."

[15] Andromeda was daughter of Cepheus, king of Ethiopia, which was being ravaged by a sea monster. Cepheus learned that the only cure was to expose Andromeda to the monster, which he did, chaining her to a rock on the shore. She was rescued by the hero Perseus. Andromeda was conventionally portrayed as white, but it is nevertheless odd that Philip, the macho European, should identify himself with an African – and an African woman at that.

For guiding so much torment to my soul.

Cardinal. My much wrong'd Prince! you need not wish to kill
By ways more certain, than by upbraiding me
With my too credulous, shamefull past misdeeds.

Philip. If that wou'd kill, I'de weary out my tongue
With an eternal repetition of thy Treachery; –
Nay, and it shou'd forget all other language,
But Traytor! Cardinal! which I wou'd repeat,
Till I had made my self as raging mad,
As the wild Sea, when all the Winds are up!
And in that Storm, I might forget my grief.

Cardinal. Wou'd I cou'd take the killing Object from your Eyes.

Philip. Oh *Alonzo*, to add to my distraction
Must I find thee a sharer in my Fate!

Alonzo. It is my duty, Sir, to dye with you. –
But Sir, my Princess
Has here – a more than equal claim to grief;
And fear for her dear safety, will deprive me
Of this poor life, that shou'd have been your Sacrifice.

Enter Zarrack *with a Dagger; gazes on* Philip.

Philip. Kind Murderer, welcome! quickly free my soul!
And I will kiss the Sooty hand that wounds me.

Zarrack. Oh, I see you can be humble.

Philip. Humble! I'le be as gentle as a Love-sick Youth,
When his dear Conqu'ress sighs a hope into him,
If thou wilt kill me! – Pity me, and kill me.

Zarrack. I hope to see your own hand do that office.

Philip. Oh thou wert brave indeed,
If thou wou'dst lend me but the use of one!

Zarrack. You'l want a Dagger then.

Philip. By Heaven no, I'de run it down my throat,
Or strike my pointed fingers through my breast.

Zarrack. Ha, ha, ha, what pity 'tis you want a hand.

Enter Osmin.

Philip. Osmin! sure thou wilt be so kind to kill me!
Thou hadst a soul was humane.

Osmin. Indeed I will not, Sir, you are my King!   *Unbinds him.*

Philip. What mean'st thou?

Osmin. To set you free, my Prince!

Philip. Thou art some Angel sure, in that dark Cloud.

Zarrack. What mean'st thou, Traytor!

Osmin. Wait till your eyes inform you.

Cardinal. Good Gods! what mean'st thou!

Osmin. Sir, arm your hand with this.   *Gives* Philip *a Sword, goes*

Zarrack. Thou art half damn'd for this!   *to undoe* Alonzo.

    I'le to my Prince! –

Philip. I'le stop you on your way, – lye there; – your tongue   *Kills him.*

    Shall tell no tales to day: – Now Cardinal – but hold,

    I scorn to strike thee whilst thou art unarm'd,

    Yet so thou didst to me;

    For which I have not leisure now to kill thee.

    – Here, take thy liberty; – nay do not thank me,

    By Heaven I do not mean it as a grace.

Osmin. My Lord, take this; –   *To* Alonzo *and*

    And this – to arm your Highness.   *the Cardinal.*

Alonzo. Thou dost amaze me!

Osmin. Keep in your wonder with your doubts, my Lord.

Philip. We cannot doubt, whilst we're thus fortify'd –   *Looking on*

    Come *Osmin*, let us fall upon the Guards.   *his Sword.*

Osmin. There are no Guards, Great Sir, but what are yours;

    And see – your Friend I've brought to serve ye too.   *Opens a back door.*

Enter Leonora *and Women,* Ordonio, Sebastian, Antonio, *&c.*

Philip. My dearest Sister safe!

Leonora. Whilst in your presence, Sir, and you thus Arm'd,

Osmin. The Moor approaches, – now be ready all.

Philip. That name I never heard with joy till now;

    Let him come on, and arm'd with all his Powers,

    Thus singly I defie him.   *Draws.*

Enter Abdelazer.

Osmin *secures*
the door.

Abdelazer. Hah! betray'd! and by my Slaves! by *Osmin* too!

Philip. Now thou damn'd Villain! true born Son of Hell!

    Not one of thy Infernal Kin shall save thee.

Abdelazer. Base Coward Prince!

    Whom the admiring world mistakes for brave;

When all thy boasted Valour, fierce and hot
As was thy Mother in her height of Lust,
Can with the aid of all these – treacherous Swords
Take but a single life! – but such a life,
As amongst all their store the envying Gods
Has not another such to breath in man.

Philip. Vaunt on, thou monstrous Instrument of Hell!
For I'm so pleas'd to have thee in my power,
That I can hear thee number up thy sins,
And yet be calm, whilst thou art near damnation:

Abdelazer. Thou ly'st, thou canst not keep thy temper in;
For hadst thou so much bravery of mind,
Thou'dst fight me singly; which thou dar'st not do.

Philip. Not dare!
By Heaven if thou wert twenty Villains more,
And I had all thy weight of sins about me,
I durst thus venture on; – forbear, *Alonzo.*

Alonzo. I will not, Sir.

Philip. I was indeed too rash; 'tis such a Villain,
As shou'd receive his death from nought but Slaves.

Abdelazer. Thou'st reason, Prince! nor can they wound my body,
More then I've done thy Fame; for my first step
To my Revenge, I whor'd the Queen thy Mother.

Philip. Death! though this I knew before, yet the hard word
Runs harshly through my heart; –
If thou hadst murder'd fifty Royal *Ferdinands*,
And with inglorious Chains as many years
Had loaded all my limbs, 't had been more pardonable
Then this Eternal stain upon my name:
– Oh thou hast breath'd thy worst of venom now.

Abdelazer. My next advance, was poisoning of thy Father.

Philip. My Father poison'd! and by thee! thou Dog,
Oh that thou hadst a thousand lives to lose,
Or that the world depended on thy single one,
That I might make a Victim
Worthy to offer up to his wrong'd Ghost, –
But stay, – there's something in thy count of sins untold,
That I must know; not that I doubt, by Heaven,
That I am *Philip*'s Son. –

Abdelazer. Not for thy ease, but to declare my malice,

Know Prince, I made thy amorous Mother
Proclaim thee Bastard, when I miss'd of killing thee.
Philip. Gods! let me contain my rage!
Abdelazer. I made her too, betray the credulous Cardinal;
   And having then no farther use of her,
   Satiated with her Lust,
   I set *Roderigo* on to murder her:
   Thy death had next succeeded; and thy Crown
   I wou'd have laid at *Leonora*'s feet.
Alonzo. How! durst you love the Princess!
Abdelazer. Fool, durst! had I been born a Slave,
   I durst with this same Soul do any thing:
   Yes! and the last sense that will remain about me,
   Will be my Passion for that charming Maid,
   Whom I'de enjoy e're now, but for thy Treachery.   *To Osmin.*
Philip. Deflowr'd my Sister! Heaven punish me Eternally
   If thou out-liv'st the minute thou'st declar'd it.
Abdelazer. I will, in spight of all that thou canst do:
   – Stand off, Fool-hardy Youth, if thou'dst be safe,
   And do not draw thy certain ruine on,
   Or think that e're this hand was arm'd in vain.
Philip. Poor angry Slave, how I contemn thee now.
Abdelazer. As humble Huntsmen do the generous Lion;
   Now thou dar'st see me lash my sides, and roar,
   And bite my snare in vain; who with one look,
   (Had I been free) hadst shrunk into the Earth
   For shelter from my Rage:
   And like that noble Beast, though thus betray'd,
   I've yet an awfull fierceness in my looks,
   Which makes thee fear t'approach, and 'tis at distance
   That thou dar'st kill me: for come but in my reach,
   And with one grasp, I wou'd confound thy hopes.
Philip. I'le let thee see how vain thy boastings are,
   And unassisted by one single rage,
   Thus – make an easie passage to thy heart.

        Runs on him, all the rest do the like in the same minute: Abdelazer
            aims at the Prince, and kills Osmin: *and falls dead himself.*

– Dye with thy sins unpardon'd, and forgotten. –   *Shout within.*
Alonzo. Great Sir, your Throne and Kingdom want you now;

Your People rude with joy do fill each Street,
And long to see their King, – whom Heaven preserve. *Kneels.*
All. Long live *Philip* King of *Spain*: –
Philip. I thank ye all; – and now my dear *Alonzo*,
Receive the recompence of all thy sufferings,
Whilst I create thee Duke of *Salamancha*.
Alonzo. Thus low I take the bounty from your hands. *Kneels.*
Leonora. Rise Sir, my Brother now has made us equal.
Cardinal. And shall this joyfull day, that has restor'd you
To all the Glories of your Birth and merits,
That has restor'd all *Spain* the greatest Treasure
That ever happy Monarchy possess'd,
Leave only me unhappy? when, Sir, my crime
Was only too much Faith: – thus low I fall,
And from that store of mercy Heaven has given you,
Implore you wou'd dispense a little here.
Philip. Rise, (though with much a-do) I will forgive you.
Leonora. Come, my dear Brother, to that glorious business
Our Birth and Fortunes call us, let us haste,
For here methinks we are in danger still.
Philip. So after Storms, the joyful Mariner
Beholds the distant wish'd-for shore afar,
And longs to bring the rich-fraught Vessel in,
Fearing to trust the faithless Seas again.

The End of the Play.

EPILOGUE. [16]

Spoken by little Mis. *Ariell*. [17]

WIth late success being blest, I'm come agen;
You see what kindness can do, Gentlemen,
Which when once Shewn, our Sex cannot refrain.
Yet spight of such a Censure, I'le proceed,
And for our Poetess will intercede:
Before, a Poet's wheadling words prevail'd,
Whose melting speech my tender heart assail'd,
And I the flattring Scriblers cause maintain'd; [18]
So by my means the Fop applauses gain'd.
'Twas wisely done to choose m' his Advocate, ⎫
Since I have prov'd to be his better Fate, ⎬
For what I lik'd, I thought you could not hate, ⎭
Respect for you Gallants, made me comply, ⎫
Though I confess he did my Passion try, ⎬
And I am too good-natur'd to deny. ⎭
But now not Pity, but my Sexes cause,
Whose Beauty does, like Monarchs, give you Laws,
Should now Command, being joyn'd with Wit, Applause.
Yet since our Beauty's power's not absolute,
She'l not the priviledge of our Sex dispute,
But does by me Submit. — Yet since you 've been

---

[16] The 1677 edition of *Abdelazer* contains no prologue. The prologue printed in the 1693 edition re-uses a prologue to Fletcher and Massinger's *The Double Marriage*, originally published in A. B.'s (Aphra Behn's?) *Covent Garden Drolery* (London, 1672), 14–15, and already reprinted as the epilogue to Behn's 1689 play *The Widdow Ranter*.

[17] Probably Anne Bracegirdle (c. 1663–1748), who was to be one of the leading actresses of her generation, retiring at the height of her powers in 1707.

[18] The Epilogue to Thomas Otway's play *Don Carlos* (June 1676) was "Spoken by a Girle," probably Bracegirdle.

For my sake kind, repeat it once again.
Your kindness, Gallants, I shall soon repay,
If you'l but favour my design to day:
Your last Applauses, like refreshing showrs,
Made me spring up and bud like early Flow'rs;
Since then I'm grown at least an Inch in height,
And shall e're long be full-blown for delight.

Written by a Friend.

FINIS.

APHRA BEHN

Oroonoko (1688)

Right Honourable

Lord *MAITLAND*.[1]

My Lord,

S *Ince the World is grown so Nice*° *and Critical upon Dedications, and will Needs be judging the Book, by the Wit of the Patron; we ought, with a great deal of Circumspection, to chuse a Person against whom there can be no Exception; and whose Wit, and Worth, truly Merits all that one is capable of saying upon that Occasion.*

    The most part of Dedications are charg'd with Flattery; and if the World knows a Man has some Vices, they will not allow one to speak of his Virtues. This, my Lord, is for want of thinking Rightly; if Men wou'd consider with Reason, they wou'd have another sort of Opinion, and Esteem of Dedications; and wou'd believe almost every Great Man has enough to make him Worthy of all that can be said of him there. My Lord, a Picture-drawer, when he intends to make a good Picture, essays the Face many Ways, and in many Lights, before he begins; that he may chuse, from the several turns of it, which is most Agreeable, and gives it the best Grace; and if there be a Scar, an ungrateful Mole, or any little Defect, they leave it out; and yet make the Picture extreamly like: But he who has the good Fortune to draw a Face that is exactly Charming in all its Parts and Features, what Colours or Agreements° *can be added to make it Finer? All that he can give is but its due; and Glories in a Piece whose Original alone gives it its Perfection. An ill Hand may diminish, but a good Hand cannot augment its Beauty. A Poet is a Painter in his way; he draws to the Life, but in another kind; we draw the*

Nice: Fastidious, hypercritical.   **Agreements:** Attractions.

---

[1] Richard, Lord Maitland (1653–95), later the fourth Earl of Lauderdale, was a steadfast supporter of the Stuarts. He went into exile after the Revolution of 1688, but was banished from James II's court at Saint-Germain because he disapproved of the ex-king's extreme Catholic policy. He translated Virgil into English verse. A manuscript of the translation (eventually published in 1737) was consulted by Dryden during his translation of Virgil.

Nobler part, the Soul and Mind; the Pictures of the Pen Shall out-last those of the Pencil°; and even Worlds themselves. 'Tis a Short Chronicle of those Lives that possibly wou'd be forgotten by other Historians, or lye neglected there, however deserving an immortal Fame; for Men of eminent Parts° are as Exemplary as even Monarchs themselves; and Virtue is a noble Lesson to be learn'd, and 'tis by Comparison we can Judge and Chuse. 'Tis by such illustrious Presidents,° as your Lordship, the World can be Better'd and Refin'd; when a great part of the lazy Nobility shall, with Shame, behold the admirable Accomplishments of a Man so Great, and so Young.

Your Lordship has Read innumerable Volumes of Men, and Books; not Vainly for the gust° of Novelty, but Knowledge, excellent Knowledge: Like the industrious Bee, from every Flower you return Laden with the precious Dew, which you are sure to turn to the Publick Good. You hoard no one Perfection, but lay it all out in the Glorious Service of your Religion and Country; to both which you are a useful and necessary Honour: They both want such Supporters; and 'tis only Men of so elevated Parts, and fine Knowledge; such noble Principles of Loyalty and Religion this Nation Sighs for.² Where shall we find a Man so Young, like St. Augustine,³ in the midst of all his Youth and Gaiety, Teaching the World divine Precepts, true Nations of Faith, and Excellent Morality, and, at the same time, be also a perfect Pattern of all that accomplish a Great Man? You have, my Lord, all that refin'd Wit that Charms, and the Affability that Obliges; a Generosity that gives a Lustre to your Nobility; that Hospitality, and Greatness of Mind, that ingages the World; and that admirable Conduct, that so well Instructs it. Our Nation ought to regret and bemoan their Misfortunes, for not being able to claim the Honour of the Birth of a Man who is so fit to serve his Majesty,

---

Pencil: paintbrush	**Parts:** Abilities	**Presidents:** Precedents
gust: Appetite		

---

² At this point, a copy of this text in the possession of the Bodleian library has a passage that was canceled from all other surviving texts: "*Where is it amongst all our Nobility we shall find so great a Champion for the Catholick Church? With what Divine Knowledge who have writ in Defence of the Faith! How unanswerably have you clear'd all these Intricacies in Religion, which even the Gownmen have left Dark and Difficult! With what unbeaten Arguments you convince, the Faithless, and instruct the Ignorant!*" The passage was presumably suppressed because its support of Catholicism was politically sensitive. Despite this passage, it seems most unlikely that Behn herself was a Catholic. For fuller discussion of the Bodleian text, see Mary Ann O'Donnell, *Aphra Behn: An Annotated Bibliography of Primary and Secondary Sources* (New York: Garland, 1986), 144–48. "Gownmen" are clergymen.

³ In his youth, St. Augustine (354–430) was at first a devotee of the Roman orator and philosopher Cicero, and then of the Manichean religion, which held that the universe was a battleground between a good and an evil deity. He converted to Christianity in 386, in his early thirties, and was thus hardly the theological infant prodigy that Behn claims.

and his Kingdoms, in all Great and Publick Affairs: And to the Glory of Your Nation be it spoken, it produces more considerable Men, for all fine Sence, Wit, Wisdom, Breeding, and Generosity (for the generality of the Nobility) than all other Nations can Boast, and the Fruitfulness of your Virtues sufficiently make amends for the Barrenness of your Soil: Which however cannot be incommode°
to your Lordship; since your Quality, and the Veneration that the Commonalty naturally pay their Lords, creates a flowing Plenty there — that makes you Happy. And to compleat your Happiness, my Lord, Heaven has blest you with a Lady,[4] *to whom it has given all the Graces, Beauties, and Virtues of her Sex; all the Youth, Sweetness of Nature; of a most illustrious Family; and who is a most rare Example to all Wives of Quality, for her eminent Piety, Easiness, and Condescention;*[5] *and as absolutely merits Respect from all the World, as she does that Passion and Resignation° she receives from your Lordship; and which is, on her part, with so much Tenderness return'd. Methinks your tranquil Lives are an Image of the new Made and Beautiful Pair in Paradise: And 'tis the Prayers and Wishes of all, who have the Honour to know you, that it may Eternally so continue, with Additions of all the Blessings this World can give you.*

My Lord, the Obligations I have to some of the Great Men of Your Nation, particularly to your Lordship, gives me an Ambition of making my Acknowledgments, by all the Opportunities I can; and such humble Fruits, as my Industry produces, I lay at your Lordships Feet. This is a true Story,[6] *of a Man Gallant enough to merit your Protection; and, had he always been so Fortunate, he had not made so Inglorious an end: The Royal Slave I had the Honour to Know in my Travels to the other World; and though I had none above me in that Country, yet I wanted power to preserve this Great Man. If there be any thing that seems Romantick°, I beseech your Lordship to consider, these Countries do, in all things, so far differ from ours, that they produce unconceivable Wonders; at least, they appear so to us, because New and Strange. What I have mention'd I have taken care shou'd be Truth, let the Critical Reader judge as he pleases. 'Twill be no Commendation to the Book, to assure your Lordship I writ it in a few Hours,*

---

incommode: inconvenient   **Resignation:** submission, compliance
Romantick: imaginary

---

[4] Anne Campbell (1658–1734), the fiercely Protestant daughter of the ninth Earl of Argyll, who had participated in the Rye House Plot against Charles II in 1683 and the Duke of Monmouth's rebellion against James II in 1685. In 1684, her husband was deprived of his office of Lord Justice General because of suspicion that he was implicated in Argyll's schemes.

[5] "Courteous disregard of difference of rank or position" (*OED*).

[6] Several characters in *Oroonoko* are based on historical figures, but we have no record of a slave revolt corresponding to the events of Behn's narrative.

though it may serve to Excuse some of its Faults of Connexion; for I never rested my Pen a Moment for Thought: 'Tts purely the Merit of my Slave that must render it worthy of the Honour it begs; and the Author of that of Subscribing herself,

My Lord,
Your Lordship's most oblig'd
and obedient Servant,
A. BEHN.

THE

HISTORY

OF THE

𝕽𝖔𝖞𝖆𝖑 𝕾𝖑𝖆𝖛𝖊.

I Do not pretend, in giving you the History of this *Royal Slave*, to entertain my Reader with the Adventures of a feign'd *Hero*, whose Life
and Fortunes Fancy may manage at the Poets Pleasure; nor in relating
the Truth, design to adorn it with any Accidents, but such as arriv'd° in
earnest to him: And it shall come simply into the World, recommended by
its own proper Merits, and natural Intrigues; there being enough of Reality
to support it, and to render it diverting, without the Addition of Invention.

I was my self an Eye-Witness, to a great part, of what you will find here
set down,[7] and what I cou'd not be Witness of, I receiv'd from the Mouth
of the chief Actor in this History, the *Hero* himself, who gave us the whole
Transactions of his Youth; and though I shall omit, for Brevity's sake, a
thousand little Accidents of his Life, which, however pleasant to us, where
History was scarce, and Adventures very rare; yet might prove tedious and
heavy to my Reader, in a World where he finds Diversions for every Minute,
new and strange: But we who were perfectly charm'd with the Character
of this great Man, were curious to gather every Circumstance of his Life.

The Scene of the last part of his Adventures lies in a Colony in *America*,
called *Surinam*,[8] in the *West-Indies*.

---

arriv'd: happened

---

[7] It seems certain that Aphra Behn did visit Surinam, perhaps as a government spy,
probably in 1663–64. See Janet Todd, *The Secret Life of Aphra Behn*, revised ed. (London:
Pandora, 2000), 38–66.

[8] An English colony on the northern coast of South America. It had been repeatedly
settled by Europeans, with a short-lived British colony from 1643 to 1645. A more durable
British colony was established in 1650 by Anthony Rous and Francis, Lord Willoughby
of Parham (1613?–66). During the Second Dutch War, it was captured by the Dutch,
then recaptured by the English, and later ceded to the Dutch in the Treaty of Breda in
1667.

But before I give you the Story of this *Gallant Slave*, 'tis fit I tell you
the manner of bringing them to these new *Colonies*; for those they make
use of there, are not *Natives* of the place;[9] for those we live with in perfect Amity, without daring to command 'em; but on the contrary, caress
'em with all the brotherly and friendly Affection in the World; trading
with 'em for their Fish, Venison, Buffilo's, Skins, and little Rarities; as
Marmosets, a sort of *Monkey* as big as a Rat or Weesel, but of a marvellous
and delicate shape, and has Face and Hands like an Humane Creature:
and *Cousheries*,[10] a little Beast in the form and fashion of a Lion, as big
as a Kitten; but so exactly made in all parts like that noble Beast, that it
is it in *Minature*: Then for little *Parakeetoes*, great Parrots, *Muckaws*,° and
a thousand other Birds and Beasts of wonderful and surprizing Forms,
Shapes, and Colours. For Skins of prodigious Snakes, of which there are
some threescore Yards in length; as is the Skin of one that may be seen at
His Majesty's *Antiquaries*.[11] Where are also some rare Flies,[12] of amazing
Forms and Colours, presented to 'em by my self; Some as big as my Fist,
some less; and all of various Excellencies, such as Art cannot imitate. Then
we trade for Feathers, which they order into all Shapes, make themselves
little short Habits of 'em, and glorious Wreaths for their Heads, Necks,
Arms and Legs, whose Tinctures are unconceivable. I had a Set of these
presented to me, and I gave 'em to the King's Theatre, and it was the Dress
of the *Indian Queen*,[13] infinitely admir'd by Persons of Quality; and were

Muckaws: macaws

---

[9] The British did enslave Native Americans in some colonies, but mortality rates were
very high (see, e.g., Richard Ligon, *A True and Exact History of the Island of Barbados*
[1655] [London, 1673], 54). Du Tertre asserts that the Caribs were too lazy to be enslaved
(I, 485).

[10] The lion tamarin monkey. See Antoine Biet, *Voyage de la France équinoxiale* (Paris,
1664), 430; Breton gives the word as *coucìri* (*Dictionnaire caraïbe-français* [Auxerre, 1665]).
According to Biet, the tamarins "are no bigger than squirrels, and have a head and a
face like that of a lion" (341). According to Warren, "The *Cusharee* is black, less than
a *Marmazet*, and shap'd every way perfectly like a *Lyon*" (*An Impartial Description of
Surinam* [London, 1667], 14; below, 334).

[11] Probably the museum of the Royal Society.

[12] "Flies we have of so many kindes, (from two inches long with the great hornes, which
we keep in boxes, and are shewed by *John Tredescan* [Tradescant] amongst his rarities) to
the least Atome" (Ligon, 63). *Flies* can mean any winged insect: Behn probably means
butterflies.

[13] A lavishly costumed heroic play by Sir Robert Howard and John Dryden, first performed
by the King's Company at its Bridges Street theatre in January 1664. The titular character
is the villainess of the play (not, as is sometimes carelessly asserted, the heroine): She
has usurped the throne of the young Montezuma in Mexico. It is not clear whether the
feathers were used at the first performance or at a revival: see Todd, *Secret Life*, 73. The
stage directions contain no description of Zempoalla's costume, though the opening of
Act V calls for "*four Priests in habits of white and red Feathers*" (California Dryden, VIII).

unimitable. Besides these, a thousand little Knacks, and Rarities in Nature, and some of Art; as their Baskets, Weapons, Aprons, etc. We dealt with 'em with Beads of all Colours, Knives, Axes, Pins and Needles; which they us'd only as Tools to drill Holes with in their Ears, Noses and Lips,[14] where they hang a great many little things; as long Beads, bits of Tin, Brass, or Silver, beat thin; and any shining Trincket. The Beads they weave into Aprons about a quarter of an Ell° long, and of the same breadth; working them very prettily in Flowers of several Colours of Beads; which Apron they wear just before 'em, as *Adam* and *Eve* did the Fig-leaves;[15] the Men wearing a long Stripe of Linen, which they deal with us for. They thread these Beads also on long Cotton-threads, and make Girdles to tie their Aprons to, which come twenty times, or more, about the Waste; and then cross, like a Shoulder-belt, both ways, and round their Necks, Arms and Legs. This Adornment, with their long black Hair, and the Face painted in little Specks or Flowers here and there, makes 'em a wonderful Figure to behold.[16] Some of the Beauties which indeed are finely shap'd, as almost all are, and who have pretty Features, are very charming and novel; for they have all that is called Beauty, except the Colour, which is a reddish Yellow; or after a new Oiling, which they often use to themselves, they are of the colour of a new Brick, but smooth, soft and sleek. They are extream modest and bashful, very shy, and nice° of being touch'd. And though they are all thus naked, if one lives for every among 'em, there is not to be seen an indecent Action, or Glance;[17] and being continually us'd to see one another so unadorn'd, so like our first Parents before the Fall, it seems as if they had no Wishes; there being nothing to heighten Curiosity, but all you can see, you see at once, and every Moment see; and where there is no Novelty, there can be no Curiosity. Not but I have seen a handsom young *Indian*, dying for Love of a very beautiful young *Indian* Maid; but all his Courtship was, to fold his Arms, pursue her with his Eyes, and Sighs were all his

---

ell: 45 inches   **nice:** fastidious

[14] Body piercing is described in Rochefort, 257.
[15] It was common to compare the New World and its almost naked inhabitants to Eden. Dryden refers to "guiltless *Men*" (*To My Honored Friend, Dr. Charleton*, l. 13, in California Dryden, I), though Milton in *Paradise Lost* compares Adam and Eve to the Native Americans when they have lost their "first naked glory" and hidden their genitals (9.1114–18, in Alastair Fowler, ed., *Paradise Lost* [London: Longman, 1971]. Du Tertre describes the paradisal nakedness and happiness of the Native Americans (I, 357), but then describes the flaws of their culture, including deceitful, diabolically inspired priests.
[16] On Native American body painting, see Rochefort, 254–56.
[17] Warren (23; below, 335–36) and Biet (389) both report on the lasciviousness of the Native Americans, though Warren states that they did not kiss.

Language: While she, as if no such Lover were present; or rather, as if she desired none such, carefully guarded her Eyes from beholding him; and never approach'd him, but she look'd down with all the blushing Modesty I have seen in the most severe and cautious of our World. And these People represented to me an absolute *Idea* of the first State of Innocence, before Man knew how to sin: And 'tis most evident and plain; that simple Nature is the most harmless, inoffensive and vertuous Mistress. 'Tis she alone, if she were permitted, that better instructs the World, than all the Inventions of Man: Religion wou'd here but destroy that Tranquillity, they possess by Ignorance; and Laws wou'd but teach 'em to know Offence, of which now they have no Notion. They once made Mourning and Fasting for the Death of the *English* Governor, who had given his Hand to come on such a Day to 'em, and neither came, nor sent; believing, when once a Man's Word was past, nothing but Death cou'd or shou'd prevent his keeping it:[18] And when they saw he was not dead, they ask'd him, what Name they had for a Man who promis'd a thing he did not do? The Governor told them, Such a man, was a *Lyar*, which was a Word of Infamy to a Gentleman. Then one of 'em reply'd, *Governor, you are a Lyar, and guilty of that Infamy.* They have a Native Justice, which knows no Fraud; and they understand no Vice, or Cunning, but when they are taught by the *White Men.* They have Plurality of Wives, which, when they grow old, they serve those that succeed 'em, who are young; but with a Servitude easie and respected; and unless they take Slaves in War, they have no other Attendants.

Those on that *Continent* where I was, had no King; but the oldest War-Captain was obey'd with great Resignation.

A War-Captain is a Man who has lead them on to Battel with Conduct,° and Success; of whom I shall have Occasion to speak more hereafter, and of some other of their Customs and Manners, as they fall in my way.

With these People, as I said, we live in perfect Tranquillity, and good Understanding, as it behooves us to do; they knowing all the places where to seek the best Food of the Country, and the Means of getting it; and for very small and unvaluable Trifles, supply us with what 'tis impossible for

---

Conduct: good generalship

---

[18] "The very words that import lying, falshood, treason, dissimulations, covetousnes [*sic*], envie, detraction, and pardon, were never heard of amongst them" (Montaigne "Of the Caniballes" in *Essays*, trans. John Florio [1603] [London, 1613], 102; below, 290). Though generally hostile to the Caribs, le Sieur de la Borde notes that they are without lies ('sans mensonges's, *Relation de l'Origine, Moeurs, Coustumes, Religion, Guerres et Voyages des Caraibes* [n.p., 1684], 3). In Swift's *Gulliver's Travels*, the Houyhnhms have no word for falsehood.

us to get; for they do not only in the Wood, and over the *Sevana's*,[19] in Hunting, supply the parts of Hounds, by swiftly scouring through those almost impassable places; and by the meer Activity of their Feet, run down the nimblest Deer, and other eatable Beasts: But in the water, one wou'd think they were Gods of the Rivers, or Fellow-Citizens of the Deep; so rare an Art they have in Swimming, Diving, and almost Living in Water; by which they command the less swift Inhabitants of the Floods. And then for Shooting; what they cannot take, or reach with their Hands, they do with Arrows; and have so admirable an Aim, that they will split almost an Hair; and at any distance that an Arrow can reach, they will shoot down Oranges, and other Fruit, and only touch the Stalk with the Dart's Points, that they may not hurt the Fruit. So that they being, on all Occasions, very useful to us, we find it absolutely necessary to caress 'em as Friends, and not to treat 'em as Slaves; nor dare we do other, their Numbers so far surpassing ours in that *Continent*.°

Those then whom we make use of to work in our Plantations of Sugar, are *Negro's, Black*-Slaves altogether; which are transported thither in this manner.

Those who want Slaves, make a Bargain with a Master, or Captain of a Ship, and contract to pay him so much a-piece, a matter of twenty Pound a Head for as many as he agrees for, and to pay for em when they shall be deliver'd on such a Plantation: So that when there arrives a Ship laden with Slaves, they who have so contracted, go a-board, and receive their Number by Lot; and perhaps in one Lot that may be for ten, there may happen to be three or four Men; the rest, Women and Children: Or be there more or less of either Sex, you are oblig'd to be contented with your Lot.

Coramantien,[20] a Country of *Blacks* so called, was one of those places in which they found the most advantageous Trading for these Slaves; and thither most of our great Traders in that Merchandice traffick'd; for that Nation is very war-like and brave; and having a continual Campaign, being always in Hostility with one neighbouring Prince or other, they had the fortune to take a great many Captives; for all they took in Battel, were sold as Slaves; at least, those common Men who cou'd not ransom themselves.

Continent: land

---

[19] Savannahs. "A treeless plain; properly, one of those found in various parts of tropical America" (*OED*).

[20] A trading post on the coast of what is now Ghana, used by English and Dutch slave traders. The region is described in Ogilby, *Africa*, 431. All slaves shipped from this fort were referred to as Cormantines.

Of these Slaves so taken, the General only has all the profit; and of these
Generals, our Captains and Masters of Ships buy all their Freights.

The King of *Coramantien* was himself a Man of a Hundred and odd
Years old, and had no Son, though he had many beautiful *Black*-Wives; for
most certainly, there are Beauties that can charm of that Colour.[21] In his
younger Years he had had many gallant Men to his Sons, thirteen of which
died in Battel, conquering when they fell; and he had only left him for
his Successor, one Grand-Child, Son to one of these dead Victors; who,
as soon as he cou'd bear a Bow in his Hand, and a Quiver at his Back,
was sent into the Field, to be trained up by one of the oldest Generals,
to War; where, from his natural Inclination to Arms, and the Occasions
given him, with the good Conduct of the old General, he became, at the
Age of Seventeen, one of the most expert Captains, and bravest Soldiers,
that ever saw the Field of *Mars*:[22] So that he was ador'd as the Wonder of
all that World, and the Darling of the Soldiers. Besides, he was adorn'd
with a native Beauty so transcending all those of his gloomy Race, that he
strook an Awe and Reverence, even in those that knew not his Quality; as
he did in me, who beheld him with Surprize and Wonder, when afterwards
he arriv'd in our World.

He had scarce arriv'd at his Seventeenth Year, when fighting by his
Side, the General was kill'd with an Arrow in his Eye, which the Prince
Oroonoko[23] (for so was this gallant *Moor*[24] call'd) very narrowly avoided; nor
had he, if the General, who saw the Arrow shot, and perceiving it aim'd at
the Prince, had not bow'd his Head between, on purpose to receive it in
his own Body rather than it shou'd touch that of the Prince, and so saved
him.

'Twas then, afflicted as *Oroonoko* was, that he was proclaim'd General in
the old Man's place; and then it was, at the finishing of that War, which

---

[21] Richard Ligon describes an encounter with some beautiful black women slaves "of such
shapes, as would have puzzelld *Albert Durer*, the great Mr of Proportion, but to have
imitated; and *Tition* [*sic*], or *Andrea de Sarta*, for softnes of muscles, and Curiositie of
Colouring, though with a studied diligence; and a love both to the partie and the worke"
(15).

[22] The Roman god of war, equivalent to the Greek Ares.

[23] Probably derived from the South American river, the Orinoco (sometimes spelt
Oroonoko).

[24] In ancient times, the Mauri were the inhabitants of Mauretania, a region of North Africa
in parts of what are now Morocco and Algeria. Later, the term was applied generally to
the Moslems of northwest Africa. As late as the seventeenth century, these people were
frequently assumed to be black, and the term was therefore extended to black Africans,
as in *Titus Andronicus* and *Othello*.

had continu'd for two Years, that the Prince came to Court; where he had hardly been a Month together, from the time of his fifth Year, to that of Seventeen; and 'twas amazing to imagine where it was he learn'd so much Humanity;° or, to give his Accomplishments a juster Name, where 'twas he got that real Greatness of Soul, those refin'd Notions of true Honour, that absolute Generosity,²⁵ and that Softness that was capable of the highest Passions of Love and Gallantry, whose Objects were almost continually fighting Men, or those mangl'd, or dead; who heard no Sounds, but those of War and Groans: Some part of it we may attribute to the Care of a *French.* Man of Wit and Learning;²⁶ who finding it turn to very good Account to be a sort of Royal Tutor to this young *Black,* & perceiving him very ready, apt, and quick of Apprehension, took a great pleasure to teach him Morals, Language and Science; and was for it extreamly belov'd and valu'd by him. Another Reason was, He lov'd, when he came from War, to see all the *English* Gentlemen that traded thither; and did not only learn their Language, but that of the *Spaniards*° also, with whom he traded afterwards for Slaves.

I have often seen and convers'd with this great Man, and been a Witness to many of his mighty Actions; and do assure my Reader, the most Illustrious Courts cou'd not have produc'd a braver Man, both for Greatness of Courage and Mind, a Judgment more solid, a Wit more quick, and a Conversation more sweet and diverting. He knew almost as much as if he had read much: He had heard of, and admir'd the *Romans*; he had heard of the late Civil Wars in *England,* and the deplorable Death of our great Monarch;²⁷ and wou'd discourse of it with all the Sense, and Abhorrence of the Injustice imaginable. He had an extream good and graceful Mien, and all the Civility of a well-bred great Man. He had nothing of Barbarity in his Nature, but in all Points address'd° himself, as if his Education had been in some *European* Court.

Humanity: civility, courtesy **Spaniards:** i.e., Portuguese
address'd: conducted

---

²⁵ Literally goodness of race (in the familial sense); here, nobility of conduct.
²⁶ In 1688, the year of *Oroonoko,* Behn published a translation of the French writer Fontenelle's *The History of Oracles, and the Cheats of the Pagan Priests.* By mocking the fraudulence of pagan religious practices, Fontenelle implied that Christianity was equally fraudulent. This was a popular practice among religious skeptics; for example, the Englishman Charles Blount. Fontenelle may have inspired the figure of the French tutor, and his work perhaps influenced Behn's account of the deceitful practices of the Indian priests.
²⁷ The two civil wars (1642–1648), which resulted in the execution of Charles I in 1649 and led to the Protectorate of Oliver Cromwell.

This great and just Character of *Oronoko* gave me an extream Curiosity
to see him, especially when I knew he spoke, *French* and *English*, and that I
cou'd talk with him. But though I had heard so much of him, I was as greatly
surpriz'd when I saw him, as if I had heard nothing of him; so beyond all
Report I found him. He came into the Room, and address'd himself to me,
and some other Women, with the best Grace in the World. He was pretty
tall, but of a Shape the most exact that can be fansy'd: The most famous
Statuary° cou'd not form the Figure of a Man more admirably turn'd from
Head to Foot. His Face was not of that brown, rusty Black which most of
that Nation are, but a perfect Ebony, or polish'd Jett. His Eyes were the
most awful° that cou'd be seen, and very piercing; the White of 'em being
like Snow, as were his Teeth. His Nose was rising and *Roman*, instead of
African and flat.[28] His Mouth, the finest shap'd that cou'd be seen; far from
those great turn'd Lips, which are so natural to the rest of the *Negroes.* The
whole Proportion and Air of his Face was so noble, and exactly form'd,
that, bating his Colour, there cou'd be nothing in Nature more beautiful,
agreeable and handsome. There was no one Grace wanting, that bears the
Standard of true Beauty: His Hair came down to his Shoulders, by the Aids
of Art; which was, by pulling it out with a Quill, and keeping it comb'd;

Statuary: sculptor   **awfull:** awe-inspiring

---

[28] Europeans were very aware of the nasal differences between themselves and black
Africans, though it was sometimes believed that Africans artificially flattened their chil-
drens' noses to conform to their ideals of beauty (e.g., Rochefort, 201): even the nose
may be a cultural artifact, rather than a racial sign. Du Tertre, for example, relates the
case of an African slave woman who was persuaded not to flatten the nose of her first
baby. She was, however, so horrified by the infant's ugliness that she surreptitiously
modified the nose of her second child (I, 508). Villault claims that well-born inhabitants of the Gold Coast seldom have flat noses, because their mothers do not carry their
babies with their faces against their shoulders (Nicolas Villault, Sieur de Bellefond, A
Relation of the Coasts of Africk Called Guinee [1669] [London, 1670], 157). Conversely,
non-European races drew praise if their noses conformed to the European model. In a
passage that Behn probably knew, for example, William Penn writes of the Pennsylvania
Indians: "the thick Lip and flat Nose, so frequent to the *East–Indians* and *Blacks*, are
not common to them; for I have seen as comely *European*-like Faces among them, of
both, as on your side the Sea; and truly an *Italian* Complexion hath not much more of
the White, and the Noses of several of them have as much of the *Roman*" ([Richard
Blome], *The Present State of His Majesties Isles and Territories in America* [London, 1687],
96; taken from William Penn, *A Letter from William Penn . . . To the Committee of the
Free Society of Traders of that Province, residing in London* [London, 1683], 5). Du Tertre
notes the "nez aquilin" of the half-Native American son of General Thomas Warner
(I, 508).

of which he took particular Care.[29] Nor did the Perfections of his Mind come short of those of his Person; for his Discourse was admirable upon almost any Subject; and who-ever had heard him speak, wou'd have been convinc'd of their Errors, that all fine Wit is confin'd to the *White* Men, especially to those of *Christendom*; and wou'd have confess'd that *Oroonoko* was as capable even of reigning well, and of governing as wisely, had as great a Soul, as politick Maxims°, and was as sensible of Power as any Prince civiliz'd in the most refin'd Schools of Humanity and Learning, or the most Illustrious Courts.

This Prince, such as I have describ'd him, whose Soul and Body were so admirably adorn'd, was (while yet he was in the Court of his Grandfather) as I said, as capable of Love, as 'twas possible for a brave and gallant Man to be; and in saying that, I have nam'd the highest Degree of Love; for sure, great Souls are most capable of that Passion.

I have already said, the old General was kill'd by the shot of an Arrow, by the Side of this Prince, in Battel; and that *Oroonoko* was made General. This old dead *Hero* had one only Daughter left of his Race;° a Beauty that, to describe her truly, one need say only, she was Female to the noble Male; the beautiful *Black Venus*, to our young *Mars*;[30] as charming in her Person as he, and of delicate Vertues. I have seen an hundred *White* Men sighing after her, and making a thousand Vows at her feet, all vain, and unsuccessful: And she was, indeed, too great for any, but a Prince of her own Nation to adore.

Oroonoko coming from the Wars, (which were now ended) after he had made his Court to his Grandfather, he thought in Honour he ought to

---

politick Maxims: judicious principles   **Race:** Family

[29] Oroonoko resembles the perfectly formed heroes of French romance. Compare the description of the Moorish prince Juba in La Calprenède's *Cleopatra*: "[T]hey had never seen one better shaped among all the persons of his Sex; all the lines of it so evenly regular, as it was too hard for the skilfullest desire to mend any thing about it; his complexion was something brown, his eyes black, but full of such a sparkling vivacity, as it required a steady eye to behold them without shrinking at the lustre; his hair of the same colour, being very long, and curling naturally, fell in large annulets [ringlets] upon his shoulders; in fine, his whole composure carried so compleat a Symmetry, as it would have pos'd Envy's self to have found fault" (Part I, Book iv, 97 [irregular pagination]).

[30] Venus was the Roman goddess of love and Mars the god of war. Their Greek equivalents were Aphrodite and Ares. According to Book VIII of the *Odyssey*, Ares committed adultery with Aphrodite while her unappealing husband, the lame craftsman-god Hephaestus, was away. He, however, had contrived a wonderful gold net, which fell on the lovers and trapped them in the act.

make a Visit to *Imoinda*, the Daughter of his Foster-father, she dead General; and to make some Excuses to her, because his Preservation was the Occasion of her Father's Death; and to present her with those Slaves that had been taken in this last Battel, as the Trophies of her Father's Victories. When he came, attended by all the young Soldiers of any Merit, he was infinitely surpriz'd at the Beauty of this fair Queen of Night, whose Face and Person was so exceeding all he had ever beheld, that lovely Modesty with which she receiv'd him, that Softness in her Look, and Sighs, upon the melancholy Occasion of this Honour that was done by so great a Man as *Oroonoko*, and a Prince of whom she had heard such admirable things; the Awfulness° wherewith she receiv'd him, and the Sweetness of her Words and Behaviour while he stay'd, gain'd a perfect Conquest over his fierce Heart, and made him feel, the Victor cou'd be subdu'd. So that having made his first Complements, and presented her an hundred and fifty Slaves in Fetters, he told her with his Eyes, that he was not insensible of her Charms; while *Imoinda*, who wish'd for nothing more than so glorious a Conquest, was pleas'd to believe, she understood that silent Language of new-born Love; and from that Moment, put on all her Additions to Beauty.

The prince return'd to Court with quite another Humour than before; and though he did not speak much of the fair *Imoinda*, he had the pleasure to hear all his Followers speak of nothing but the Charms of that Maid; insomuch that, even in the Presence of the old King, they were extolling her, and heightning, if possible, the Beauties they had found in her: So that nothing else was talk'd of, no other Sound was heard in every Corner where there were Whisperers, but *Imoinda! Imoinda!*

'Twill be imagin'd *Oroonoko* stay'd not long before he made his second Visit; nor, considering his Quality, not much longer before he told her, he ador'd her. I have often heard him say, that he admir'd° by what strange Inspiration he came to talk things so soft, and so passionate, who never knew Love, nor was us'd to the Conversation° of Women; but (to use his own Words) he said, Most happily, some new, and till then unknown Power instructed his Heart and Tongue in the Language of Love, and at the same time, in favour of him, inspir'd *Imoinda* with a Sense of his Passion. She was touch'd with what he said and return'd it all in such Answers as went to his very Heart, with a Pleasure unknown before: Nor did he use those Obligations ill, that Love had done him; but turn'd all his happy Moments to the best advantage; and as he knew no Vice, his Flame aim'd at nothing but Honour, if such a distinction may be made in Love;

Awfulness: awe   **admir'd:** wondered   **Conversation:** company

and especially in that Country, where Men take to themselves as many as they can maintain; and where the only Crime and Sin with Woman is, to turn her off, to abandon her to Want, Shame and Misery: Such ill Morals are only practis'd in *Christian*-Countries, where they prefer the bare Name of Religion; and, without Vertue or Morality, think that's sufficient. But *Oroonoko* was none of those Professors; but as he had right Notions of Honour, so he made her such Propositions as were not only and barely such; but, contrary to the Custom of his Country, he made her Vows, she shou'd be the only woman he wou'd possess while he liv'd; that no Age or Wrinkles shou'd incline him to change, for her Soul wou'd be always fine, and always young; and he shou'd have an eternal *Idea* in his Mind of the Charms she now bore, and shou'd look into his Heart for that *Idea*, when he cou'd find it no longer in her Face.

After a thousand Assurances of his lasting Flame, and her eternal Empire over him, she condescended to receive him for her Husband; or rather, receiv'd him, as the greatest Honour the God's cou'd do her.

There is a certain Ceremony in these Cases to be observ'd, which I forgot to ask him how perform'd; but 'twas concluded on both sides, that, in Obedience to him, the Grand-father was to be first made acquainted with the Design: for they pay a most absolute Resignation° to the Monarch, especially when he is a Parent also.

On the other side, the old King, who had many Wives, and many Concubines, wanted not Court-Flatterers to insinuate in his Heart a thousand tender Thoughts for this young Beauty; and who represented her to his Fancy, as the most charming he had ever possess'd in all the long Race of his numerous Years. At this Character° his old Heart, like an extinguish'd Brand, most apt to take Fire, felt new Sparks of Love, and began to kindle; and now grown to his second Childhood, long'd with Impatience to behold this gay thing, with whom, alas! he cou'd but innocently play. But how he shou'd be confirm'd she was this *Wonder*, before he us'd his Power to call her to Court (where Maidens never came, unless for the King's private Use) he was next to consider; and while he was so doing, he had Intelligence brought him, that *Imoinda* was most certainly Mistress to the Prince *Oroonoko*. This gave him some *Shagrien*;° however, it gave him also an Opportunity, one Day, when the Prince was a-hunting, to wait on a Man of Quality, as his Slave and Attendant, who shou'd go and make a Present to *Imoinda*, as from the Prince; he shou'd then, unknown, see

Resignation: obedience   **Character:** description
Shagrien: chagrin, acute annoyance

this fair Maid, and have an Opportunity to hear what Message she wou'd return the Prince for his Present; and from thence gather the state of her Heart, and degree of her Inclination. This was put in Execution, and the old Monarch saw, and burnt: He found her all he had heard, and wou'd not delay his Happiness, but found he shou'd have some Obstacle to overcome her Heart; for she express'd her Sense of the Present the Prince had sent her, in terms so sweet, so soft and pretty, with an Air of Love and Joy that cou'd not be dissembl'd; insomuch that 'twas past doubt whether she lov'd *Oroonoko* entirely. This gave the old King some Affliction; but he salv'd it with this, that the Obedience the People pay their King, was not at all inferior to what they pay'd their Gods: And what Love would not oblige *Imoinda* to do, Duty wou'd compel her to.

He was therefore no sooner got to his Apartment, but he sent the Royal Veil to *Imoinda*; that is, the Ceremony of Invitation; he sends the Lady, he has a Mind to honour with his Bed, a Veil, with which she is cover'd, and secur'd for the King's Use; and 'tis Death to disobey; besides, held a most impious Disobedience.

'Tis not to be imagin'd the Surprize and Grief that seiz'd this lovely Maid at this News and Sight. However, as Delays in these Cases are dangerous, and Pleading worse than Treason; trembling, and almost fainting, she was oblig'd to suffer her self to be cover'd, and led away.

They brought her thus to Court; and the King, who had caus'd a very rich Bath to be prepar'd, was led into it, where he sate under a Canopy, in State, to receive this long'd for Virgin; whom he having commanded shou'd be brought to him, they (after dis-robing her) led her to the Bath, and making fast the Doors, left her to descend. The King, without more Courtship, bad her throw off her Mantle, and come to his Arms. But *Imoinda*, all in Tears, threw her self on the Marble, on the Brink of the Bath, and besought him to hear her. She told him, as she was a Maid, how proud of the Divine Glory she should have been of having it in her power to oblige her King: but as by the Laws, he cou'd not; and from his Royal Goodness, wou'd not take from any Man his wedded Wife: so she believ'd she shou'd be the Occasion of making him commit a great Sin, if she did not reveal her State and Condition; and tell him, she was anothers, and cou'd not be so happy to be his.

The King, enrag'd at this Delay, hastily demanded the Name of the bold Man, that had marry'd a Woman of her Degree, without his Consent. *Imoinda*, seeing his Eyes fierce, and his Hands tremble; whether with Age, or Anger, I know not; but she fansy'd the last, almost repented she had said so much, for now she fear'd the Storm wou'd fall on the Prince; she therefore said a thousand things to appease the raging of his Flame, and to prepare him to hear who it was with Calmness; but before she spoke, he imagin'd who she meant, but wou'd not seem to do so, but commanded her to lay aside her Mantle, and suffer her self to receive his Caresses; or, by his Gods, he swore, that happy Man whom she was going to name shou'd die, though it were even *Oroonoko* himself. *Therefore* (said he) *deny this Marriage, and swear thy self a Maid. That* (reply'd *Imoinda*) *by all our Powers I do; for I am not yet known to my Husband.* 'Tis enough (said the King;) *'tis enough to satisfie both my Conscience, and my Heart.* And rising from his Seat, he went, and led her into the Bath; it being in vain for her to resist.

In this time the Prince, who was return'd from Hunting, went to visit his *Imoinda*, but found her gone; and not only so, but heard she had receiv'd the Royal Veil. This rais'd him to a Storm; and in his Madness, they had much ado to save him from laying violent Hands on himself. Force first prevail'd, and then Reason: They urg'd all to him, that might oppose his Rage; but nothing weigh'd so greatly with him as the King's Old Age uncapable of injuring him with *Imoinda*. He wou'd give way to that Hope, because it pleas'd him most, and flatter'd best his Heart. Yet this serv'd not altogether to make him cease his different Passions, which sometimes rag'd within him, and sometimes softned into Showers. 'Twas not enough to appease him, to tell him, his Grand-father was old, and cou'd not that way injure him, while he retain'd that awful Duty which the young Men are us'd there to pay to their grave Relations. He cou'd not be convinc'd he had no Cause to sigh and mourn for the Loss of a Mistress, he cou'd not with all his Strength and Courage retrieve. And he wou'd often cry, *O my Friends! were she in wall'd Cities, or confin'd from me in Fortifications of the greatest Strength; did Inchantments or Monsters detain her from me, I wou'd venture through any Hazard to free her; But here, in the Arms of a feeble old Man, my Youth, my violent Love, my Trade in Arms, and all my vast Desire of Glory, avail me nothing: Imoinda is as irrecoverably lost to me, as if she were snatch'd by the cold Arms of Death: Oh! she is never to be retriev'd. If I wou'd wait tedious Years, till Fate shou'd bow the old King to his Grave; even that wou'd not leave me Imoinda free; but still that Custom that makes it so vile a Crime for a Son to marry his Father's Wives or Mistresses, wou'd hinder my Happiness; unless I wou'd either ignobly set an ill President° to my Successors, or abandon my Country, and fly with her to some unknown World, who never heard our Story.*

President: precedent

But it was objected to him, that his Case was not the same; for *Imoinda* being his lawful Wife, by solemn Contract, 'twas he was the injur'd Man, and might, if he so pleas'd, take *Imoinda* back, the Breach of the Law being on his Grand-father's side; and that if he cou'd circumvent him, and redeem her from the *Otan*,³¹ which is the Palace of the King's Women, a sort of *Seraglio*, it was both just and lawful for him so to do.

This Reasoning had some force upon him, and he shou'd have been entirely comforted, but for the Thought that she was possess'd by his Grand-father. However, he lov'd so well, that he was resolv'd to believe what most favour'd his Hope; and to endeavour to learn from *Imoinda's* own Mouth, what only she cou'd satisfie him in; whether she was robb'd of that Blessing, which was only due to his Faith and Love. But as it was very hard to get a Sight of the Women, for no Men ever enter'd into the *Otan*, but when the King went to entertain himself with some one of his Wives, or Mistresses; and 'twas Death at any other time, for any other to go in; so he knew not how to contrive to get a Sight of her.

While *Oroonoko* felt all the Agonies of Love, and suffer'd under a Torment the most painful in the World, the old King was not exempted from his share of Affliction. He was troubl'd for having been forc'd by an irresistable Passion, to rob his Son³² of a Treasure, he knew, cou'd not but be extreamly dear to him, since she was the most beautiful that ever had been seen; and had besides, all the Sweetness and Innocence of Youth and Modesty, with a Charm of Wit surpassing all. He found that, however she was forc'd to expose her lovely Person to his wither'd Arms, she, cou'd only sigh and weep there, and think of *Oroonoko*; and often-times cou'd not forbear

---

³¹ Janet Todd compares *otan* with "*oda*, the Turkish term for a room in a seraglio, or the Persian *otagh*, a tent or pavilion" (Behn [1992–96], III, 448), and notes "In the Akan languages of the Gold Coast, *odammaa* and *odan* signify a small hut or room" (Janet Todd, ed., *Oroonoko* [London: Penguin, 2003], 85, n. 39). Behn could have found the Turkish term in Jean Baptiste Tavernier, *A New Relation of the Inner-Part of the Grand Seignior's Seraglio* [1675] (London, 1684), 35. *Odas* were, however, rather asexual places, being classrooms in which palace pages were instructed by eunuchs in Islam. *Otan* is the name of a region in present-day Nigeria and of a sacred stone. Villault describes polygamy in West Africa (alleging that the wives are perfectly content with the system): "A good Merchant, or Officer, will have twenty or thirty, according to his abilities. The King of *Fetu's* Son-in-law had forty, by whom he had a douzain of daughters, fourteen to the douzain of the other Sex, and kept constantly a hundred Slaves to attend them" (155); the king of Fetu "has as many Wives as he pleases, who are all disposed into several appartements, with whom he dines or sups sometimes as he thinks good" (238). According to Ogilby the King of Benin had a thousand wives. The wives of his dead father were guarded in a cloister by eunuchs (*Africa*, 475).

³² Actually grandson, but son could loosely mean "male descendant."

speaking of him, though her Life were, by Custom, forfeited by owning her Passion. But she spoke not of a Lover only, but of a Prince dear to him, to whom she spoke; and of the Praises of a Man, who, till now, fill'd the old Man's Soul with Joy at every Recital of his Bravery, or even his Name. And 'twas this Dotage on our young *Hero*, that gave *Imoinda* a thousand Privileges to speak of him, without offending; and this Condescention° in the old King, that made her take the Satisfaction of speaking of him so very often.

Besides, he many times enquir'd how the Prince bore himself; and those of whom he ask'd, being entirely Slaves to the Merits and Vertues of the Prince, still answer'd what they thought conduc'd best to his Service; which was, to make the old King fansy that the Prince had no more Interest in *Imoinda*, and had resign'd her willingly to the Pleasure of the King; that he diverted himself with his Mathematicians, his Fortifications, his Officers, and his Hunting.

This pleas'd the old Lover, who fail'd not to report these things again to *Imoinda*, that she might, by the Example of her young Lover, withdraw her Heart, and rest better contented in his Arms. But however she was forc'd to receive this unwelcome News, in all Appearance, with Unconcern, and Content, her Heart was bursting within, and she was only happy when she cou'd get alone, to vent her Griefs and Moans with Sighs and Tears.

What Reports of the Prince's Conduct were made to the King, he thought good to justifie as far as possibly he cou'd by his Actions; and when he appear'd in the Presence of the King, he shew'd a Face not at all betraying his Heart: So that in a little time the old Man, being entirely convinc'd that he was no longer a Lover of *Imoinda*, he carry'd him with him, in his Train, to the *Otan*, often to banquet with his Mistress. But as soon as he enter'd, one Day, into the Apartment of *Imoinda*, with the King, at the first Glance from her Eyes, notwithstanding all his determin'd Resolution, he was ready to sink in the place where he stood; and had certainly done so, but for the Support of *Aboan*, a young Man, who was next to him; which, with his Change of Countenance, had betray'd him, had the King chanc'd to look that way. And I have observ'd, 'tis a very great Error in those, who laugh when one says, *A* Negro *can change Colour*; for I have seen 'em as frequently blush, and look pale, and that as visibly as ever I saw in the most beautiful *White*. And 'tis certain that both these Changes were evident, this Day, in both these Lovers. And *Imoinda*, who saw with some Joy the Change in the Prince's Face, and found it in her own, strove

Condescention: disregard of his superiority

to divert the King from beholding either, by a forc'd Caress, with which she met him; which was a new Wound in the Heart of the poor dying Prince. But as soon as the King was busy'd in looking on some fine thing of *Imoinda*'s making, she had time to tell the Prince with her angry, but Love-darting Eyes, that she resented° his Coldness, and bemoan'd her own miserable Captivity. Nor were his Eyes silent, but answer'd hers again, as much as Eyes cou'd do, instructed by the most tender, and most passionate Heart that ever lov'd: And they spoke so well, and so effectually, as *Imoinda* no longer doubted, but she was the only Delight, and the Darling of that Soul she found pleading in 'em its Right of Love, which none was more willing to resign than she. And 'twas this powerful Language alone that in an Instant convey'd all the Thoughts of their Souls to each other; that they both found, there wanted but Opportunity to make them both entirely happy. But when he saw another Door open'd by *Onahal*, former old Wife of the King's, who now had Charge of *Imoinda*; and saw the Prospect of a Bed of State made ready, with Sweets and Flowers for the Dalliance of the King; who immediately led the trembling Victim from his Sight, into that prepar'd Repose. What Rage! what wild Frenzies seiz'd his Heart! which forcing to keep within Bounds, and to suffer without Noise, it became the more insupportable, and rent his Soul with ten thousand Pains. He was forc'd to retire, to vent his Groans; where he fell down on a Carpet, and lay struggling a long time, and only breathing now and then, – O *Imoinda*! When *Onahal* had finish'd her necessary Affair within, shutting the Door, she came forth to wait, till the King call'd; and hearing some one sighing in the other Room, she pass'd on, and found the Prince in that deplorable Condition, which she thought needed her Aid: She gave him Cordials, but all in vain; till finding the nature of his Disease, by his Sighs, and naming *Imoinda*. She told him, he had not so much Cause as he imagin'd, to afflict himself; for if he knew the King so well as she did, he wou'd not lose a Moment in Jealousie, and that she was confident that *Imoinda* bore, at this Minute, part in his Affliction. *Aboan* was of the same Opinion; and both together, perswaded him to re-assume his Courage; and all sitting down on the Carpet, the Prince said so many obliging things to *Onahal*, that he half perswaded her to be of his Party. And she promis'd him, she wou'd thus far comply with his just Desires, that she wou'd let *Imoinda* know how faithful he was, what he suffer'd, and what he said.

This Discourse lasted till the King call'd, which gave *Oroonoko* a certain Satisfaction; and with the Hope *Onahal* had made him conceive, he assum'd

resented: felt keenly

a Look as gay as 'twas possible a Man in his Circumstances cou'd do; and presently after, he was call'd in with the rest who waited without. The King commanded Musick to be brought, and several of his young Wives and Mistresses came all together by his Command, to dance before him; where *Imoinda* perform'd her Part with an Air and Grace so passing all the rest, as her Beauty was above 'em; and receiv'd the Present, ordain'd as a Prize. The Prince was every Moment more charm'd with the new Beauties and Graces he beheld in this fair One: And while he gaz'd, and she danc'd, *Onahal* was retir'd to a Window with *Aboan*.

This *Onahal*, as I said, was one of the Cast-Mistresses° of the old King; and 'twas these (now past their Beauty) that were made Guardians, or Governants° to the new, and the young Ones; and whose Business it was, to teach them all those wanton Arts of Love, with which they prevail'd and charm'd heretofore in their Turn; and who now treated the triumphing happy Ones with all the Severity, as to Liberty and Freedom, that was possible, in revenge of those Honours they rob them of; envying them those Satisfactions, those Gallantries and Presents, that were once made to themselves, while Youth and Beauty lasted, and which they now saw pass regardless by,[33] and pay'd only to the Bloomings. And certainly, nothing is more afflicting to a decay'd Beauty, than to behold in it self declining Charms, that were once ador'd; and to find those Caresses paid to new Beauties, to which once she laid a Claim; to hear 'em whisper as she passes by, *That once was a delicate° Woman*. These abandon'd Ladies therefore endeavour to revenge all the Despights,° and Decays of Time, on these flourishing happy Ones. And 'twas this Severity, that gave *Oroonoko* a thousand Fears he shou'd never prevail with *Onahal*, to see *Imoinda*. But, as I said, she was now retir'd to a Window with *Aboan*.

This young Man was not only one of the best Quality, but a Man extreamly well made, and beautiful; and coming often to attend the King to the *Otan*, he had subdu'd the Heart of the antiquated *Onahal*, which had not forgot how pleasant it was to be in Love: And though she had some Decays in her Face, she had none in her Sence and Wit; she was there agreeable still, even to *Aboan's* Youth; so that he took pleasure in entertaining her with Discourses of Love. He knew also, that to make his Court to these She-Favourites, was the way to be great; these being the Persons that do all Affairs and Business at Court. He had also observ'd that she had given him Glances more tender and inviting, than she had done to others

---

Cast-mistresses: discarded mistresses   Governants: duennas
delicate: beautiful   Despights: injuries

[33] Emended from "pass were regardless by".

of his Quality: And now, when he saw that her Favour cou'd so absolutely oblige the Prince, he fail'd not to sigh in her Ear, and to look with Eyes all soft upon her, and give her Hope that she had made some Impressions on his Heart. He found her pleas'd at this, and making a thousand Advances to him; but the Ceremony ending, and the King departing, broke up the Company for that Day, and his Conversation.

Aboan fail'd not that Night to tell the Prince of his Success, and how advantageous the Service of *Onahal* might be to his Amour with *Imoinda*. The Prince was overjoy'd with this good News, and besought him, if it were possible, to caress her so, as to engage her entirely; which he cou'd not fail to do, if he comply'd with her Desires: *For then* (said the Prince) *her Life lying at your Mercy, she must grant you the Request you make in my Behalf.* Aboan understood him; and assur'd him, he would make Love so effectually, that he wou'd defie the most expert Mistress of the Art, to find out whether he dissembl'd it, or had it really. And 'twas with Impatience they waited the next Opportunity of going to the *Otan*.

The Wars came on, the Time of taking the Field approach'd, and 'twas impossible for the Prince to delay his going at the Head of his Army, to encounter the Enemy: So that every Day seem'd a tedious Year, till he saw his *Imoinda*; for he believ'd he cou'd not live, if he were forc'd away without being so happy. 'Twas with Impatience therefore, that he expected the next Visit the King wou'd make; and, according to his Wish, it was not long.

The Parley of the Eyes of these two Lovers had not pass'd so secretly, but an old jealous Lover cou'd spy it; or rather, he wanted not Flatterers, who told him, they observ'd it: So that the Prince was hasten'd to the Camp, and this was the last Visit he found he shou'd make to the *Otan*; he therefore urg'd *Aboan* to make the best of this last Effort, and to explain himself so to *Onahal*, that she, deferring her Enjoyment of her young Lover no longer, might make way for the Prince to speak to *Imoinda*.

The whole Affair being agreed on between the Prince and *Aboan*, they attended the King, as the Custom was, to the *Otan*; where, while the whole Company was taken up in beholding the Dancing, and antick° Postures the Women Royal made, to divert the King, *Onahal* singl'd our *Aboan*, whom she found most pliable to her Wish. When she had him where she believ'd she cou'd not be heard, she sigh'd to him, and softly cry'd, *Ah*, Aboan! *When will you be sensible of my Passion? I confess it with my Mouth, because I wou'd not give my Eyes the Lye; and you have but too much already perceiv'd they have confess'd my Flame: Nor wou'd I have you believe, that because I am*

antick: bizarre

the abandon'd Mistress of a King, I esteem my self altogether divested of Charms. No, Aboan; *I have still a Rest of Beauty enough engaging, and have learn'd to please too well, not to be desirable. I can have Lovers still, but will have none but* Aboan. *Madam* (reply'd the half-feigning Youth) *you have already, by my Eyes, found, you can still conquer; and I believe 'tis in pity of me, you condescend to this kind Confessions, But, Madam, Words are us'd to be so small a part of our Country-Courtship, that 'tis rare one can get so happy an Opportunity as to tell one's Heart; and those few Minutes we have are forc'd to be snatch'd for more certain Proofs of Love, than speaking and sighing; and such I languish for.*

He spoke this with such a Tone, that she hop'd it true, and cou'd not forbear believing it; and being wholly transported with Joy, for having subdu'd the finest of all the King's Subjects to her Desires, she took from her Ears two large Pearls, and commanded him to wear 'em in his. He wou'd have refus'd 'em, crying, *Madam, these are not the Proofs of your Love that I expect; 'tis Opportunity, 'tis a Lone-hour only, that can make me happy.* But forcing the Pearls into his Hand, she whisper'd softly to him, *Oh! Do not fear a Woman's Invention, when Love sets her a-thinking.* And pressing his Hand, she cry'd, *This Night you shall be happy. Come to the Gate of the Orange-Groves, behind the* Otan; *and I will be ready, about Mid-night, to receive you.* 'Twas thus agreed, and she left him, that no notice might be taken of their speaking together.

The Ladies were still dancing, and the King, laid on a Carpet, with a great deal of pleasure, was beholding them, especially *Imoinda*; who that Day appear'd more lovely than ever, being enliven'd with the good Tidings *Onahal* had brought her of the constant Passion the Prince had for her. The Prince was laid on another Carpet, at the other end of the Room, with his Eyes fix'd on the Object of his Soul; and as she turn'd, or mov'd, so did they, and she alone gave his Eyes and Soul their Motions: Nor did *Imoinda* employ her Eyes to any other Use, than in beholding with infinite Pleasure the Joy she produc'd in those of the Prince. But while she was more regarding him, than the Steps she took, she chanc'd to fall; and so near him, as that leaping with extream force from the Carpet, he caught her in his Arms as she fell; and 'twas visible to the whole Presence, the Joy where with he receiv'd her: He clasp'd her close to his Bosom, and quite forgot that Reverence that was due to the Mistress of a King, and that Punishment that is the Reward of a Boldness of this nature; and had not the Presence of Mind of *Imoinda* (fonder of his Safety, than her own) befriended him, in making her spring from his Arms, and fall into her Dance again, he had, at that Instant, met his Death; for the old King, jealous to the last degree, rose up in Rage, broke all the Diversion, and led *Imoinda* to her

Apartment, and sent out Word to the Prince, to go immediately to the Camp; and that if he were found another Night in Court, he shou'd suffer the Death ordain'd for disobedient Offenders.

You may imagine how welcome this News was to *Oroonoko*, whose unseasonable Transport and Caress of *Imoinda* was blam'd by all Men that lov'd him; and now he perceiv'd his Fault, yet cry'd, *That for such another Moment, he wou'd be content to die.*

All the *Otan* was in disorder about this Accident; and *Onahal* was particularly concern'd, because on the Prince's Stay depended her Happiness; for she cou'd no longer expect that of *Aboan.* So that, e'er they departed, they contriv'd it so, that the Prince and he shou'd come both that Night to the Grove of the *Otan*, which was all of Oranges and Citrons; and that there they shou'd wait her Orders.

They parted thus, with Grief enough, till Night; leaving the King in possession of the lovely Maid. But nothing cou'd appease the Jealousie of the old Lover: He wou'd not be impos'd on, but wou'd have it, that *Imoinda* made a false Step on purpose to fall into *Oroonoko's* Bosom, and that all things look'd like a Design on both sides, and 'twas in vain she protested her Innocence: He was old and obstinate, and left her more than half assur'd that his Fear was true.

The King going to his Apartment, sent to know where the Prince was, and if he intended to obey his Command. The Messenger return'd, and told him, he found the Prince pensive, and altogether unpreparing for the Campaign; that he lay negligently on the Ground, and answer'd very little. This confirm'd the Jealousie of the King, and he commanded that they shou'd very narrowly and privately watch his Motions; and that he shou'd not stir from his Apartment, but one Spy or other shou'd be employ'd to watch him: So that the Hour approaching, wherein he was to go to the Citron Grove; and taking only *Aboan* along with him, he leaves his Apartment, and was watch'd to the very Gate of the *Otan*; where he was seen to enter, and where they left him, to carry back the Tidings to the King.

Oroonoko and *Aboan* were no sooner enter'd, but *Onahal* led the Prince to the Apartment of *Imoinda*; who, not knowing any thing of her Happiness, was laid in Bed. But *Onahal* only left him in her Chamber, to make the best of his Opportunity, and took her dear *Aboan* to her own; where he shew'd the heighth of Complaisance° for his Prince, when, to give him an Opportunity, he suffer'd himself to be caress'd in Bed by *Onahal.*

The Prince softly waken'd *Imoinda*, who was not a little surpriz'd with Joy to find him there; and yet she trembl'd with a thousand Fears. I believe,

---

Complaisance: Obligingness

he omitted saying nothing to this young Maid, that might perswade her to suffer him to seize his own, and take the Rights of Love; and I believe she was not long resisting those Arms, where she so long'd to be; and having Opportunity, Night and Silence, Youth, Love and Desire, he soon prevail'd; and ravish'd in a Moment, what his old Grand-father had been endeavouring for so many Months.

'Tis not to be imagin'd the Satisfaction of these two young Lovers; nor the Vows she made him, that she remain'd a spotless Maid, till that Night; and that what she did with his Grand-father, had robb'd him of no part of her Virgin-Honour, the Gods, in Mercy and Justice, having reserv'd that for her plighted Lord, to whom of Right it belong'd. And 'tis impossible to express the Transports he suffer'd, while he listen'd to a Discourse so charming, from her lov'd Lips; and clasp'd that Body in his Arms, for whom he had so long languish'd; and nothing now afflicted him, but his suddain Departure from her; for he told her the Necessity, and his Commands; but shou'd depart satisfy'd in this, That since the old King had hitherto not been able to deprive him of those Enjoyments which only belong'd to him, he believ'd for the future he wou'd be less able to injure him; so that, abating the Scandal of the Veil, which was no otherwise so, than that she was Wife to another: He believ'd her safe, even in the Arms of the King, and innocent; yet wou'd he have ventur'd at the Conquest of the World, and have given it all, to have had her avoided that Honour of receiving the *Royal Veil.* 'Twas thus, between a thousand Caresses, that both bemoan'd the hard Fate of Youth and Beauty, so liable to that cruel Promotion: 'Twas a Glory that cou'd well have been spar'd here, though desir'd, and aim'd at by all the young Females of that Kingdom.

But while they were thus fondly employ'd, forgetting how Time ran on, and that the Dawn must conduct him far away from his only Happiness, they heard a great Noise in the *Otan,* and unusual Voices of Men; at which the Prince, starting from the Arms of the frighted *Imoinda,* ran to a little Battel-Ax he us'd to wear by his Side; and having not so much leisure, as to put on his Habit, he oppos'd himself against some who were already opening the Door, which they did with so much Violence, that *Oroonoko* was not able to defend it; but was forc'd to cry out with a commanding Voice, *Whoever ye are that have the Boldness to attempt to approach this Apartment thus rudely, know, that I, the Prince* Oroonoko, *will revenge it with the certain Death of him that first enters: Therefore stand back, and know, this place is sacred to Love, and me this Night; to Morrow 'tis the King's.*

This he spoke with a Voice so resolv'd and assur'd, that they soon retir'd from the Door, but cry'd, *'Tis by the King's Command we are come; and being satisfy'd by the Voice, O Prince, as much as if we had enter'd, we can report to the King the Truth of all his Fears, and leave thee to provide for thy own Safety, as thou art advis'd by thy Friends.*

At these Words they departed, and left the Prince to take a short and sad Leave of his *Imoinda*; who trusting in the strength of her Charms, believ'd she shou'd appease the Fury of a jealous King, by saying, She was surpriz'd, and that it was by force of Arms he got into her Apartment. All her Concern now was for his Life, and therefore she hasten'd him to the Camp; and with much a-do, prevail'd on him to go: Nor was it she alone that prevail'd, *Aboan* and *Onahal* both pleaded, and both assur'd him of a Lye that shou'd be well enough contriv'd to secure *Imoinda*. So that, at last, with a Heart sad as Death, dying Eyes, and sighing Soul, *Oroonoko* departed, and took his way to the Camp.

It was not long after the King in Person came to the *Otan*; where beholding *Imoinda* with Rage in his Eyes, he upbraided her Wickedness and Perfidy, and threatning her Royal Lover, she fell on her Face at his Feet, bedewing the Floor with her Tears, and imploring his Pardon for a Fault which she had not with her Will committed; as *Onahal*, who was also prostrate with her, cou'd testifie: That, unknown to her, he had broke into her Apartment, and ravish'd her. She spoke this much against her Conscience; but to save her own Life, 'twas absolutely necessary she shou'd feign this Falsity. She knew it cou'd not injure the Prince, he being fled to an Army that wou'd stand by him, against any Injuries that shou'd assault him. However, this last Thought of *Imoinda*'s being ravish'd, chang'd the Measures of his Revenge; and whereas before he design'd to be himself her Executioner, he now resolv'd she shou'd not die. But as it is the greatest Crime in nature amongst 'em to touch a Woman, after having been possess'd by a Son, a Father, or a Brother; so now he look'd on *Imoinda* as a polluted thing, wholly unfit for his Embrace; nor wou'd he resign her to his Grand-son, because she had receiv'd the *Royal Veil*. He therefore removes her from the *Otan*, with *Onahal*; whom he put into safe Hands, with Order they shou'd be both sold off, as Slaves, to another Country, either *Christian*, or *Heathen*; 'twas no matter where.

This cruel Sentence, worse than Death, they implor'd, might be revers'd; but their Prayers were vain, and it was put in Execution accordingly, and that with so much Secrecy, that none, either without, or within the *Otan*, knew any thing of their Absence, or their Destiny.

The old King, nevertheless, executed this with a great deal of Reluctancy; but he believ'd he had made a very great Conquest over himself, when he had once resolv'd, and had perform'd what he resolv'd. He believ'd now, that his Love had been unjust; and that he cou'd not expect the Gods, or Captain of the Clouds, (as they call the unknown Power) shou'd suffer a better Consequence from so ill a Cause. He now begins to hold *Oroonoko* excus'd; and to say, he had Reason for what he did: And now every Body cou'd assure the King, how passionately *Imoinda* was belov'd by the Prince; even those confess'd it now, who said the contrary before his Flame was abated. So that the King being old, and not able to defend himself in War, and having no Sons of all his Race remaining alive, but only this, to maintain him on his Throne; and looking on this as a Man disoblig'd, first by the Rape° of his Mistress, or rather, Wife; and now by depriving of him wholly of her, he feard, might make him desperate, and do some cruel thing, either to himself, or his old Grand-father, the Offender; he began to repent him extreamly of the Contempt he had, in his Rage, put on *Imoinda*. Besides, he consider'd he ought in Honour to have kill'd her, for this Offence, if it had been one: He ought to have had so much Value and Consideration for a Maid of her Quality, as to have nobly put her to death; and not to have sold her like a common Slave, the greatest Revenge, and the most disgraceful of any; and to which they a thousand times prefer Death, and implore it; as *Imoinda* did, but cou'd not obtain that Honour. Seeing therefore it was certain that *Oroonoko* wou'd highly resent this Affront, he thought good to make some Excuse for his Rashness to him; and to that End he sent a Messenger to the Camp, with Orders to treat with him about the Matter, to gain his Pardon, and to endeavour to mitigate his Grief; but that by no means he shou'd tell him, she was sold, but secretly put to death; for he knew he shou'd never obtain his Pardon for the other.

When the Messenger came, he found the Prince upon the point of Engaging with the Enemy; but as soon as he heard of the Arrival of the Messenger, he commanded him to his Tent, where he embrac'd him, and receiv'd him with Joy; which was soon abated, by the down-cast Looks of the Messenger, who was instantly demanded the Cause by *Oroonoko*, who, impatient of Delay, ask'd a thousand Questions in a Breath; and all concerning *Imoinda*: But there needed little Return, for he cou'd almost answer himself of all he demanded, from his Sighs and Eyes. At last, the Messenger casting himself at the Prince's Feet, and kissing them, with all the Submission of a Man that had something to implore which he dreaded to utter, he besought him to hear with Calmness what he had to deliver to him, and to call up all his noble and Heroick Courage, to encounter with his Words, and defend himself against the ungrateful things he must relate.

Rape: abduction

Oroonoko reply'd, with a deep Sigh, and a languishing Voice, – *I am arm'd against their worst Efforts–; for I know they will tell me*, Imoinda *is no more –; and after that, you may spare the rest*. Then, commanding him to rise, he laid himself on a Carpet, under a rich Pavillion, and remain'd a good while silent, and was hardly heard to sigh. When he was come a little to himself, the Messenger ask'd him leave to deliver that part of his Embassy, which the Prince had not yet devin'd: And the Prince cry'd, *I permit thee* – Then he told him the Affliction the old King was in, for the Rashness he had committed in his Cruelty to *Imoinda*; and how he daign'd to ask Pardon for his Offence, and to implore the Prince wou'd not suffer that Loss to touch his Heart too sensibly, which now all the Gods cou'd not restore him, but might recompence him in Glory, which he begg'd he wou'd pursue; and that Death, that common Revenger of all Injuries, wou'd soon even the Account between him, and a feeble old Man.

Oroonoko bad him return his Duty to his Lord and Master; and to assure him, there was no Account of Revenge to be adjusted between them; if there were, 'twas he was the Aggressor, and that Death wou'd be just, and, maugre° his Age, wou'd see him righted; and he was contented to leave his Share of Glory to Youths more fortunate, and worthy of that Favour from the Gods. That henceforth he wou'd never lift a Weapon, or draw a Bow; but abandon the small Remains of his Life to Sighs and Tears, and the continual Thoughts of what his Lord and Grand-father had thought good to send out of the World, with all that Youth, that Innocence; and Beauty.[34]

After having spoken this, whatever his greatest Officers, and Men of the best Rank cou'd do, they cou'd not raise him from the Carpet, or perswade him to Action, and Resolutions of Life; but commanding all to retire, he shut himself into his Pavillion all that Day, while the Enemy was ready to engage; and wondring at the Delay, the whole Body of the chief of the Army then address'd themselves to him, and to whom they had much a-do to get Admittance. They fell on their Faces at the Foot of his Carpet; where they lay, and besought him with earnest Prayers and

---

maugre: despite

[34] In the *Iliad*, the Greek hero Achilles withdraws from the fighting at Troy after the Greek leader Agamemnon has robbed him of the slave girl who had been given to him as a prize. The situation was much imitated; for example, in La Calprenède's *Cleopatra* and (under its influence) Dryden's *The Indian Queen* and *The Conquest of Granada*. There is no need to assume a specific allusion to the *Iliad*, as David Hoegberg does ("Caesar's Toils: Allusion and Rebellion in *Oroonoko*," *Eighteenth-Century Fiction* 7 [1995], 239–58 [241–43]).

Tears, to lead 'em forth to Battel, and not let the Enemy take Advantages of them; and implor'd him to have regard to his Glory, and to the World, that depended on his Courage and Conduct. But he made no other Reply to all their Supplications but this, That he had now no more Business for Glory; and for the World, it was a Trifle not worth his Care. *Go*, (continu'd he, sighing) *and divide it amongst you; and reap with joy what you so vainly prize, and leave me to my more welcome Destiny.*

They then demanded what they shou'd do, and whom he wou'd constitute° in his Room, that the Confusion of ambitious Youth and Power might not ruin their Order, and make them a Prey to the Enemy. He reply'd, He wou'd not give himself the Trouble————; but wish'd 'em to chuse the bravest Man amongst 'em, let his Quality or Birth be what it wou'd: *For, O my Friends* (said he!) *it is not Titles make Men brave, or good; or Birth that bestows Courage and Generosity, or makes the Owner happy. Believe this, when you behold* Oroonoko, *the most wretched, and abandon'd by Fortune, of all the Creation of the Gods.* So turning himself about, he wou'd make no more Reply to all they cou'd urge or implore.

The Army beholding their Officers return unsuccessful, with sad Faces, and ominous Looks, that presag'd no good Luck, suffer'd a thousand Fears to take Possession of their Hearts, and the Enemy to come even upon 'em, before they wou'd provide for their Safety, by any Defence; and though they were assur'd by some, who had a mind to animate 'em, that they shou'd be immediately headed by the Prince, and that in the mean time *Aboan* had Orders to command as General; yet they were so dismay'd for want of that great Example of Bravery, that they cou'd make but a very feeble Resistance; and at last, down-right, fled before the Enemy, who pursu'd 'em to the very Tents, killing 'em: Nor cou'd all *Aboan's* Courage, which that Day gain'd him immortal Glory, shame 'em into a Manly Defence of themselves. The Guards that were left behind, about the Prince's Tent, seeing the Soldiers flee before the Enemy, and scatter themselves all over the Plain, in great Disorder, made such Out-cries as rouz'd the Prince from his amorous Slumber, in which he had remain'd bury'd for two Days, without permitting any Sustenance to approach him: But, in spight of all his Resolutions, he had not the Constancy of Grief to that Degree, as to make him insensible of the Danger of his Army; and in that Instant he leap'd from his Couch, and cry'd, – *Come, if we must die, let us meet Death the noblest Way; and 'twill be more like* Oroonoko *to encounter him at an Army's Head, opposing the Torrent of a conquering Foe, than lazily, on a Couch,*

constitute: appoint

to wait his lingering Pleasure, and die every Moment by a thousand wrecking°
Thoughts; or be tamely taken by an Enemy, and led a whining, Love-sick Slave,
to adorn the Triumphs of Jamoan, *that young Victor, who already is enter'd*
beyond the Limits I had prescrib'd him.

While he was speaking, he suffer'd his People to dress him for the Field; and sallying out of his Pavillion, with more Life and Vigour in his Countenance than ever he shew'd, he appear'd like some Divine Power descended to save his Country from Destruction; and his People had purposely put on[35] him all things that might make him shine with most Splendor, to strike a reverend° Awe into the Beholders. He flew into the thickest of those that were pursuing his Men; and being animated with Despair, he fought as if he came on purpose to die, and did such things as will not be believ'd that Humane Strength cou'd perform; and such as soon inspir'd all the rest with new Courage, and new Order: And now it was, that they began to fight indeed; and so, as if they wou'd not be out-done, even by their ador'd *Hero*; who turning the Tide of the Victory, changing absolutely the Fate of the Day, gain'd an entire Conquest;[36] and *Oroonoko* having the good Fortune to single out *Jamoan*, he took him Prisoner with his own Hand, having wounded him almost to death.

This *Jamoan* afterwards became very dear to him, being a Man very gallant, and of excellent Graces, and fine Parts; so that he never put him amongst the Rank of Captives, as they us'd to do, without distinction, for the common Sale, or Market; but kept him in his own Court, where he retain'd nothing of the Prisoner, but the Name, and return'd no more into his own Country, so great an Affection he took for *Oroonoko*; and by a thousand Tales and Adventures of Love and Gallantry, flatter'd his Disease of Melancholy and Languishment; which I have often heard him say, had certainly kill'd him, but for the Conversation of this Prince and *Aboan*, the *French* Governor he had from his Childhood, of whom I have

---

wrecking: racking   **reverend:** reverent

[35] Early editions read "put him on" (incited him to). The emendation seems to be demanded by the context.

[36] Securing victory single-handed is a standard accomplishment of the hero of the French prose romance and of the more critically observed successors in the Restoration heroic play. The archetypally invincible seventeenth-century romantic hero is Artaban, one of the many heroes of La Calprenède's *Cleopatra*. In one battle, he honorably defends his captors against pirates: "as if there secretly lodg'd a fatality in his Sword to all that opposed him, he carried it to no part of the fight, wherein he did not cut down Enemies in heaps, and change the fortunes of both parties, with a prodigious promptitude" (Part III, Book iv, 261). Oroonoko's ultimate misfortune is to be a hero of romantic narrative in a world ruled by the lies of commerce.

spoken before, and who was a Man of admirable Wit, great Ingenuity and Learning; all which he had infus'd into his young Pupil. This *French*-Man was banish'd out of his own Country, for some Heretical Notions he held; and though he was a Man of very little Religion, he had admirable Morals, and a brave Soul.

After the total Defeat of *Jamoan*'s Army, which all fled, or were left dead upon the Place, they spent some time in the Camp; *Oroonoko* chusing rather to remain a while there in his Tents, than enter into a Place, or live in a Court where he had so lately suffer'd so great a Loss. The Officers therefore, who saw and knew his Cause of Discontent, invented all sorts of Diversions and Sports, to entertain their Prince: So that what with those Amuzements abroad, and others at home, that is, within their Tents, with the Perswasions, Arguments and Care of his Friends and Servants that he more peculiarly priz'd, he wore off in time a great part of that *Shagrien*, and Torture of Despair, which the first Effects[37] of *Imoinda*'s Death had given him: Insomuch as having receiv'd a thousand kind Embassies from the King, and Invitations to return to Court, he obey'd, though with no little Reluctancy; and when he did so, there was a visible Change in him, and for a long time he was much more melancholy than before. But Time lessens all Extreams, and reduces 'em to *Mediums* and Unconcern; but no Motives or Beauties, though all endeavour'd it, cou'd engage him in any sort of Amour, though he had all the Invitations to it, both from his own Youth, and others Ambitions and Designs.

Oroonoko was no sooner return'd from this last Conquest, and receiv'd at Court with all the Joy and Magnificence that cou'd be express'd to a young Victor, who was not only return'd triumphant, but belov'd like a Deity, when there arriv'd in the Port an *English* Ship.

This Person had often before been in these Countries, and was very well known to *Oroonoko*, with whom he had traffick'd for Slaves, and had us'd to do the same with his Predecessors.

This Commander was a Man of a finer sort of Address, and Conversation, better bred, and more engaging, than most of that sort of Men are; so that he seem'd rather never to have been bred out of a Court, than almost all his Life at Sea. This Captain therefore was always better receiv'd at Court, than most of the Traders to those Countries were; and especially by *Oroonoko*, who was more civiliz'd, according to the *European* Mode, than any other had been, and took more Delight in the *White* Nations; and, above all, Men of Parts and Wit. To this Captain he sold abundance of his Slaves;

---

[37] Emended from "Efforts."

and for the Favour and Esteem he had for him, made him many Presents, and oblig'd him to stay at Court as long as possibly he cou'd. Which the Captain seem'd to take as a very great Honour done him, entertaining the Prince every Day with Globes and Maps, and Mathematical Discourses and Instruments; eating, drinking, hunting and living with him with so much Familiarity, that it was not to be doubted, but he had gain'd very greatly upon the Heart of this gallant young Man. And the Captain, in Return of all these mighty Favours, besought the Prince to honour his Vessel with his Presence, some Day or other, to Dinner, before he shou'd set Sail; which he condescended to accept, and appointed his Day. The Captain, on his part, fail'd not to have all things in a Readiness, in the most magnificent Order he cou'd possibly: And the Day being come, the Captain, in his Boat, richly adorn'd with Carpets and Velvet-Cushions, row'd to the Shoar to receive the Prince; with another Long-Boat, where was plac'd all his Musick and Trumpets, with which *Oroonoko* was extreamly delighted; who met him on the Shoar, attended by his *French* Governor, *Jamoan, Aboan*, and about an hundred of the noblest of the Youths of the Court: And after they had first carry'd the Prince on Board, the Boats fetch'd the rest off; where they found a very splendid Treat, with all sorts of fine Wines; and were as well entertain'd, as 'twas possible in such a place to be.

The Prince having drunk hard of Punch, and several Sorts of Wine, as did all the rest (for great Care was taken, they shou'd want nothing of that part of the Entertainment) was very merry, and in great Admiration of the Ship, for he had never been in one before; so that he was curious of beholding every place, where he decently might descend. The rest, no less curious, who were not quite overcome with Drinking, rambl'd at their pleasure *Fore* and *Aft*, as their Fancies guided 'em: So that the Captain, who had well laid his Design before, gave the Word, and seiz'd on all his Guests; they clapping great Irons suddenly on the Prince, when he was leap'd down in the Hold, to view that part of the Vessel; and locking him fast down, secur'd him. The same Treachery was us'd to all the rest; and all in one Instant, in several places of the Ship, were lash'd fast in Irons, and betray'd to Slavery. That great Design over, they set all Hands to work to hoise° Sail; and with as treacherous and fair a Wind, they made from the Shoar with this innocent and glorious Prize, who thought of nothing less than such an Entertainment.[38]°

---

hoise: hoist   **Entertainment:** reception

---

[38] A similar case of kidnapping is narrated in Du Tertre II, 494, and Rochefort, 323, where the victims are Native Americans.

Some have commended this Act, as brave, in the Captain; but I will spare my Sence of it, and leave it to my Reader, to judge as he pleases.

It may be easily guess'd, in what manner the Prince resented this Indignity, who may be best resembl'd to a Lion taken in a Toil;° so he rag'd, so he struggl'd for Liberty, but all in vain; and they had so wisely manag'd his Fetters, that he cou'd not use a Hand in his Defence, to quit himself of a Life that wou'd by no Means endure Slavery; nor cou'd he move from the Place, where he was ty'd, to any solid part of the Ship, against which he might have beat his Head, and have finish'd his Disgrace that way: So that being deprived of all other means, he resolved to perish for want of Food: And pleased at last with that Thought, and toil'd and tired by Rage and Indignation, he laid himself down, and sullenly resolved upon dying, and refused all things that were brought him.

This did not a little vex the Captain, and the more so, because, he found almost all of 'em of the same Humour; so that the loss of so many brave Slaves, so tall and goodly to behold, wou'd have been very considerable: He therefore order'd one to go from him (for he wou'd not be seen himself) to *Oroonoko*, and to assure him he was afflicted for having rashly done so unhospitable a Deed, and which cou'd not be now remedied, since they were far from shore; but since he resented it in so high a nature, he assur'd him he wou'd revoke his Resolution, and set both him and his Friends a-shore on the next Land they shou'd touch at; and of this the Messenger gave him his Oath, provided he wou'd resolve to live: And *Oroonoko*, whose Honour was such as he never had violated a Word in his Life himself, much less a solemn Asseveration; believ'd in an instant what this Man said, but reply'd, He expected for a Confirmation of this, to have his shameful Fetters dismiss'd. This Demand was carried to the *Captain*, who return'd him answer, That the Offence had been so great which he had put upon the Prince, that he durst not trust him with Liberty while he remained in the Ship, for fear lest by a Valour natural to him, and a Revenge that would animate that Valour, he might commit some Outrage fatal to himself and the *King* his Master, to whom his Vessel did belong. To this *Oroonoko* replied, he would engage his Honour to behave himself in all friendly Order and Manner, and obey the Command of the *Captain*, as he was Lord of the *King*'s Vessel, and General of those Men under his Command.

This was deliver'd to the still doubting *Captain*, who could not resolve to trust a *Heathen* he said, upon his Parole,° a Man that had no sence or

Toil: net   Parole: word

notion of the God that he Worshipp'd. *Oroonoko* then replied, He was very sorry to hear that the *Captain* pretended to the Knowledge and Worship of any *Gods*, who had taught him no better Principles, than not to Credit as he would be Credited: but they told him the Difference of their Faith occasion'd that Distrust: For the *Captain* had protested to him upon the Word of a *Christian*, and sworn in the Name of a Great *GOD*; which if he shou'd violate, he would expect eternal Torment in the World to come. *Is that all the Obligation he has to be Just to his Oath,* replied *Oroonoko? Let him know I Swear by my Honour, which to violate, wou'd not only render me contemptible and despised by all brave and honest Men, and so give my self perpetual pain, but it wou'd be eternally offending and diseasing all Mankind, harming, betraying, circumventing and outraging all Men; but Punishments hereafter are suffer'd by ones self; and the World takes no cognizances whether this* God *have revenged 'em, or not, 'tis done so secretly, and deferr'd so long: While the Man of no Honour, suffers every moment the scorn and contempt of the honester World, and dies every day ignominiously in his Fame, which is more valuable than Life: I speak not this to move Belief, but to shew you how you mistake, when you imagine, That he who will violate his Honour, will keep his Word with his* Gods. So turning from him with a disdainful smile, he refused to answer him, when he urg'd him to know what Answer he shou'd carry back to his *Captain*; so that he departed without saying any more.

The *Captain* pondering and consulting what to do, it was concluded that nothing but *Oroonoko*'s Liberty wou'd encourage any of the rest to eat, except the *French*-man, whom the *Captain* cou'd not pretend to keep Prisoner, but only told him he was secured because he might act something in favour of the Prince, but that he shou'd be freed as soon as they came to Land. So that they concluded it wholly necessary to free the Prince from his Irons, that he might show himself to the rest; that they might have an Eye upon him, and that they cou'd not fear a single Man.

This being resolv'd, to make the Obligation the greater, the Captain himself went to *Oroonoko*; where, after many Complements, and Assurances of what he had already promis'd, he receiving from the Prince his *Parole*, and his Hand, for his good Behaviour, dismiss'd his Irons, and brought him to his own Cabin; where, after having treated and repos'd him a while, for he had neither eat nor slept in four Days before, he besought him to visit those obstinate People in Chains, who refus'd all manner of Sustenance; and intreated him to oblige 'em to eat, and assure 'em of their Liberty the first Opportunity.

Oroonoko, who was too generous,° not to give Credit to his Words, shew'd himself to his People, who were transported with Excess of Joy at the sight of their Darling Prince; falling at his Feet, and kissing and embracing 'em; believing, as some Divine Oracle, all he assur'd 'em. But he besought 'em to bear their Chains with that Bravery that became those whom he had seen act so nobly in Arms; and that they cou'd not give him greater Proofs of their Love and Friendship, since 'twas all the Security the Captain (his Friend) cou'd have, against the Revenge, he said, they might possibly justly take, for the Injuries sustain'd by him. And they all, with one Accord, assur'd him, they cou'd not suffer enough, when it was for his Repose and Safety.

After this they no longer refus'd to eat, but took what was brought 'em, and were pleas'd with their Captivity, since by it they hop'd to redeem the Prince, who, all the rest of the Voyage, was treated with all the Respect due to his Birth, though nothing cou'd divert his Melancholy; and he wou'd often sigh for *Imoinda*, and think this a Punishment due to his Misfortune, in having left that noble Maid behind him, that fatal Night, in the *Otan*, when he fled to the Camp.

Possess'd with a thousand Thoughts of past Joys with this fair young Person, and a thousand Griefs for her eternal Loss, he endur'd a tedious Voyage, and at last arriv'd at the Mouth of the River of *Surinam*, a Colony belonging to the King of *England*, and where they were to deliver some part of their Slaves. There the Merchants and Gentlemen of the Country going on Board, to demand those Lots of Slaves they had already agreed on; and, amongst those, the Over-seers of those Plantations where I then chanc'd to be, the Captain, who had given the Word, order'd his Men to bring up those noble Slaves in Fetters, whom I have spoken of; and having put 'em, some in one, and some in other Lots, with Women and Children (which they call *Pickaninies*,)[39] they sold 'em off, as Slaves, to several Merchants and Gentlemen; not putting any two in one Lot, because they wou'd separate 'em far from each other; not daring to trust em together, lest Rage and Courage, shou'd put 'em upon contriving some great Action, to the Ruin of the Colony.

Oroonoko was first seiz'd on, and sold to our Over-seer, who had the first Lot, with seventeen more of all sorts and sizes, but not one of Quality

---

generous: noble

---

[39] Black African babies. A West African Negro derivative of the Spanish diminutive *pequeñin* (very small; a small child) or its Portuguese equivalent *pequenino*.

with him. When he saw this, he found what they meant; for, as I said, he understood *English* pretty well; and being wholly unarm'd and defenceless, so as it was in vain to make any Resistance, he only beheld the Captain with a Look all fierce and disdainful, upbraiding him with Eyes, that forc'd Blushes on his guilty Cheeks, he only cry'd, in passing over the Side of the Ship, *Farewel, Sir: 'Tis worth my Suffering, to gain so true a Knowledge both of you, and of your Gods by whom you swear.* And desiring those that held him to forbear their pains, and telling 'em he wou'd make no Resistance, he cry'd, *Come, my Fellow-Slaves; let us descend, and see if we can meet with more Honour and Honesty in the next World we shall touch upon.* So he nimbly leap'd into the Boat, and shewing no more Concern, suffer'd himself to be row'd up the River, with his seventeen Companions.

The Gentleman that bought him was a young *Cornish* Gentleman, whose Name was *Trefry*;[40] a Man of great Wit, and fine Learning, and was carry'd into those Parts by the Lord–Governor, to manage all his Affairs. He reflecting on the last Words of *Oroonoko* to the Captain, and beholding the Richness of his Vest,° no sooner came into the Boat, but he fix'd his Eyes on him; and finding something so extraordinary in his Face, his Shape and Mien, a Greatness of Look, and Haughtiness in his Air, and finding he spoke *English*, had a great mind to be enquiring into his Quality and Fortune; which, though *Oroonoko* endeavour'd to hide, by only confessing he was above the Rank of common Slaves, *Trefry* soon found he was yet something greater than he confess'd; and from that Moment began to conceive so vast an Esteem for him, that he ever after lov'd him as his dearest Brother, and shew'd him all the Civilities due to so great a Man.

Trefry was a very good Mathematician, and a Linguist; cou'd speak *French* and *Spanish*, and in the three Days they remain'd in the Boat (for so long were they going from the Ship, to the Plantation) he entertain'd *Oroonoko* so agreeably with his Art and Discourse, that he was no less pleas'd with *Trefry*, than he was with the Prince; and he thought himself, at least, fortunate in this, that since he was a Slave, as long as he wou'd suffer himself to remain so, he had a Man of so excellent Wit and Parts for a Master: So that before they had finish'd their Voyage up the River, he made no scruple of declaring to *Trefry* all his Fortunes, and most part of

---

Vest: robe

[40] Perhaps Lord Willoughby's agent in his Surinam plantation, as well as manager of St John's Hill. In a letter of 1662 Trefry calls Byam "our noble Governor" (*Historical Manuscripts Commissions, 10th Report*, 6, Bouverie MSS; cited in Janet Todd, ed., *Oroonoko*, [2003], 86, n. 62). Behn, however, makes the men antagonists.

what I have here related, and put himself wholly into the Hands of his new Friend, whom he found resenting all the Injuries were done him, and was charm'd with all the Greatnesses of his Actions; which were recited with that Modesty, and delicate Sence, as wholly vanquish'd him, and subdu'd him to his Interest. And he promis'd him on his Word and Honour, he wou'd find the Means to re-conduct him to his own Country again: assuring him, he had a perfect Abhorrence of so dishonourable an Action; and that he wou'd sooner have dy'd, than have been the Author of such a Perfidy. He found the Prince was very much concern'd to know what became of his Friends, and how they took their Slavery; and *Trefry* promis'd to take care about the enquiring after their Condition, and that he shou'd have an Account of 'em.

Though, as *Oroonoko* afterwards said, he had little Reason to credit the Words of a *Backearary*,[41] yet he knew not why; but he saw a kind of Sincerity, and awful Truth in the Face of *Trefry*; he saw an Honesty in his Eyes, and he found him wise and witty enough to understand Honour; for it was one of his Maxims, *A Man of Wit cou'd not be a Knave or Villain.*

In their passage up the River, they put in at several Houses for Refreshment; and ever when they landed, numbers of People wou'd flock to behold this Man; not but their Eyes were daily entertain'd with the sight of Slaves, but the Fame of *Oroonoko* was gone before him, and all People were in Admiration of his Beauty. Besides, he had a rich Habit on, in which he was taken, so different from the rest, and which the Captain cou'd not strip him of, because he was forc'd to surprize his Person in the Minute he sold him. When he found his Habit made him liable, as he thought, to be gaz'd at the more, he begg'd *Trefry* to give him something more befitting a Slave; which he did, and took off his Robes. Nevertheless, he shone through all; and his *Osenbrigs*[42] (a sort of brown *Holland* Suit he had on) cou'd not conceal the Graces of his Looks and Mien; and he had no less Admirers, than when he had his dazeling Habit on: The Royal Youth appear'd in spight of the Slave, and People cou'd not help treating him after a different manner, without designing it: As soon as they approach'd him, they venerated and esteem'd him; his Eyes insensibly commanded Respect, and his Behaviour insinuated it into every Soul. So that there was nothing talk'd of but this young and gallant Slave, even by those who yet knew not that he was a Prince.

---

[41] A white man. OED gives the word as *buckra*, with many variant spellings. It occurs in Tryon as *Bacchararo* and in *Great Newes from the Barbadoes* as *Baccararoes*; Thomas Tryon, *Friendly Advice to the Gentlemen Planters of the East and West Indies* ([London], 1684), 151; *Great Newes from the Barbadoes* (London, 1676), 10.

[42] Osnaburgs; garments made from a kind of coarse linen, originally made in Osnabrück.

I ought to tell you, that the *Christians* never buy any Slaves but they give 'em some Name of their own, their native ones being likely very barbarous, and hard to pronounce; so that Mr. *Trefry* gave *Oroonoko* that of *Cæsar*;[43] which Name will live in that Country as long as that (scarce more) glorious one of the great *Roman*; for 'tis most evident, he wanted° no part of the Personal Courage of that *Cæsar*, and acted things as memorable, had they been done in some part of the World replenish'd with People, and Historians, that might have given him his due. But his Misfortune was, to fall in an obscure World, that afforded only a Female Pen to celebrate his Fame; though I doubt not but it had liv'd from others Endeavours, if the *Dutch*, who, immediately after his Time, took that Country,[44] had not kill'd, banish'd and dispers'd all those that were capable of giving the World this great Man's Life much better than I have done. And Mr. *Trefry*, who design'd it, dy'd before he began it; and bemoan'd himself for not having undertook it in time.

For the future therefore, I must call *Oroonoko, Cæsar*, since by that Name only he was known in our Western World, and by that Name he was receiv'd on Shoar at *Parham-House*,[45] where he was destin'd a Slave. But if the King himself (God bless him) had come a-shore, there cou'd not have been greater Expectations by all the whole Plantation, and those neighbouring ones, than was on ours at that time; and he was receiv'd more like a Governor, than a Slave. Notwithstanding, as the Custom was, they assign'd him his Portion of Land,[46] his House, and his Business, up in the Plantation. But as it was more for Form, than any Design, to put him to his Task, he endur'd no more of the Slave but the Name, and remain'd some Days in the House, receiving all Visits that were made him, without stirring towards that part of the Plantation where the *Negroes* were.

---

wanted: lacked

---

[43] In La Calprenède's *Cleopatra*, the African prince Juba becomes a slave in Rome and is given the name Coriolanus by Julius Caesar. Owners generally gave new, culturally familiar names to their slaves. Classical names, such as Caesar, Pompey, or Nero, were not uncommon. Oroonoko's new name carries obvious irony, for Julius Caesar was betrayed and murdered by his friends; like Oroonoko's, his death – from multiple stab wounds – involved severe mutilation of his body.

[44] The Dutch captured Surinam in 1667. It was recaptured by the English, but ceded to the Dutch in the Treaty of Breda, in return for New York (New Amsterdam).

[45] On Lord Willoughby's estate of Parham Hill, named after Parham in Suffolk, his ancestral estate.

[46] Slaves were assigned plots of land, from which they were expected to support themselves. See Warren, 19 (below, 335).

At last, he wou'd needs go view his Land, his House, and the Business assign'd him. But he no sooner came to the Houses of the Slaves, which are like a little Town by it self, the *Negroes* all having left Work, but they all came forth to behold him, and found he was that Prince who had, at several times, sold most of 'em to these Parts; and, from a Veneration they pay to great Men, especially if they know 'em, and from the Surprize and Awe they had at the sight of him, they all cast themselves at his Feet, crying our, in their Language, *Live, O King*! *Long live, O King*! And kissing his Feet, paid him even Divine Homage.

Several *English* Gentlemen were with him; and what Mr. *Trefry* had told 'em, was here confirm'd; of which he himself before had no other Witness than *Cæsar* himself: But he was infinitely glad to find his Grandure confirm'd by the Adoration of all the Slaves.

Cæsar troubl'd with their Over-Joy, and Over-Ceremony, besought 'em to rise, and to receive him as their Fellow-Slave; assuring them, he was no better. At which they set up with one Accord a most terrible and hidious Mourning and condoling, which he and the *English* had much a-do to appease; but at last they prevail'd with 'em, and they prepar'd all their barbarous Musick, and every one kill'd and dress'd something of his own Stock (for every Family has their Land a-part, on which, at their leisure-times they breed all eatable things;) and clubbing it together, made a most magnificent Supper, inviting their *Grandee*[47] *Captain*, their *Prince*, to honour it with his Presence; which he did, and several *English* with him; where they all waited on him, some playing, others dancing before him all the time, according to the Manners of their several Nations; and with unwearied Industry, endeavouring to please and delight him.

While they sat at Meat Mr. *Trefry* told *Cæsar*, that most of these young *Slaves* were undon in Love, with a fine she *Slave*, whom they had had about Six Months on their Land; the *Prince*, who never heard the Name of *Love* without a Sigh, nor any mention of it without the Curiosity of examining further into that tale, which of all Discourses was most agreeable to him, asked, how they came to be so Unhappy, as to be all Undon for one fair *Slave*? *Trefry*, who was naturally Amorous, and lov'd to talk of Love as well as any body, proceeded to tell him, they had the most charming Black that ever was beheld on their *Plantation*, about Fifteen or Sixteen Years old, as

---

[47] Originally a Spanish or Portuguese nobleman of the highest rank (*OED*); more generally, any important person.

he guest;° that, for his part, he had done nothing but Sigh for her ever since she came; and that all the white Beautys he had seen, never charm'd him so absolutely as this fine Creature had done; and that no Man, of any Nation, ever beheld her, that did not fall in Love with her; and that she had all the *Slaves* perpetually at her Feet; and the whole Country resounded with the Fame of *Clemene*,[48] for so, said he, we have Christ'ned her: But she denys us all with such a noble Disdain, that 'tis a Miracle to see, that she, who can give such eternal Desires, shou'd herself be all Ice, and all Unconcern. She is adorn'd with the most Graceful Modesty that ever beautifyed Youth; the softest Sigher – that, if she were capable of Love, one would swear she languish'd for some absent happy Man; and so retir'd, as if she fear'd a Rape even from the God of Day; or that the Breezes would steal Kisses from her delicate Mouth. Her Task of Work some sighing Lover every day makes it his Petition to perform for her, which she excepts blushing, and with reluctancy, for fear he will ask her a Look for a Recompence, which he dares not presume to hope; so great an Awe she strikes into the Hearts of her Admirers. *I do not wonder*, replied the Prince, *that* Clemene *shou'd refuse Slaves, being as you say so Beautiful, but wonder how she escapes those who can entertain her as you can do; or why, being your Slave, you do not oblige her to yield. I confess*, said *Trefry, when I have, against her will, entertain'd her with Love so long, as to be transported with my Passion; even above Decency, I have been ready to make use of those advantages of Strength and Force Nature has given me. But oh! she disarms me, with that Modesty and Weeping so tender and so moving, that I retire, and thank my Stars she overcame me.* The Company laught at his Civility to a *Slave*, and *Cæsar* only applauded the nobleness of his Passion and Nature; since that Slave might be Noble, or, what was better, have true Notions of Honour and Vertue in her. Thus past they this

---

guest: guessed

[48] Whereas Oroonoko's new name, Caesar, has specific historical associations, Imoinda is simply given a conventional, generalized pastoral or neoclassical name. Behn calls Lady Mary Compton "Clemena" in her "Pastoral Pindarick on the Marriage of the Right Honourable the Earle of Dorset and Midlesex, to the Lady Mary Compton." Many of Molière's plays (such as *Les Fâcheux* and *Le Misanthrope*) contain characters called Clymène, Climène, or Célimène. The name is derived from the Greek name Clymene, which means famous or infamous, and is therefore perhaps appropriate to the context in which it is introduced – "the whole Country resounded with the Fame of *Clemene*" – and to Behn's presentation of herself as custodian of her characters' fame. None of the many classical bearers of this name, however, seems particularly appropriate. They include the putative mother of Homer and the mother of Phaëthon, who unsuccessfully tried to drive the chariot of his father, the sun god Helios.

Night, after having received, from the *Slaves*, all imaginable Respect and Obedience.

The next Day *Trefry* ask'd *Cæsar* to walk, when the heat was allay'd, and designedly carried him by the Cottage of the *fair Slave*; and told him, she whom he spoke of last Night liv'd there retir'd. *But*, says he, *I would not wish you to approach, for, I am sure, you will be in Love as soon as you behold her*. *Cæsar* assur'd him, he was proof against all the Charms of that Sex; and that if he imagin'd his Heart cou'd be so perfidious to Love again, after *Imoinda*, he believ'd he shou'd tear it from his Bosom: They had no sooner spoke, but a little shock Dog,[49] that *Clemene* had presented her, which she took great Delight in, ran out; and she, not knowing any body was there, ran to get it in again, and bolted out on those who were just Speaking of her: When seeing them, she wou'd have run in again; but *Trefry* caught her by the Hand, and cry'd, Clemene, *however you fly a Lover, you ought to pay some Respect to this Stranger*: (pointing to *Cæsar*) But she, as if she had resolv'd never to raise her Eyes to the Face of a Man again, bent 'em the more to the Earth, when he spoke, and gave the *Prince* the Leasure to look the more at her. There needed no long Gazing, or Consideration, to examin who this fair Creature was; he soon saw *Imoinda* all over her; in a Minute he saw her Face, her Shape, her Air, her Modesty, and all that call'd forth his Soul with Joy at his Eyes, and left his Body destitute of almost Life; it stood without Motion, and, for a Minute, knew not that it had a Being; and, I believe, he had never come to himself, so opprest he was with over-Joy, if he had not met with this Allay,° that he perceiv'd *Imoinda* fall dead in the Hands of *Trefry*: this awaken'd him, and he ran to her aid, and caught her in his Arms, where, by degrees, she came to herself; and 'tis needless to tell with what transports, what extasies of Joy, they both a while beheld each other, without Speaking; then Snatcht each other to their Arms; then Gaze again, as if they still doubted whether they possess'd the Blessing: They Graspt, but when they recovered their Speech, 'tis not to be imagin'd, what tender things they exprest to each other; wondering what strange Fate had brought 'em again together. They soon inform'd each other of their Fortunes, and equally bewail'd their Fate; but, at the same time, they mutually protested, that even Fetters and Slavery were Soft and Easy; and wou'd be supported with Joy and Pleasure, while they cou'd be so happy to possess each other, and to be able to make good their Vows.

Allay: hindrance

---

[49] A dog with long, shaggy hair, especially a poodle. Imoinda has been given a pet specifically associated with languid European ladies of fashion.

Cæsar swore he disdain'd the Empire of the World, while he cou'd behold his *Imoinda*; and she despis'd Grandure and Pomp, those Vanities of her Sex, when she cou'd Gaze on *Oroonoko*. He ador'd the very Cottage where she resided, and said, That little Inch of the World wou'd give him more Happiness than all the Universe cou'd do; and she vow'd, It was a Pallace, while adorn'd with the Presence of *Oroonoko*.

Trefry was infinitely pleas'd with this Novel,° and found this *Clemene* was the Fair Mistress of whom *Cæsar* had before spoke; and was not a little satisfied, that Heaven was so kind to the *Prince*, as to sweeten his Misfortunes by so lucky an Accident; and leaving the Lovers to themselves, was impatient to come down to *Parham House*, (which was on the same *Plantation*) to give me an Account of what had hapned. I was as impatient to make these Lovers a Visit, having already made a Friendship with *Cæsar*; and from his own Mouth learn'd what I have related, which was confirmed by his French-man, who was set on Shore to seek his Fortunes; and of whom they cou'd not make a Slave, because a Christian; and he came daily to *Parham Hill* to see and pay his Respects to his Pupil *Prince*: So that concerning and intresting my self, in all that related to *Cæsar*, whom I had assur'd of Liberty, as soon as the Governor arriv'd, I hasted presently to the Place where the Lovers were, and was infinitely glad to find this Beautiful young *Slave* (who had already gain'd all our Esteems, for her Modesty and her extraordinary Prettyness) to be the same I had heard *Cæsar* speak so much of. One may imagine then, we paid her a treble Respect; and though from her being carv'd in fine Flowers and Birds all over her Body,[50] we took her to be of Quality before, yet, when we knew *Clemene* was *Imoinda*, we cou'd not enough admire her.

I had forgot to tell you, that those who are Nobly born of that Country, are so delicately Cut and Rac'd° all over the fore-part of the Trunk of their Bodies, that it looks as if it were Japan'd; the Works being raised like high Poynt round the Edges of the Flowers: Some are only Carv'd with a little Flower, or Bird, at the Sides of the Temples, as was *Cæsar*; and those who

---

Novel: new turn of events   **Rac'd:** cut

---

[50] "The Women of this place ... cut on their Skins divers Shapes of Beasts, afterwards anointing the gashes with a certain Herb that makes the Marks never wear out. This manner of Ornament they highly esteem" (Ogilby, *Africa*, 359); "[T]hey cut and carve their skins about their ears, and temples, which rising up in little blisters, they paint them over with divers colours, and fancy it a great addition to their beauty" (Villault, 149).

are so Carv'd over the Body, resemble our Ancient *Picts*,[51] that are figur'd in the Chronicles, but these Carvings are more delicate.

From that happy Day *Cæsar* took *Clemene* for his Wife, to the general Joy of all People; and there was as much Magnificence as the Country wou'd afford at the Celebration of this Wedding: and in a very short time after she conceiv'd with Child; which made *Cæsar* even adore her, knowing he was the last of his Great Race. This new Accident made him more Impatient of Liberty, and he was every Day treating with *Trefry* for his and *Clemene's* Liberty; and offer'd either Gold, or a vast quantity of Slaves, which shou'd be paid before they let him go, provided he cou'd have any Security that he shou'd go when his Ransom was paid: They fed him from Day to Day with Promises, and delay'd him, till the Lord Governor shou'd come; so that he began to suspect them of falshood, and that they wou'd delay him till the time of his Wives delivery, and make a Slave of that too, For all the Breed is theirs to whom the Parents belong: This Thought made him very uneasy, and his Sullenness gave them some Jealousies° of him; so that I was oblig'd, by some Persons, who fear'd a Mutiny (which is very Fatal sometimes in those Colonies, that abound so with Slaves, that they exceed the Whites in vast Numbers) to discourse with *Cæsar*, and to give him all the Satisfaction I possibly cou'd; they knew he and *Clemene* were scarce an Hour in a Day from my Lodgings; that they eat with me, and that I oblig'd 'em in all things I was capable of: I entertain'd him with the Lives[52] of the Romans, and great Men, which charmd him to my Company; and her, with teaching her all the pretty Works° that I was Mistress of; and telling her Stories of Nuns, and endeavoring to bring her to the knowledge of the

---

Jealousies: suspicions   **Works:** ornamental needlework

---

[51] An ancient people of north Britain, who lost their distinct identity in the 9th century CE after their kingdom merged with that of the Scots. The Latin word *Picti* is identical with the word for "painted people," but may simply be a Latinized version of an unfamiliar foreign name; the fourth-century Latin poet Claudian, however, refers to the Picts' habit of tattooing themselves. In the context of New World culture, ancient British body adornment is mentioned by Rochefort (256) and Godwyn (*The Negro's & Indians Advocate* [London, 1680], 34–35). The second edition of Thomas Hariot's *A Brief and True Report of the New Found Land of Virginia* (1590) contains illustrated comparisons of the markings of the Virginian Native Americans and those of the Picts.

[52] The first edition reads "Loves." A new translation of Plutarch's *Parallel Lives* of Romans and Greeks, overseen by Dryden, had been published in 1683. When he rebels, Oroonoko is given false confidence by the example of Hannibal, frequently mentioned by Plutarch. Bacon, the self-destructive heroic fantasist of Behn's *The Widdow Ranter* (1689), is also seduced by the example of characters in Plutarch.

true God. But of all Discourses *Cæsar* lik'd that the worst, and wou'd never be reconcil'd to our Notions of the Trinity,[53] of which he ever made a Jest; it was a Riddle, he said, wou'd turn his Brain to conceive, and one cou'd not make him understand what Faith was. However, these Conversations fail'd not altogether so well to divert him, that he lik'd the Company of us Women much above the Men; for he cou'd not Drink; and he is but an ill Companion in that Country that cannot: So that obliging him to love us very well, we had all the Liberty of Speech with him, especially my self, whom he call'd his *Great Mistress*; and indeed my Word wou'd go a great way with him. For these Reasons, I had Opportunity to take notice to him, that he was not well pleas'd of late, as he us'd to be; was more retir'd and thoughtful; and told him, I took it Ill he shou'd Suspect we would break our Words with him, and not permit both him, and *Clemene* to return to his own Kingdom, which was not so long a way, but when he was once on his Voyage he wou'd quickly arrive there. He made me some Answers that shew'd a doubt in him, which made me ask him, what advantage it wou'd be to doubt? it would but give us a Fear of him, and possibly compel us to treat him so as I shou'd be very loath to behold: that is, it might occasion his Confinement. Perhaps this was not so Luckily spoke of me, for I perceiv'd he resented that Word, which I strove to Soften again in vain: However, he assur'd me, that whatsoever Resolutions he shou'd take, he wou'd Act nothing upon the White-People; and as for my self, and those upon that *Plantation* where he was, he wou'd sooner forfeit his eternal Liberty, and Life it self, than lift his Hand against his greatest Enemy on that Place:

---

[53] The Trinity was a notoriously hard concept for primitive peoples to grasp. Ogilby notes that the inhabitants of Cape Verde "hold the *Christian* Religion in great abomination, affirming, that God who giveth all things, and can do what he pleaseth, and causes Thunder, Lightning, Rain and Wind, is Omnipotent, and needs neither praying to, nor to be set forth in so mysterious a way as that of the Trinity" (*Africa*, 353). Of the Native Americans, Thomas Gage writes, "The mystery of the Trinity, and of the incarnation of Christ, and our redemption by him is too hard for them" (*The English-American his Travail by Sea and Land* [London, 1648], 150). In *De Promulgatione Evangelii* (Cologne, 1596) Acosta argues that all converts should be instructed in the Trinity (5.4); in 1578, he was instrumental in the burning of Francisco de la Cruz, a friar who had argued that the Native Americans did not have to believe in the Trinity to be saved. The Trinity, however, was also a prime target for the mockery of free-thinkers. See, e.g., Charles Blount, "*Concerning the* Arrians, Trinitaries *and Councils*" [1678], in Charles Blount, [Charles] Gildon, et al. *The Oracles of Reason* (London, 1693), 97–105. In 1697 Thomas Aikenhead was hanged in Edinburgh for heresies that included denial of the Trinity. Depending on the seventeenth-century reader's point of view, Oroonoko's anti-Trinitarianism marks him either as a pre-Christian primitive or an advanced post-Christian thinker.

He besought me to suffer no Fears upon his Account, for he cou'd do nothing that Honour shou'd not dictate; but he accus'd himself for having suffer'd Slavery so long; yet he charg'd that weakness on Love alone, who was capable of making him neglect even Glory it self; and, for which, now he reproches himself every moment of the Day. Much more to this effect he spoke, with an Air impatient enough to make me know he wou'd not be long in Bondage; and though he suffer'd only the Name of a Slave, and had nothing of the Toil and Labour of one, yet that was sufficient to render him Uneasy; and he had been too long Idle, who us'd to be always in Action, and in Arms: He had a Spirit all Rough and Fierce, and that cou'd not be tam'd to lazy Rest; and though all endeavors were us'd to exercise himself in such Actions and Sports as this World afforded, as Running, Wrastling, Pitching the Bar,[54] Hunting and Fishing, Chasing and Killing *Tigers*[55] of a monstrous Size, which this Continent affords in abundance; and wonderful *Snakes*, such as *Alexander* is reported to have incounter'd at the River of *Amazons*,[56] and which *Cæsar* took great Delight to overcome; yet these were not Actions great enough for his large Soul, which was still panting after more renown'd Action.

Before I parted that Day with him, I got, with much ado, a Promise from him to rest yet a little longer with Patience, and wait the coming of the Lord Governor, who was every Day expected on our Shore; he assur'd me he wou'd, and this Promise he desired me to know was given perfectly in Complaisance to me, in whom he had an intire Confidence.

After this, I neither thought it convenient to trust him much out of our View, nor did the Country who fear'd him; but with one accord it was advis'd to treat him Fairly, and oblige him to remain within such a compass, and that he shou'd be permitted, as seldom as cou'd be, to go up to the Plantations of the Negroes; or, if he did, to be accompany'd by some that shou'd be rather in appearance Attendants than Spys. This Care was for some time taken, and *Cæsar* look'd upon it as a Mark of extraordinary Respect, and was glad his discontent had oblig'd 'em to be more observant to him; he received new assurance from the Overseer, which was confirmed to him by the Opinion of all the Gentlemen of the Country, who made their court to him: During this time that we had his Company more frequently

---

[54] Throwing a thick rod of iron or wood.

[55] Big cats, such as jaguars or panthers. Biet was shown a tiger skin by an Indian who had killed the animal with a knife (343). Warren tells of a boastful and over-confident huntsman who was killed by a tiger, and of a more successful tiger hunter, John Millar (12–13; below, ooo).

[56] Quintus Curtius Rufus, *The History of Alexander the Great* 6.4. See also 10.1.

than hitherto we had had, it may not be unpleasant to relate to you the Diversions we entertain'd him with, or rather he us.

My stay was to be short in that Country, because my Father dy'd at Sea, and never arriv'd to possess the Honour was design'd him, (which was Lieutenant-General of Six and thirty Islands, besides the Continent of *Surinam*) nor the advantages he hop'd to reap by them;[57] so that though we were oblig'd to continue on our Voyage, we did not intend to stay upon the Place: Though, in a Word, I must say thus much of it, That certainly had his late Majesty, of sacred Memory,[58] but seen and known what a vast and charming World he had been Master of in that Continent°, he would never have parted so Easily with it to the *Dutch*. 'Tis a Continent whose vast Extent was never yet known, and may contain more Noble Earth than all the Universe besides; for, they say, it reaches from East to West; one Way as far as *China*, and another to *Peru:* It affords all things both for Beauty and Use; 'tis there Eternal Spring, always the very Months of *April, May* and *June*; the Shades are perpetual, the Trees, bearing at once all degrees of Leaves and Fruit, from blooming Buds to ripe Autumn;[59] Groves of Oranges, Limons, Citrons, Figs, Nutmegs, and noble Aromaticks, continually bearing their Fragrancies. The Trees appearing all like Nosegays adorn'd with Flowers of different kind; some are all White, some Purple, some Scarlet, some Blew, some Yellow; bearing, at the same time, Ripe Fruit and Blooming Young, or producing every Day new. The very Wood of all these Trees have an intrinsick Value above common Timber; for they are, when cut, of different Colours, glorious to behold; and bear a Price considerable, to inlay withal. Besides this, they yield rich Balm, and Gums; so that we make our Candles of such an Aromatick Substance, as does not only give a sufficient Light, but, as they Burn, they cast their Perfumes all about. Cedar is the common Firing,° and all the Houses are built with it. The very Meat we eat, when set on the Table, if it be Native, I mean of the Country, perfumes the whole Room; especially a little Beast call'd an *Armadilly*, a thing which I can liken to nothing so well as a *Rhinoceros*; 'tis all in white Armor so joynted, that it

---

Continent: mainland country   Firing: fuel

---

[57] It seems likely that Behn's father was Bartholomew Johnson, a barber of Canterbury. See Jane Jones, "New Light on the Background and Early Life of Aphra Behn," *Notes and Queries* 37, no. 235 (1990), 288–93. The post of lieutenant-general was, in fact, held by William Byam. The governor of Surinam, Lord Willoughby, did die at sea, in a hurricane.

[58] Charles II, who had died in 1685.

[59] "There is a constant Spring and Fall... Some [trees] have always Blossoms, and the several degrees of fruit at once" (Warren, 5; below, 332). The absence of seasonal cycle is also described in Ogilby, *America* (London, 167), 607.

moves as well in it, as if it had nothing on; this Beast is about the bigness of a Pig of Six Weeks old. But it were endless to give an Account of all the divers Wonderfull and Strange things that Country affords, and which we took a very great Delight to go in search of; though those adventures are oftentimes Fatal and at least Dangerous: But while we had *Cæsar* in our Company on these Designs we fear'd no harm, nor suffer'd any.

As soon as I came into the Country, the best House in it was presented me, call'd St. *John's Hill*.[60] It stood on a vast Rock of white Marble, at the Foot of which the River ran a vast depth down, and not to be descended on that side; the little Waves still dashing and washing the foot of this Rock, made the softest Murmurs and Purlings in the World; and the Opposite Bank was adorn'd with such vast quantities of different Flowers eternally Blowing,° and every Day and Hour new, fenc'd behind 'em with lofty Trees of a Thousand rare Forms and Colours, that the Prospect was the most ravishing[61] that Fancy[62] can create. On the Edge of this white Rock, towards the River, was a Walk or Grove of Orange and Limon[63] Trees, about half the length of the Mall[64] here, whose Flowery and Fruit-bearing Branches meet at the top, and hinder'd the Sun, whose Rays are very fierce there, from entering a Beam into the Grove; and the cool Air that came from the River made it not only fit to entertain People in, at all the hottest Hours of the Day, but refresh'd the sweet Blossoms, and made it always Sweet and Charming; and sure the whole Globe of the World cannot show so delightful a Place as this Grove was: Not all the Gardens of boasted *Italy* can produce a Shade to outvie this, which Nature had joyn'd with Art to render so exceeding Fine; and 'tis a marvel to see how such vast Trees, as big as English Oaks, cou'd take footing on so solid a Rock, and in so little Earth, as cover'd that Rock; but all things by Nature there are Rare, Delightful and Wonderful. But to our Sports.

Sometimes we wou'd go surprizing, and in search of young *Tigers* in their Dens, watching when the old Ones went forth to forage for Prey; and oftentimes we have been in great Danger, and have fled apace for our

---

Blowing: blooming

---

60 A plantation owned by Sir Robert Harley, near Parham Hill.

61 The 1688 editions have "raving," which is altered in the third to "ravishing."

62 "Sands" in the 1688 editions. Some later editions emend it to "Fancy," which seems more apposite.

63 A common seventeenth-century spelling, corresponding to that in French.

64 Emended in the third edition from "Marl hear." The Mall is next to St James's Park and was a fashionable walk. It is the setting for scenes in J. D.'s comedy *The Mall* (1674) and Sir George Etherege's *The Man of Mode* (1676), where its voguish character is greatly stressed.

Lives, when surpriz'd by the Dams. But once, above all other times, we went on this Design, and *Cæsar* was with us, who had no sooner stol'n a young *Tiger* from her Nest, but going off, we incounter'd the Dam, bearing a Buttock of a Cow, which he[65] had torn off with his mighty Paw, and going with it towards his *Den*; we had only four Women, *Cæsar*, and an English Gentleman, Brother to *Harry Martin*, the great *Oliverian*;[66] we found there was no escaping this inrag'd and ravenous Beast. However, we Women fled as fast as we cou'd from it; but our Heels had not sav'd our Lives, if *Cæsar* had not laid down his *Cub*, when he found the *Tiger* quit her Prey to make the more speed towards him; and taking Mr. *Martin*'s Sword desir'd him to stand aside, or follow the Ladies. He obey'd him, and *Cæsar* met this monstrous Beast of might, size, and vast Limbs, who came with open Jaws upon him; and fixing his Awful stern Eyes full upon those of the Beast, and putting himself into a very steddy and good aiming posture of Defence, ran his Sword quite through his Breast down to his very Heart, home to the Hilt of the Sword; the dying Beast stretch'd forth her Paw, and going to grasp his Thigh, surpris'd with Death in that very moment, did him no other harm than fixing her long Nails in his Flesh very deep, feebly wounded him, but cou'd not grasp the Flesh to tear off any. When he had done this, he hollow'd° to us to return; which, after some assurance of his Victory, we did, and found him lugging out the Sword from the Bosom of the *Tiger*, who was laid in her Bloud on the Ground; he took up the *Cub*, and with an unconcern, that had nothing of the Joy or Gladness of a Victory, he came and laid the Whelp at my Feet: We all extreamly wonder'd at his Daring, and at the Bigness of the Beast, which was about the highth of an Heifer, but of mighty, great, and strong Limbs.

Another time, being in the Woods, he kill'd a *Tiger*, which had long infested that part, and born away abundance of Sheep and Oxen, and other things, that were for the support of those to whom they belong'd; abundance of People assail'd this Beast, some affirming they had shot her with several Bullets quite through the Body, at several times; and some swearing they shot her through the very Heart, and they believ'd she was a Devil rather

---

hollow'd: shouted

---

[65] The mother tiger is described both in masculine and in feminine pronouns. The inconsistency is almost certainly due simply to a misprint in a particularly erratic section of the text. Later editions emend the masculine pronouns.

[66] Henry Martin or Marten (1602–1680), one of the signatories of Charles I's death warrant, was in fact a republican opponent of Cromwell. His brother George Marten died in Surinam in 1666.

than a Mortal thing. *Cæsar*, had often said, he had a mind to encounter this Monster, and spoke with several Gentlemen who had attempted her; one crying, I shot her with so many poyson'd Arrows, another with his Gun in this part of her, and another in that; so that he remarking all these Places where she was shot, fancy'd still he shou'd overcome her, by giving her another sort of a Wound than any had yet done; and one day said (at the Table) *What Trophies and Garlands Ladies will you make me, if I bring you home the Heart of this Ravenous Beast, that eats up all your Lambs and Pigs?* We all promis'd he shou'd be rewarded at all our Hands. So taking a Bow, which he chus'd out of a great many, he went up in the Wood, with two Gentlemen, where he imagin'd this Devourer to be; they had not past very far in it, but they heard her Voice, growling and grumbling, as if she were pleas'd with something she was doing. When they came in view, they found her muzzling in the Belly of a new ravish'd Sheep, which she had torn open; and seeing herself approach'd, she took fast hold of her Prey, with her fore Paws, and set a very fierce raging Look on *Cæsar*, without offering to approach him; for fear, at the same time, of loosing what she had in Possession. So that *Cæsar* remain'd a good while, only taking aim, and getting an opportunity to shoot her where he design'd; 'twas some time before he cou'd accomplish it, and to wound her, and not kill her, wou'd but have enrag'd her more, and indanger'd him: He had a Quiver of Arrows at his side, so that if one fail'd he cou'd be supply'd; at last, retiring a little, he gave her opportunity to eat, for he found she was Ravenous, and fell too as soon as she saw him retire; being more eager of her Prey than of doing new Mischiefs. When he going softly to one side of her, and hiding his Person behind certain Herbage that grew high and thick, he took so good aim, that, as he intended, he shot her just into the Eye, and the Arrow was sent with so good a will, and so sure a hand, that it stuck in her Brain, and made her caper, and become mad for a moment or two; but being seconded by another Arrow, he fell dead upon the Prey: *Cæsar* cut him[67] Open with a Knife, to see where those Wounds were that had been reported to him, and why he did not Die of 'em. But I shall now relate a thing that possibly will find no Credit among Men, because 'tis a Notion commonly receiv'd with us, That nothing can receive a Wound in the Heart and Live; but when the Heart of this courageous Animal was taken out, there were Seven Bullets of Lead in it, and the Wounds seam'd[68] up with great Scars, and she liv'd with the Bullets a great while, for it was long since they were shot: This

---

[67] The sex of the second tiger is also inconsistently described.
[68] Marked with lines or indentations; "Said of a scar, wound, etc." (*OED*).

Heart the Conqueror brought up to us, and 'twas a very great Curiosity, which all the Country came to see; and which gave *Cæsar* occasion of many fine Discourses; of Accidents in War, and Strange Escapes.

At other times he wou'd go a Fishing; and discoursing on that Diversion, he found we had in that Country a very Strange Fish, call'd, a *Numb Eel*,[69] (an *Eel* of which I have eaten) that while it is alive, it has a quality so Cold,[70] that those who are Angling, though with a Line of never so great a length, with a Rod at the end of it, it shall, in the same minute the Bait is touched by this *Eel*, seize him or her that holds the Rod with benumb'dness, that shall deprive 'em of Sense, for a while; and some have fall'n into the Water, and others drop'd as dead on the Banks of the Rivers where they stood, as soon as this Fish touches the Bait. *Cæsar* us'd to laugh at this, and believ'd it impossible a Man cou'd loose his Force at the touch of a Fish; and cou'd not understand that Philosophy, that a cold Quality should be of that Nature: However, he had a great Curiosity to try whether it wou'd have the same effect on him it had on others, and often try'd, but in vain; at last, the sought for Fish came to the Bait, as he stood Angling on the Bank; and instead of throwing away the Rod, or giving it a sudden twitch out of the Water, whereby he might have caught both the *Eel*, and have dismist the Rod, before it cou'd have too much Power over him; for Experiment sake, he grasp'd it but the harder, and fainting fell into the River; and being still possest of the Rod, the Tide carry'd him senseless as he was a great way, till an *Indian* Boat took him up; and perceiv'd, when they touch'd him, a Numbness seize them, and by that knew the Rod was in his Hand; which, with a Paddle (that is, a short Oar) they struck away, and snatch'd it into the Boat, *Eel* and all. If *Cæsar* were almost Dead, with the effect of this Fish, he was more so with that of the Water, where he had remain'd the space of going a League; and they found they had much a-do to bring him back to Life: But, at last, they did, and brought him home, where he was in a few Hours well Recover'd and Refresh'd; and not a little Asham'd to find he shou'd be overcome by an *Eel*; and that all the People, who heard his Defiance, wou'd Laugh at him. But we cheared him up; and he, being convinc'd, we had the *Eel* at Supper; which was a quarter of an Ell about, and most delicate Meat; and was of the more Value, since it cost so Dear, as almost the Life of so gallant a Man.

[69] Electric eel, described in Warren (below, 331).
[70] Aristotle had argued that matter consists of combinations of four qualities: hot, cold, moist, and dry.

About this time we were in many mortal Fears, about some Disputes the *English* had with the *Indians*; so that we cou'd scarce trust our selves, without great Numbers, to go to any *Indian* Towns, or Place, where they abode; for fear they shou'd fall upon us, as they did immediately after my coming away; and that it was in the possession of the *Dutch*, who us'd 'em not so civilly as the *English*; so that they cut in pieces all they cou'd take, getting into Houses, and hanging up the Mother, and all her Children about her; and cut a Footman, I left behind me, all in Joynts, and nail'd him to Trees.

This feud began while I was there; so that I lost half the satisfaction I propos'd, in not seeing and visiting the *Indian* Towns. But one Day, bemoaning of our Misfortunes upon this account, *Cæsar* told us; we need not Fear; for if we had a mind to go, he wou'd undertake to be our Guard: Some wou'd, but most wou'd not venture; about Eighteen of us resolv'd, and took Barge; and, after Eight Days, arriv'd near an *Indian* Town: But approaching it, the Hearts of some of our Company fail'd, and they wou'd not venture on Shore; so we Poll'd who wou'd, and who wou'd not: For my part, I said, If *Cæsar* wou'd, I wou'd go, he resolv'd, so did my Brother, and my Woman, a Maid of good Courage. Now none of us speaking the Language of the People, and imagining we shou'd have a half Diversion in Gazing only; and not knowing what they said, we took a Fisherman that liv'd at the Mouth of the River, who had been a long Inhabitant there, and oblig'd him to go with us: But because he was known to the *Indians*, as trading among 'em; and being, by long Living there, become a perfect *Indian* in Colour, we, who resolv'd to surprize 'em, by making 'em see something they never had seen, (that is, White People) resolv'd only my self, my Brother, and Woman shou'd go; so *Cæsar*, the Fisherman, and the rest, hiding behind some thick Reeds and Flowers, that grew on the Banks, let us pass on towards the Town, which was on the Bank of the River all along. A little distant from the Houses, or Hutts; we saw some Dancing, others busy'd in fetching and carrying of Water from the River: They had no sooner spy'd us, but they set up a loud Cry, that frighted us at first; we thought it had been for those that should Kill us, but it seems it was of Wonder and Amazement. They were all Naked, and we were Dress'd, so as is most commode° for the hot Countries, very Glittering and Rich; so that we appear'd extreamly fine; my own Hair was cut short, and I had a Taffaty° Cap, with Black Feathers, on my Head; my Brother was in a Stuff° Sute, with Silver Loops and Buttons, and abundance of

commode: convenient **Taffaty:** taffeta **Stuff:** light woollen cloth

Green Ribon; this was all infinitely surprising to them, and because we saw them stand still, till we approach'd 'em, we took Heart and advanc'd; came up to 'em, and offer'd 'em our Hands; which they took, and look'd on us round about, calling still for more Company; who came swarming out, all wondering, and crying out *Tepeeme*; taking their Hair up in their Hands, and spreading it wide to those they call'd out too; as if they would say (as indeed it signify'd) *Numberless Wonders*, or not to be recounted, no more than to number the Hair of their Heads.[71] By degrees they grew more bold, and from gazing upon us round, they touch'd us; laying their Hands upon all the Features of our Faces, feeling our Breasts and Arms, taking up one Petticoat, then wondering to see another; admiring our Shooes and Stockings, but more our Garters, which we gave 'em; and they ty'd about their Legs, being Lac'd with Silver Lace at the ends, for they much Esteem any shining things: In fine, we suffer'd 'em to survey us as they pleas'd, and we thought they wou'd never have done admiring° us. When *Cæsar*, and the rest, saw we were receiv'd with such wonder, they came up to us; and finding the *Indian* Trader whom they knew, (for 'tis by these Fishermen, call'd *Indian* Traders, we hold a Commerce with 'em; for they love not to go far from home, and we never go to them) when they saw him therefore they set up a new Joy; and cry'd, in their Language, *Oh! here's our* Tiguamy, *and we shall now know whether those things can speak:* So advancing to him, some of 'em gave him their Hands, and cry'd, *Amora Tiguamy*, which is as much as, *How do you*, or *Welcome Friend*;[72] and all, with one din, began to gabble to him, and ask'd, If we had Sense, and Wit? if we cou'd talk of affairs of Life, and War, as they cou'd do? if we cou'd Hunt, Swim, and

---

admiring: wondering at

---

[71] Many writers commented on the Caribs' inability to count higher than twenty (the number of their fingers and toes) or indeed not so high. Warren relates that the natives of Surinam can sometimes count to double or treble the number of their digits, "but their Arithmetick is quickly at a loss, and then they Cry out *Ounsa awara* that is, like the Hair of ones Head, innumerable" (26; see below, 337). See also Ogilby, *America*, 616; Rochefort, 264. According to Biet, followed by Behn, the word for innumerable is *tapoüimé* ("much" [396]). See Bernard Dhuicq, "New Evidence of Aphra Behn's Stay in Surinam," *Notes and Queries*, 42, no. 224 (1979), 524–25. Whereas these commentators simply stress mathematical naïveté, Behn is concerned (as throughout the story) with the relationship between mathematical and linguistic culture: She expresses a failure to describe in terms of a failure to count. In his *Essay Concerning Human Understanding* (1690), John Locke (who owned a copy of *Oroonoko*) was to use the mathematical limitations of the Native Americans to demonstrate the dependence of numerical skills upon numerical vocabulary (2.16.6).

[72] According to Biet, *amoré* means "you" (430, 432) and thence "good day" ("it's you!") (398, 407); *tigami* means "child" (414). See Dhuicq, 525.

do a thousand things they use? He answer'd 'em, We cou'd. Then they invited us into their Houses, and dress'd Venison and Buffelo for us; and, going out, gathered a Leaf of a Tree, call'd a *Sarumbo* Leaf,[73] of Six Yards long, and spread it on the Ground for a Table-Cloth; and cutting another in pieces instead of Plates, setting us on little bow *Indian* Stools, which they cut out of one intire piece of Wood, and Paint, in a sort of Japan Work: They serve every one their Mess° on these pieces of Leaves, and it was very good, but too high season'd with Pepper. When we had eat, my Brother, and I, took out our Flutes, and play'd to 'em, which gave 'em new Wonder; and I soon perceiv'd, by an admiration, that is natural to these People; and by the extream Ignorance and Simplicity of 'em, it were not difficult to establish any unknown or extravagant Religion in among them; and to impose any Notions or Fictions upon 'em.[74] For seeing a Kinsman of mine set some Paper a Fire, with a Burning-glass, a Trick they had never before seen, they were like to have Ador'd him for a God; and beg'd he wou'd give them the Characters or Figures of his Name, that they might oppose it against Winds and Storms; which he did, and they held it up in those Seasons, and fancy'd it had a Charm to conquer them; and kept it like a Holy Relique.[75] They are very Superstitious, and call'd him the Great *Peeie*,[76] that is, *Prophet*. They show'd us their *Indian Peeie*, a Youth of about Sixteen Years old, as handsom as Nature cou'd make a Man. They consecrate a beautiful Youth from his Infancy, and all Arts are us'd to compleat him in the finest manner, both in Beauty and Shape:

Mess: course

---

[73] "[T]heir napery [table linen] is the Leaves of Trees" (Warren, 24; below, 336). Biet gives *chalombo* as the word for the leaf of a tree (416).

[74] One of many passages in *Oroonoko* indicating Behn's skepticism about religious questions.

[75] Behn again stresses that Native American culture does not have the symbolic resources that sustain European power. Other writers also ascribe to the Native Americans an ingenuously material or superstitious view of written symbols. Rochefort notes that they regard letters as messengers and spies: "fearing one day the eye and tongue of one of these Letters, they hid it under a stone, that they might freely eat some Melons of their Masters" (273). Biet records that they imagine that written paper speaks (362).

[76] The term occurs as "*Peeaios*" in Harcourt (26) and as "*Peeies*" in Warren (26, below, 338), though these authors provide little information about their practices. The priests are termed "Piayes" in Biet, 385–388, and "Boyez" in Du Tertre, 364, and Rochefort, 274. According to Du Tertre the priests "approach the patient, feel, press, and handle the afflicted part, constantly blowing on it, and sometimes pull out (or seem to pull out) palm thorns as long as a finger, little bones, snake teeth, and splinters of wood, persuading the patient that they have caused the pain.... Thus the poor patient is cured more by imagination than in reality, and is enchanted rather than freed from illusion" (II, 368). Du Tertre, however, sees the process as diabolic rather than merely fraudulent.

He is bred to all the little Arts and cunning they are capable of; to all the
Legerdemain Tricks, and Slight of Hand, whereby he imposes upon the
Rabble; and is both a Doctor in Physick and Divinity. And by these Tricks
makes the Sick believe he sometimes eases their Pains; by drawing from
the afflicted part little Serpents, or odd Flies, or Worms, or any Strange
thing; and though they have besides undoubted good Remedies, for almost
all their Diseases, they cure the Patient more by Fancy than by Medicines;
and make themselves Fear'd, Lov'd, and Reverenc'd. This young *Peeie* had
a very young Wife, who seeing my Brother kiss her, came running and
kiss'd me; after this, they kiss'd one another, and made it a very great Jest,
it being so Novel; and new Admiration and Laughing went round the
Multitude, that they never will forget that Ceremony, never before us'd or
known. *Cæsar* had a mind to see and talk with their War *Captains*, and
we were conducted to one of their Houses; where we beheld several of
the great *Captains*, who had been at Councel: But so frightful a Vision
it was to see 'em no Fancy can create; no such Dreams can represent so
dreadful a Spectacle. For my part I took 'em for Hobgoblins, or Fiends,
rather than Men; but however their Shapes appear'd, their Souls were
very Humane and Noble; but some wanted their Noses, some their Lips,
some both Noses and Lips, some their Ears, and others Cut through each
Cheek, with long Slashes; through which their Teeth appear'd; they had
several (other) formidable Wounds and Scars, or rather Dismemberings;
they had *Comitias*,[77] or little Aprons before 'em; and Girdles of Cotton,
with their Knives naked, stuck in it; a Bow at their Backs, and a Quiver of
Arrows on their Thighs; and most had Feathers on their Heads of divers
Colours. They cry'd, *Amora Tigame* to us, at our entrance, and were pleas'd
we said as much to 'em; they seated us, and gave us Drink of the best Sort;
and wonder'd, as much as the others had done before, to see us. *Cæsar*
was marvelling as much at their Faces, wondering how they shou'd all be
so Wounded in War; he was Impatient to know how they all came by
those frightful Marks of Rage or Malice, rather than Wounds got in Noble
Battel: They told us, by our Interpreter, That when any War was waging,
two Men chosen out by some old *Captain*, whose Fighting was past, and
who cou'd only teach the Theory of War, those two Men were to stand
in Competition for the Generalship, or Great War Captain; and being
brought before the old Judges, now past Labour, they are ask'd, What they
dare do to shew they are worthy to lead an Army? When he, who is first

---

[77] Biet glosses *camisa* as a general word for clothing (*linge*, 419). In Raymond Breton the
word is *camicha*.

ask'd, making no Reply, Cuts of his Nose, and throws it contemptably°
on the Ground; and the other does something to himself that he thinks
surpasses him, and perhaps deprives himself of Lips and an Eye; so they
Slash on till one gives out, and many have dy'd in this Debate.[78] And 'its
by a passive Valour they shew and prove their Activity; a sort of Courage
too Brutal to be applauded by our Black Hero; nevertheless he express'd
his Esteem of 'em.

In this Voyage *Cæsar* begot so good an understanding between the *Indians* and the *English*, that there were no more Fears, or Heart-burnings°
during our stay; but we had a perfect, open, and free Trade with 'em: Many
things Remarkable, and worthy Reciting, we met with in this short Voyage; because *Cæsar* made it his Business to search out and provide for our
Entertainment, especially to please his dearly Ador'd *Imoinda*, who was
a sharer in all our Adventures; we being resolv'd to make her Chains as
easy as we cou'd, and to Compliment the Prince in that manner that most
oblig'd him.

As we were coming up again, we met with some *Indians* of strange
Aspects; that is, of a larger Size, and other sort of Features, than those of our
Country: Our *Indian Slaves*,[79] that Row'd us, ask'd 'em some Questions, but
they cou'd not understand us; but shew'd us a long Cotton String, with several Knots on it; and told us, they had been coming from the Mountains so

---

contemptably: contemptuously   Heart-burnings: resentments

[78] Initiation into military command did involve rituals of endurance, such as scarification
or whipping; see Rochefort. 314–15; Du Tertre II, 377; Biet, 378; Warren, 24 (below,
336). Describing ritual killing of prisoners of war, Rochefort records that the executioner
"caus'd himself to be mangl'd and slash'd, and cut in several parts of the body, as a
Trophey of Valour" (379). No recorded ritual, however, parallels Behn's, though there
is a parallel in a southern Indian custom recorded by the sixteenth-century Portuguese
traveller Duarte Barbosa. At the end of a twelve-year reign, the King of Quilacare would
immolate himself: "before all the people he takes some very sharp knives, and begins to
cut off his nose, and then his ears, and his lips, and all his members, and as much flesh
off himself as he can; and he throws it away very hurriedly, until so much of his blood
is spilled that he begins to faint, and then he cuts his throat himself" (cited in Sir James
George Frazer, *The Golden Bough*, abridged and ed. Robert Fraser [Oxford: Oxford
University Press, 1994], 246). An Italian translation of Barbosa's work was included in
Giovanni Battista Ramusio's much-reprinted *Navigationi* (1550), but it is not clear that
Behn could have known it (Giovanni Battista Ramusio, *Navigazioni e Viaggi*, ed. Marica
Milanesi, 6 vols. [Turin: Einaudi, 1978–88], II, 667–68). Perhaps she invented the ritual,
because the recorded initiation rituals did not sufficiently reflect her interest in the use
of the body as an economic unit.

[79] An inconsistency. Behn had earlier stated that Indians were not enslaved. See above, 127
and n. 9.

many Moons as there were Knots;[80] they were habited in Skins of a strange
Beast, and brought along with 'em Bags of Gold Dust; which, as well as
they cou'd give us to understand, came streaming in little small Chanels
down the high Mountains, when the Rains fell; and offer'd to be the con-
voy to any Body, or Persons, that wou'd go to the Mountains. We carry'd
these Men up to *Parham*, where they were kept till the Lord Governour
came: And because all the Country was mad to be going on this Golden
Adventure, the Governour, by his Letters, commanded (for they sent some
of the Gold to him) that a Guard shou'd be set at the Mouth of the River
of *Amazons*, (a River so call'd, almost as broad as the River of *Thames*)[81]
and prohibited all People from going up that River, it conducting to those
Mountains of Gold. But we going off for *England* before the Project was
further prosecuted, and the Governour being drown'd in a Hurricane,[82]
either the Design dy'd, or the *Dutch* have the Advantage of it: And 'tis to
be bemoan'd what his Majesty lost by loosing that part of *America.*

Though this digression is a little from my Story, however since it contains
some Proofs of the Curiosity and Daring of this great Man, I was content
to omit nothing of his Character.

It was thus, for sometime we diverted him; but now *Imoinda* began to
shew she was with Child, and did nothing but Sigh and Weep for the
Captivity of her Lord, her Self, and the Infant yet Unborn; and believ'd,
if it were so hard to gain the Liberty of Two, 'twou'd be more difficult
to get that for Three. Her Griefs were so many Darts in the great Heart
of *Cæsar*; and taking his Opportunity one *Sunday*, when all the Whites
were overtaken in Drink, as there were abundance of several Trades, and

---

[80] Biet (363, 397) and Rochefort (275) describe the use of knots, though in a reverse fashion:
For example, twenty days before an event, twenty knots would be tied in a cord: and
one would be untied with the passing of each day. Behn's version is more suggestive
of a culture without any capacity for abstract number: The numbers exist only in the
knots, and there is no word or idea for them. Knotted cords were not necessarily, in
fact, mathematically rudimentary; in Peru, such cords (*quipus*) could constitute complex
abaci, used in large-scale land administration. See Thomas Crump, *The Anthropology
of Numbers* (Cambridge: Cambridge University Press, 1990), 42–43; Georges Ifrah, *The
Universal History of Numbers: From Prehistory to the Invention of the Computer*, trans.
David Bellos et al. (London: Harvill Press, 1998), 68–71.

[81] The Amazon is, of course, far wider than the Thames, reaching a width of approximately
200 miles. On describing his arrival at Surinam, Biet notes that the estuary of the Surinam
River was as broad as that of the Seine at Honfleur (260)

[82] Lord Willoughby died at sea in a hurricane in 1666. According to the hostile Du
Tertre, who accused Willoughby of planning to exterminate all the French settlers in the
Caribbean, "this horrible tempest aborted all the detestable designs of Lord Willoughby"
(IV, 102).

Slaves for Four Years,° that Inhabited among the *Negro* Houses; and *Sunday* was their Day of Debauch, (otherwise they were a sort of Spys upon *Cæsar;*) he went pretending out of Goodness to 'em, to Feast amongst 'em; and sent all his Musick, and order'd a great Treat for the whole Gang, about Three Hundred *Negros*; and about a Hundred and Fifty were able to bear Arms, such as they had, which were sufficient to do Execution with Spirits° accordingly: For the *English* had none but rusty Swords, that no Strength cou'd draw from a Scabbard; except the People of particular Quality, who took care to Oyl 'em and keep 'em in good Order: The Guns also, unless here and there one, or those newly carri'd from *England*, wou'd do no good or harm; for 'tis the Nature of that County to Rust and Eat up Iron, or any Metals, but Gold and Silver. And they are very Unexpert at the Bow, which the *Negros* and *Indians* are perfect Masters of.

    Cæsar, having singl'd out these Men from the Women and Children, made an Harangue to 'em of the Miseries, and Ignominies of Slavery; counting up all their Toyls and Sufferings, under such Loads, Burdens, and Drudgeries, as were fitter for Beasts than Men; Senseless Brutes, than Humane Souls. He told 'em it was not for Days, Months, or Years, but for Eternity; there was no end to be of their Misfortunes: They suffer'd not like Men who might find a Glory, and Fortitude in Oppression; but like Dogs that lov'd the Whip and Bell,[83] and fawn'd the more they were beaten: That they had lost the Divine Quality of Men, and were become insensible Asses, fit only to bear; nay worse: an Ass, or Dog, or Horse having done his Duty, cou'd lye down in Retreat, and rise to Work again, and while he did his Duty indur'd no Stripes; but Men, Villanous, Senseless Men, such as they, Toyl'd on all the tedious Week till Black *Friday*;° and then, whether they Work'd or not, whether they were Faulty or Meriting, they promiscuously, the Innocent with the Guilty, suffer'd the infamous Whip, the sordid Stripes, from their Fellow *Slaves* till their Blood trickled from all Parts of their Body; Blood, whose every drop ought to be Reveng'd with a Life of some of those Tyrants, that impose it; *And why*, said he, *my dear Friends and Fellow-sufferers, shou'd we be Slaves to an unknown People? Have they Vanquish'd us Nobly in Fight? Have they Won us in Honourable Battel? And are we, by the chance of War, become their Slaves? This wou'd not anger a Noble Heart, this wou'd not animate a Souldiers Soul; no, but we are Bought and*

Slaves for four years: indentured servants
do Execution with Spirits: fight courageously
Black Friday: day set aside for punishment

---

[83] Used in training dogs, and often used as symbols of fawning servility (as in Act V of Otway's comedy *The Souldiers Fortune* [1680]).

Sold like Apes, or Monkeys, to be the Sport of Women, Fools and Cowards; and the Support of Rogues, Runagades°, that have abandon'd their own Countries, for Rapin, Murders, Thefts and Villanies: Do you not hear every Day how they upbraid each other with infamy of Life, below the Wildest Salvages°; and shall we render Obedience to such a degenerate Race, who have no one Humane Vertue left, to distinguish 'em from the vilest Creatures? Will you, I say, suffer the Lash from such Hands? They all Reply'd. with one accord, *No, no, no*; Cæsar *has spoke like a Great Captain; like a Great King.*

After this he wou'd have proceeded, but was interrupted by a tall *Negro* of some more Quality than the rest, his Name was *Tuscan*; who Bowing at the Feet of *Cæsar*, cry'd, *My Lord, we have listen'd with joy and Attention to what you have said; and, were we only Men, wou'd follow so great a Leader through the World: But oh! consider, we are Husbands and Parents too, and have things more dear to us than Life, our Wives and Children unfit for Travel, in these unpassable Woods, Mountains and Bogs; we have not only difficult Lands to overcome, but Rivers to Wade, and Monsters to Incounter; Ravenous Beasts of Prey –* To this, *Cæsar* Reply'd, *That Honour was the First Principle in Nature, that was to be Obey'd; but as no Man wou'd pretend to that, without all the Acts of Vertue, Compassion, Charity, Love, Justice and Reason; he found it not inconsistent with that, to take an equal Care of their Wives and Children, as they wou'd of themselves; and that he did not Design, when he led them to Freedom, and Glorious Liberty, that they shou'd leave that better part of themselves to Perish by the Hand of the Tyrant's Whip: But if there were a Woman among them so degenerate from Love and Vertue to chuse Slavery before the pursuit of her Husband, and with the hazard of her Life, to share with him in his Fortunes; that such an one ought to be Abandon'd, and left as a Prey to the common Enemy.*

To which they all Agreed, – and Bowed. After this, he spoke of the Impassable Woods and Rivers; and convinc'd 'em, the more Danger, the more Glory. He told them that he had heard of one *Hannibal* a great Captain, had Cut his Way through Mountains of solid Rocks;[84] and shou'd a few Shrubs oppose them; which they cou'd Fire before 'em? No, 'twas a trifling Excuse to Men resolv'd to die, or overcome. As for Bogs, they are with a little Labour fill'd and harden'd; and the Rivers cou'd be no Obstacle, since they Swam by Nature; at least by Custom, from their First Hour of their Birth: That when the Children were Weary they must carry

---

Runagades: renegades, deserters   **Slavages:** savages

---

[84] In 218 BCE the Carthaginian general Hannibal crossed the Alps on his way to invade Italy. On reaching an impassable barrier of rock, he weakened it with fire and vinegar. See Livy 21.37.

them by turns, and the Woods and their own Industry wou'd afford them Food. To this they all assented with Joy.

Tuscan then demanded, What he wou'd do? He said, they wou'd Travel towards the Sea; Plant a New Colony, and Defend it by their Valour; and when they cou'd find a Ship, either driven by stress of Weather, or guided by Providence that way, they wou'd Sieze it, and make it a Prize, till it had Transported them to their own Countries; at least, they shou'd be made Free in his Kingdom, and be Esteem'd as his Fellow-sufferers, and Men that had the Courage, and the Bravery to attempt, at least, for Liberty; and if they Dy'd in the attempt it wou'd be more brave, than to Live in perpetual Slavery.

They bow'd and kiss'd his Feet at this Resolution, and with one accord Vow'd to follow him to Death. And that Night was appointed to begin their March; they made it known to their Wives, and directed them to tie their Hamaca° about their Shoulder, and under their Arm like a Scarf; and to lead their Children that cou'd go, and carry those that cou'd not. The Wives who pay an intire Obedience to their Husbands obey'd, and stay'd for 'em, where they were appointed: The Men stay'd but to furnish themselves with what defensive Arms they cou'd get; and All met at the Rendezvous, where *Cæsar* made a new incouraging Speech to 'em, and led 'em out.

But, as they cou'd not march far that Night, on Monday early, when the Overseers went to call 'em all together, to go to Work, they were extreamly surpris'd, to find not one upon the Place, but all fled with what Baggage they had. You may imagine this News was not only suddenly spread all over the *Plantation*, but soon reach'd the Neighbouring ones; and we had by Noon about Six hundred Men, they call the *Militia* of the County, that came to assist us in the persute of the Fugitives: But never did one see so comical an Army march forth to War. The Men, of any fashion, wou'd not concern themselves, though it were almost the common Cause; for such Revoltings are very ill Examples, and have very fatal Consequences often-times in many Colonies: But they had a Respect for *Cæsar*, and all hands were against the *Parhamites*, as they call'd those of *Parham Plantation*; because they did not, in the first place, love the Lord Governor; and secondly, they wou'd have it, that *Cæsar* was Ill us'd, and Baffl'd° with; and 'tis not impossible but some of the best in the Country was of his Council in this Flight, and depriving us of all the *Slaves*; so that they of the better sort wou'd not meddle in the matter. The Deputy Governor, of whom I have had no great

Hamaca: hammock   Baffl'd: cheated

occasion to speak, and who was the most Fawning fair-tongu'd Fellow in
the World, and one that pretended the most Friendship to *Cæsar*, was now
the only violent Man against him; and though he had nothing, and so need
fear nothing, yet talk'd and look'd bigger than any Man: He was a Fellow,
whose Character is not fit to be mention'd with the worst of the *Slaves*.
This Fellow wou'd lead his Army forth to meet *Cæsar*, or rather to persue
him; most of their Arms were of those sort of cruel Whips they call *Cat with
Nine Tayls*; some had rusty useless Guns for show; others old Basket-hilts,°
whose Blades had never seen the Light in this Age; and others had long
Staffs, and Clubs. Mr. *Trefry* went along, rather to be a Mediator than a
Conqueror, in such a Batail; for he foresaw, and knew, if by fighting they
put the *Negroes* into dispair; they were a sort of sullen Fellows, that wou'd
drown, or kill themselves, before they wou'd yield, and he advis'd that fair
means was best: But *Byam*[85] was one that abounded in° his own Wit, and
wou'd take his own Measures.

It was not hard to find these Fugitives; for as they fled they were forc'd
to fire and cut the Woods before 'em, so that Night or Day they persu'd
'em by the light they made, and by the path they had clear'd: But as soon
as *Cæsar* found he was persu'd, he put himself in a Posture of Defence,
placing all the Women and Children in the Reer; and himself, with *Tuscan*
by his side, or next to him, all promising to Dye or Conquer. Incourag'd
thus, they never stood to Parley, but fell on Pell-mell upon the *English*,
and kill'd some, and wounded a good many; they having recourse to their
Whips, as the best of their Weapons: And as they observ'd no Order, they
perplex'd the Enemy so sorely, with Lashing 'em in the Eyes; and the
Women and Children, seeing their Husbands so treated, being of fearful
Cowardly Dispositions, and hearing the *English* cry out, *Yield and Live,
Yield and be Pardon'd*; they all run in amongst their Husbands and Fathers,
and hung about 'em, crying out, *Yield, yield; and leave* Cæsar *to their Revenge*;
that by degrees the *Slaves* abandon'd *Cæsar*, and left him only *Tuscan* and
his Heroick *Imoinda*; who, grown big as she was, did nevertheless press
near her Lord, having a Bow, and a Quiver full of poyson'd Arrows, which
she manag'd with such dexterity, that she wounded several, and shot the
Governor into the Shoulder; of which Wound he had like to have Dy'd,

---

Basket-hilts: swords with protective metal hilts
abounded in: was full of

---

[85] William Byam, Deputy Governor of Surinam, who administered it in Lord Willoughby's
absence. He is praised as a man of honor by Warren (6) and Biet (e.g., 263), but attacked
for his dictatorial ways by Robert Sanford. After the surrender of Surinam, Byam became
governor of Antigua, where he died c. 1670.

but that an *Indian* Woman, his Mistress, suck'd the Wound, and cleans'd it from the Venom: But however, he stir'd not from the Place till he had Parly'd with *Cæsar*, who he found was resolv'd to dye Fighting, and wou'd not be Taken; no more wou'd *Tuscan*, or *Imoinda*. But he, more thirsting after Revenge of another sort, than that of depriving him of Life, now made use of all his Art of talking, and dissembling; and besought *Cæsar* to yield himself upon Terms, which he himself should propose, and should be Sacredly assented to and kept by him: He told him, It was not that he any longer fear'd him, or cou'd believe the force of Two Men, and a Young Heroin, cou'd overcome all them, with all the Slaves now on their side also; but it was the vast Esteem he had for his Person; the desire he had to serve so Gallant a Man; and to hinder himself from the Reproach hereafter, of having been the occasion of the Death of a *Prince*, whose Valour and Magnanimity deserv'd the Empire of the World. He protested to him, he look'd upon this Action, as Gallant and Brave; however tending to the prejudice of his Lord and Master, who wou'd by it have lost so considerable a number of *Slaves*; that this Flight of his shou'd be look'd on as a heat of Youth, and rashness of a too forward Courage, and an unconsider'd impatience of Liberty, and no more; and that he labour'd in vain to accomplish that which they wou'd effectually perform, as soon as any Ship arriv'd that wou'd touch on his Coast. *So that if you will be pleas'd,* continued he, *to surrender your self, all imaginable Respect shall be paid you; and your Self, your Wife, and Child, if it be here born, shall depart free out of our Land.* But *Cæsar* wou'd hear of no Composition; though *Byam* urg'd, If he persu'd, and went on in his Design, he wou'd inevitably Perish, either by great *Snakes*, wild Beasts, or Hunger; and he ought to have regard to his Wife, whose Condition required ease, and not the fatigues of tedious Travel; where she cou'd not be secur'd from being devoured. But *Cæsar* told him, there was no Faith in the White Men, or the Gods they Ador'd; who instructed 'em in Principles so false, that honest Men cou'd not live amongst 'em; though no People profess'd so much, none perform'd so little; that he knew what he had to do, when he dealt with Men of Honour; but with them a Man ought to be eternally on his Guard, and never to Eat and Drink with *Christians* without his Weapon of Defence in his Hand; and, for his own Security, never to credit one Word they spoke. As for the rashness and inconsiderateness of his Action he wou'd confess the Governor is in the right; and that he was asham'd of what he had done, in endeavoring to make those Free, who were by Nature *Slaves*, poor wretched Rogues, fit to be us'd as *Christians* Tools; Dogs, treacherous and cowardly, fit for such Masters; and they wanted only but to be whipt into the knowledge of the *Christian Gods* to be the vilest of all creeping things; to learn to Worship such Deities as had not Power to make 'em Just, Brave, or Honest. In fine, after a thousand things of this Nature, not fit here to be recited, he told *Byam*, he had rather Dye than Live upon the same Earth with such Dogs. But *Trefry* and *Byam* pleaded and protested together so much, that *Trefry* believing the *Governor* to mean what he said; and speaking very cordially himself, generously put himself into *Cæsar*'s Hands, and took him aside, and perswaded him, even with Tears, to Live, by Surrendring himself, and to name his Conditions. *Cæsar* was overcome by his Wit and Reasons, and in consideration of *Imoinda*; and demanding what he desir'd, and that it shou'd be ratify'd by their Hands in Writing,[86] because he had perceiv'd that was the common way of contract between Man and Man, amongst the Whites: All this was perform'd, and *Tuscan*'s Pardon was put in, and they Surrender to the Governor, who walked peaceably down into the *Plantation* with 'em, after giving order to bury their dead. *Cæsar* was very much toyl'd with the bustle of the Day; for he had fought like a Fury, and what Mischief was done he and *Tuscan* perform'd alone; and gave their Enemies a fatal Proof that they durst do any thing, and fear'd no mortal Force.

But they were no sooner arriv'd at the Place, where all the Slaves receive their Punishments of Whipping, but they laid Hands on *Cæsar* and *Tuscan*, faint with heat and toyl; and, surprising them, Bound them to two several Stakes, and Whipt them in a most deplorable and inhumane Manner, rending the very Flesh from their Bones; especially *Cæsar*, who was not perceiv'd to make any Mone, or to alter his Face, only to roul his Eyes on the Faithless *Governor*, and those he believ'd Guilty, with Fierceness and Indignation; and, to compleat his Rage, he saw every one of those *Slaves*, who, but a few Days before, Ador'd him as something more than Mortal, now had a Whip to give him some Lashes, while he strove not to break his Fetters; though if he had, it were impossible: But he pronounced a Woe and Revenge from his Eyes, that darted Fire, that 'twas at once both Awful and Terrible to behold.

When they thought they were sufficiently Reveng'd on him, they unty'd him, almost Fainting, with loss of Blood, from a thousand Wounds all over his Body; from which they had rent his Cloaths, and led him Bleeding and Naked as he was; and loaded him all over with Irons; and then rubbed his Wounds, to compleat their Cruelty, with *Indian Pepper*, which had like to have made him raving Mad; and, in this Condition, made him so fast to

[86] Compare the Native Americans' superstitious awe of writing (above, 171 and n. 74). Europeans are distinguished from other cultures by their symbolic systems: writing, historical narrative, and mathematics (Oroonoko is first attracted by the English captains "Mathematical Discourses and Instruments" [150]). All these systems are abused for the purposes of violent deception.

the Ground that he cou'd not stir, if his Pains and Wounds wou'd have given him leave. They spar'd *Imoinda*, and did not let her see this Barbarity committed towards her Lord, but carry'd her down to *Parham*, and shut her up; which was not in kindness to her, but for fear she shou'd Dye with the Sight, or Miscarry; and then they shou'd loose a young *Slave*, and perhaps the Mother.

You must know, that when the News was brought on Monday Morning, that *Cæsar* had betaken himself to the Woods, and carry'd with him all the *Negroes*. We were possess'd with extream Fear, which no perswasions cou'd Dissipate, that he wou'd secure himself till Night; and then, that he wou'd come down and Cut all our Throats. This apprehension made all the Females of us fly down the River, to be secur'd; and while we were away, they acted this Cruelty: For I suppose I had Authority and Interest enough there, had I suspected any such thing, to have prevented it; but we had not gon many Leagues, but the News over-took us that *Cæsar* was taken, and Whipt like a common *Slave*. We met on the River with Colonel *Martin*, a Man of great Gallantry, Wit, and Goodness, and whom I have celebrated in a Character of my New *Comedy*,[87] by his own Name, in memory of so brave a Man: He was Wise and Eloquent; and, from the fineness of his Parts, bore a great Sway over the Hearts of all the *Colony:* He was a Friend to *Cæsar*, and resented this false Dealing with him very much. We carried him back to *Parham*, thinking to have made an Accomodation; when we came, the First News we heard was, that the *Governor* was Dead of a Wound *Imoinda* had given him; but it was not so well: But it seems he wou'd have the Pleasure of beholding the Revenge he took on *Cæsar*; and before the cruel Ceremony was finish'd, he drop'd down; and then they perceiv'd the Wound he had on his Shoulder, was by a venom'd Arrow; which, as I said, his *Indian* Mistress heal'd, by Sucking the Wound.

We were no sooner Arriv'd, but we went up to the *Plantation* to see *Cæsar*, whom we found in a very Miserable and Unexpressable Condition; and I have a Thousand times admired how he liv'd, in so much tormenting Pain. We said all things to him, that Trouble, Pitty, and Good Nature cou'd suggest; Protesting our Innocency of the Fact, and our Abhorance of such Cruelties. Making a Thousand Professions of Services to him, and Begging as many Pardons for the Offenders, till we said so much, that he believ'd we had no Hand in his ill Treatment; but told us, he cou'd never Pardon *Byam*; as for *Trefry*, he confess'd he saw his Grief and Sorrow, for his Suffering, which he cou'd not hinder, but was like to have been beaten

---

[87] Behn's *The Younger Brother* was first performed in 1696, with alterations by Charles Gildon. Its hero is called George Marteen.

down by the very *Slaves*, for Speaking in his Defence: But for *Byam*, who was their Leader, their Head; – and shou'd, by his Justice, and Honor, have been an Example to 'em. – For him, he wish'd to Live, to take a dire Revenge of him, and said, *It had been well for him, if he had Sacrific'd me, instead of giving me the contemptable Whip.* He refus'd to Talk much, but Begging us to give him our Hands; he took 'em, and Protested never to lift up his, to do us any Harm. He had a great Respect for Colonel *Martin*, and always took his Counsel, like that of a Parent; and assur'd him, he wou'd obey him in any thing, but his Revenge on *Byam*. *Therefore, said he, for his own Safety, Let him speedily dispatch me; for if I cou'd dispatch my self, I wou'd not, till that Justice were done to my injur'd Person, and the contempt of a Souldier: No, I wou'd not kill my self, even after a Whiping, but will be content to live with that Infamy, and be pointed at by every grining Slave, till I have compleated my Revenge; and then you shall see that* Oroonoko *scorns to live with the Indignity that was put on* Cæsar[88]. All we cou'd do cou'd get no more Words from him; and we took care to have him put immediately into a healing Bath, to rid him of his Pepper; and order'd a Chirurgeon[89] to anoint him with healing Balm, which he suffer'd, and in some time he began to be able to Walk and Eat; we fail'd not to visit him every Day, and, to that end, had him brought to an apartment at *Parham*.

The *Governor* was no sooner recover'd, and had heard of the menaces of *Cæsar*, but he call'd his Council; who (not to disgrace them, or Burlesque the Government there) consisted of such notorious Villains as *Newgate* never transported;[90] and possibly originally were such, who understood neither the Laws of God or *Man*; and had no sort of Principles to make 'em worthy the Name of Men:[91] But, at the very Council Table, wou'd Contradict and Fight with one another; and Swear so bloodily that 'twas terrible to hear, and see 'em. (Some of 'em were afterwards Hang'd, when the *Dutch* took possession of the place; others sent off in Chains: But calling these special Rulers of the Nation together, and requiring their Counsel in this weighty Affair, they all concluded, that (Damn 'em) it might be their own Cases;

---

[88] Oroonoko here reclaims his cultural identity as an African.

[89] From the Greek *cheirourgos* (lit. hand-worker). The original form of *surgeon*.

[90] Newgate was a London prison. The moral and social worthlessness of colonists was the subject of much indignant comment (in, for example, Behn's *The Widdow Ranter*). Dryden complained that Britain sent to the colonies "the draughts [sewage] of dungeons, and the stench of stews [brothels]" (*The Hind and the Panther* [1687] 2.560, in California Dryden, III).

[91] A characteristic example of cultural role reversal, for this charge was more usually levelled against the Native Americans. Biet, for example, claims that the Indians have neither religion nor civil law (359–61); Sepúlveda claims that they are less than human.

and that *Cæsar* ought to be made an Example to all the *Negroes*, to fright 'em from daring to threaten their Betters, their Lords and Masters;[92] and, at this rate, no Man was safe from his own *Slaves*; and concluded, *nemine contradicente*° that *Cæsar* shou'd be Hang'd.

Trefry then thought it time to use his Authority; and told *Byam* his Command did not extend to his Lord's *Plantation*; and that *Parham* was as much exempt from the Law as *White-hall*;[93] and that they ought no more to touch the Servants of the Lord − (who there represented the King's Person) than they cou'd those about the King himself; and that *Parham* was a Sanctuary; and though his Lord were absent in Person, his Power was still in Being there; which he had intrusted with him, as far as the Dominions of his particular *Plantations* reach'd, and all that belong'd to it; the rest of the *Country*, as *Byam* was Lieutenant to his Lord, he might exercise his Tyranny upon. *Trefry* had others as powerful, or more, that int'rested themselves in *Cæsar*'s Life, and absolutely said, He shou'd be Defended. So turning the *Governor*, and his wise Council, out of Doors, (for they sate at *Parham-house*) they set a Guard upon our Landing Place, and wou'd admit none but those we call'd Friends to us and *Cæsar*.

The *Governor* having remain'd wounded at *Parham*, till his recovery was compleated, *Cæsar* did not know but he was still there; and indeed, for the most part, his time was spent there; for he was one that lov'd to Live at other Peoples Expence; and if he were a Day absent, he was Ten present there; and us'd to Play, and Walk, and Hunt, and Fish, with *Cæsar*. So that *Cæsar* did not at all doubt, if he once recover'd Strength, but he shou'd find an opportunity of being Reveng'd on him: Though, after such a Revenge, he cou'd not hope of Live; for if he escap'd the Fury of the *English* Mobile,° who perhaps woud have been glad of the occasion to have kill'd him, he was resolv'd not to survive his Whipping; yet he had, some tender Hours, a repenting Softness, which he called his fits of Coward; wherein he struggled with Love for the Victory of his Heart, which took part with his charming *Imoinda* there; but, for the most part, his time was past in melancholy Thought, and black Designs; he consider'd, if he shou'd do this Deed, and Dye, either in the Attempt, or after it, he left his lovely

---

nemine contradicente: no-one opposing
Mobile: mob (Lat. *mobile vulgus*, the fickle crowd)

---

[92] Note that Behn thinks exclusively in terms of class distinctions when contrasting Oroonoko with his white oppressors.
[93] Whitehall Palace was the principal residence of British rulers from 1529 to 1698, when it was largely destroyed by fire.

Imoinda a Prey, or at best a *Slave*, to the inrag'd Multitude; his great Heart cou'd not indure that Thought. *Perhaps*, said he, *she may be first Ravished by every Brute; exposed first to their nasty Lusts, and then a shameful Death*. No; he could not Live Moment under that Apprehension, too insupportable to be born. These were his Thoughts, and his silent Arguments with his Heart, as he told us afterwards; so that now resolving not only to kill *Byam*, but all those he thought had inrag'd him; pleasing his great Heart with the fancy'd Slaughter he shou'd make over the whole Face of the *Plantation*. He first resolv'd on a Deed, that (however Horrid it at first appear'd to us all) when we had heard his Reasons, we thought it Brave and Just: Being able to Walk, and, as he believ'd, fit for the Execution of his great Design, he beg'd *Trefry* to trust him into the Air, believing a Walk wou'd do him good; which was granted him, and taking *Imoinda* with him, as he us'd to do in his more happy and calmer Days, he led her up into a Wood, where, after (with a thousand Sighs, and long Gazing silently on her Face, while Tears gusht, in spight of him, from his Eyes) he told her his Design first of Killing her, and then his Enemies, and next himself, and the impossibility of Escaping, and therefore he told her the necessity of Dying; he found the Heroick Wife faster pleading for Death than he was to propose it, when she found his fix'd Resolution; and, on her Knees, besought him, not to leave her a Prey to his Enemies. He (griev'd to Death) yet pleased at her noble Resolution, took her up, and imbracing her, with all the passion and Languishment of a dying Lover, drew his Knife to kill this Treasure of his Soul, this Pleasure of his Eyes; while Tears trickl'd down his Cheeks, hers were Smiling with Joy she shou'd dye by so noble a Hand, and be sent in her own Country,[94] (for that's their Notion of the next World) by him she so tenderly Lov'd, and so truly Ador'd in this; for Wives have a respect for their Husbands equal to what any other People pay a Deity; and when a Man finds any occasion to quit his Wife, if he love her, she dyes by his Hand; if not, he sells her, or suffers some other to kill her. It being thus, you may believe the Deed was soon resolv'd on; and 'tis not to be doubted, but the Parting, the eternal Leave taking of Two such Lovers, so greatly Born, so Sensible,° so Beautiful, so Young, and so Fond, must be very Moving, as the Relation of it was to me afterwards.

　　All that Love cou'd say in such cases, being ended; and all the intermitting Irresolutions being adjusted, the Lovely, Young, and Ador'd Victim lays

---

Sensible:　sensitive

[94] See Ligon, 51; Warren, 20 (below, 335).

her self down, before the Sacrificer; while he, with a Hand resolv'd, and a
Heart breaking within, gave the Fatal Stroke; first, cutting her Throat, and
then severing her, yet Smiling, Face from that Delicate Body, pregnant as it
was with Fruits of tend' rest Love. As soon as he had done, he laid the Body
decently on Leaves and Flowers; of which he made a Bed, and conceal'd it
under the same cover-lid of Nature; only her Face he left yet bare to look
on: But when he found she was Dead, and past all Retrieve, never more to
bless him with her Eyes, and soft Language; his Grief swell'd up to Rage;
he Tore,° he Rav'd he Roar'd, like some Monster of the Wood, calling on
the lov'd Name of *Imoinda*; a thousand times he turn'd the Fatal Knife that
did the Deed, toward his own Heart, with a Resolution to go immediately
after her; but dire Revenge, which now was a thousand times more fierce
in his Soul than before, prevents him; and he wou'd cry out, *No; since I have
sacrificed* Imoinda *to my Revenge, shall I loose that Glory which I have purchas'd
so dear, as at the Price of the fairest, dearest softest Creature that ever Nature
made? No, no*! Then, at her Name, Grief wou'd get the ascendant° of Rage,
and he wou'd lye down by her side, and water her face with showers of
Tears, which never were wont to fall from those Eyes: And however bent
he was on his intended Slaughter, he had not power to stir from the Sight
of this dear Object, now more Belov'd, and more Ador'd than ever.

He remain'd in this deploring Condition for two Days, and never rose
from the Ground where he had made his sad Sacrifice; at last, rousing
from her side, and accusing himself with living too long, now *Imoinda*
was dead; and that the Deaths of those barbarous Enemies were deferr'd
too long, he resolv'd now to finish the great Work; but offering° to rise,
he found his Strength so decay'd, that he reel'd to and fro, like Boughs
assail'd by contrary Winds; so that he was forced to lye down again, and
try to summons all his Courage to his Aid; he found his Brains turn round,
and his Eyes were dizzy; and Objects appear'd not the same to him they
were wont to do; his Breath was short; and all his Limbs surprised with a
Faintness he had never felt before. He had not Eat in two Days, which was
one occasion of this Feebleness, but excess of Grief was the greatest; yet
still he hop'd he shou'd recover Vigour to act his Design; and lay expecting
it yet six Days longer; still mourning over the dead Idol of his Heart, and
striving every Day to rise, but cou'd not.

In all this time you may believe we were in no little affliction for *Cæsar*,
and his Wife; some were of Opinion he was escap'd never to return; others
thought some Accident had hap'ned to him: But however, we fail'd not to

Tore: ranted   **Ascendant:** upper hand   **offering:** attempting

send out an hundred People several ways to search for him; a Party, of about forty, went that way he took; among whom was *Tuscan*, who was perfectly reconcil'd to *Byam*; they had not gon very far into the Wood, but they smelt an unusual Smell, as of a dead Body; for Stinks must be very noisom that can be distinguish'd among such a quantity of Natural Sweets, as every Inch of that Land produces. So that they concluded they shou'd find him dead, or somebody that was so; they past on towards it, as Loathsom as it was, and made such a rusling among the Leaves that lye thick on the Ground, by continual Falling, that *Cæsar* heard he was approach'd; and though he had, during the space of these eight Days, endeavor'd to rise, but found he wanted Strength, yet looking up, and seeing his Pursuer, he rose, and reel'd to a Neighbouring Tree, against which he fix'd his Back; and being within a dozen Yards of those that advanc'd, and saw him; he call'd out to them, and bid them approach no nearer, if they wou'd be safe: So that they stood still, and hardly believing their Eyes, that wou'd perswade them that it was *Cæsar* that spoke to 'em, so much was he alter'd; they ask'd him, What he had done with his Wife? for they smelt a Stink that almost struck them dead. He, pointing to the dead Body, sighing, cry'd, *Behold her there*; they put off the Flowers that cover'd her with their Sticks, and found she was kill'd; and cry'd out, *Oh Monster ! that hast murther'd thy Wife:* Then asking him, Why he did so cruel a Deed? He replied, he had no leasure to answer impertinent Questions; *You may go back*, continued he, *and tell the Faithless Governor, he may thank Fortune that I am breathing my last; and that my Arm is too feeble to obey my Heart, in what it had design'd him*: But his Tongue faultering, and trembling, he cou'd scarce end what he was saying. The *English* taking Advantage by his Weakness, cry'd, *Let us take him alive by all means:* He heard 'em; and, as if he had reviv'd from a Fainting, or a Dream, he cry'd out, *No, Gentlemen, you are deceiv'd; you will find no more Cæsars to be Whipt; no more find a Faith in me: Feeble as you think me, I have Strength yet left to secure me from a second Indignity.* They swore all a-new, and he only shook his Head, and beheld them with Scorn; then they cry'd out, *Who will venture on this single Man? Will no body?* They stood all silent while *Cæsar* replied, *Fatal will be the Attempt to the first Adventurer; let him assure himself,* and, at that Word, held up his Knife in a menacing Posture, *Look ye, ye faithless Crew,* said he, *'tis not Life I seek, nor am I afraid of Dying*; and, at that Word, cut a piece of Flesh from his own Throat, and threw it at 'em, *yet still I wou'd Live if I cou'd, till I had perfected my Revenge. But oh! it cannot be; I feel Life gliding from my Eyes and Heart; and, if I make not haste, I shall yet fall a Victim to the shameful Whip.* At that, he rip'd up his own Belly; and took his Bowels and pull'd 'em out, with what Strength he cou'd; while some, on their Knees imploring, besought him to hold his Hand. But when they saw him tottering, they cry'd out, *Will none venture on him?* A bold *English* cry'd, *Yes, if he were the Devil;* (taking Courage when he saw him almost Dead) and swearing a horrid Oath for his farewell to the World; he rush'd on *Cæsar*, with his Arm'd Hand met him so fairly, as stuck him to the Heart, and he fell Dead at his Feet. *Tuscan* seeing that, cry'd out, *I love thee, oh* Cæsar; *and therefore will not let thee Dye, if possible*: And, running to him, took him in his Arms; but, at the same time, warding a Blow that *Cæsar* made at his Bosom, he receiv'd it quite through his Arm; and *Cæsar* having not the Strength to pluck the Knife forth, though he attempted it, *Tuscan* neither pull'd it out himself, nor suffer'd it to be pull'd out; but came down with it sticking in his Arm; and the reason he gave for it was, because the Air shou'd not get into the Wound: They put their Hands across, and carried *Cæsar* between Six of 'em, fainted as he was; and they thought Dead, or just Dying; and they brought him to *Parham*, and laid him on a Couch, and had the Chirurgeon immediately to him, who drest his Wounds, and sow'd up his Belly, and us'd means to bring him to Life, which they effected. We ran all to see him; and, if before we thought him so beautiful a Sight, he was now so alter'd, that his Face was like a Death's Head black'd over; nothing but Teeth, and Eyeholes: For some Days we suffer'd no body to speak to him, but caused Cordials to be poured down his Throat, which sustained his Life; and in six or seven Days he recover'd his Senses: For, you must know, that Wounds are almost to a Miracle cur'd in the *Indies*; unless Wounds in the Legs, which rarely ever cure.

When he was well enough to speak, we talk'd to him; and ask'd him some Questions about his Wife, and the Reasons why he kill'd her; and he then told us what I have related of that Resolution, and of his Parting; and he besought us, we would let him Dye, and was extreamly Afflicted to think it was possible he might Live; he assur'd us, if we did not Dispatch him, he wou'd prove very Fatal to a great many. We said all we cou'd to make him Live, and gave him new Assurances; but he begg'd we wou'd not think so poorly of him, or of his love to *Imoinda*, to imagine we cou'd Flatter him to Life again; but the Chirurgeon assur'd him, he cou'd not Live, and therefore he need not Fear. We were all (but *Cæsar*) afflicted at this News; and the Sight was gashly;° his Discourse was sad; and the earthly Smell about him so strong, that I was perswaded to leave the Piace for some time; (being my self but Sickly, and very apt to fall into Fits of

gashly: ghastly

dangerous Illness upon any extraordinary Melancholy) the Servants, and *Trefry*, and the Chirurgeons, promis'd all to take what possible care they cou'd of the Life of *Cæsar*; and I, taking Boat, went with other Company to Colonel *Martin*'s, about three Days Journy down the River; but I was no sooner gon, but the *Governor* taking *Trefry*, about some pretended earnest Business, a Days Journy up the River; having communicated his Design to one *Banister*,[95] a wild *Irish* Man, and one of the Council; a Fellow of absolute Barbarity, and fit to execute any Villany, but was Rich. He came up to *Parham*, and forcibly took *Cæsar*, and had him carried to the same Post where he was Whip'd; and causing him to be ty'd to it, and a great Fire made before him, he told him, he shou'd Dye like a Dog, as he was. *Cæsar* replied, this was the first piece of Bravery that ever *Banister* did; and he never spoke Sence till he pronounc'd that Word; and, if he wou'd keep it, he wou'd declare, in the other World, that he was the only Man, of all the Whites, that ever he heard speak Truth. And turning to the Men that bound him, he said, *My Friends, am I to Dye, or to be Whip'd?* And they cry'd, *Whip'd! no; you shall not escape so well*: And then he replied, smiling, *A Blessing on thee*; and assur'd them, they need not tye him, for he wou'd stand fixt, like a Rock; and indure Death so as shou'd encourage them to Dye. *But if you Whip me*, said he, *be sure you tye me fast.*

He had learn'd to take Tobaco; and when he was assur'd he should Dye, he desir'd they would give him a Pipe in his Mouth, ready Lighted, which they did; and the Executioner came, and first cut off his Members, and threw them into the Fire; after that, with an ill-favoured Knife, they cut his Ears, and his Nose, and burn'd them; he still Smoak'd on, as if nothing had touch'd him; then they hack'd off one of his Arms, and still he bore up, and held his Pipe; but at the cutting off the other Arm, his Head sunk, and his Pipe drop'd; and he gave up the Ghost,[96] without a Groan, or a Reproach. My Mother and Sister were by him all the while, but not suffer'd to save him; so rude and wild were the Rabble, and so inhumane were the Justices, who stood by to see the Execution, who after paid dearly enough for their Insolence. They cut *Cæsar* in Quarters, and sent them to several of the chief *Plantations*: One Quarter was sent to Colonel *Martin*, who refus'd it; and swore, he had rather see the Quarters of *Banister*, and the *Governor* himself, than those of *Cæsar*, on his *Plantations*; and that he cou'd govern

---

[95] Major James Bannister negotiated with the Dutch after the ceding of Surinam. He went to Jamaica in 1671, where he was made major general and given responsibility for the militia. He was murdered in 1673.

[96] A common seventeenth-century expression for dying. There is no need to assume an allusion to the death of Christ (Mark 15:37, 39; Luke 23:46; John 19:30).

his *Negroes* without Terrifying and Grieving them with frightful Spectacles of a mangl'd King.

Thus Dy'd this Great Man; worthy of a better Fate, and a more sublime Wit than mine to write his Praise; yet, I hope, the Reputation of my Pen is considerable enough to make his Glorious Name to survive to all Ages; with that of the Brave, the Beautiful, and the Constant *Imoinda*.

FINIS.

Oroonoko (1696)

THOMAS SOUTHERNE (1660–1746) scored great successes with his sprightly comedy, *Sir Anthony Love* (1690), and his tragedies, *The Fatal Marriage* (1694) and *Oroonoko*. His other plays were less successful, though his dark and innovative comedies, *The Wives' Excuse* (1691) and *The Maid's Last Prayer* (1693), have won modern admirers, the former being successfully staged at Stratford in 1994. Via John Hawkesworth's 1759 revision, Southerne's *Oroonoko* substantially influenced 'Biyi Bandele's *Oroonoko*, which premiered at Stratford in 1999. Coincidentally, all Southerne's hits were inspired by Behn's prose fiction (*Sir Anthony Love* by *The Lucky Mistake* and *The Fatal Marriage* by *The History of the Nun*).

The principal actors in *Oroonoko* were:

- John Verbruggen (d. 1708), Oroonoko. Verbruggen was one of the leading young actors of his generation, especially after the actors' secession in 1695. He created the part of Mirabell in Congreve's *The Way of the World.*
- George Powell (1668?–1714), Aboan. Powell was one of the leading actors of his generation, though he was a difficult man with a drink problem and some reputation for hamming.
- Joseph Williams (b. c. 1663), Lieutenant Governor. Williams was a star actor with a large range. Although he predominantly played heroes in tragedy and comedy, he could also play villains in the former and fools in the latter.
- Jane Rogers (d. 1718), Imoinda. She specialized in virtuous, vulnerable, and sentimental roles.
- Frances Maria Knight (fl. 1682?–1724), Widow Lackitt. She excelled at playing scheming or passionately lustful beauties, both in comedy and tragedy. The present casting is unusual.

• Susanna Verbruggen (c. 1667–1703), Charlot Welldon. She was the wife of John Verbruggen and the widow of the murdered actor William Mountfort (d. 1692). A vivacious and versatile comedienne, she often took breeches roles, although she did not quite have the figure for them.

Oroonoko :

A

TRAGEDY

As it is Acted at the

𝕿𝖍𝖊𝖆𝖙𝖗𝖊-𝕽𝖔𝖞𝖆𝖑,

By His MAJESTY'S SERVANTS.

Written by *THO. SOUTHERNE.*

– Quo fata trabunt, virtus secura sequetur.   Lucan.[1]

Virtus recludens immeritis mori
Cælum, negatâ tentat iter viâ.   Hor. Od. 2. lib. 3[2]

LONDON:

Printed for *H. Playford* in the *Temple-Change.*
B. Tooke at the *Middle-Temple-Gate.* And
S. Buckley at the *Dolphin* against St. *Dunstan's*
Church in *Fleetstreet.*

M DC XC VI.

---

[1] "Where the fates [draw], virtue will follow without fear" (Lucan, *Pharsalia* 2.287).
[2] "Virtue, opening heaven to those unworthy of death, attempts its path along a way denied to others" (Horace, *Odes* 3.2.21–22).

WILLIAM

Duke of Devonshire, &c.[3]

Lord Steward of His Majesty's Houshold, Knight
of the Most Noble Order of the Garter, and
One of His Majesty's Most Honourable Privy
Council.

MY LORD,

THE Best part of the Fortune of my last Play (*The Innocent Adultery*)[4]
was, that it gave me an Opportunity of making my self known to
Your Grace. You were pleased to countenance the Advances which I had
been a great while directing and aiming at You, and have since encourag'd
me into an Industry, which, I hope, will allow me in this Play to own (which
is the only way I can) the great Obligations I have to You.

I stand engag'd to Mrs. *Behn* for the Occasion of a most Passionate Distress in my Last Play; and in a Conscience that I had not made her a
sufficient Acknowledgment, I have run further into her Debt for *Oroonoko*,
with a Design to oblige me to be honest; and that every one may find me
out for Ingratitude, when I don't say all that's fit for me upon that Subject.
She had a great Command of the Stage; and I have often wonder'd that she
would bury her Favourite Hero in a *Novel*, when she might have reviv'd him
in the *Scene.*° She thought either that no Actor could represent him; or she
could not bear him represented: And I believe the last, when I remember
what I have heard from a Friend of hers,[5] That she always told his Story,
more feelingly, than she writ it. Whatever happen'd to him at *Surinam*,
he has mended his Condition in *England.* He was born here under Your

---

Scene: stage

[3] William Cavendish, Duke of Devonshire (1641–1707), was a leading Whig politician,
who had opposed James II and taken a prominent part in his overthrow.
[4] The subtitle of Southerne's tragedy *The Fatal Marriage* (1694). Like *Oroonoko*, it inter-
wove tragedy and comedy; its tragic part was also derived from one of Behn's short
fictions, *The History of the Nun.*
[5] Perhaps Charles Gildon.

Grace's Influence; and that has carried his Fortune farther into the World, than all the Poetical Stars that I could have sollicited for his Success. It was Your Opinion, *My Lord*, that directed me to Mr. *Verbruggen*; and it was his Care to maintain Your Opinion, that directed, the Town to me, the Better Part of it, the People of Quality; whose Favours as I am proud of I shall always be industrious to preserve.

My Lord, I know the Respect and Reverence which in this Address I ought to appear in before You, who are so intimate with the Ancients, so general a Knower of the several Species of Poetry, and so Just a Judge in the Trials of this kind. You have an Absolute Power to Arraign and Convict, but a prevailing Inclination to Pardon and Save; and from the Humanity of Your Temper, and the true Knowledge of the Difficulties of succeeding this way, never aggravate or insist upon Faults

> − *Quas aut incuria fudit*,[6]
> *Aut humana parùm cavit Natura.* −
>
> Hor. Art. Poet.

to our Condemnation, where they are Venial, and not against the Principles of the Art we pretend to. *Horace*, who found it so, says,

> − *Gratia Regum*
> *Pieriis tentata modis.*[7]

The Favour of Great Men is the Poets Inheritance, and all Ages have allow'd 'em to put in their Claim; I only wish that I had Merit enough to prefer me to Your Grace: That I might deserve in some measure that Patronage which You are pleased to bestow on me: That I were a *Horace* for such a *Mecænas*.[8] That I could describe what I admire; and tell the World what I really think, That as You possess those Infinite Advantages of Nature and Fortune in so Eminent a degree; that as You so far excel in the Perfections of Body and Mind, You were design'd and fashion'd a Prince, to be the Honour of the Nation, and the Grace and Ornament of the Court. *Sir*, In the Fulness of Happiness and Blessings which You

---

[6] "Which inattention has let slip, or where human nature has been careless" (Horace, *Art of Poetry*, ll. 352–53).

[7] "The favour of kings was sought with the strains of the Muses" (Horace, *Art of Poetry*, ll. 404–05).

[8] Caius Maecenas (d. 8 BCE) was an associate of the Emperor Augustus, who supported Virgil, Horace, Propertius, and other writers. He is the archetype of the literary patron.

enjoy, I can only bring in my Wishes for the Continuance of 'em; they shall constantly be devoted to you, with all the Services of,

MY LORD,

Your Grace's most Obliged, most
Thankful, and most Humble Servant,

Tho. Southerne.

PROLOGUE to *Oroonoko.*

Sent by an Unknown Hand.   And Spoken by Mr. *Powell.*

AS when in Hostile Times two Neighbouring States
    Strive by themselves, and their Confederates;
The War at first is made with awkard° Skill,
And Soldiers clumsily each other kill:
Till time at length their untaught Fury tames,
And into Rules their heedless Rage reclaims:
Then every Science by degrees is made
Subservient to the Man-destroying Trade:
Wit, Wisdom, Reading, Observation, Art;
A well-turn'd Head to guide a Generous Heart.
So it may prove with our Contending Stages,[9]
If you will kindly but supply their Wages:
Which you with ease may furnish, by retrenching
Your Superfluities of Wine and Wenching.
Who'd grudge to spare from Riot and hard Drinking,
To lay it out on means to mend his thinking?
To follow such Advice you shou'd have leisure,
Since what refines your Sense, refines your Pleasure:
Women grown tame by Use[10] each Fool can get,
But Cuckolds all are made by Men of Wit.
To Virgin Favours Fools have no pretence:
For Maidenheads were made for Men of Sense.
'Tis not enough to have a Horse well bred,
To shew his Mettle, he must be well fed:

---

awkard: awkward

---

[9] There had been a theatrical monopoly in London from 1682 to 1695. Then, a group of aggrieved actors formed a breakaway company, discontented with the tactics of the manager, Christopher Rich. Southerne's play was acted by Rich's company. The prologue draws a parallel between the war of the theaters and that currently in progress between England and France.

[10] Women whom extensive sexual experience has turned into easy conquests.

Nor is it all in Provender and Breed,
He must be try'd and strain'd, to mend his speed:
A Favour'd Poet, like a Pamper'd Horse,
Will strain his Eye-balls out to win the Course.
Do you but in your Wisdoms vote it fit
To yield due Succors to this War of Wit,
The Buskin[11] with more grace shall tread the Stage,
Love sigh in softer Strains, Heroes less Rage:
Satyr shall show a Triple Row of Teeth,
And Comedy shall laugh your Fops to death:
Wit shall resume, and Pegasus[12] *shall foam,*
And soar in search of Ancient Greece *and* Rome.
And since the Nation's in the Conquering Fit;[13]
As you by Arms, we'll vanquish France *in Wit:*
The Work were over, cou'd our Poets write
With half the Spirit that our Soldiers fight.

Persons Represented.

M E N.

	BY
Oroonoko,	*Mr. Verbruggen.*
Aboan,	*Mr. Powell.*
Lieutenant Governor of *Surinam,*	*Mr. Williams.*
Blandford,	*Mr. Harland.*
Stanmore,	*Mr. Horden.*
Jack Stanmore,	*Mr. Mills.*
Capt. Driver,	*Mr. Ben. Johnson.*
Daniel, *Son to Widow* Lackitt,	*Mr. Mich. Lee.*
Hottman,	*Mr. Sympson.*

---

[11] The boot (*cothurnus*) worn by Greek tragic actors; a metonym for tragedy itself. It was frequently opposed to the sock (light shoe) worn in Greek comedy.
[12] In Greek myth, a winged horse ridden by the hero Bellerophon. A common image for poetic exaltation.
[13] England and its allies were at war with France, which supported the claims of James II. The capture of Namur in 1695 was their first major success for some years.

Planters, Indians, Negroes, Men, Women, and Children.

W O M E N.

	BY
Imoinda,	*Mrs. Rogers.*
Widow Lackitt,	*Mrs. Knight.*
Charlot Welldon, *in Man's Cloaths*,	*Mrs. Verbruggen.*
Lucy Welldon, *her Sister*,	*Mrs. Lucas.*

The S C E N E *Surinam*, a Colony in the *West-Indies;* at the Time of the Action of this Tragedy, in the Possession of the *English.*

OROONOKO.

ACT I. SCENE I.

Enter Welldon *following* Lucy.

Lucy. What will this come to? What can it end in? You have persuaded me to leave dear *England*, and dearer *London*, the place of the World most worth living in, to follow you a Husband-hunting into *America:* I thought Husbands grew in these Plantations.

Welldon. Why so they do, as thick as Oranges, ripening one under another: Week after week they drop into some Woman's mouth: 'Tis but a little patience, spreading your Apron in expectation, and one of 'em will fall into your Lap at last.

Lucy. Ay, so you say indeed.

Welldon. But you have left dear *London*, you say: Pray what have you left in *London* that was very dear to you, that had not left you before?

Lucy. Speak for your self, Sister.

Welldon. Nay, I'll keep you in countenance. The Young Fellows, you know, the dearest part of the Town, and without whom *London* had been a Wilderness to you and me, had forsaken us a great while.

Lucy. Forsaken us! I don't know that they ever had us.

Welldon. Forsaken us the worst way, Child; that is, did not think us worth having; they neglected us, no longer design'd upon us, they were tir'd of us. Women in *London* are like the Rich Silks, they are out of fashion a great while before they wear out. –

Lucy. The Devil take the Fashion, I say.

Welldon. You may tumble° 'em over and over at their first coming up, and never disparage° their Price; but they fall upon wearing immediately, lower and lower in their value, till they come to the Broker at last.

tumble: rumple   **disparage:** lower

Lucy. Ay, ay, that's the Merchant they deal with. The Men would have us at their own scandalous Rates: Their Plenty makes 'em wanton; and in a little time, I suppose, they won't know what they would have of the Women themselves.

Welldon. O, yes, they know what they wou'd have. They wou'd have a Woman give the Town a Pattern of her Person and Beauty, and not stay in it so long to have the whole Piece worn out. They wou'd have the Good Face only discover'd, and not the Folly, that commonly goes along with it. They say there is a vast Stock of Beauty in the Nation, but a great part of it lies in unprofitable hands; therefore for the good of the Publick, they wou'd have a Draught made once a Quarter, send the decaying Beauties for Breeders into the Country, to make room for New Faces to appear, to countenance the Pleasures of the Town.

Lucy. 'Tis very hard, the Men must be young as long as they live, and poor Women be thought decaying and unfit for the Town at One or Two and twenty. I'm sure we were not Seven Years in *London.*

Welldon. Not half the time taken notice of, Sister. The Two or Three last Years we could make nothing of it, even in a Vizard-Masque;[14] not in a Vizard-Masque, that has cheated many a man into an old acquaintance. Our Faces began to be as familiar to the Men of Intrigue, as their Duns,° and as much avoided. We durst not appear in Publick Places, and were almost grudg'd a Gallery in the Churches:[15] Even there they had their Jests upon us, and cry'd, She's in the right on't, good Gentlewoman, since no man considers her Body, she does very well indeed to take care of her Soul.

Lucy. Such unmannerly fellows there will always be.

Welldon. Then, you may remember, we were reduc'd to the last necessity, the necessity of making silly Visits to our civil[16] Acquaintance, to bring us into tolerable Company. Nay, the young Inns-of-Court Beaus,[17] of but one Term's standing in the Fashion, who knew no body, but as they were shewn 'em by the Orange-Women,[18] had Nicknames for us: How often have they laugh'd out, There goes my Landlady; Is not she come to let Lodgings° yet?

Duns: creditors   **let Lodgings:** prostitute herself

---

[14] A mask covering the whole face. It became increasingly associated with prostitutes.
[15] Galleries in churches were places where the fashionable displayed themselves.
[16] A clichéd term of praise, variously meaning "humane," "polite," or "sexually obliging."
[17] Law students at one of the four Inns of Court.
[18] Sellers of oranges in the theater, popularly associated with prostitution and procuring.

Lucy. Young Coxcombs° that knew no better.

Welldon. And that we must have come to. For your part, what Trade cou'd you set up in? You wou'd never arrive at the Trust and Credit of a Guinea-Bawd:[19] You wou'd have too much Business of your own, ever to mind other Peoples.

Lucy. That is true indeed.

Welldon. Then, as a certain sign that there was nothing more to be hop'd for, the Maids at the Chocolate Houses found us out, and laugh'd at us: Our *Billet-doux*° lay there neglected for Waste-Paper: We were cry'd down so low we cou'd not pass upon the City; and became so notorious in our galloping way, from one end of the Town to t'other,[20] that at last we cou'd hardly compass a competent change of Petticoats to disguize us to the Hackney-Coachmen:[21] And then it was near walking a-foot indeed.

Lucy. Nay, that I began to be afraid of.

Welldon. To prevent which, with what Youth and Beauty was left, some Experience, and the small Remainder of Fifteen hundred Pounds apiece, which amounted to bare Two hundred between us both, I persuaded you to bring your person for a Venture to the *Indies*. Every thing has succeeded in our Voyage: I pass for your Brother: One of the Richest Planters here happening to dye just as we landed, I have claim'd Kindred with him: So, without making his Will, he has left us the Credit of his Relation to trade upon: We pass for his Cousins, coming here to *Surinam* chiefly upon his Invitation: We live in Reputation; have the best Acquaintance of the place; and we shall see our account in't, I warrant you.

Lucy. I must rely upon you –

Enter Widow Lackitt.

Widow. Mr *Welldon*, your Servant. Your Servant, Mrs. *Lucy*. I am an Ill Visitor, but 'tis not too late, I hope, to bid you welcome to this side of the world. *Salutes* Lucy.

Coxcombs: conceited fools   **Billet-doux:** love letters

[19] The guinea was a gold coin, whose original value was twenty shillings. It was the standard fee for a procuress.

[20] The city was the commercial area of London; the town was the fashionable residential area.

[21] The hackney was a four-wheeled coach drawn by two horses, which could take six passengers.

Welldon. Gad so, I beg your Pardon, Widow, I shou'd have done the Civilities of my House before: but, as you say, 'tis not too late, I hope. –

Going to kiss her.

Widow. What! You think now this was a civil way of begging a Kiss; and by my Troth, if it were, I see no harm in't; 'tis a pitiful Favour indeed that is not worth asking for: Tho I have known a Woman speak plainer before now, and not understood neither.

Welldon. Not under my Roof. Have at you, Widow. –

Widow. Why, that's well said, spoke like a Younger Brother, that deserves to have a Widow. –   *He kisses her.*

You're a Younger Brother[22] I know, by your kissing.

Welldon. How so, pray?

Widow. Why, you kiss as if you expected to be paid for't. You have Birdlime[23] upon your Lips. You stick so close, there's no getting rid of you.

Welldon. I am a-kin to a Younger Brother.

Widow. So much the better: We Widows are commonly the better for Younger Brothers.

Lucy. Better, or worse, most of you. But you won't be much better for him, I can tell you. –   *Aside.*

Welldon. I was a Younger Brother; but an Uncle of my Mother's has maliciously left me an Estate, and, I'm afraid, spoil'd my Fortune.

Widow. No, no; an Estate will never spoil your Fortune. I have a good Estate my self, thank Heaven, and a kind Husband that left it behind him.

Welldon. Thank Heaven, that took him away from it, Widow, and left you behind him.

Widow. Nay, Heav'ns Will must be done; he's in a better place.

Welldon. A better place for you, no doubt on't: Now you may look about you; chuse for your self, Mrs. *Lackitt*, that's your business; for I know you design to marry again.

Widow. O dear! Not I, I protest and swear; I don't design it: But I won't swear neither; one does not know what may happen to tempt one.

Welldon. Why, a lusty young Fellow may happen to tempt you.

---

[22] The eldest son inherited the bulk of the estate, with younger brothers generally receiving a modest sum or income. The younger brother in search of a rich wife is a standard figure in comedy of this period; for example, Vanbrugh's *The Relapse* (1696) and Farquhar's *The Beaux' Stratagem* (1707).

[23] A sticky substance that was spread on twigs to catch birds.

Widow. Nay, I'll do nothing rashly: I'll resolve against nothing. The Devil, they say, is very busy upon these occasions; especially with the Widows. But if I am to be tempted, it must be with a Young Man, I promise you – Mrs. *Lucy,* Your Brother is a very pleasant Gentleman: I came about Business to him, but he turns every thing into Merriment.

Welldon. Business, Mrs. *Lackitt.* Then, I know, you wou'd have me to your self. Pray leave us together, Sister.   *Exit* Lucy.
What am I drawing upon my self here?   *Aside.*

Widow. You have taken a very pretty House here; every thing so neat about you already. I hear you are laying out for a Plantation.

Welldon. Why, yes truly, I like the Countrey, and wou'd buy a Plantation, if I cou'd, reasonably.

Widow. O! by all means, reasonably.

Welldon. If I cou'd have one to my mind, I wou'd think of settling among you.

Widow. O! you can't do better. Indeed we can't pretend to have so good company for you, as you had in *England*; but we shall make very much of you. For my own part, I assure you, I shall think my self very happy to be more particularly known to you.

Welldon. Dear Mrs. *Lackitt,* you do me too much Honour.

Widow. Then as to a Plantation, Mr. *Welldon,* you know I have several to dispose of. Mr. *Lackitt,* I thank him, has left me, though I say it, the Richest Widow upon the place; therefore I may afford to use you better than other people can. You shall have one upon any reasonable terms.

Welldon. That's a fair Offer indeed.

Widow. You shall find me as easy as any body you can have to do with, I assure you. Pray try me, I wou'd have you try me, Mr. *Welldon.* Well, I like that Name of yours exceedingly, Mr. *Welldon.*

Welldon. My Name!

Widow. O exceedingly! If any thing cou'd persuade me to alter my own Name, I verily believe nothing in the world wou'd do it so soon, as to be call'd Mrs. *Welldon.*

Welldon. Why, indeed *Welldon* does found something better than *Lackitt.*

Widow. O! a great deal better. Not that there is so much in a Name neither. But I don't know, there is something: I shou'd like mightily to be call'd Mrs. *Welldon.*

Welldon. I'm glad you like my Name.

Widow. Of all things. But then there's the misfortune; one can't change ones Name, without changing ones Condition.

Welldon. You'l hardly think it worth that, I believe.

Widow. Think it worth what, Sir? Changing my Condition? Indeed, Sir, I
  think it worth every thing. But, alas! Mr. *Welldon*, I have been a Widow
  but Six Months; 'tis too soon to think of changing ones Condition yet;
  indeed it is: Pray don't desire it of me: Not but that you may persuade
  me to any thing, sooner than any Person in the world. –

Welldon. Who, I, Mrs. *Lackitt*?

Widow. Indeed you may, Mr. *Welldon*, sooner than any man living. Lord,
  there's a great deal in saving a Decency: I never minded it before: Well,
  I'm glad you spoke first to excuse my Modesty. But what, Modesty means
  nothing, and is the Virtue of a Girl, that does not know what she would
  be at: A Widow should be wiser. Now I will own to you; but I won't
  confess neither; I have had a great Respect for you a great while: I beg
  your Pardon, Sir, and I must declare to you, indeed I must, if you desire
  to dispose of all I have in the world, in an Honourable Way, which I
  don't pretend to be any way deserving your consideration, my Fortune
  and Person, if you won't understand me without telling you so, are both
  at your service. Gad so! another time –

Stanmore *enters to 'em.*

Stanmore. So, Mrs. *Lackitt*, your Widowhood is waning apace. I see which
  way 'tis going. *Welldon*, you're a happy man. The Women and their
  Favours come home to you.

Widow. A fiddle of favour, Mr. *Stanmore*: I am a lone Woman, you know
  it, left in a great deal of Business; and Business must be followed or lost.
  I have several Stocks and Plantations upon my hands, and other things
  to dispose of, which Mr. *Welldon* may have occasion for.

Welldon. We were just upon the brink of a Bargain, as you came in.

Stanmore. Let me drive it on for you.

Welldon. So you must, I believe, you or somebody for me.

Stanmore. I'll stand by you: I understand more of this business, than you
  can pretend to.

Welldon. I don't pretend to't; 'tis quite out of my way indeed.

Stanmore. If the Widow gets you to her self, she will certainly be too hard
  for you: I know her of old: She has no Conscience in a Corner; a very
  Jew in a bargain, and would circumcise you to get more of you.

Welldon. Is this true, Widow?

Widow. Speak as you find, Mr. *Welldon*: I have offer'd you very fair:
  Think upon't, and let me hear of you: The sooner the better, Mr.
  Welldon. –   *Exit.*

Stanmore. I assure you, my Friend, she'll cheat you if she can.

Welldon. I don't know that; but I can cheat her, if I will.

Stanmore. Cheat her? How?

Welldon. I can marry her; and then I'm sure I have it in my power to cheat her.

Stanmore. Can you marry her?

Welldon. Yes, faith, so she says: Her pretty Person and Fortune (which, one with the other, you know, are not contemptible) are both at my service.

Stanmore. Contemptible! very considerable, I'gad; very desirable: Why, she's worth Ten thousand Pounds, man; a clear Estate: No charge upon't, but a boobily Son: He indeed was to have half; but his Father begot him, and she breeds him up, not to know or have more than she has a mind to: And she has a mind to something else, it seems.

Welldon. There's a great deal to be made of this. –   *Musing.*

Stanmore. A handsome Fortune may be made on't; and I advise you to't, by all means.

Welldon. To marry her! an old, wanton Witch! I hate her.

Stanmore. No matter for that: Let her go to the Devil for you. She'll cheat her Son of a good Estate for you: That's a Perquisite of a Widow's Portion always.

Welldon. I have a design, and will follow her at least, till I have a Pen'worth of the Plantation.

Stanmore. I speak as a friend, when I advise you to marry her. For 'tis directly against the Interest of my own Family. My Cousin *Jack* has belabour'd her a good while that way.

Welldon. What! Honest *Jack*! Ill not hinder him. I'll give over the thoughts of her.

Stanmore. He'll make nothing on't; she does not care for him. I'm glad you have her in your power.

Welldon. I may be able to serve him.

Stanmore. Here's a Ship come into the River; I was in hopes it had been from *England.*

Welldon. From *England*!

Stanmore. No, I was disappointed; I long to see this hand some Cousin of yours: The Picture you gave me of her has charm'd me.

Welldon. You'll see whether it has flatter'd her or no, in a little time. If she recover'd of that Illness that was the reason of her staying behind us, I know she will come with the first opportunity. We shall see her, or hear of her death.

Stanmore. We'll hope the best. The Ships from *England* are expected every day.

Welldon. What Ship is this?

Stanmore. A Rover, a Buccaneer,[24] a Trader in Slaves: That's the Commodity we deal in, you know. If you have a curiosity to see our manner of marketting, I'll wait upon you.

Welldon. We'll take my Sister with us. –   *Exeunt.*

SCENE II. *An Open Place.*

Enter Lieutenant-Governor *and* Blandford.

Governor. There's no resisting your Fortune, *Blandford*; you draw all the Prizes.

Blandford. I draw for our Lord Governor, you know; his Fortune favours me.

Governor. I grudge him nothing this time; but if Fortune had favour'd me in the last Sale, the Fair Slave had been mine; *Clemene* had been mine.

Blandford. Are you still in love with her?

Governor. Every day more in love with her.

> *Enter Captain* Driver, *teaz'd and pull'd about by Widow* Lackitt *and several Planters. Enter at another door* Welldon, Lucy, Stanmore.

Widow. Here have I six Slaves in my Lot, and not a Man among 'em; all Women and Children; what can I do with 'em, Captain? Pray consider. I am a Woman my self, and can't get my own Slaves, as some of my Neighbours do.

1st Planter. I have all Men in mine: Pray, Captain, let the Men and Women be mingled together, for Procreation-sake, and the good of the Plantation.

2nd Planter. Ay, ay, a Man and a Woman, Captain, for the good of the Plantation.

Captain. Let 'em mingle together and be damn'd, what care I? Would you have me pimp for the good of the Plantation?

1st Planter. I am a constant Customer, Captain.

Widow. I am always Ready Money to you, Captain.

1st Planter. For that matter, Mistress, my Money is as ready as yours.

Widow. Pray hear me, Captain.

Captain. Look you, I have done my part by you; I have brought the number of Slaves you bargain'd for; if your Lots have not pleas'd you, you must draw again among your selves.

[24] A rover is a pirate ship in general; a buccaneer is more specifically associated with coastal raids, especially in the West Indies.

3rd Planter. I am contented with my Lot.

4th Planter. I am very well satisfied.

3rd Planter. We'll have no drawing again.

Captain. Do you hear, Mistress? You may hold your tongue: For my part, I expect my Money.

Widow. Captain, No body questions or scruples the Payment. But I won't hold my tongue; 'tis too much to pray and pay too: One may speak for ones own, I hope.

Captain. Well, what wou'd you say?

Widow. I say no more than I can make out.

Captain. Out with it then.

Widow. I say, things have not been so fair carry'd as they might have been. How do I know how you have juggled together in my absence? You drew the Lots before I came, I'm sure.

Captain. That's your own fault, Mistress; you might have come sooner.

Widow. Then here's a Prince, as they say, among the Slaves, and you set him down to go as a common Man.

Captain. Have you a mind to try what a Man he is? You'll find him no more than a common Man at your business.

Widow. Sir, You're a scurvy Fellow to talk at this rate to me. If my Husband were alive, Gadsbodykins, you wou'd not use me so.

Captain. Right, Mistress, I would not use you at all.

Widow. Not use me! Your Betters every Inch of you, I wou'd have you to know, wou'd be glad to use me, Sirrah. Marry come up here, who are you, I trow? You begin to think your self a Captain, forsooth, because we call you so. You forget your self as fast as you can; but I remember you; I know you for a pitiful paltry Fellow, as you are; an Upstart to Prosperity; one that is but just come acquainted with Cleanliness, and that never saw Five Shillings of your own, without deserving to be hang'd for 'em.

Governor. She has giv'n you a Broadside, Captain; You'll stand up to her.

Captain. Hang her, Stink-pot, I'll come no near.[25]

Widow. By this good light, it wou'd make a Woman do a thing she never design'd; Marry again, tho she were sure to repent it, to be reveng'd of such a –

Jack Stanmore. What's the matter, Mrs. *Lackitt*? Can I serve you?

Widow. No, no, you can't serve me: You are for serving your self, I'm sure. Pray go about your business, I have none for you: You know I have told you so. Lord! how can you be so troublesome? nay, so unconscionable,

---

[25] Nearer: the original, but now obsolete, sense (as the comparative of *nigh*).

to think that every Rich Widow must throw her self away upon a Young Fellow that has nothing?

Stanmore. Jack, You are answer'd, I suppose.

Jack Stanmore. I'll have another pluck at her.

Widow. Mr. *Welldon,* I am a little out of order; but pray bring your Sister to dine with me. Gad's my life, I'm out of all patience with that pitiful Fellow: My flesh rises° at him: I can't stay in the place where he is. –   *Exit.*

Blandford. Captain, You have us'd the Widow very familiarly.

Captain. This is my way; I have no design, and therefore am not over civil. If she had ever a handsome Daughter to wheedle her out of: Or if I cou'd make any thing of her Booby Son.

Welldon. I may improve that hint, and make something of him.   *Aside.*

Governor. She's very Rich.

Captain. I'm rich my self. She has nothing that I want: I have no Leaks to stop. Old Women are Fortune-Menders. I have made a good Voyage, and wou'd reap the fruits of my labour, We plow the deep, my Masters, but our Harvest is on shore. I'm for a Young Woman.

Stanmore. Look about, Captain, there's one ripe, and ready for the Sickle.

Captain. A Woman indeed! I will be acquainted with her: Who is she?

Welldon. My Sister, Sir.

Captain. Wou'd I were a-kin to her: If she were my Sister, she shou'd never go out of the Family. What say you, Mistress? You expect I should marry you, I suppose.

Lucy. I shan't be disappointed, if you don't.   *Turning away.*

Welldon. She won't break her heart, Sir.

Captain. But I mean –   *Following her.*

Welldon. And I mean –   *Going between him and* Lucy.

That you must not think of her without marrying.

Captain. I mean so too.

Welldon. Why then your meaning's out.

Captain. You're very short.

Welldon. I will grow, and be taller for you.

Captain. I shall grow angry, and swear.

Welldon. You'll catch no fish then.[26]

Captain. I don't well know whether he designs to affront me, or no.

---

flesh rises: I have gooseflesh

---

[26] "If you swear, you'll catch no fish" (proverbial).

Stanmore. No, no, he's a little familiar; 'tis his way.

Captain. Say you so? Nay, I can be as familiar as he, if that be it. Well, Sir, look upon me full: What say you? How do you like me for a Brother-in-law?

Welldon. Why yes, faith, you'll do my business,   *Turning him about.* If we can agree about my Sister's.

Captain. I don't know whether your Sister will like me, or not: I can't say much to her: But I have Money enough: And if you are her Brother, as you seem to be a-kin to her; I know that will recommend me to you.

Welldon. This is your Market for Slaves; my Sister is a Free Woman, and must not be dispos'd of in publick. You shall be welcome to my House, if you please: And, upon better acquaintance, if my Sister likes you, and I like your Offers, –

Captain. Very well, Sir, I'll come and see her.

Governor. Where are the Slaves, Captain? They are long a coming.

Blandford. And who is this Prince that's fallen to my Lot, for the Lord Governor? Let me know something of him, that I may treat him accordingly; who is he?

Captain. He's the Devil of a Fellow, I can tell you; a Prince every Inch of him: You have paid dear enough for him, for all the good he'll do you: I was forc'd to clap him in Irons, and did not think the Ship safe neither. You are in hostility with the *Indians*, they say; they threaten you daily: You had best have an eye upon him.

Blandford. But who is he?

Governor. And how do you know him to be a Prince?

Captain. He is Son and Heir to the great King of *Angola*,[27] a mischievous Monarch in those parts, who, by his good will, wou'd never let any of his Neighbours be in quiet. This Son was his General, a plaguy fighting Fellow: I have formerly had dealings with him for Slaves, which he took Prisoners, and have got pretty roundly by him. But the Wars being at an end, and nothing more to be got by the Trade of that Countrey, I made bold to bring the Prince along with me.

Governor. How could you do that?

Blandford. What! steal a Prince out of his own Countrey? Impossible!

Captain. 'Twas hard indeed; but I did it. You must know, this *Oroonoko* –

Blandford. Is that his Name?

---

[27] A kingdom in West Africa, occupied by the Portuguese; Southerne was perhaps aware that Coramantien was not an African kingdom. For a description of the Angolan slave trade, see Ogilby, *Africa*, 562.

Captain. Ay, *Oroonoko.*

Governor. *Oroonoko.*

Captain. Is naturally inquisitive about the Men and Manners of the White
   Nations. Because I could give him some account of the other Parts of the
   World, I grew very much into his favour: In return of so great an Honour,
   you know I cou'd do no less upon my coming away, than invite him on
   board me: Never having been in a Ship, he appointed his time, and I
   prepared my Entertainment: He came the next Evening as privately as
   he cou'd, with about some Twenty along with him. The Punch went
   round; and as many of his Attendants as wou'd be dangerous, I sent
   dead drunk on shore; the rest we secur'd: And so you have the Prince
   Oroonoko.

1st Planter. Gad-a-mercy, Captain, there you were with him, I'faith.

2nd Planter. Such men as you are fit to be employ'd in Publick Affairs: The
   Plantation will thrive by you.

3rd Planter. Industry shou'd be encourag'd.

Captain. There's nothing done without it, Boys. I have made my Fortune
   this way.

Blandford. Unheard-of Villany!

Stanmore. Barbarous Treachery!

Blandford. They applaud him for't.

Governor. But, Captain, methinks you have taken a great deal of pains for
   this Prince *Oroonoko*; why did you part with him at the common rate of
   Slaves?

Captain. Why, Lieutenant-Governor, I'll tell you; I did design to carry
   him to *England*, to have show'd him there; but I found him troublesome
   upon my hands, and I'm glad I'm rid of him. – Oh, ho, here they come.

   *Black Slaves, Men, Women, and Children, pass across the Stage by
      two and two; Aboan, and others of Oroonoko's Attendants
      two and two; Oroonoko last of all in Chains.*

Lucy. Are all these Wretches Slaves?

Stanmore. All sold, they and their Posterity all Slaves.

Lucy. O miserable Fortune!

Blandford. Most of 'em know no better; they were born so, and only change
   their Masters. But a Prince, born only to Command, betray'd and
   sold! My heart drops blood for him.[28]

Captain. Now, Governor, here he comes, pray observe hime.

---

[28] Note the emphasis on class and on class culture. It is abhorrent to enslave a prince; the
   common slaves endure no worse conditions than they did at home.

Oroonoko. So, Sir, You have kept your Word with me.

Captain. I am a better Christian, I thank you, than to keep it with a Heathen.

Oroonoko. You are a Christian, be a Christian still:
If you have any God that teaches you
To break your Word, I need not curse you more:
Let him cheat you, as you are false to me.
You faithful Followers of my better Fortune!
We have been Fellow-Soldiers in the Field;   *Embracing*
Now we are Fellow-Slaves. This last farewell.   *his Friends.*
Be sure of one thing that will comfort us,
Whatever World we next are thrown upon,
Cannot be worse than this.   *All Slaves go off, but* Oroonoko.

Captain. You see what a Bloody Pagan he is, Governor; but I took care that none of his Followers should be in the same Lot with him, for fear they shou'd undertake some desperate action, to the danger of the Colony.

Oroonoko. Live still in fear; it is the Villains Curse,
And will revenge my Chains: Fear ev'n me,
Who have no pow'r to hurt thee. Nature abhors,
And drives thee out from the Society
And Commerce of Mankind, for Breach of Faith.
Men live and prosper but in Mutual Trust,
A Confidence of one another's Truth:
That thou hast violated. I have done.
I know my Fortune, and submit to it.

Governor. Sir, I am sorry for your Fortune, and wou'd help it, if I cou'd.

Blandford. Take off his Chains. You know your condition; but you are fall'n into Honourable Hands: You are the Lord Governor's Slave, who will use you nobly: In his absence it shall be my care to serve you.

Blandford applying to him.

Oroonoko. I hear you, but I can believe no more.

Governor. Captain, I'm afraid the world won't speak so honourably of this action of yours, as you wou'd have 'em.

Captain. I have the Money. Let the world speak and be damn'd, I care not.

Oroonoko. I wou'd forget my self.   Be satisfied,   *To* Blandford.
I am above the rank of common Slaves.
Let that content you.   The Christian there, that knows me,
For his own sake will not discover more.

Captain. I have other matters to mind. You have him, and much good may do you with your Prince.   *Exit.*

The Planters pulling and staring at Oroonoko.

Blandford. What wou'd you have there? you stare as if you never saw a Man
　　before. Stand further off.　　　　　　　　　　　　　　*Turns 'em away.*
Oroonoko. Let 'em stare on. I am unfortunate, but not asham'd
　　Of being so: No, let the Guilty blush,
　　The White Man that betray'd me: Honest Black
　　Disdains to change its Colour.　I am ready:
　　Where must I go? Dispose me as you please.
　　I am not well acquainted with my Fortune,
　　But must learn to know it better: So I know, you say:
　　Degrees make all things easy.
Blandford. All things shall be easy.
Oroonoko. Tear off this Pomp, and let me know my self:
　　The slavish Habit best becomes me now.
　　Hard Fare, and Whips, and Chains may overpow'r
　　The frailer flesh, and bow my Body down.
　　But there's another, Nobler Part of Me,
　　Out of your reach, which you can never tame.
Blandford. You shall find nothing of this wretchedness
　　You apprehend. We are not Monsters all.
　　You seem unwilling to disclose your self:
　　Therefore for fear the mentioning your Name
　　Should give you new disquiets, I presume
　　To call you *Cæsar.*
Oroonoko. I am my self; but call me what you please.
Stanmore. A very good Name, *Cæsar.*
Governor. And very fit for his great Character.
Oroonoko. Was *Cæsar* then a Slave?
Governor. I think he was; to Pirates[29] too: He was a great Conqueror, but
　　unfortunate in his Friends. –
Oroonoko. His Friends were Christians?
Blandford. No.
Oroonoko. No! that's strange.
Governor. And murder'd by 'em.
Oroonoko. I wou'd be *Cæsar* there. Yet I will live.

---

[29] Southerne improves the connection between Oroonoko and Julius Caesar, who was
　　similarly captured at sea by pirates. As soon as he was ransomed, however, he pursued
　　his former captors and executed them. See Suetonius, *Caesar* 4, 74, and Plutarch, *Cæsar*,
　　1.3–2.4).

Blandford. Live to be happier.

Oroonoko. Do what you will with me.

Blandford. I'll wait upon you, attend, and serve   *Exit with* Oroonoko.
you.

Lucy. Well, if the Captain had brought this Prince's Countrey along with him, and wou'd make me Queen of it, I wou'd not have him, after doing so base a thing.

Welldon. He's a man to thrive in the world, Sister: He'll make you the better Jointure.

Lucy. Hang him, nothing can prosper with him.

Stanmore. Enquire into the great Estates, and you will find most of 'em depend upon the same Title of Honesty: The men who raise 'em first are much of the Captain's Principles.

Welldon. Ay, ay, as you say, let him be damn'd for the good of his Family. Come, Sister, we are invited to dinner.

Governor. *Stanmore*, You dine with me.   *Exeunt Omnes.*

ACT II. SCENE I. *Widow* Lackitt'*s House.*

Widow Lackitt, Welldon.

Welldon. This is so great a Favour, I don't know how to receive it.

Widow. O dear Sir! you know how to receive and how to return a Favour, as well as any body, I don't doubt it: 'Tis not the first you have had from our Sex, I suppose.

Welldon. But this is so unexpected.

Widow. Lord, how can you say so, Mr. *Welldon?* I won't believe you. Don't I know you handsome Gentlemen expect every thing that a Woman can do for you? And by my troth you're in the right on't: I think one can't too much for a Handsome Gentleman; and so you shall find it.

Welldon. I shall never have such an Offer again, that's certain: What shall I do? I am mightily divided. –   *Pretending a*

Widow. Divided! O dear, I hope not so, Sir,   *concern.*
If I marry, truly I expect to have you to my self.

Welldon. There's no danger of that, Mrs. *Lackitt.* I am divided in my thoughts. My Father upon his Death bed oblig'd me to see my Sister dispos'd of, before I married my self. 'Tis that sticks upon me. They say indeed Promises are to be broken or kept; and I know 'tis a foolish thing to be tied to a Promise; but I can't help it: I don't know how to get rid of it.

Widow. Is that all?

Welldon. All in all to me. The Commands of a dying Father, you know, ought to be obey'd.

Widow. And so they may.

Welldon. Impossible, to do me any good.

Widow. They shan't be your hindrance. You wou'd have a Husband for your Sister, you say: He must be very well to pass too in the world, I suppose?

Welldon. I wou'd not throw her away.

Widow. Then marry her out of hand to the Sea-Captain you were speaking of.

Welldon. I was thinking of him, but 'tis to no purpose: She hates him.

Widow. Does she hate him? Nay, 'tis no matter, an Impudent Rascal as he is, I wou'd not advise her to marry him.

Welldon. Can you think of no body else?

Widow. Let me see.

Welldon. Ay, pray do: I shou'd be loth to part with my good fortune in you for so small a matter as a Sister: But you find how it is with me.

Widow. Well remembred, I'faith: Well, if I thought you wou'd like of it, I have a Husband for her: What do you think of my Son?

Welldon. You don't think of it your self.

Widow. I protest but I do: I am in earnest, if you are. He shall marry her within this half hour, if you'll give your consent to it.

Welldon. I give my consent! I'll answer for my Sister, she shall have him: You may be sure I shall be glad to get over the difficulty.

Widow. No more to be said then, that difficulty is over. But I vow and swear you frightned me, Mr. *Welldon.* If I had not had a Son now for your Sister, what must I have done, do you think? Were not you an ill natur'd thing to boggle° at a Promise? I cou'd break twenty for you.

Welldon. I am the more oblig'd to you: But this Son will save all.

Widow. He's in the house; I'll go and bring him my self.   *Going.*
You wou'd do well to break the business to your. Sister: She's within, I'll send her to you. –   *Going again, comes back.*

Welldon. Pray do.

Widow. But d'you hear? Perhaps she may stand upon her Maidenly Behaviour, and blush, and play the fool, and delay: But don't be answer'd so: What! she is not a Girl at these years: Shew your Authority, and tell

---

boggle: take fright at

her roundly, she must be married immediately. I'll manage my Son, I
warrant you. – *Goes out in haste.*

Welldon. The Widow's in haste, I see: I thought I had laid a rub in the
road, about my Sister: But she has stept over that. She's making way for
her self as fast as she can; but little thinks where she is going: I cou'd tell
her she is going to play the fool: But people don't love to hear of their
faults: Besides, that is not my business at present.

So, Sister, I have a Husband for you. – *Enter Lucy.*

Lucy. With all my heart: I don't know what Confinement Marriage may
be to the Men, but I'm sure the Women have no liberty without it. I am
for any thing that will deliver me from the care of a Reputation, which
I begin to find impossible to preserve.

Welldon. I'll ease you of that care: You must be married immediately.

Lucy. The sooner the better; for I am quite tir'd of setting up for a Husband.
The Widow's foolish Son is the man, I suppose.

Welldon. I consider'd your Constitution, Sister; and finding you wou'd have
occasion for a Fool, I have provided accordingly.

Lucy. I don't know what occasion I may have for a Fool when I'm married:
But I find none but Fools have occasion to marry.

Welldon. Since he is to be a Fool then, I thought it better for you to have
one of his Mother's making than your own; 'twill save you the trouble.

Lucy. I thank you; you take a great deal of pains for me: But, pray tell me,
what are you doing for your self all this while?

Welldon. You were never true to your own secrets, and therefore I won't
trust you with mine. Only remember this, I am your elder Sister, and
consequently laying my Breeches aside, have as much occasion for a
Husband as you can have. I have a Man in my eye, be satisfied.

Enter Widow Lackitt, *with her Son* Daniel.

Widow. Come, *Daniel*, hold up thy head, Child: Look like a Man: You
must not take it as you have done. Gad's my life! there's nothing to be
done with twirling your Hat, Man.

Daniel. Why, Mother, what's to be done then?

Widow. Why look me in the face, and mind what I say to you!

Daniel. Marry, who's the fool then? what shall I get by minding what you
say to me?

Widow. Mrs. *Lucy*, the Boy is bashful, don't discourage him: Pray come a
little forward, and let him salute you. *Going between*
Lucy and Daniel.

Lucy. A fine Husband I am to have truly. *To* Welldon.

Widow. Come, *Daniel*, you must be acquainted with this Gentlewoman.

Daniel. Nay, I'm not proud, that is not my fault: I am presently acquainted when I know the Company; but this Gentlewoman is a stranger to me.

Widow. She is your Mistress; I have spoke a good word for you; make her a Bow, and go and kiss her.

Daniel. Kiss her! Have a care what you say; I warrant she scorns your words. Such Fine Folk are not us'd to be slopt and kiss'd. Do you think I don't know that, Mother?

Widow. Try her, try her, Man.   Daniel *bows, she thrust*
Why that's well done; go nearer her.   *him forward.*

Daniel. Is the Devil in the Woman? Why so I can go nearer her, if you would let a body alone.   *To his Mother.*
Cry you mercy, for sooth; my Mother is always shaming one before company: She wou'd have me as unmannerly as her self, and offer to kiss you.   *To* Lucy.

Welldon. Why, won't you kiss her?

Daniel. Why, pray, may I?

Welldon. Kiss her, Kiss her, Man.

Daniel. Marry, and I will. *Kisses her.* Gadsooks! she kisses rarely! An' please you, Mistress, and seeing my Mother will have it so, I don't much care if I kiss you again, for sooth.   *Kisses her again.*

Lucy. Well, how do you like me now?

Daniel. Like you! marry, I don't know. You have bewitch'd me, I think: I was never so in my born days before.

Widow. You must marry this Fine Woman, *Daniel.*

Daniel. Hey day! marry her! I was never married in all my life. What must I do with her then, Mother?

Widow. You must live with her, eat and drink with her, go to bed with her, and sleep with her.

Daniel. Nay, marry, if I must go to bed with her, I shall never sleep, that's certain: She'll break me of my rest, quite and clean, I tell you before hand. As for eating and drinking with her, why I have a good stomach, and can play my part in any company. But how do you think I can go to bed to a Woman I don't know?

Welldon. You shall know her better.

Daniel. Say you so, Sir?

Welldon. Kiss her again.   Daniel *Kisses* Lucy.

Daniel. Nay, kissing I find will make us presently acquainted. We'll steal into a Corner to practise a little, and then I shall be able to do any thing.

Welldon. The Young Man mends apace.

Widow. Pray don't baulk him.

Daniel. Mother, Mother, if you'll stay in the room by me, and promise not
to leave me, I don't care for once if I venture to go to bed with her.

Widow. There's a good Child; go in and put on thy best Cloaths; pluck up
a spirit; I'll stay in the room by thee. She won't hurt thee, I warrant thee.

Daniel. Nay, as to that matter, I'm not afraid of her: I'll give her as
good as she brings: I have a *Rowland* for her *Oliver*,[30] and so you may
tell her.   *Exit.*

Widow. Mrs *Lucy*, we shan't stay for you: You are in a readiness, I suppose.

Welldon. She's always ready to do what I wou'd have her, I must say that
for my Sister.

Widow. 'T will be her own another day. Mr. *Welldon*, we'll marry 'em out
of hand, and then –

Welldon. And then, Mrs. *Lackitt*, look to your self. –   *Exeunt.*

SCENE II.

Oroonoko *and* Blandford.

Oroonoko. You grant I have good reason to suspect
   All the professions you can make to me.

Blandford. Indeed you have.

Oroonoko. The Dog that sold me did profess as much
   As you can do. – But yet I know not why, –
   Whether it is because I'm fall'n so low,
   And have no more to fear. – That is not it:
   I am a Slave no longer than I please.
   'Tis something nobler. – Being just my self,
   I am inclining to think others so:
   'Tis that prevails upon me to believe you.

Blandford. You may believe me.

Oroonoko. I do believe you.
   From what I know of you, you are no Fool:
   Fools only are the Knaves, and live by Tricks.
   Wise men may thrive without 'em, and be honest.

Blandford. They won't all take your counsel. –   *Aside.*

Oroonoko. You know my Story, and you say you are
   A Friend to my Misfortunes: That's a name
   Will teach you what you owe your self and me.

---

[30] Give as good as one gets. Roland and Oliver were heroes of *The Song of Roland*.

Blandford. I'll study to deserve to be your Friend.
When once our Noble Governor arrives,
With him you will not need my Interest:
He is too generous not to feel your wrongs.
But be assur'd I will employ my pow'r,
And find the means to send you home again.

Oroonoko. I thank you, Sir. – My honest, wretched Friends!
Their Chains are heavy: They have hardly found   *Sighing.*
So kind a Master. May I ask you, Sir,
What is become of 'em? Perhaps I shou'd not.
You will forgive a Stranger.

Blandford. I'll enquire and use my best endeavours, where they are,
To have 'em gently us'd.

Oroonoko. Once more I thank you.
You offer every Cordial that can keep
My Hopes alive, to wait a better day.
What Friendly Care can do, you have apply'd.
But, Oh! I have a Grief admits no Cure.

Blandford. You do not know, Sir, –

Oroonoko. Can you raise the dead?
Pursue and overtake the Wings of Time?
And bring about again the Hours, the Days,
The Years that made me happy.

Blandford. That is not to be done.

Oroonoko. No, there is nothing to be done for me.   *Kneeling and*
Thou God ador'd! thou ever-glorious Sun!   *kissing the Earth.*
If she be yet on Earth, send me a Beam
Of thy All-seeing Power to light me to her.
Or if thy Sister Goddess has preferr'd
Her Beauty to the skies to be a Star;
O tell me where she shines, that I may stand
Whole Nights, and gaze upon her.

Blandford. I am rude, and interrupt you.

Oroonoko. I am troublesome:
But pray give me your Pardon.   My swoll'n Heart
Bursts out its passage, and I must complain.
O! can you think of nothing dearer to me?
Dearer than Liberty, my Countrey, Friends,
Much dearer, than my Life? that I have lost.
The tend' rest, best belov'd, and loving Wife.

Blandford. Alas! I pity you.

Oroonoko. Do, pity me:
   Pity's a-kin to Love; and every thought
   Of that soft kind is welcome to my Soul.
   I wou'd be pity'd here.

Blandford. I dare not ask more than you please to tell me: but if you
   Think it convenient to let me know
   Your Story, I dare promise you to bear
   A part in your Distress, is not assist you.

Oroonoko. Thou honest-hearted man! I wanted such,
   Just such a Friend as thou art, that would sit
   Still as the night, and let me talk whole days
   Of my *Imoinda.* O! I'll tell thee all
   From first to last; and pray observe me well.

Blandford. I will most heedfully.

Oroonoko. There was a Stranger in my Father's Court,
   Valu'd and honour'd much: He was a White,
   The first I ever saw of your Complexion:
   He chang'd his gods for ours, and so grew great;
   Of many Virtues, and so fam'd in Arms,
   He still commanded all my Father's Wars.
   I was bred under him. One Fatal Day,
   The Armies joining, he before me stept,
   Receiving in his breast a Poyson'd Dart
   Levell'd at me; He dy'd within my Arms.
   I've tir'd you already.

Blandford. Pray go on.

Oroonoko. He left an only Daughter, whom he brought
   An Infant to *Angola.*   When I came
   Back to the Court, a happy Conqueror;
   Humanity oblig'd me to condole
   With this sad Virgin for a Father's Loss,
   Lost for my safety.   I presented her
   With all the Slaves of Battel to attone
   Her Father's Ghost.   But when I saw her Face,
   And heard her speak, I offer'd up my self
   To be the Sacrifice.   She bow'd and blush'd;
   I wonder'd and ador'd.   The Sacred Pow'r
   That had subdu'd me, then inspir'd my Tongue,
   Inclin'd her Heart; and all our Talk was Love.

Blandford. Then you were happy.

Oroonoko. O! I was too happy.

    I marry'd her: And though my Countrey's Custom

    Indulg'd the Privilege of many Wives,

    I swore my self never to know but her.

    She grew with Child, and I grew happier still.

    O my *Imoinda!* but it cou'd not last.

    Her fatal Beauty reach'd my Father's[31] Ears:

    He sent for her to Court, where, cursed Court!

    No Woman comes, but for his Amorous Use.

    He raging to possess her, she was forc'd

    To own her self my Wife.   The furious King

    Started at Incest: But grown desperate,

    Not daring to enjoy what he desir'd,

    In mad Revenge, which I cou'd never learn,

    He Poyson'd her, or sent her far, far off,

    Far from my hopes ever to see her more.

Blandford. Most barbarous of Fathers! the sad Tale

    Has struck me dumb with wonder.

Oroonoko. I have done.

    I'le trouble you no farther: now and then,

    A Sigh will have its way; that shall be all.

Enter Stanmore.

Stanmore. Blandford, the Lieutenant Governour is gone to your Plantation. He desires you wou'd bring the Royal Slave with you. The sight of his fair Mistriss, he says, is an Entertainment for a Prince; he wou'd have his opinion of her.

Oroonoko. Is he a Lover?

Blandford. So he says himself: he flatters a beautifull Slave, that I have, and calls her Mistress.

Oroonoko. Must he then flatter her to call her Mistriss?

    I pity the proud Man, who thinks himself

    Above being in love: what, tho' she be a Slave,

    She may deserve him.

Blandford. You shall judge of that, when you see her, Sir.

Oroonoko. I go with you. Exeunt.

---

[31] Rather than grandfather, as in Behn. Sexual rivalry between fathers and sons was common in Restoration drama (e.g., in Dryden's *The Assignation* [1672] and *Aureng-Zebe* [1675]).

SCENE III. *A Plantation.*

Lieutenant Governour following Imoinda.

Governour. I have disturb'd you, I confess my fault,
  My fair *Clemene*, but begin again,
  And I will listen to your mournfull Song,
  Sweet as the soft complaining Nightingales:
  While every Note calls out my trembling Soul,
  And leaves me silent, as the Midnight Groves,
  Only to shelter you, sing, sing agen,
  And let me wonder at the many ways
  You have to ravish me.
Imoinda. O! I can weep
  Enough for you, and me, if that will please you.
Governour. You must not weep: I come to dry your Tears,
  And raise you from your Sorrow. Look upon me:
  Look with the Eyes of kind indulging Love,
  That I may have full cause for what I say:
  I come to offer you your liberty,
  And be my self the Slave. You turn away.   *Following her.*
  But every thing becomes you. I may take
  This pretty hand: I know your Modesty
  Wou'd draw it back: but you wou'd take it ill;
  If I shou'd let it go, I know you wou'd.
  You shall be gently forc'd to please your self;
  That you will thank me for.   *She struggles, and gets her hand*
                                from him, then he offers to kiss her.
  Nay if you struggle with me, I must take. –
Imoinda. You may, my life, that I can part with freely.   *Exit.*
        Enter Blandford, Stanmore, Oroonoko *to him.*
Blandford. So, Governour, we don't disturb you, I hope: your Mistriss
  has left you: you were making Love, she's thankfull for the Honour, I
  suppose.
Governour. Quite insensible to all I say, and do:
  When I speak to her, she sighs, or weeps,
  But never answers me as I wou'd have her.
Stanmore. There's something nearer than her Slavery, that touches her.
Blandford. What do her fellow Slaves say of her? cann't they find the
  cause?

Governour. Some of 'em, who pretend to be wiser than the rest, and hate
    her, I suppose, for being us'd better than they are, will needs have it that
    she's with Child.

Blandford. Poor wretch! if it be so, I pity her:
    She has lost a husband, that perhaps was dear
    To her; and then you cannot-blame her.

Oroonoko. If it be so, indeed you cannot blame her.   *Sighing.*

Governour. No, no, it is not so: if it be so,
    If still must love her: and desiring still,
    If must enjoy her.

Blandford. Try what you can do with fair means, and wellcome.

Governour. I'll give you ten Slaves, for her.

Blandford. You know she is our Lord Governour's: but if I could Dispose
    of her, I wou'd not now, especially to you.

Governour. Why not to me?

Blandford. I mean against her Will.   You are in love with her.
    And we all know what your desires wou'd have:
    Love stops at nothing but possession.
    Were she within your pow'r, you do not know
    How soon you wou'd be tempted to forget
    The Nature of the Deed, and, may be, act
    A violence, you after wou'd repent.

Oroonoko. 'Tis Godlike in you to protect the weak.

Governour. Fye, fye, I wou'd not force her. Tho' she be
    A Slave, her Mind is free, and shou'd consent.

Oroonoko. Such Honour will engage her to consent:
    And then, if you'r in love, she's worth the having.
    Shall we not see this wonder?

Governour. Have a care;
    You have a Heart, and she has conquering Eyes.

Oroonoko. I have a Heart: but if it cou'd be false
    To my first Vows, ever to love agen,
    These honest Hands shou'd tear it from my Breast,
    And throw the Traytor from me.   O! *Imoinda!*
    Living or dead, I can be only thine.

Blandford. Imoinda was his Wife: She's either dead,
    Or living dead to him: forc't from his Arms
    By an inhuman Father.   Another time
    I'le tell you all.   *To* Governour *and* Stanmore.

Stanmore. Hark! the Slaves have done their work;
  And now begins their Evening merriment.
Blandford. The Men are all in love with fair *Clemene*
  As much as you are: and the Women hate her,
  From an instinct of natural jealousie.
  They sing, and dance, and try their little tricks
  To entertain her, and divert her sadness.
  May be she is among 'em: shall we see?   *Exeunt.*
                    The Scene drawn shews the Slaves, Men, Women, and
                    Children upon the Ground, some rise and dance, others
                                        sing the following Songs.

A SONG. By an unknown hand.

Sett by Mr. *Courtevill*,[32] and sung by the Boy to *Miss Cross*.[33]

I.

A Lass there lives upon the Green,
Cou'd I her Picture draw;
A brighter Nymph was never seen,
That looks, and reigns a little Queen,
And keeps the Swains in awe.

II.

Her Eyes are Cupid's *Darts, and Wings,*
Her Eyebrows are his Bow;
Her Silken Hair the Silver Strings,
Which sure and swift destruction brings
To all the Vale below.

III.

If Pastorella's *dawning Light*
Can warm, and wound us so:
Her Noon will shine so piercing bright,
Each glancing beam will kill outright,
And every Swain subdue.

[32] Raphael Courteville (d. c. 1735), an organist, composer, and singer.
[33] As Jordan and Love suggest, this was probably Jemmy Bowen (b. c. 1685), the leading boy
  singer of the 1690s. In two other plays of 1696 he sang with Letitia Cross (c. 1677–1737),
  an actress, dancer, and leading girl singer of the time.

A SONG, by Mr. *Cheek*.[34]

Sett by Mr. *Courtevill*, and sung by Mr. *Leveridge*.[35]

I.

Bright Cynthia's *Pow'r divinely great,*
What Heart is not obeying?
A thousand Cupids *on her wait,*
And in her Eyes are playing.

II.

She seems the Queen of Love to reign,
For She alone dispences
Such Sweets, as best can entertain
The Gust° of all the Senses.

III.

Her Face a charming prospect brings;
Her Breath gives balmy Blisses:
I hear an Angel, when she sings,
And taste of Heaven in Kisses.

IV.

Four Senses thus she feasts with joy,
From Nature's richest Treasure:
Let me the other Sense employ,
And I shall dye with pleasure.

During the Entertainment, the Governour, Blandford,
Stanmore, Oroonoko, *enter as Spectators; that ended,*
Captain Driver, Jack Stanmore, *and several Planters.*
enter with their Swords drawn.   *A Bell rings.*

Captain. Where are you, Governour? make what hast you can
   To save your self, and the whole Colony.
   I bid 'em ring the Bell.
Governour. What's the matter?

Gust: taste, relish

[34] Thomas Cheek, who supplied songs and a prologue for several plays, including Southerne's *The Wives Excuse.*
[35] Richard Leveridge (c. 1670–1758), a bass singer and song composer.

Jack Stanmore. The *Indians* are come down upon us:
   They have plunder'd some of the Plantations already,
   And are marching this way, as fast as they can.
Governour. What can we do against 'em?
Blandford. We shall be able to make a stand,
   Till more Planters come in to us.
Jack Stanmore. There are a great many more without,
   If you wou'd show your self, and put us in order.
Governour. There's no danger of the White Slaves,[36] they'll not stir:
   Blandford, and *Stanmore* come you along with me:
   Some of you stay here to look after the Black-Slaves.

> *All go out but the Captain, and 6 Planters, who all at*
> *once seize* Oroonoko.

1st Planter. Ay, ay, let us alone.
Captain. In the first place we secure you, Sir, as an Enemy to the
   Government.
Oroonoko. Are you there, Sir, you are my constant Friend.
1st Planter. You will be able to do a great deal of mischief.
Captain. But we shall prevent you: bring the Irons hither. He has the
   malice of a Slave in him, and wou'd be glad to be cutting his Masters
   Throats, I know him. Chain his hands and feet, that he may not run
   over to 'em: if they have him, they shall carry him on their backs, that I
   can tell 'em.

> *As they are chaining him,* Blandford *enters, runs to 'em.*

Blandford. What are you doing there?
Captain. Securing the main chance: this is a bosom enemy.
Blandford. Away you Brutes: I'll answer with my life for his behaviour; so
   tell the Governour.
Captain ⎫Well, Sir, so we will. {   *Exeunt Captain and*
Planter. ⎭   *Planters.*
Oroonoko. Give me a Sword and I'll deserve your trust.

> *A Party of* Indians *enter, hurrying* Imoinda *among the Slaves;*
> *another Party of* Indians *sustains 'em retreating, follow'd*
> *at a distance by the Governour with the Planters:*
> Blandford, Oroonoko *joyn 'em.*

---

[36] Criminals and political prisoners were sent to the West Indies as slaves during Cromwell's
protectorate and during the Restoration. Indentured white servants were also commonly
called "white slaves"; see *Oxford History of the British Empire*, I, 230.

Blandford. Hell, and the Devil! they drive away our Slaves before our Faces.
  Governour, can you stand tamely by, and suffer this? *Clemene*, Sir, your
  Mistriss is among 'em.
Governour. We throw our selves away, in the attempt to rescue 'em.
Oroonoko. A Lover cannot fall more glorious,
  Than in the cause of Love. He that deserves
  His Mistress's favour wonnot stay behind:
  I'le lead you on, be bold, and follow me.
          Oroonoko *at the head of the Planters, falls upon the*
          Indians *with a great shout, beats 'em off.*

        Imoinda *enters.*

Imoinda. I'm tost about by my tempestuous Fate,
  And no where must have rest; *Indians*, or *English!*
  Whoever has me, I am still a Slave.
  No matter whose I am, since I am no more,
  My Royal Masters; Since I'm his no more.
  O I was happy! nay, I will be happy,
  In the dear thought that I am still his Wife,
  Tho' far divided from him.   *Draws off to a corner of the Stage.*

After a shout, enter the Governour with Oroonoko,
  Blandford, Stanmore, *and the Planters.*

Governour. Thou glorious Man! thou something greater sure
  Than *Cæsar* ever was! that single Arm
  Has sav'd us all: accept our general thanks.
All bow to Oroonoko.
  And what we can do more to recompense
  Such noble services, you shall command.
  Clemene too shall thank you, – she is safe –
  Look up, and bless your brave deliverer.
        Brings Clemene *forward, looking down on the ground.*
Oroonoko. Bless me indeed!
Blandford. You start!
Oroonoko. O all you Gods!
  Who govern this great World, and bring about
  Things strange, and unexpected, can it be?
Governour. What is't you stare at so?

Oroonoko. Answer me some of you, you who have power,
And have your Senses free: or are you all
Struck thro' with wonder too?   *Looking still fixt on her.*
Blandford. What wou'd you know?
Oroonoko. My Soul steals from my Body thro' my Eyes:
All that is left of life, I'll gaze away.
And die upon the Pleasure.
Governour. This is strange!
Oroonoko. If you but mock me with her Image here:[37]
If she be not *Imoinda* –   *She looks upon him, and falls into*
Ha! she faints!   *a Swoon, he runs to her.*
Nay, then it must be she: it is *Imoinda:*
My Heart confesses her, and leaps for joy,
To welcome her to her own Empire here.
I feel her all, in every part of me.
O! let me press her in my eager Arms,
Wake her to life, and with this kindling Kiss
Give back that Soul, she only sent to me.   *Kisses her.*
Governour. I am amaz'd!
Blandford. I am as much as you.
Oroonoko. Imoinda! O! thy *Oroonoko* calls.

Imoinda *coming to life.*

Imoinda. My *Oroonoko*! O! I can't believe
What any Man can say.   But if I am
To be deceiv'd, there's something in that Name,
That Voice, that Face,   *Staring on him.*
O! if I know my self, I cannot be mistaken.

Runs, and embraces Oroonoko.

Oroonoko. Never here;
You cannot be mistaken: I am yours,
Your *Oroonoko*, all that you wou'd have,
Your tender loving Husband.
Imoinda. All indeed
That I wou'd have: my Husband! then I am
Alive, and waking to the Joys I feel:

---

[37] With her characteristic mingling of the heroic and the banal, Behn has Oroonoko find
Imoinda as she is chasing a pet dog. Here, the lovers' meeting follows Oroonoko's
greatest moment of heroism.

They were so great, I cou'd not think 'em true.
But I believe all that you say to me:
For Truth it self, and everlasting Love
Grows in this Breast, and pleasure in these arms.

Oroonoko. Take, take me all: enquire into my heart,
(You know the way to every secret there)
My Heart, the sacred treasury of Love:
And if, in absence, I have mis-employ'd
A Mite° from the rich store: if I have spent
A Wish, a Sigh, but what I sent to you:
May I be curst to wish, and sigh in vain,
And you not pity me.

Imoinda. O! I believe,
And know you by my self.   If these sad Eyes,
Since last we parted, have beheld the Face
Of any Comfort; or once wish'd to see
The light of any other Heaven, but you:
May I be struck this moment blind, and lose
Your blessed sight, never to find you more.

Oroonoko. Imoinda! O! this separation
Has made you dearer, if it can be so,
Than you were ever to me.   You appear
Like a kind Star to my benighted Steps,
To guide me on my way to happiness:
I cannot miss it now.   Governour, Friend,
You think me mad: but let me bless you all,
Who, any way, have been the Instruments
Of finding her again.   *Imoinda*'s found!
And every thing, that I wou'd have in her.

Embracing her in the most passionate Fondness.

Stanmore. Where's your Mistriss now, Governour?
Governour. Why, where most Men's Mistrisses are forc'd to be sometimes,
With her Husband, it seems: but I won't lose her so.   *Aside.*
Stanmore. He has fought lustily for her, and deserves her, I'll say that for
him.
Blandford. Sir we congratulate your happiness: I do most heartily.
Governour. And all of us: but how it comes to pass –

Mite: a coin of the least value

Oroonoko. That will require more precious time than I can spare you now.
   I have a thousand things to ask of her,
   And she as many more to know of me.
   But you have made me happier, I confess,
   Acknowledge it, much happier, than I
   Have words, or pow'r to tell you.   Captain, you,
   Ev'n you, who most have wrong'd me, I forgive.
   I won't say you have betray'd me now:
   I'll think you but the minister of Fate,
   To bring me to my lov'd *Imoinda* here.
Imoinda. How, how shall I receive you? how be worthy
   Of such Endearments, all this tenderness?
   These are the Transports of Prosperity,
   When Fortune smiles upon us.
Oroonoko. Let the Fools, who follow Fortune, live upon her smiles.
   All our Prosperity is plac'd in Love.
   We have enough of that to make us happy.
   This little spot of Earth you stand upon,
   Is more to me, than the extended Plains
   Of my great Father's Kingdom. Here I reign
   In full delights, in Joys to Pow'r unknown;
   Your Love my Empire, and your Heart my Throne.   *Exeunt.*

ACT III.

SCENE I.

Aboan *with several Slaves,* Hottman.

Hottman. What! to be Slaves to Cowards! Slaves to Rogues!
   Who cann't defend themselves!
Aboan. Who is this Fellow? he talks as if he were acquainted With our
   design: is he one of us? *Aside to his own Gang.*
Slave. Not yet: but he will be glad to make one, I believe.
Aboan. He makes a mighty noise.
Hottman. Go, sneak in Corners; whisper out your Griefs,
   For fear your Masters hear you: cringe and crouch
   Under the bloody whip, like beaten Currs,
   That lick their Wounds, and know no other cure.

All, wretches all! you feel their cruelty,
As much as I can feel, but dare not groan.
For my part, while I have a Life and Tongue,
I'll curse the Authors of my Slavery.
Aboan. Have you been long a Slave?
Hottman. Yes, many years.
Aboan. And do you only curse?
Hottman. Curse? only curse? I cannot conjure,
  To raise the Spirits up of other Men:
  I am but one.   O! for a Soul of fire,
  To warm, and animate our common Cause,
  And make a body of us: then I wou'd
  Do something more than curse.
Aboan. That body set on Foot, you wou'd be one,
  A limb, to lend it motion.
Hottman. I wou'd be the Heart of it: the Head, the Hand, and Heart.
  Wou'd I cou'd see the day.
Aboan. You will do all your self.
Hottman. I wou'd do more, than I shall speak: but I may find a time.
Aboan. The time may come to you; be ready for't.
  Methinks he talks too much: I'll know him more,
  Before I trust him farther.
Slave. If he dares half what he says, he'll be of use to us.

Enter Blandford to 'em.

Blandford. If there be any one among you here,
  That did belong to *Oroonoko*, speak,
  I come to him.
Aboan. I did belong to him: *Aboan*, my Name.
Blandford. You are the Man I want; pray, come with me.   *Exeunt.*

SCENE II.

Oroonoko *and* Imoinda.

Oroonoko. I do not blame my Father for his Love:
  (Tho' that had been enough to ruine me)
  'Twas Nature's fault, that made you like the Sun,
  The reasonable worship of Mankind:
  He cou'd not help his Adoration.

Age had not lock'd his Sences up so close,
But he had Eyes, that open'd to his Soul,
And took your Beauties in: he felt your pow'r,
And therefore I forgive his loving you.
But when I think on his Barbarity,
That cou'd expose you to so many Wrongs;
Driving you out to wretched Slavery,
Only for being mine; then I confess,
I wish I cou'd forget the Name of Son,
That I might curse the Tyrant.

Imoinda. I will bless him, for I have found you here: Heav'n only knows.
What is reserv'd for us: but if we ghess
The future by the past, our Fortune must.
Be wonderfull, above the common Size,
Of good or ill; it must be in extreams:
Extreamly happy, or extreamly wretched.

Oroonoko. 'Tis in our pow'r to make it happy now.

Imoinda. But not to keep it so.   *Enter* Blandford *and* Aboan.

Blandford. My Royal Lord! I have a Present for you.

Oroonoko. Aboan!

Aboan. Your lowest Slave.

Oroonoko. My try'd and valu'd Friend.
This worthy Man always prevents my wants:
I only wish'd, and he has brought thee to me.
Thou art surpriz'd: carry thy duty there;

                              Aboan *goes to* Imoinda
                              and falls at her Feet.

While I acknowledge mine, how shall I thank you.

Blandford. Believe me honest to your interest,
And I am more than paid.   I have secur'd,
That all your Followers shall be gently us'd.
This Gentleman, your chiefest Favourite,
Shall wait upon your Person, while you stay among us.

Oroonoko. I owe every thing to you.

Blandford. You must not think you are in Slavery.

Oroonoko. I do not find I am.

Blandford. Kind Heaven has miraculously sent
Those Comforts, that may teach you to expect
Its farther care, in your deliverance.

Oroonoko. I sometimes think my self, Heav'n is concern'd
   For my deliverance.
Blandford. It will be soon:
   You may expect it.   Pray, in the mean time,
   Appear as chearfull as you can among us.
   You have some Enemies, that represent
   You dangerous, and wou'd be glad to find
   A Reason, in your discontent, to fear:
   They watch your looks.   But there are honest Men,
   Who are your Friends: You are secure in them.
Oroonoko. I thank you for your caution.
Blandford. I will leave you.
   And be assur'd, I wish your liberty.   *Exit.*
Aboan. He speaks you very fair.
Oroonoko. He means me fair.
Aboan. If he should not, my Lord.
Oroonoko. If, he should not:
   I'll not suspect his Truth: but if I did,
   What shall I get by doubting?
Aboan. You secure, not to be disappointed: but besides,
   There's this advantage in suspecting him:
   When you put off the hopes of other men,
   You will rely upon your God-like self:
   And then you may be sure of liberty.
Oroonoko. Be sure of liberty! what dost thou mean;
   Advising to rely upon my self?
   I think I may be sure on't: we must, wait:
   'Tis worth a little patience.   *Turning to* Imoinda
Aboan. O my Lord!
Oroonoko. What dost thou drive at?
Aboan. Sir, another time,
   You wou'd have found it sooner: but I see
   Love has your Heart, and takes up all your thoughts.
Oroonoko. And canst thou blame me?
Aboan. Sir, I must not blame you.
   But as our fortune stands, there is a Passion
   (Your pardon Royal Mistriss, I must speak:)
   That wou'd become you better than your Love:
   A brave resentment; which inspir'd by you,
   Might kindle, and diffuse a generous rage

Among the Slaves, to rouze and shake our Chains,
And struggle to be free.

Oroonoko. How can we help our selves?

Aboan. I knew you, when you wou'd have found a way.
How, help our selves! the very *Indians* teach us:
We need but to attempt our Liberty,
And we may carry it.   We have Hands sufficient,
Double the number of our Masters force,
Ready to be employ'd.   What hinders us
To set 'em then at work? we want but you,
To head our enterprize, and bid us strike.

Oroonoko. What wou'd you do?

Aboan. Cut our Oppressors Throats.

Oroonoko. And you wou'd have me joyn in your design of Murder?

Aboan. It deserves a better Name:
But be it what it will, 'tis justified
By self-defence, and natural liberty.

Oroonoko. I'll hear no more on't.

Aboan. I am sorry for't.

Oroonoko. Nor shall you think of it.

Aboan. Not think of it!

Oroonoko. No, I command you not.

Aboan. Remember Sir,
You are a Slave your self, and to command,
Is now anothers right. Not think of it!
Since the first moment they put on my Chains,
I've thought of nothing but the weight of 'em,
And how to throw 'em off: can yours sit easie?

Oroonoko. I have a sense of my condition,
As painfull, and as quick, as yours can be.
I feel for my *Imoinda* and my self;
Imoinda much the tenderest part of me.
But though I languish for my liberty,
I wou'd not buy it at the Christian Price
Of black Ingratitude: they shannot say,
That we deserv'd our Fortune by our Crimes.
Murder the Innocent!

Aboan. The Innocent!

Oroonoko. These men are so, whom you wou'd rise against:
If we are Slaves, they did not make us Slaves;

But bought us in an honest way of trade:
As we have done before 'em, bought and sold
Many a wretch, and never thought it wrong.
They paid our Price for us, and we are now
Their Property, a part of their Estate,
To manage as they please.   Mistake me not,
I do not tamely say, that we should bear
All they could lay upon us: but we find
The load so light, so little to be felt,
(Considering they have us in their power,
And may inflict what grievances they please)
We ought not to complain.

Aboan. My Royal Lord!
You do not know the heavy Grievances,
The Toyls, the Labours, weary Drudgeries,
Which they impose; Burdens, more fit for Beasts,
For senseless Beasts to bear, than thinking Men.
Then if you saw the bloody Cruelties,
They execute on every slight offence;
Nay sometimes in their proud, insulting sport:
How worse than Dogs, they lash their fellow Creatures:
Your heart wou'd bleed for 'em. O cou'd you know
How many Wretches lift their Hands and Eyes
To you, for their Relief.[38]

Oroonoko. I pity 'em,
And wish I cou'd with honesty do more.

Aboan. You must do more, and may, with honesty.
O Royal Sir, remember who you are,
A Prince, born for the good of other Men:
Whose God-like Office is to draw the Sword
Against Oppression, and set free Mankind:
And this, I'm sure, you think Oppression now.
What tho' you have not felt these miseries,
Never believe you are oblig'd to them:
They have their selfish reasons, may be, now,

---

[38] Southerne's emphasis again differs from Behn's. In Behn, Oroonoko himself denounces the cruelties of slavery, which he himself has not witnessed; here, the initially uninformed and complacent hero is instructed in the cruelties of the slave's condition by one who has experienced them. Southerne's denunciation of cruelty to slaves does not, however, necessarily imply a denunciation of slavery itself.

For using of you well: but there will come
A time, when you must have your share of 'em.
Oroonoko. You see how little cause I have to think so:
    Favour'd in my own Person, in my Friends;
    Indulg'd in all that can concern my care,
    In my *Imoinda*'s soft Society.   *Embracing her.*
Aboan. And therefore wou'd you lye contented down,
    In the forgetfulness, and arms of Love,
    To get young Princes for 'em?
Oroonoko. Say'st thou! ha!
Aboan. Princes, the Heirs of Empire, and the last
    Of your illustrious Lineage, to be born
    To pamper up their Pride, and be their Slaves?
Oroonoko. Imoinda! save me, save me from that thought.
Imoinda. There is no safety from it: I have long
    Suffer'd it with a Mother's labouring pains;
    And can no longer. Kill me, kill me now,
    While I am blest, and happy in your love;
    Rather than let me live to see you hate me:
    As you must hate me; me, the only cause;
    The Fountain of these flowing miseries:
    Dry up this Spring of Life, this pois'nous Spring,
    That swells so fast, to overwhelm us all.
Oroonoko. Shall the dear Babe, the eldest of my hopes,
    Whom I begot a Prince, be born a Slave?
    The treasure of this Temple was design'd
    T'enrich a Kingdom Fortune: shall it here
    Be seiz'd upon by vile unhallow'd hands,
    To be employ'd in uses most prophane?
Aboan. In most unworthy uses; think of that;
    And while you may, prevent it.   O my Lord!
    Rely on nothing that they say to you.
    They speak you fair, I know, and bid you wait.
    But think what 'tis to wait on promises:
    And promises of Men, who know no tye
    Upon their words, against their interest:
    And where's their interest in freeing you?
Imoinda. O! where indeed, to lose so many Slaves?
Aboan. Nay grant this Man, you think so much your Friend,
    Be honest, and intends all that he says:

He is but one; and in a Government,
Where, he confesses, you have Enemies,
That watch your looks: what looks can you put on,
To please these men, who are before resolv'd
To read 'em their own own way? alas! my Lord!
If they incline to think you dangerous,
They have their knavish Arts to make you so.
And then who knows how far their cruelty
May carry their revenge?

Imoinda. To every thing,
That does belong to you; your Friends, and me;
I shall be torn from you, forc't away,
Helpless, and miserable: shall I live
To see that day agen?

Oroonoko. That day shall never come.

Aboan. I know you are perswaded to believe
The Governour's arrival will prevent
These mischiefs, and bestow your liberty:
But who is sure of that? I rather fear
More mischiefs from his coming: he is young,
Luxurious, passionate, and amorous:
Such a Complexion, and made bold by power,
To countenance all he is prone to do;
Will know no bounds, no law against his Lusts:
If, in a fit of his Intemperance,
With a strong hand, he should resolve to seize,
And force my Royal Mistress from your Arms,
How can you help your self?

Oroonoko. Ha! thou hast rouz'd
The Lion in his den, he stalks abroad,
And the wide Forrest trembles at his roar.
I find the danger now: my Spirits start
At the alarm, and from all quarters come
To Man my Heart, the Citadel of love.
Is there a power on Earth to force you from me?
And shall I not resist it? not strike first
To keep, to save you? to prevent that curse?
This is your Cause, and shall it not prevail?
O! you were born all ways to conquer me.

Now I am fashion'd to thy purpose: speak,
What Combination, what Conspiracy,
Woud'st thou engage me in? I'le undertake
All thou woud'st have me now for liberty,
For the great Cause of Love and Liberty.

Aboan. Now, my great Master, you appear your self.
And since we have you joyn'd in our design,
It cannot fail us. I have muster'd up
The choicest Slaves, Men who are sensible
Of their condition, and seem most resolv'd:
They have their several parties.

Oroonoko. Summon 'em,
Assemble 'em: I will come forth, and shew
My self among 'em: if they are resolv'd,
I'le lead their formost resolutions.

Aboan. I have provided those will follow you.

Oroonoko. With this reserve in our proceeding still,
The means that lead us to our liberty,
Must not be bloody.

Aboan. You command in all.
We shall expect you, Sir.

Oroonoko. You shannot long.

> *Exeunt Oroonoko and Imoinda at one Door,*
> *Aboan at another.*

SCENE III.

Welldon coming in before Mrs. Lackitt.

Widow. These unmannerly *Indians* were something unseasonable, to disturb us just in the nick, Mr. *Welldon*: but I have the Parson within call still, to doe us the good turn.

Welldon. We had best stay a little I think, to see things settled agen, had not we? Marriage is a serious thing you know.

Widow. What do you talk of a serious thing, Mr. *Welldon*? I think you have sound me sufficiently serious: I have marry'd my Son to your Sister, to pleasure you: and now I come to claim your promise to me, you tell me marriage is a serious thing.

Welldon. Why, is it not?

Widow. Fidle fadle, I know what it is: 'tis not the first time I have been
marry'd, I hope: but I shall begin to think, you don't design to do fairly
by me, so I shall.

Welldon. Why indeed, Mrs *Lackitt*, I am afraid I can't do as fairly as I wou'd
by you. 'Tis what you must know, first or last; and I shou'd be the worst
man in the world to conceal it any longer; therefore I must own to you,
that I am marry'd already.

Widow. Marry'd! you don't say so I hope! how have you the Conscience
to tell me such a thing to my face! have you abus'd me then, fool'd and
cheated me? What do you take me for, Mr. *Welldon*? do you think I am
to be serv'd at this rate? but you shan't find me the silly creature, you
think me: I wou'd have you to know, I understand better things, than to
ruine my Son without a valuable consideration. If I can't have you, I can
keep my Money. Your Sister shan't have the catch of him, she expected:
I won't part with a Shilling to 'em.

Welldon. You made the match your self, you know, you can't blame
me.

Widow. Yes, yes, I can, and do blame you: you might have told me before
you were marry'd.

Welldon. I wou'd not have told you now; but you follow'd me so close, I
was forc'd to't: indeed I am marry'd in *England*; but 'tis, as if I were not;
for I have been parted from my Wife a great while: and to do reason
on both sides, we hate one another heartily. Now I did design, and will
marry you still, if you'll have a little patience.

Widow. A likely business truly.

Welldon. I have a Friend in *England* that I will write to, to poyson my Wife,
and then I can marry you with a good Conscience, if you love me, as you
say you do; you'll consent to that, I'm sure.

Widow. And will he do it, do you think?

Welldon. At the first word, or he is not the Man I take him to be.

Widow. Well, you are a dear Devil, Mr. *Welldon*: and wou'd you poyson
your Wife for me?

Welldon. I wou'd do any thing for you.

Widow. Well, I am mightily oblig'd to you. But 'twill be a great while
before you have an answer of your Letter.

Welldon. 'Twill be a great while indeed.

Widow. In the mean time, Mr. *Welldon* –

Welldon. Why in the mean time – Here's company: we'll settle that within.
I'll follow you.   *Exit* Widow.

Enter Stanmore.

Stanmore. So Sir, you carry your business swimmingly: you have stolen a
 Wedding, I hear.

Welldon. Ay, my Sister is marry'd: and I am very near being run away
 with my self.

Stanmore. The Widow will have you then.

Welldon. You come very seasonably to my rescue: *Jack Stanmore* is to be
 had, I hope.

Stanmore. At half an hours warning.

Welldon. I must advise with you.   *Exeunt.*

SCENE IV.

Oroonoko *with* Aboan, Hottman, *Slaves.*

Oroonoko. Impossible! nothing's impossible:
 We know our strength only by being try'd.
 If you object the Mountains, Rivers, Woods
 Unpassable, that lie before our March:
 Woods we can set on fire: we swim by nature:
 What can oppose us then, but we may tame?
 All things submit to vertuous industry:
 That we can carry with us, that is ours.

Slave. Great Sir, we have attended all you said,
 With silent joy and admiration:
 And, were we only Men, wou'd follow such,
 So great a Leader, thro' the untry'd World.
 But, oh! consider we have other Names,
 Husbands and Fathers, and have things more dear
 To us, than Life, our Children, and our Wives,
 Unfit for such an expedition:
 What must become of them?

Oroonoko. We wonnot wrong
 The virtue of our Women, to believe
 There is a Wife among 'em, wou'd refuse
 To share her Husband's fortune.   What is hard,
 We must make easie to 'em in our Love: while we live,
 And have our Limbs, we can take care for them;
 Therefore I still propose to lead our march

Down to the Sea, and plant a Colony:
Where, in our native innocence, we shall live
Free, and be able to defend our selves;
Till stress of weather, or some accident
Provide a Ship for us.

Aboan. An accident! the luckiest accident presents it self:
The very Ship, that brought and made us Slaves,
Swims in the River still; I see no cause
But we may seize on that.

Oroonoko. It shall be so:
There is a justice in it pleases me.
Do you agree to it?   *To the Slaves.*

Omnes. We follow you.

Oroonoko. You do not relish it.   *To* Hottman.

Hottman. I am afraid
You'll find it difficult, and dangerous.

Aboan. Are you the Man to find the danger first?
You shou'd have giv'n example.   Dangerous!
I thought you had not understood the word;
You, who wou'd be the Head, the Hand, and Heart:
Sir, I remember you, you can talk well;
I wonnot doubt but you'll maintain your word.

Oroonoko. This Fellow is not right, I'll try him further.   *To* Aboan.
The danger will be certain to us all:
And Death most certain in miscarrying.
We must expect no mercy, if we fail:
Therefore our way must be not to expect:
We'll put it out of expectation,
By Death upon the place, or Liberty.
There is no mean, but death or Liberty.
There's no Man here, I hope, but comes prepar'd
For all that can befall him.

Aboan. Death is all:
In most conditions of humanity
To be desir'd, but to be shun'd in none:
The remedy of many; wish of some;
And certain end of all.
If there be one among us, who can fear
The face of Death appearing like a Friend,
As in this cause of Honour Death must be:

How will he tremble, when he sees him drest
In the wild fury of our Enemies,
In all the terrors of their cruelty?
For now if we shou'd fall into their hands,
Cou'd they invent a thousand murd'ring ways,
By racking Torments, we shou'd feel 'em all.
Hottman. What will become of us?
Oroonoko. Observe him now.   *To* Aboan *concerning* Hottman.
   I cou'd die altogether, like a Man:
   As you, and you, and all of us may do:
   But who can promise for his bravery
   Upon the Rack? where fainting, weary life,
   Hunted thro' every Limb, is forc'd to feel
   An agonizing death of all its parts?
   Who can bear this? resolve to be empal'd?
   His Skin flead off, and roasted yet alive?
   The quivering flesh torn from his broken Bones,
   By burning Pincers? who can bear these Pains?
Hottman. They are not to be born.   *Discovering all the*
                                                confusion of fear.

Oroonoko. You see him now, this Man of mighty words!
Aboan. How his Eyes roul!
Oroonoko. He cannot hide his fear:
   I try'd him this way, and have found him out.
Aboan. I cou'd not have believ'd it. Such a Blaze,
   And not a spark of Fire!
Oroonoko. His violence,
   Made me suspect him first: now I'm convinc'd.
Aboan. What shall we do with him?
Oroonoko. He is not fit –
Aboan. Fit! hang him, he is only fit to be
   Just what he is, to live and die a Slave:
   The base Companion of his servile Fears.
Oroonoko. We are not safe with him.
Aboan. Do you think so?
Oroonoko. He'll certainly betray us.
Aboan. That he shan't:
   I can take care of that: I have a way
   To take him off his evidence:
Oroonoko. What way?

Aboan. I'll stop his mouth before you, stab him here,
    And then let him inform.   *Going to stab* Hottman,
                                             Oroonoko *holds him.*

Oroonoko. Thou art not mad?
Aboan. I wou'd secure our selves.
Oroonoko. It shannot be this way; nay cannot be:
    His Murder wou'd alarm all the rest,
    Make 'em suspect us of Barbarity,
    And, may be, fall away from our design.
    We'll not set out in Blood: we have, my Friends,
    This Night to furnish what we can provide,
    For our security, and just defence.
    If there be one among us, we suspect
    Of baseness, or vile fear, it will become
    Our common care, to have our Eyes on him:
    I wonnot name the Man.
Aboan. You ghess at him.   *To* Hottman.
Oroonoko. To morrow, early as the breaking day,
    We rendezvous behind the Citron Grove.
    That Ship secur'd, we may transport our selves
    To our respective homes: my Fathers Kingdom
    Shall open her wide arms to take you in,
    And nurse you for her own, adopt you all,
    All, who will follow me.
Omnes. All, all follow you.
Oroonoko. There I can give you all your liberty;
    Bestow its Blessings, and secure 'em yours.
    There you shall live with honour, as becomes
    My Fellow-sufferers, and worthy Friends:
    This if we do succeed: But if we fall
    In our attempt, 'tis nobler still to dye,
    Than drag the galling yoke of slavery.   *Exeunt Omnes.*

ACT IV.

SCENE I.

Welldon *and* Jack Stanmore.

Welldon. You see, honest *Jack,* I have been industrious for you: you must
take some pains now to serve your self.

Jack Stanmore. Gad, Mr. *Welldon*, I have taken a great deal of pains: And if the Widow speaks honestly, faith and troth, She'll tell you what a pains-taker I am.

Welldon. Fie, fie, not me: I am her Husband you know: She won't tell me what pains you have taken with her: Besides, she takes you for me.

Jack Stanmore. That's true: I forgot you had marry'd her. But if you knew all –

Welldon. 'Tis no matter for my knowing all: if she does –

Jack Stanmore. Ay, ay, she does know, and more than ever she knew since she was a woman, for the time; I will be bold to say: for I have done –

Welldon. The Devil take you, you'll never have done.

Jack Stanmore. As old as she is, she has a wrincle[39] behind more than she had, I believe – For I have taught her, what she never knew in her life before.

Welldon. What care I what wrincles she has? or what you have taught her? If you'll let me advise you, you may; if not, you may prate on, and ruine the whole design.

Jack Stanmore. Well, well, I have done.

Welldon. No body, but your Cozin, and you, and I, know any thing of this matter. I have marry'd Mrs. *Lackitt*; and put you to bed to her, which she knows nothing of, to serve you: in two or three days I'll bring it about so, to resign up my claim, with her consent, quietly to you.

Jack Stanmore. But how will you do it?

Welldon. That must be my business: in the mean time, if you should make any noise, 'twill come to her Ears, and be impossible to reconcile her.

Jack Stanmore. Nay, as for that, I know the way to reconcile her, I warrant you.

Welldon. But how will you get her Money? I am marry'd to her.

Jack Stanmore. That I don't know indeed.

Welldon. You must leave it to me, you find, all the pains I shall put you to, will be to be silent: you can hold your Tongue for two or three days?

Jack Stanmore. Truly, not well, in a matter of this nature: I should be very unwilling to lose the reputation of this nights work, and the pleasure of telling.

Welldon. You must mortifie that vanity a little: you will have time enough to brag, and lie of your Manhood, when you have her in a bare-fac'd condition to disprove you.

---

[39] Pun on the meaning of *wrinkle* as "trick."

Jack Stanmore. Well, I'll try what I can do: the hopes of her Money must do it.

Welldon. You'll come at night again? 'tis your own business.

Jack Stanmore. But you have the credit on't.

Welldon. 'Twill be your own another day, as the Widow says. Send your Cozin to me: I want his advise.

Jack Stanmore. I want to be recruited, I'm sure, a good Breakfast, and to Bed: She has rock'd my Cradle sufficiently.   *Exit.*

Welldon. She wou'd have a Husband; and if all be, as he says, she has no reason to complain: but there's no relying on what the Men say upon these occasions: they have the benefit of their bragging, by recommending their abilities to other Women: theirs is a trading Estate, that lives upon credit, and increases by removing it out of one Bank into another. Now poor Women have not these opportunities: we must keep our stocks dead by us, at home, to be ready for a purchase, when it comes, a Husband, let him be never so dear, and be glad of him: or venture our Fortunes abroad on such rotten security, that the principal and interest, nay very often our persons are in danger. If the Women wou'd agree (which they never will) to call home their Effects, how many proper Gentlemen wou'd (sneak into another way of living, for want of being responsible in this? then Husbands wou'd be cheaper. Here comes the Widow, she'll tell truth: she'll not bear false Witness against her own interest, I know.

Enter Widow Lackitt.

Welldon. Now, Mrs. *Lackitt.*

Widow. Well, well, *Lackitt*, or what you will now; now I am marry'd to you: I am very well pleas'd with what I have done, I assure you.

Welldon. And with what I have done too, I hope.

Widow. Ah! Mr. *Welldon*! I say nothing, but you're a dear Man, and I did not think it had been in you.

Welldon. I have more in me than you imagine.

Widow. No, no, you can't have more than I imagine: 'tis impossible to have more: you have enough for any Woman, in an honest way, that I will say for you.

Welldon. Then I find you are satisfied.

Widow. Satisfied! no indeed; I'm not to be satisfied, with you or without you: to be satisfied, is to have enough of you; now, 'tis a folly to lye: I shall never think I can have enough of you. I shall be very fond° of you:

Fond: foolishly affectionate

wou'd you have me fond of you? What do you do to me, to make me love you so well?

Welldon. Can't you tell what?

Widow. Go; there's no speaking to you: you bring all the Blood of ones body into ones face, so you do: why do you talk so?

Welldon. Why, how do I talk?

Widow. You know how: but a little colour becomes me, I believe: how do I look to day?

Welldon. O! most lovingly, most amiably.

Widow. Nay, this can't be long a secret, I find, I shall discover it by my Countenance.

Welldon. The Women will find you out, you look so cheerfully.

Widow. But do I, do I really look so cheerfully, so amiably? there's no such paint in the World as the natural glowing of a Complexion. Let 'em find me out, if they please, poor Creatures, I pity 'em: they envy me, I'm sure, and wou'd be glad to mend their looks upon the same occasion. The young jilflirting Girls, forsooth, believe nobody must have a Husband, but themselves; but I wou'd have 'em to know there are other things to be taken care of, besides their green Sickness.[40]

Welldon. Ay, sure, or the Physicians wou'd have but little practise.

Widow. Mr. *Welldon*, what must I call you. I must have somes pretty fond name or other for you: what shall I call you?

Welldon. I thought you lik'd my own name.

Widow. Yes, yes, I like it, but I must have a nick-name for you: most Women have nick-names for their Husbands –

Welldon. Cuckold.

Widow. No, no, but 'tis very pretty before company; it looks negligent, and is the fashion, you know.

Welldon. To be negligent of their Husbands, it is indeed.

Widow. Nay then, I won't be in the fashion; for I can never be negligent of dear Mr. *Welldon*: and to convince you, here's something to encourage you not to be negligent of me.

Gives him a Purse and a little Casket.

Five hundred pounds in Gold in this; and Jewels to the value of five hundred pounds more in this.

Welldon opens the Casket.

Welldon. Ay, marry, this will encourage me indeed.

---

[40] An iron-deficiency anaemia in young women, falsely believed to be curable by sexual intercourse.

Widow. There are comforts in marrying an elderly Woman, Mr. *Welldon.*
Now a young Woman wou'd have fancy'd she had paid you with her
person, or had done you the favour.

Welldon. What do you talk of young Women? you are as young as any of
'em, in every thing, but their folly and ignorance.

Widow. And do you think me so? but I have no reason to suspect you. Was
not I seen at your house this Morning, do you think?

Welldon. You may venture again: you'll come at night, I suppose.

Widow. O dear! at night? so soon?

Welldon. Nay, if you think it so soon.

Widow. O! no, it is not for that Mr. *Welldon*, but –

Welldon. You won't come then.

Widow. Won't! I don't say, I won't: that is not a word for a Wife:
If you command me –

Welldon. To please your self.

Widow. I will come to please you.

Welldon. To please your self, own it.

Widow. Well, well, to please my self then, you're the strangest Man in the
world, nothing can scape you: you'll to the bottom of every thing.

Enter Daniel, Lucy *Following.*

Daniel. What wou'd you have? what do you follow me for?

Lucy. Why, may'nt I follow you? I must follow you now all the World
over.

Daniel. Hold you, hold you there: not so far by a mile or two; I have
enough of your Company already, byrlady; and something to spare: you
may go home to your Brother, an you will, I have no farther to do with
you.

Widow. Why, *Daniel*, Child, thou are not out of thy wits sure, art thou?

Daniel. Nay, marry, I don't know; but I am very near it, I believe: I am
alter'd for the worse mightily since you saw me; and she has been the
cause of it there.

Widow. How so, Child?

Daniel. I told you before what wou'd come on't, of putting me to bed to a
strange Woman: but you wou'd not be said nay.

Widow. She is your Wife now, Child, you must love her.

Daniel. Why, so I did, at first.

Widow. But you must love her always.

Daniel. Always! lov'd her as long as I cou'd, Mother, and as long as loving
was good, I believe, for I find now I don't care a fig for her.

Lucy. Why, you lubberly,° slovenly, misbegotten Blockhead –

Widow. Nay, Mistriss *Lucy*, say any thing else, and spare not: but as to his begetting, that touches me, he is as honestly begotten, tho' I say it, that he is the worse agen.[41]

Lucy. I see all good nature is thrown away upon you –

Widow. It was so with his Father before him: he takes after him.

Lucy. And therefore I will use you, as you deserve, you Tony.[42]

Widow. Indeed he deserves bad enough; but don't call him out of his name, his name is *Daniel*, you know.

Daniel. She may call me Hermophrodite, if she will, For I hardly know whether I'm a Boy or a Girl.

Welldon. A Boy, I warrant thee, as long as thou liv'st.

Daniel. Let her call me what she pleases, Mother, 'tis not her Tongue that I am afraid of.

Lucy. I will make such a Beast of thee, such a Cuckold!

Widow. O, pray, no, I hope; do nothing rashly, Mrs. *Lucy.*

Lucy. Such a Cuckold will I make of thee!

Daniel. I had rather be a Cuckold, than what you wou'd make of me in a week, I'm sure: I have no more Manhood left in me already, than there is, saving the mark, in one of my Mothers old under Petticoats here.

Widow. Sirrah, Sirrah, meddle with your Wife's Petticoats, and let your Mother's alone, you ungracious Bird,° you.					*Beats him.*

Daniel. Why is the Devil in the Woman? what have I said now? Do you know, if you were ask'd, I trow? but you are all of a bundle; ev'n hang together; he that unties you, makes a Rod for his own tail; and so he will find it, that has any thing to do with you.

Widow. Ay, Rogue enough, you shall find it: I have a Rod for your Tail still.

Daniel. No, Wife and I care not.

Widow. I'll swinge° you into better manners, you Booby.

Beats him off, Exit.

Welldon. You have consummated our project upon him.

Lucy. Nay, if I have a limb of the Fortune, I care not who has the whole body of the Fool.

---

lubberly: loutish   **bird:** youngster   **swinge:** beat

---

[41] So much the worse for being the true child of his foolish father (Thomas Southerne, *Oroonoko*, ed. Maximillian E. Novak and David Stuart Rodes (Lincoln: University of Nebraska Press, 1976), 83).

[42] A simpleton; perhaps from the character of Antonio in Middleton and Rowley's *The Changeling.*

Welldon. That you shall, and a large one, I promise you.

Lucy. Have you heard the news? they talk of an English Ship in the River.

Welldon. I have heard on't: and am preparing to receive it, as fast as I can.

Lucy. There's something the matter too with the Slaves, Some disturbance or other; I don't know what 'tis.

Welldon. So much the better still: We fish in troubled waters: We shall have fewer Eyes upon us. Pray, go you home, and be ready to assist me in your part of the design.

Lucy. I can't fail in mine.   *Exit*

Welldon. The Widow has furnish'd me, I thank her, to carry it on. Now I have got a Wife, 'tis high time to think of getting a Husband. I carry my fortune about me; A thousand Pounds in Gold and Jewels. Let me see – 'Twill be a considerable trust:[43] And I think, I shall lay it out to advantage.

Enter Stanmore.

Stanmore. So *Welldon, Jack* has told me his success; and his hopes of marrying the Widow by your means.

Welldon. I have strain'd a point, *Stanmore*, upon your account, to be serviceable to your Family.

Stanmore. I take it upon my account; and am very much oblig'd to you. But here we are all in an uproar.

Welldon. So they say, what's the matter?

Stanmore. A Mutiny among the Slaves: *Oroonoko* is at the head of 'em, Our Governour is gone out with his rascally Militia against 'em, what it may come to no body knows.

Welldon. For my part, I shall do as well as the rest: but I'm concern'd for my Sister, and Cozen, whom I expect in the Ship from *England.*

Stanmore. There's no danger of 'em.

Welldon. I have a thousand pounds here, in Gold and Jewels, for my Cozens use, that I wou'd more particularly take care of: 'tis too great a summ to venture at home; and I wou'd not have her wrong'd of it: therefore, to secure it, I think my best way will be, to put it into your keeping.

Stanmore. You have a very good opinion of my honesty.

                                            Takes the Purse and Casket.

Welldon. I have indeed, if any thing shou'd happen to me, in this bustle, as no body is secure of accidents, I know you will take my Cozen into your protection and care.

Stanmore. You may be sure on't.

---

[43] "An estate committed to the charge of trustees" (*OED*).

Welldon. If you hear she is dead, as she may be, then I desire you to accept of the Thousand Pound, as a Legacy, and Token of my Friendship; my Sister is provided for.

Stanmore. Why, you amaze me: but you are never the nearer dying, I hope, for makeing your Will?

Welldon. Not a jot; but I love to be before-hand with Fortune. If she comes safe; this is not a place for a single Woman, you know; Pray see her marryed as soon as you can.

Stanmore. If she be as handsom as her Picture, I can promise her a Husband.

Welldon. If you like her, when you see her, I wish nothing so much as to have you marry her your self.

Stanmore. From what I have heard of her, and my Engagements to you, it must be her Fault, if I don't: I hope to have her from your own Hand.

Welldon. And I hope to give her to you, for all this.

Stanmore. Ay, ay, hang these melancholy Reflections. Your Generosity has engag'd all my Services.

Welldon. I always thought you worth making a Friend.

Stanmore. You shan't find your good Opinion thrown away upon me: I am in your Debt, and shall think so as long as I live.   *Exeunt.*

SCENE II.

Enter on one side of the Stage Oroonoko, Aboan, *with the Slaves,* Imoinda *with a Bow and Quiver, the Women, some leading, others carrying their Children upon their Backs.*

Oroonoko. The Women, with their Children, fall behind.
  Imoinda You must not expose your self:
  Retire, my Love: I almost fear for you.
Imoinda. I fear no Danger: Life, or Death, I will enjoy with you.
Oroonoko. My Person is your Guard.
Aboan. Now, Sir, blame your self: if you had not prevented my cutting his Throat, that Coward there had not discover'd us; He comes now to upbraid you.

Enter on the other side Governour, talking to Hottman, *with his Rabble.*

Governour. This is the very thing I would have wisht.
  Your honest Service to the Government   *To* Hottman.
  Shall be rewarded with your Liberty.

Aboan. His honest Service! call it what it is,
   His Villany, the Service of his Fear:
   If he pretends to honest Services,
   Let him stand out, and meet me, like a Man.   *Advancing.*
Oroonoko. Hold, you: And you who come against us, hold;
   I charge you in a general good to all,
   And wish I cou'd command you, to prevent
   The bloody Havock of the murdering Sword.
   I wou'd not urge Destruction uncompell'd:
   But if you follow Fate, you find it here.
   The Bounds are set, the Limits of our Lives:
   Between us lyes the gaping Gulph of Death,
   To swallow all: who first advances –   *Enter the Captain with his Crew.*
Captain. Here, here, here they are, Governour: What! seize upon my Ship!
   Come, Boys, fall on –   *Advancing first,* Oroonoko *kills him.*
Oroonoko. Thou art fall'n indeed. Thy own Blood be upon thee.
Governour. Rest it there: he did deserve his Death.
   Take him away.   *The Body remov'd.*
   You see, Sir, you and those mistaken Men
   Must be our Witnesses, we do not come
   As Enemies, and thirsting for your Blood.
   If we desir'd your Ruin, the Revenge
   Of our Companions Death, had pusht it on.
   But that we over-look, in a Regard
   To common Safety, and the publick Good.
Oroonoko. Regard that publick good: draw off your Men;
   And leave us to our Fortune: We're resolv'd.
Governour. Resolv'd, on what? your Resolutions
   Are broken, overturn'd, prevented, lost:
   What Fortune now can you raise out of 'em?
   Nay, grant we shou'd draw off, what can you do?
   Where can you move? What more can you resolve?
   Unless it be to throw your selves away.
   Famine must eat you up, if you go on.
   You see, our Numbers cou'd with Ease compel
   What we request: And what do we request?
   Only to save your selves?
       The Women with their Children gathering about the Men.
Oroonoko. I'le hear no more.
Women. Hear him, hear him. He takes no care of us.

Governour. To those poor wretches who have been seduc'd,
   And led away, to all, and every one,
   We offer a full Pardon –
Oroonoko. Then fall on.   *Preparing to Engage.*
Governour. Lay hold upon't, before it be too late,
   Pardon and Mercy.

       The Women clinging about the Men, they leave Oroonoko,
            and fall upon their Faces crying out for Pardon.

Slaves. Pardon, Mercy, Pardon.
Oroonoko. Let 'em go all: now, Governour, I see,
   I own the Folly of my Enterprise,
   The Rashness of this Action, and must blush
   Quite thro' this Vail of Night, a whitely Shame,
   To think I cou'd design to make those free,
   Who were by Nature Slaves; Wretches design'd
   To be their Masters Dogs, and lick their Feet.
   Whip, whip 'em to the Knowledge of your Gods,
   Your Christian Gods, who suffer you to be
   Unjust, dishonest, cowardly, and base,
   And give 'em your Excuse for being so.
   I wou'd not live on the same Earth with Creatures,
   That only have the Faces of their Kind:
   Why shou'd they look like Men, who are not so?
   When they put off their Noble Natures, for
   The groveling qualities of down-cast Beasts,
   I wish they had their Tails.[44]
Aboan. Then we shou'd know 'em.
Oroonoko. We were too few before for Victory:
   We're still enow to dye.   *To* Imoinda, Aboan.

              Blandford *Enters.*

Governour. Live, Royal Sir;
   Live, and be happy long on your own Terms:
   Only consent to yield, and you shall have
   What Terms you can propose, for you, and yours.
Oroonoko. Consent to yield! shall I betray my self?
Governour. Alas! we cannot fear, that your small Force,

---

[44] This is the only passage in the Behn and Southerne texts that implies contempt for the
   black African's essential character. Yet Oroonoko is describing the loss, not the absence,
   of human character, and he is himself a black African.

The Force of two, with a weak Womans Arm,
Shou'd Conquer us. I speak in the regard
And Honour of your Worth, in my desire
And forwardness to serve so great a Man.
I wou'd not have it lie upon my Thoughts,
That I was the occasion of the fall
Of such a Prince, whose Courage carried on
In a more Noble Cause, wou'd well deserve
The Empire of the World.

Oroonoko. You can speak fair.

Governour. Your Undertaking, tho' it wou'd have brought
So great a loss to us, we must all say
Was generous, and noble; and shall be
Regarded only as the Fire of Youth,
That will break out sometimes in Gallant Souls
We'll think it but the Natural Impulse,
A rash impatience of Liberty:
No otherwise.

Oroonoko. Think it what you will.
I was not born to render an Account
Of what I do, to any but my self.   Blandford *comes forward.*

Blandford. I'm glad you have proceeded by fair means.   *To the Governour.*
I came to be a Mediator.

Governour. Try what you can work upon him.

Oroonoko. Are you come against me too?

Blandford. Is this to come against you?   *Offering his Sword to* Oroonoko.
Unarm'd to put my self into your Hands?
I come, I hope, to serve you.

Oroonoko. You have serv'd me;
I thank you for't: And I am pleas'd to think
You were my Friend, while I had need of one:
But now 'tis past; this farewell; and be gone.   *Embraces him.*

Blandford. It is not past, and I must serve you still.
I wou'd make up these Breaches, which the Sword
Will widen more; and close us all in Love.

Oroonoko. I know what I have done, and I shou'd be
A Child to think they ever can Forgive:
Forgive! Were there but that, I wou'd not live
To be Forgiven: Is there a Power on Earth,
That I can ever need forgiveness from?

Blandford. You sha' not need it.

Oroonoko. No, I wonnot need it.

Blandford. You see he offers you your own Conditions, or you, and
yours.

Oroonoko. I must Capitulate?°

Precariously Compound, on stinted° Terms,

To save my Life?

Blandford. Sir, he Imposes none.

You make 'em for your own Security.

If your great Heart cannot descend to treat,

In adverse Fortune, with an Enemy:

Yet sure, your Honour' safe, you may accept

Offers of Peace, and Safety from a Friend.

Governour. He will rely on what you say to him: *To* Blandford.

Offer him what you can, I will confirm,

And make all good: Be you my Pledge of Trust.

Blandford. I'le answer with my Life for all he says.[45]

Governour. Ay, do, and pay the Forfeit if you please.   *Aside.*

Blandford. Consider, Sir, can you consent to throw

That Blessing from you, you so hardly found,   (*Of* Imoinda.)

And so much valu'd once?

Oroonoko. Imoinda! Oh!

'Tis She that holds me on this Argument

Of tedious Life: I cou'd resolve it soon,

Were this curst Being only in Debate.

But my *Imoinda* struggles in my Soul:

She makes a Coward of me: I Confess

I am afraid to part with Her in Death:

And more afraid of Life to lose Her here.

Blandford. This way you must lose her, think upon

The weakness of her Sex, made yet more weak

With her Condition, requiring Rest,

And soft Indulging Ease, to nurse your Hopes,

And make you a glad Father.

Capitulate: discuss terms of surrender   **stinted:** limited

---

[45] Whereas Behn's Oroonoko ingenuously trusts in the written word, Southerne's relies
on an oath. Behn is showing how advanced symbolic systems may themselves be the
instruments of barbarity; Southerne is lamenting the decay of a world dominated by
feudal values of the word, trust, and service (key and recurrent terms in both plots).

Oroonoko. There I feel a Father's Fondness, and a Husband's Love:
 They seize upon my Hart, strain all its strings,
 To pull me to 'em, from my stern resolve.
 Husband, and Father! All the melting Art
 Of Eloquence lives in those softning Names.
 Methinks I see the Babe, with Infant Hands,
 Pleading for Life, and begging to be born:
 Shall I forbid his Birth? Deny him Light?
 The Heavenly Comforts of all cheering Light?
 And make the Womb the Dungeon of his Death?
 His Bleeding Mother his sad Monument?
 These are the Calls of Nature, that call loud,
 They will be heard, and Conquer in their Cause:
 He must not be a Man, who can resist 'em.
 No, my *Imoinda*! I will venture all
 To save thee, and that little Innocent.
 The World may be a better Friend to him,
 Than I have found it. Now I yield my self: *Gives up his Sword.*
 The Conflict's past, and we are in your Hands.
                    Several Men get about Oroonoko, *and* Aboan, *and seize 'em.*
Governour. So you shall find you are: Dispose of them,
 As I commanded you.
Blandford. Good Heaven forbid! You cannot mean –
Governour. This is not your Concern.
                              To Blandford *who goes to* Oroonoko.
 I must take care of you.   *To* Imoinda.
Imoinda. I'm at the end
 Of all my Care: Here I will die with him.   *Holding* Oroonoko.
Oroonoko. You shall not force her from me.   *He holds her.*
Governour. Then I must   *They force her from him.*
 Try other means, and Conquer Force by Force:
 Break, cut off his Hold, bring her away.
Imoinda. I do not ask to Live, kill me but here.
Oroonoko. O Bloody Dogs! Inhumane Murderers.
                    Imoinda *forc't out of one Door by the Governour, and others.*
                    Oroonoko *and* Aboan *hurried out of another.*
                                              Exeunt Omnes.

ACT V.

SCENE I.

Enter Stanmore, Lucy, Welldon [in woman's clothes].

Stanmore. 'Tis strange we cannot hear of him: Can no body give an account of him?

Lucy. Nay, I begin to despair: I give him for gone.

Stanmore. Not so I hope.

Lucy. There are so many disturbances in this devilish Country! Wou'd we had never seen it.

Stanmore. This is but a cold welcome for you, Madam, after so troublesome a Voyage.

Welldon. A cold Welcome indeed, Sir, without my Cousin *Welldon*, He was the best Friend I had in the World.

Stanmore. He was a very good Friend of yours indeed, Madam.

Lucy. They have made him away, Murder'd him for his Mony, I believe, he took a considerable Sum out with him, I know, that has been his Ruin.

Stanmore. That has done him no Injury, to my knowledge: For this Morning he put into my Custody what you speak of, I suppose a Thousand Pounds, for the use of this Lady.

Welldon. I was always oblig'd to him: and he has shown his Care of me, in placing my little Affairs in such Honourable Hands.

Stanmore. He gave me a particular charge of you, Madam, very particular, so particular, that you will be surpriz'd when I tell you.

Welldon. What, pray Sir.

Stanmore. I am engag'd to get you a Husband, I promis'd that before I saw you; and now I have seen you, you must give me leave to offer you my self.

Lucy. Nay, Cozen, never be coy upon the matter, to my Knowledge my Brother always design'd you for this Gentleman.

Stanmore. You hear, Madam, he has given me his Interest, and 'tis the Favour I wou'd have begg'd of him.   Lord! you are so like him –

Welldon. That you are oblig'd to say you like me for his Sake.

Stanmore. I shou'd be glad to love you for your own.

Welldon. If I shou'd consent to the fine things you can say to me, how wou'd you look at last, to find 'em thrown away upon an old Acquaintance?

Stanmore. An old Acquaintance!

Welldon. Lord, how easily are you Men to be impos'd upon! I am no Cozen newly arriv'd from *England*, not I; but the very *Welldon* you wot of.

Stanmore. Welldon!

Welldon. Not murdered, nor made away, as my Sister wou'd have you believe, but am in very good Health, your old friend in Breeches that was, and now your humble Servant in Petticoats.

Stanmore. I'm glad we have you agen. But what service can you do me in Petticoats, pray?

Welldon. Can't you tell what?

Stanmore. Not I, by my troth: I have found my Friend, and lost my Mistress, it seems, which I did not expect from your Petticoats.

Welldon. Come, come, you have had a Friend of your Mistress long enough, 'tis high time now to have a Mistress of your Friend.

Stanmore. What do you say?

Welldon. I am a Woman, Sir.

Stanmore. A Woman!

Welldon. As arrant a Woman as you wou'd have had me but now, I assure you.

Stanmore. And at my Service?

Welldon. If you have any for me in Petticoats.

Stanmore. Yes, yes, I shall find you employment.

Welldon. You wonder at my proceeding, I believe.

Stanmore. 'Tis a little extraordinary, indeed.

Welldon. I have taken some pains to come into your Favour.

Stanmore. You might have had it cheaper a great deal.

Welldon. I might have marry'd you in the Person of my English Cozen, but cou'd not consent to cheat you, ev'n in the thing I had a mind to.

Stanmore. 'Twas done as you do every thing.

Welldon. I need not tell you, I made that little Plot, and carry'd it on only for this Opportunity. I was resolv'd to see whether you lik't me as a Woman, or not: if I had found you indifferent, I wou'd have indeavour'd to have been so too: but you say you like me, and therefore I have ventur'd to discover° the truth.

Stanmore. Like you! I like you so well, that I'm afraid you won't think Marriage a proof on't: shall I give you any other?

***

discover: reveal

Welldon. No, no, I'm inclin'd to believe you, and that shall convince me. At more leisure I'le satisfie you how I came to be in Mans Cloaths, for no ill I assure you, tho' I have happen'd to play the Rogue in 'em: They have assisted me in marrying my Sister, and have gone a great way in befriending your Cozen *Jack* with the Widow. Can you forgive me for pimping for your Family?

Enter Jack Stanmore.

Stanmore. So, *Jack*, what News with you?

Jack Stanmore. I am the forepart of the Widow, you know, She's coming after with the body of the Family, the young Squire in her hand, my Son-in-Law, that is to be, with the Help of Mr. *Welldon.*

Welldon. Say you so, Sir?   *Clapping* Jack *upon the back.*

Enter Widow Lackitt *with her Son* Daniel.

Widow. So, Mrs. *Lucy*, I have brought him about agen, I have Chastis'd him, I have made him as supple as a Glove for your wearing, to pull on, or throw off, at your pleasure. Will you ever Rebell again? Will you, Sirrah? But come, come, down on your Marrow Bones, and ask her forgiveness.   Daniel *Kneels.*

Say after me, pray forsooth Wife.

Daniel. Pray forsooth Wife.

Lucy. Well, well, this is a Day of good Nature, and so I take you into Favour: But first take the Oath of Allegiance.[46]

He kisses her Hand, and rises.

If ever you do so agen –

Daniel. Nay Marry if I do, I shall have the worst on't.

Lucy. Here's a Stranger, forsooth, wou'd be glad to be known to you, a Sister of mine, pray salute her.   *Starts at* Welldon.

Widow. Your Sister! Mrs. *Lucy*! what do you mean? This is your Brother, Mr. *Welldon*; do you think I do not know Mr. *Welldon?*

Lucy. Have a care what you say: This Gentleman's about Marrying her: You may spoil all.

Widow. Fiddle faddle, what! You wou'd put a trick upon me.

---

[46] Oath of loyalty to a sovereign, required of those who held public office. The oath of allegiance to William III proved troublesome for those who still felt bound by their oath to James, and a substantial number of people refused to swear; they were known as non-jurors.

Welldon. No faith, Widow, the Trick is over, it has taken sufficiently, and now I will reach you the Trick, to prevent your being Cheated another time.

Widow. How! Cheated, Mr. *Welldon*!

Welldon. Why, ay, you will always take things by the wrong Handle, I see you will have me Mr. *Welldon*: I grant you, I was Mr. *Welldon* a little while to please you, or so: But Mr. *Stanmore* here has perswaded me into a Woman agen.

Widow. A Woman! Pray let me speak with you.   *Drawing her aside.*
  You are not in earnest, I hope? A Woman!

Welldon. Really a Woman.

Widow. Gads my Life! I could not be cheated in every thing: I know a Man from a Woman at these Years, or the Devil's in't. Pray, did not you marry me?

Welldon. You wou'd have it so.

Widow. And did not I give you a Thousand Pounds this Morning?

Welldon. Yes indeed, 'twas more than I deserv'd: But you had your Penniworth for your Penny, I suppose: You seem'd to be pleas'd with your Bargain.

Widow. A rare Bargain I have made on't, truly. I have laid out my Money to fine purpose upon a Woman.

Welldon. You wou'd have a Husband, and I provided for you as well as I cou'd.

Widow. Yes, yes, you have provided for me.

Welldon. And you have paid me very well for't, I thank you.

Widow. 'Tis very well; I may be with Child too, for ought I know, and may go look for the Father.

Welldon. Nay, if you think so, 'tis time to look about you indeed. Ev'n make up the matter as well as you can, I advise you as a Friend, and let us live Neighbourly and Lovingly together.

Widow. I have nothing else for it, that I know now.

Welldon. For my part, Mrs. *Lackitt*, your Thousand Pounds will Engage me not to laugh at you. Then my Sister is Married to your Son, he is to have half your Estate, I know; and indeed they may live upon it, very comfortably to themselves, and very creditably to you.

Widow. Nay, I can blame no body but my self.

Welldon. You have enough for a Husband still, and that you may bestow upon honest *Jack Stanmore*.

Widow. Is he the Man then?

Welldon. He is the Man you are oblig'd to.

Jack Stanmore. Yes, Faith, Widow, I am the Man: I have done fairly by
you, you find, you know what you have to trust to before hand.

Widow. Well, well, I see you will have me, ev'n Marry me, and make an
end of the business.

Stanmore. Why, that's well said, now we are all agreed, and all provided
for.   *A Servant enters to* Stanmore.

Servant. Sir, Mr. *Blandford* desires you to come to him, and bring as many
of your Friends as you can with you.

Stanmore. I come to him. You'l all go along with me. Come, young Gentleman, Marriage is the fashion, you see, you must like it now.

Daniel. If I don't, how shall I help my self?

Lucy. Nay, you may hang your self in the Noose, if you please, But you'll
never get out on't with strugling.

Daniel. Come then, let's ev'n jogg on in the old Road.
     Cuckold, or worse, I must be now contented:
     I'm not the first has marry'd, and repented.   *Exeunt.*

SCENE II.

Enter Governour *with* Blandford, *and Planters.*

Blandford. Have you no Reverence of future Fame?
     No awe upon your actions, from the Tongues,
     The censuring Tongues of Men, that will be free?
     If you confess Humanity, believe
     There is a God, or Devil, to reward
     Our doings here, do not provoke your Fate.
     The Hand of Heaven is arm'd against these Crimes,
     With hotter Thunder-Bolts, prepar'd to shoot,
     And Nail you to the Earth, a sad Example;
     A Monument of Faithless Infamy.

Enter Stanmore, J. Stanmore, Welldon, Lucy, Widow,
and Daniel.

     So, *Stanmore*, you I know, the Women too
     Will join with me: 'Tis *Oroonoko's* Cause,
     A Lover's Cause, a wretched Woman's Cause,
     That will become your Intercession.   *To the Women.*

1st Planter. Never mind 'em, Governour; he ought to be made an Example
   for the good of the Plantation.

2nd Planter. Ay, ay, 'twill frighten the Negroes from Attempting the like
   agen.

1st Planters. What rise against their Lords and Masters! At this rate no
   Man is safe from his own Slaves.

2nd Planter. No, no more he is. Therefore, one and all, Governour, we
   declare for Hanging.

Omnes Planters. Ay, ay, hang him, hang him.

Widow. What! Hang him! O! forbid it, Governour.

Welldon. ⎫
Lucy.   ⎬   We all Petition for him.

Jack Stanmore. They are for a Holy-Day; Guilty or not,
   Is not the Business, hanging is their Sport.

Blandford. We are not sure so wretched, to have these,
   The Rabble, judge for us; the changing Croud;
   The Arbitrary Guard of Fortune's Power,
   Who wait to catch the Sentence of her Frowns,
   And hurry all to ruine she Condemns.

Stanmore. So far from farther Wrong, that 'tis a shame
   He shou'd be where he is: Good Governour.
   Order his Liberty: He yielded up
   Himself, his all, at your discretion.

Blandford. Discretion! no, he yielded on your word;
   And I am made the cautionary Pledge,
   The Gage, and Hostage of your keeping it.
   Remember, Sir, he yielded on your word;
   Your Word! which honest Men will think should be
   The last resort of Truth, and trust on Earth:
   There's no Appeal beyond it, but to Heaven:
   An Oath is a recognisance to Heaven,
   Binding us over, in the Courts above,
   To plead to the Indictment of our Crimes:
   That those who 'scape this World should suffer there
   But in the common Intercourse of Men,
   (Where the dread Majesty is not Invoak'd,
   His Honour not immediately concern'd,
   Not made a Party in our Interests,)
   Our Word is all to be rely'd upon.

Widow. Come; come, You'l be as good as your Word, we know.

Stanmore. He's out of all power of doing any harm now, if he were dispos'd
 to it.

Welldon. But he is not dispos'd to it.

Blandford. To keep him, where he is, will make him soon
 Find out some desperate way to Liberty:
 He'll hang himself, or dash out his mad Brains.

Welldon. Pray try him by gentle Means: We'll all be Sureties for him.

Omnes. All, all.

Lucy. We will all answer for him now.

Governour. Well, you will have it so, do what you please,
 Just what you will with him, I give you leave.   *Exit.*

Blandford. We thank you, Sir; this way, pray come with me.   *Exeunt.*

     The Scene drawn shews Oroonoko *upon his Back, his Legs*
      and Arms stretcht out, and chain'd to the Ground.

       Enter Blandford, Stanmore. *etc.*

Blandford. O miserable Sight! help every one,
 Assist me all to free him from his Chains.
        They help him up, and bring him forward, looking down.
 Most injur'd Prince! how shall we clear our selves?
 We cannot hope you will vouchsafe to hear,
 Or credit what we say in the Defence,
 And Cause of our suspected Innocence.

Stanmore. We are not guilty of your Injuries,
 No way consenting to 'em; but abhor,
 Abominate, and loath this Cruelty.

Blandford. It is our Curse, but make it not our Crime.
 A heavy curse upon us, that we must
 Share any thing in common, ev'n the Light,
 The Elements, and Seasons, with such Men,
 Whose Principles, like the fam'd Dragons Teeth,[47]
 Scatter'd, and sown, wou'd shoot a Harvest up
 Of fighting Mischiefs, to confound themselves,
 And ruin all about 'em.

---

[47] Cadmus, founder of the ancient Greek city of Thebes, killed a monstrous serpent near
the future site of the city and was commanded by the goddess Athene to sow its teeth.
Armed men sprang up from the teeth and fought each other, until only five were left.
The survivors helped Cadmus found the city.

Stanmore. Profligates!
    Whose bold *Titanian* Impiety
    Wou'd once agen pollute their Mother Earth,
    Force her to teem with her old monstrous Brood
    Of Gyants, and forget the Race of Men.[48]
Blandford. We are not so: believe us innocent.
    We come prepar'd with all our Services,
    To offer a Redress of your base Wrongs.
    Which way shall we employ 'em?
Stanmore. Tell us, Sir, if there is any thing that can attone;
    But nothing can; that may be some amends –
Oroonoko. If you wou'd have me think you are not all
    Confederates, all accessory to
    The base Injustice of your Governour:
    If you wou'd have me live, as you appear
    Concern'd for me, if you wou'd have me live
    To thank, and bless you, there is yet a Way
    To tye me ever to your honest Love:
    Bring my *Imoinda* to me; give me her,
    To charm my Sorrows, and, if possible,
    I'le sit down with my Wrongs; never to rise
    Against my Fate, or think of Vengeance more.
Blandford. Be satisfi'd, you may depend upon us,
    We'll bring her safe to you, and suddenly.
Welldon. We wonnot leave you in so good a work.
Widow. No, no, we'll go with you.
Blandford. In the mean time
    Endeavour to forget, Sir, and forgive:
    And hope a better Fortune.   *Exeunt.*

Oroonoko *alone.*

Oroonoko. Forget! forgive! I must indeed forget,
    When I forgive: but while I am a Man,
    In Flesh, that bears, the living mark of Shame,

---

[48] In Greek mythology, the Titans were the sons of Sky (Ouranos) and Earth. One of them, Kronos, rebelled against and castrated Ouranos and supplanted him as ruler of the gods. Then when Ouranos's blood fell to the earth, it produced the Giants and the Furies. After Kronos had been supplanted by his son Zeus, there were unsuccessful rebellions against Zeus by some of the Titans and then by the Giants.

The print of these honourable Chains,
My Memory still rousing up my Wrongs,
I never can forgive this Governour;
This Villain; the disgrace of Trust, and Place,
And just Contempt of delegated Power.
What shall I do? If I declare my self,
I know him, he will sneak behind his Guard
Of Followers, and brave me in his Fears.
Else, Lyon like, with my devouring Rage,
I wou'd rush on him, fasten on his Throat,
Tear wide a Passage to his treacherous Heart,
And that way lay him open to the World.   *Pausing.*
If I shou'd turn his Christian Arts on him,
Promise him, speak him fair, flatter, and creep,
With fawning Steps, to get within his Faith;
I cou'd betray him then, as he has me.
But am I sure by that to right my self?
Lying's a certain Mark of Cowardise:
And when the Tongue forgets its Honesty,
The Heart and Hand may drop their functions too;
And nothing worthy be resolv'd, or done.
The Man must go together, bad, or good:
In one part frail, he soon grows weak in all.
Honour shou'd be concern'd in Honour's Cause.
That is not to be cur'd by Contraries,
As Bodies are, whose Health is often drawn
From rankest Poysons. Let me but find out
An honest Remedy, I have the Hand,
A ministring Hand, that will apply it Home.   *Exit.*

SCENE *the Governour's House.*

Enter Governour.

Governour. I wou'd not have her tell me, she consents:
In Favour of the Sexes Modesty,
That still shou'd be presum'd; because there is
A greater Impudence in owning it,
Than in allowing all that we can do.
This Truth I know, and yet against my self,

(So unaccountable are Lovers ways)
I talk, and lose the Opportunities,
Which Love, and she expects I shou'd employ:
Ev'n she expects: for when a Man has said
All that is fit, to save the Decency,
The Women know the rest is to be done.
I wonnot disappoint her. *Going.*

Enter to him Blandford, *the Stanmores*, Daniel, *Mrs.* Lackitt,
Welldon, *and* Lucy.

Widow. O Governorr! I'm glad we have lit upon you.
Governour. Why! what's the Matter?
Welldon. Nay, nothing extraodinary. But one good Action draws on
another. You have given the Prince his Freedom: now we come a
begging for his Wife. You won't refuse us.
Governour. Refuse you. No, no, what have I to do to refuse you?
Widow. You won't refuse to send her to him, she means.
Governour. I send her to him!
Widow. We have promis'd him to bring her.
Governour. You do very well; 'tis Kindly done of you:
Ev'n carry her to him, with all my Heart.
Lucy. You must tell us where she is.
Governour. I tell you! why, don't you know?
Blandford. Your Servants say she's in the House.
Governour. No, no, I brought her home at first indeed; but I thought it
wou'd not look well to keep her here: I remov'd her in the Hurry, only
to take care of her. What! she belongs to you: I have nothing to do
with her.
Welldon. But where is she now, Sir?
Governour. Why, Faith, I can't say certainly: you'll hear of her at *Parham*[49]
House, I suppose: there, or thereabouts: I think I sent her there.
Blandford. I'le have an Eye on him. *Aside.*
Exeunt all but the Governour.
Governour. I have ly'd my self into a little Time;
And must employ it; they'll be here agen;
But I must be before 'em. *Going out, he meets* Imoinda, *and seises her.*
Are you come!

[49] On Lord Willoughby's estate of Parham Hill, named after Parham in Suffolk, Willoughby's ancestral estate.

I'le court no longer for a Happiness
That is in mine own keeping: you may still
Refuse to grant, so I have Power to take.
The Man that asks deserves to be deny'd.

> *She disengages one hand, and draws his Sword from his*
> *side upon him, Governour starts and retires,* Blandford
> *enters behind him.*

Imoinda. He does indeed, that asks unworthily.
Blandford. You hear her, Sir, that asks unworthily.
Governour. You are no Judge.
Blandford. I am of my own Slave.
Governour. Begone, and leave us.
Blandford. When you let her go.
Governour. To fasten upon you.
Blandford. I must defend my self.
Imoinda. Help, Murder, help.

> Imoinda *retreats towards the door, favour'd by* Blandford, *when*
> *they are clos'd, she throws down the Sword, and runs out.*
> *Governour takes up the Smord, they fight, close, and fall,*
> Blandford *upon him. Servants enter, and part 'em.*

Governour. She shannot scape me so. I've gone too far,
  Not to go farther.   Curse on my delay:
  But yet she is, and shall be in my Power.
Blandford. Nay then it is the War of Honesty:
  I know you, and will save you from your self.
Governour. All come along with me.   *Exeunt.*

SCENE *the last.*

Oroonoko *enters.*

Oroonoko. To Honour bound! and yet a Slave to Love!
  I am distracted by their rival Powers,
  And both will be obey'd.   O great Revenge!
  Thou Raiser, and Restorer of faln Fame!
  Let me not be unworthy of thy Aid,
  For stopping in thy course: I still am thine:
  But can't forget I am *Imoinda*'s too.
  She calls me from my Wrongs to rescue her.
  No man condemn me, who has never felt

A womans Power, or try'd the Force of Love:
All tempers yield, and soften in those fires:
Our Honours, Interests resolving down,
Run in the gentle Current of our Joys:
But not to sink, and drown our Memory:
We mount agen to Action, like the Sun,
That rises from the Bosom of the Sea,
To run his glorious Race of Light anew,
And carry on the World. Love, Love will be
My first Ambition, and my Fame the next.

Aboan *enters bloody.*

My Eyes are turn'd against me, and combine
With my sworn Enemies, to represent
This spectacle of Honour.   *Aboan*!
My ever faithful Friend!
Aboan. I have no Name,
    That can distinguish me from the vile Earth,
    To which I'm going: a poor, abject worm,
    That crawl'd awhile upon a bustling World,
    And now am trampled to my Dust agen.
Oroonoko. I see thee gasht, and mangled.
Aboan. Spare my shame
    To tell how they have us'd me: but believe
    The Hangman's Hand wou'd have been merciful.
    Do not you scorn me, Sir, to think I can
    Intend to live under this Infamy.
    I do not come for pity, to complain.
    I've spent an honourable Life with you;
    The earliest Servant of your rising Fame,
    And wou'd attend it with my latest care:
    My life was yours, and so shall be my death.
    You must not live.
    Bending and sinking, I have dragg'd my Steps
    Thus far, to tell you that you cannot live:
    To warn you of those Ignominious wrongs,
    Whips, Rods, and all the Instruments of death,
    Which I have felt, and are prepar'd for you.
    This was the Duty that I had to pay.
    'Tis done, and now I beg to be discharg'd.

Oroonoko. What shall I do for thee?

Aboan. My Body tires,

And wonnot bear me off to Liberty:
I shall agen be taken, made a Slave.
A Sword, a Dagger yet wou'd rescue me.
I have not Strength to go to find out Death:
You must direct him to me.

Oroonoko. Here he is,   *Gives him a Dagger.*

The only present I can make thee now:
And next the honourable means of Life,
I wou'd bestow the honest means of Death.

Aboan. I cannot stay to thank you. If there is

A Being after this, I shall be yours
In the next World, your faithful Slave agen.
This is to try [*Stabs himself.*] I had a living Sense
Of all your royal Favours, but this last
Strikes through my Heart. I wonnot say farewell,
For you must follow me.   *Dyes.*

Oroonoko. In Life, and death,

The Guardian of my Honour! follow thee!
I shou'd have gone before thee: then perhaps
Thy Fate had been prevented.   All his Care
Was to preserve me from the barbarous Rage
That wrong'd him, only for being mine.
Why, why, you Gods! Why am I so accurst,
That it must be a Reason of your Wrath,
A Guilt, a Crime sufficient to the Fate
Of any one, but to belong to me?
My Friend has found it, and my Wife will soon:
My Wife! the very Fear's too much for Life:
I can't support it.   Where? *Imoinda!* Oh!

                    Going out, she meets him, running into his Arms.

Thou bosom Softness! Down of all my Cares!
I cou'd recline my thoughts upon this Breast
To a forgetfulness of all my Griefs,
And yet be happy: but it wonnot be.
Thou art disorder'd, pale, and out of Breath!
If Fate pursues thee, find a shelter here.
What is it thou woud'st tell me?

Imoinda. 'Tis in vain to call him Villain.

Oroonoko. Call him Governour: is it not so?

Imoinda. There's not another sure.

Oroonoko. Villain's the common name of Mankind here:
    But his most properly. What! what of him?
    I fear to be resolv'd, and must enquire.
    He had thee in his Power.

Imoinda. I blush to think it.

Oroonoko. Blush! to think what?

Imoinda. That I was in his Power.

Oroonoko. He cou'd not use it?

Imoinda. What can't such men do?

Oroonoko. But did he? durst he?

Imoinda. What he cou'd, he dar'd.

Oroonoko. His own Gods damn him then: for ours have none,
    No Punishment for such unheard-of Crimes.

Imoinda. This Monster, cunning in his Flatteries,
    When he had weary'd all his useless Arts,
    Leapt out, fierce as a beast of prey, to seize me.
    I trembled, fear'd.

Oroonoko. I fear, and tremble now.
    What cou'd preserve thee? what deliver thee?

Imoinda. That worthy Man, you us'd to call your Friend –

Oroonoko. Blandford.

Imoinda. Came in, and sav'd me from his Rage.

Oroonoko. He was a Friend indeed to rescue thee!
    And for his sake, I'le think it possible
    A Christian may be yet an honest man.

Imoinda. O! did you know what I have strugl'd through,
    To save me yours, sure you wou'd promise me
    Never to see me forc't from you agen.

Oroonoko. To promise thee! O! do I need to promise?
    But there is now no farther use of Words.
    Death is security for all our fears.   *Shews* Aboan's *body on the floor.*
    And yet I cannot trust him.

Imoinda. Aboan!

Oroonoko. Mangled, and torn, resolv'd to give me time
    To fit my self for what I must expect,
    Groan'd out a warning to me, and expir'd.

Imoinda. For what you must expect?

Oroonoko. Wou'd that were all.

Imoinda. What! to be butcher'd thus –

Oroonoko. Just as thou see'st.

Imoinda. By barbarous Hands, to fall at last their Prey!

Oroonoko. I have run the Race with Honour, shall I now
    Lag, and be overtaken at the Goal?

Imoinda. No.

Oroonoko. I must look back to thee.   *Tenderly.*

Imoinda. You shannot need.
    I'm always present to your purpose, say,
    Which way wou'd you dispose me?

Oroonoko. Have a care,
    Thou'rt on a Precipice, and dost not see
    Whither that question leads thee.   O! too soon
    Thou dost enquire what the assembled Gods
    Have not determin'd, and will latest doom.
    Yet this I know of Fate, this is most certain,
    I cannot, as I wou'd, dispose of thee:
    And, as I ought, I dare not.   Oh *Imoinda*!

Imoinda. Alas! that sigh! why do you tremble so?
    Nay then 'tis bad indeed, if you can weep.

Oroonoko. My Heart runs over, if my gushing Eyes
    Betray a weakness which they never knew
    Believe, thou, only thou cou'dst cause these tears.
    The Gods themselves conspire with faithless Men
    To our destruction.

Imoinda. Heaven and Earth our Foes!

Oroonoko. It is not always granted to the great,
    To be most happy: If the angry Pow'rs
    Repent their Favours, let 'em take 'em back:
    The hopes of Empire, which they gave my youth,
    By making me a Prince, I here resign.
    Let 'em quench in me all those glorious Fires,
    Which kindled at their beams: that lust of Fame,
    That Fevor of Ambition, restless still,
    And burning with the sacred Thirst of Sway,
    Which they inspir'd, to qualifie my Fate,
    And make me fit to govern under them,
    Let 'em extinguish. I submit my self
    To their high pleasure, and devoted Bow
    Yet lower, to continue still a Slave;

Hopeless of liberty: and if I cou'd
Live after it, wou'd give up Honour too,
To satisfie their Vengeance, to avert
This only Curse, the curse of losing thee.
Imoinda. If Heav'n cou'd be appeas'd, these cruel Men
Are not to be entreated, or believ'd:
O! think on that, and be no more deceiv'd.
Oroonoko. What can we do?
Imoinda. Can I do any thing?
Oroonoko. But we were born to suffer.
Imoinda. Suffer both,
Both die, and so prevent 'em.
Oroonoko. By thy Death!
O! let me hunt my travel'd Thoughts again;
Range the wide waste of desolate despair;
Start any hope.   Alas! I lose my self,
'Tis Pathless, Dark, and Barren all to me.
Thou art my only guide, my light of Life,
And thou art leaving me: Send out thy Beams
Upon the Wing; let 'em fly all around,
Discover every way: Is there a dawn,
A glimmering of comfort? the great God,
That rises on the World, must shine on us.
Imoinda. And see us set before him.
Oroonoko. Thou bespeak'st, and goes before me.
Imoinda. So I wou'd, in Love:
In the dear unsuspected part of Life,
In Death for Love.   Alas! what hopes for me?
I was preserv'd but to acquit my self,
To beg to die with you.
Oroonoko. And can'st thou ask it?
I never durst enquire into my self
About thy fate, and thou resolv'st it all.
Imoinda. Alas! my Lord! my Fate's resolv'd in yours.
Oroonoko. O! keep thee there: Let not thy Virtue shrink
From my support, and I will gather strength,
Fast as I can to tell thee –
Imoinda. I must die.
I know 'tis fit, and I can die with you.
Oroonoko. O! thou hast banisht hence a thousand fears,
Which sickned at my Heart, and quite unman'd me.

Oroonoko. Your fear's for me, I know you fear'd my strength,
  And cou'd not overcome your tenderness,
  To pass this Sentence on me: and indeed
  There you were kind, as I have always found you,
  As you have ever been: for tho' I am
  Resign'd, and ready to obey my doom,
  Methinks it shou'd not be pronounc'd by you.
Oroonoko. O! that was all the labour of my grief.
  My heart, and tongue forsook me in the strife:
  I never cou'd pronounce it.
Imoinda. I have for you, for both of us.
Oroonoko. Alas! for me! my death
  I cou'd regard as the last Scene of life,
  And act it thro' with joy, to have it done.
  But then to part with thee –
Imoinda. 'Tis hard to part:
  But parting thus, as the most happy must,
  Parting in death, makes it the easier.
  You might have thrown me off, forsaken me,
  And my misfortunes: that had been a death
  Indeed of terror, to have trembled at.
Oroonoko. Forsaken! thrown thee off!
Imoinda. But 'tis a pleasure more than life can give,
  That with unconquer'd Passion to the last,
  You struggle still, and fain wou'd hold me to you.
Oroonoko. Ever, ever, and let those stars, which are my Enemies,
  Witness against me in the other World,
  If I wou'd leave this Mansion of my Bliss,
  To be the brightest Ruler of their Skies.
  O! that we cou'd incorporate, be one,   *Embracing her.*
  One Body, as we have been long one Mind:
  That blended so, we might together mix,
  And losing thus our Beings to the World,
  Be only found to one anothers Joys.
Imoinda. Is this the way to part?
Oroonoko. Which is the way?
Imoinda. The God of Love is blind, and cannot find it.
  But quick, make haste, our Enemies have Eyes
  To find us out, and shew us the worst way
  Of parting; think on them.
Oroonoko. Why dost thou wake me?

Imoinda. O! no more of Love.
　For if I listen to you, I shall quite
　Forget my Dangers, and desire to live.
　I can't live yours.　　　　　　　　　　　　*Takes up the Dagger.*
Oroonoko. There all the Stings of Death
　Are shot into my Heart – what shall I do?
Imoinda. This Dagger will instruct you.　　　　　*Gives it him.*
Oroonoko. Ha! this Dagger!
　Like Fate, it points me to the horrid Deed.
Imoinda. Strike, strike it home, and bravely save us both.
　There is no other Safety.
Oroonoko. It must be –
　But first a dying Kiss –　　　　　　　　　　　*Kisses her.*
　This last Embrace –　　　　　　　　　　　*Embracing her.*
　And now –
Imoinda. I'm ready.
Oroonoko. O! where shall I strike?
　Is there a smallest grain of that lov'd Body
　That is not dearer to me than my Eyes,
　My bosom'd Heart, and all the life Blood there?
　Bid me cut off these Limbs, hew off these Hands,
　Dig out these Eyes, tho' I wou'd keep them last
　To gaze upon thee: but to murder thee!
　The Joy, and Charm of every ravisht Sense,
　My Wife! forbid it Nature.
Imoinda. Tis your Wife,
　Who on her knees conjures you. O! in time
　Prevent those Mischeifs that are falling on us.
　You may be hurry'd to a shameful Death,
　And I too drag'd to the vile Governour:
　Then I may cry aloud: when you are gone,
　Where shall I find a Friend agen to save me?
Oroonoko. It will be so.　　Thou unexampled Virtue!
　Thy Resolution has recover'd mine:
　And now prepare thee.
Imoinda. Thus with open Arms,
　I welcome you, and Death.

　　　　　　　　　　He drops his Dagger as he looks on her, and throws
　　　　　　　　　　　　　　　himself on the Ground.

Oroonoko. I cannot bear it.
　O let me dash against this Rock of Fate:

Dig up this Earth, tear, tear her Bowels out,
To make a Grave, deep as the Center down,
To swallow wide, and bury us together.
It wonnot be.   O! then some pitying God
(If there be one a Friend to Innocence)
Find yet a way to lay her Beauties down
Gently in Death, and save me from her Blood.
Imoinda. O rise, 'tis more than Death to see you thus.
I'le ease your Love, and do the Deed my self –

She takes up the Dagger, he rises in haste to take it from her.

Oroonoko. O! hold, I charge thee, hold.
Imoinda. Tho' I must own
It wou'd be nobler for us both from you.
Oroonoko. O! for a Whirlwind's Wing to hurry us
To yonder Cliff, which frowns upon the Flood:
That in Embraces lockt we might plunge in,
And perish thus in one anothers Arms.
Imoinda. Alas! what shout is that?
Oroonoko. I see 'em coming.
They shannot overtake us.   This last Kiss.
And now farewell.
Imoinda. Farewel, farewel for ever.
Oroonoko. I'le turn my Face away, and do it so.
Now, are you ready?
Imoinda. Now. But do not grudge me
The Pleasure in my Death of a last look,
Pray look upon me – Now I'm satisfied.
Oroonoko. So Fate must be by this

Going to stab her, he stops short, she lays her hands on his,
in order to give the blow.

Imoinda. Nay then I must assist you.
And since it is the common Cause of both,
'Tis just that both shou'd be employ'd in it.
Thus, thus 'tis finisht, and I bless my Fate,   *Stabs her self.*
That where I liv'd, I die, in these lov'd Arms.   *Dyes.*
Oroonoko. She's gone. And now all's at an End with me.
Soft, lay her down.   O we will part no more.   *Throws himself by her.*
But let me pay the tribute of my Grief,
A few sad Tears to thy lov'd Memory,
And then I follow –   *Weeps over her.*
But I stay too long.   *A noise agen.*

The Noise comes nearer.   Hold, before I go,
There's something wou'd be done. It shall be so.
And then, *Imoinda*, I'le come all to thee.   *Rises.*

> [Blandford, *and his party, enters before the Governour*
> *and his party, Swords drawn on both sides.*

Governour. You strive in vain to save him, he shall die.
Blandford. Not while we can defend him with our lives.
Governour. Where is he?
Oroonoko. Here's the Wretch whom you wou'd have.
    Put up your Swords, and let not civil broils
    Engage you in the cursed cause of one,
    Who cannot live, and now entreats to die.
    This object will convince you.
Blandford. 'Tis his Wife!   *They gather about the Body.*
    Alas! there was no other Remedy.
Governour Who did the bloody Deed?
Oroonoko. The Deed was mine:
    Bloody I know it is, and I expect
    Your Laws shou'd tell me so. Thus self-condemn'd,
    I do resign my self into your Hands,
    The Hands of Justice – But I hold the Sword
    For you – and for my self.
                    Stabs the Governour, and himself, then throws himself by
                    Imoinda's *Body.*

Stanmore. He has kill'd the Governour, and stab'd himself.
Oroonoko. 'Tis as it shou'd be now.   I have sent his Ghost
    To be a Witness of that Happiness
    In the next World, which he deny'd us here.   *Dyes.*
Blandford. I hope there is a place of Happiness
    In the next World for such exalted Virtue.
    Pagan, or Unbeliever, yet he liv'd
    To all he knew: And if he went astray,
    There's Mercy still above to set him right.
    But Christians guided by the Heavenly Ray,
    Have no excuse if we mistake our Way.

                    FINIS.

EPILOGUE,

Written by Mr. *Congreve*,[50] and Spoken by Mrs. *Verbruggen*.

Y OU *see, we try all Shapes, and Shifts, and Arts,*
    To tempt your Favours, and regain your Hearts.
We weep, and laugh, joyn mirth and grief together,
Like Rain and Sunshine mixt, in April *weather.*
Your different tasts divide our Poet's Cares:
One foot the Sock, t'other the Buskin[51] wears:
Thus, while he strives to please, he's forc'd to do't,
Like Volscius, *hip-hop, in a single Boot.*[52]
Criticks, he knows, for this may damn his Books:
But he makes Feasts for Friends, and not for Cooks.[53]
Tho' Errant-Knights of late no favour find,[54]
Sure you will be to Ladies-Errant kind.
To follow Fame, Knights-Errant make profession: ⎫
We Damsels flye, to save our Reputation: ⎬
So they, their Valour show, we, our Discretion. ⎭
To Lands of Monsters, and fierce Beasts they go: ⎫
Wee, to those Islands, where Rich Husbands grow: ⎭

---

[50] William Congreve (1670–1729), playwright.
[51] The sock and buskin represent comedy and tragedy. See above, n. 11.
[52] An allusion to a famous scene in *The Rehearsal* (1671), by the Duke of Buckingham and others, parodying the conflicts between love and honor. Prince Volscius debates whether to don his boots and depart to the army or leave them off and stay with the woman he loves. He eventually leaves, "hip hop, hip hop" (3.5.107–08), with one boot on and one off.
[53] Novak and Rodes point out an allusion to Martial, *Epigrams* IX.81: "I should prefer the dishes at my dinner to please the guests rather than the cooks" (Southerne, *Oroonoko* [1976] 125).
[54] Parts I and II of Thomas Durfey's *The Comical History of Don Quixote* (May, 1694) had succeeded, but the third (November 1695) was a failure.

Tho' they're no Monsters,° we may make 'em so.
If they're of English grow'th, they'll bear't with patience:
But save us from a Spouse of Oroonoko's *Nations!*
Then bless your Stars, you happy London *Wives,*
Who love at large, each day, yet keep your lives:
Nor envy poor Imoinda's *doating blindness,*
Who thought her Husband kill'd her out of kindness.
Death with a Husband ne'er had shewn such Charms,
Had she once dy'd° within a Lover's Arms.
Her error was from ignorance proceeding:
Poor Soul! she wanted some of our Town Breeding.
Forgive this Indians *fondness of her Spouse;*   ⎫
Their Law no Christian Liberty[55] *allows:*   ⎬
Alas! they make a Conscience of their Vows!   ⎭
If Virtue in a Heathen be a fault;
Then Damn the Heathen School, where she was taught.
She might have learn'd to Cuckold, Jilt, and Sham,
Had Covent-Garden *been in* Surinam.

FINIS.

Monsters: cuckolds   **dy'd:** experienced an orgasm

---

[55] Literally, the Christian's freedom from the law of Moses (see Galatians 5:1), but often
used ironically of morally lax behavior.

PART TWO

CONTEXTS: EUROPE, AMERICA, AND AFRICA

From *A Short Account of the Destruction of the Indies* (1542)

B ARTOLOMÉ DE LAS CASAS (1474?–1566) emigrated to Hispaniola at the age of twenty-eight, trained for the priesthood ten years later, and entered the Dominican order. He became horrified by the oppression of the Native Americans and published the *Short Account of the Destruction of the Indies* in 1542. Charles V appointed a committee to investigate his allegations, but the committee rejected them.

Las Casas's work became a key text in differentiating English moderation from the cruelty of Spain. The current translation, by Milton's nephew John Phillips, appeared at the time of Cromwell's campaign in the Caribbean, which was inspired by the belief that the Native Americans would welcome British liberation from the oppressive Spanish. Phillips' dedications, to Cromwell and "All True Englishmen," vigorously support the campaign. Thomas Gage's *The English-American* (1648) and Davenant's *The History of Sir Francis Drake* (1658), excerpted below, are associated with the same movement (which Gage played a part in inspiring).

Las Casas's work was first translated into English as *The Spanish Colonie* in 1583, at the time of the revolt of the Low Countries against Spain. Another translation, *Popery Truly Display'd in its Bloody Colours*, appeared in 1689, after the revolution that deposed the Catholic James II (which Behn is sometimes thought to have foreseen when she wrote *Oroonoko*). All three translations thus speak to a specific political moment.

The following excerpt contains an account of the kidnapping of a Native American prince in circumstances very similar to those of Oroonoko's abduction. Such accounts are common enough, but it is noteworthy how the significance of the event has changed from Phillips to Behn. For the 1656 British audience, the episode indicates the un-English treachery of an

From *The Tears of the Indies*, trans. J[ohn] P[hillips] (London, 1656) 1–3, 80–82.

alien culture. For Behn, it illustrates the morality of an alien class: a ruthless trader has the outward manners, but not the inner character, of the upper classes. It is also noteworthy that Christianity, which in Las Casas's work is opposed to the slaver's treachery, is in Behn its justification; and that, in Las Casas, the alien's assumption of a European name is a welcome sign of his cultural assimilability. Oroonoko's renaming as "Caesar" is, by contrast, full of irony.

❧

Tears of the Indies, *or Inquisition for Bloud: being the Relation of the* Spanish *Massacre there.*

In the year 1492. the *West-Indies* were discovered, in the following year they were inhabited by the *Spaniards*: a great company of the *Spaniards* going about 49 years agoe. The first place they came to, was *Hispaniola*, being a most fertile Island, and for the bignesse of it very famous, it being no less then six hundred miles in compass. Round about it lie an innumerable company of Islands, so throng'd with Inhabitants, that there is not to be found a greater multitude of people in any part of the world. The Continent is distant from this about Two hundred miles, stretching it self out in length upon the sea side for above Ten thousand miles in length. This is already found out, and more is daily discovered. These Countreys are inhabited by such a number of people, as if God had assembled and called together to this place, the greatest part of Mankinde.

This infinite multitude of people was so created by God, as that they were without fraud, without subtilty or malice, to their natural Governours most faithful and obedient. Toward the *Spaniards* whom they serve, patient, meek and peaceful, and who laying all contentious and tumultuous thoughts aside, live without any hatred or desire of revenge; the people are most delicate and tender, enjoying such a feeble constitution of body as does not permit them to endure labour, so that the Children of Princes and great persons here, are not more nice° and delicate then the Children of the meanest Countrey-man in that place. The Nation is very poor and indigent, possessing little, and by reason that they gape not after temporal goods, neither proud nor ambitious. Their diet is such that the most holy Hermite cannot feed more sparingly in the wildernesse. They go naked, only hiding the undecencies of nature, and a poor shag° mantle about an

nice: tender   **shag**: coars cloth

ell° or two long is their greatest and their warmest covering. They lie upon mats, only those who have larger fortunes, lye upon a kinde of net which is tied at the four corners, and so fasten'd to the roof, which the *Indians* in their natural language call *Hamecks*. They are of a very apprehensive and docible° wit, and capable of all good learning, and very apt to receive our Religion, which when they have but once tasted, they are carryed on with a very ardent and zealous desire to make a further progress in it; so that I have heard divers *Spaniards* confesse that they had nothing else to hinder them from enjoying heaven, but their ignorance of the true God.

To these quiet Lambs, endued with such blessed qualities, came the *Spaniards* like most cruel Tygres, Wolves, and Lions, enrag'd with a sharp and tedious hunger; for these forty years past, minding nothing else but the slaughter of these unfortunate wretches, whom with divers kinds of torments neither seen nor heard of before, they have so cruelly and inhumanely butchered, that of three millions of people which *Hispaniola* it self did contain, there are left remaining alive scarce three hundred persons. It happened afterwards when the religious persons° were gone, that there came a band of Souldiers, who according to their wonted customes of fraud and impiety, carried away captive the Prince of the Province, who (either because that name was given him by the Religious persons, or by the other *Spaniards*) was call'd *Alfonsus*; for they delight to be called by the names of the Christians, and therefore before they are informed of any thing else they desire to be baptized. By these souldiers was *Alfonsus* craftily seduced a shipboard under pretence that they would give him a Banquet; with their Prince there went seventeen other persons, for they had a confidence that the Fryers would keep the *Spaniards* from doing them any injury, for otherwise the said King would not have trusted them so far; but they were no sooner on shipboard, but the *Spaniards* hoysed up their sailes for *Hispaniola*, where they sold all the *Indians* for slaves; Now all the Region being troubled for the losse of their King and Queen, flockt to the Religious persons, and had like to have slain them; who perceiving the injustice of the *Spaniards* were very much troubled; and I do beleeve, that they had rather have lost their lives, then that the *Indians* should have suffered such an injury to the hinderance of their salvation; but the *Indians* were satisfied with the promises of the religious persons, who told them, that as soon as any ships came to the Island, they would take the first opportunity to go to *Hispaniola* and endevour to get their King and Queen set at liberty. Providence sent a

---

ell: 45 inches   **docible:** teachable
religious persons: clergymen

ship thither to confirm the condemnation of those that govern'd, by which these religious persons sent to the religious persons of *Hispaniola*, but got no redress, for the *Spaniards* there were receivers of the prey. When the religious persons, who had promised to the *Indians* that their King should return within four moneths, saw that he did not come in eight moneths, they prepared themselves for death, and to give up their lives to Christ to whom they had offer'd them before their departure out of *Hispaniola*; and so the innocent *Indians* reveng'd themselves upon the innocent Friers. For the *Indians*, believed that the religious persons were guilty of the said treachery, partly because that their promises concerning the return of their King in four moneths had prov'd so vain, partly because the *Indians* make no distinction between the religious persons and the theeving *Spaniards*.

[There follows an account of a treacherous mass kidnapping of slaves.]

JUAN GINÉS DE SEPÚLVEDA

From *Democrates Secundus* (1547)

J UAN GINÉS DE SEPÚLVEDA (1490?–1573) was the chaplain and official
chronicler of Charles V and a tutor of Philip II. *Democrates Secundus*
(1547) was written in answer to Bartolomé de Las Casas's great denunciation
of Spanish atrocities in the New World, *A Short Account of the Destruction of
the Indies* (1542). It defended the right of the Spaniards to make war on the
pagan and allegedly subhuman Native Americans; in passing, Sepúlveda
derides any temptation to idealize their primitive existence. The work was
condemned, and the royal license necessary for publication was denied.
Sepúlveda engaged in a famous "debate" in Valladolid with Las Casas,
though the antagonists never faced each other. Sepúlveda's work remained
under condemnation, and at his death he was almost forgotten.

※

With the prudence, intelligence, magnanimity, temperance, humanity, and
religion of these men [the conquistadors], now compare these less-than-
men [*homunculi*], in whom you will scarce find any traces of humanity.
They lack learning, have no use or knowledge of writing, and keep no historical records, other than a tenuous and vague memory of some events,
recorded in pictographs. They have no written laws, but only certain barbarous institutions and customs. As to virtues, if you look for temperance
and mildness, what can be hoped from people who were immoderate in
every form of intemperance and unspeakable lust, and of whom not a few fed
on human flesh? Before the Christians arrived, don't think that they lived
in leisure and in the peaceful Golden Age of the poets; on the contrary,

From Juan Ginés de Sepúlveda, *Obras completas*, ed. E. Rodríguez Peregrina and B. Cuart
Moner, III (Pozoblanco, 1995–), 65–67. My translation.

they waged almost continual war among themselves, and so ferociously that they did not value victory, unless they glutted their monstrous hunger with the flesh of enemies. Their barbarity seems all the more unnatural by contrast with the indomitably fierce Scythians,[1] who also fed on human bodies; unlike them, the Indians are so cowardly and fearful that they could scarcely bear the hostile appearance of our men. Often many thousands scattered in womanly flight and yielded to a tiny number of Spaniards, not even amounting to a hundred. . . .

[Sepúlveda here derides the pusillanimity of Montezuma and his subjects in yielding so easily to Cortés.]

The fact that some of them appear talented in certain crafts is no proof of a more human prudence, since we see small creatures such as bees and spiders fashion works which no human industry can adequately imitate.

As for what certain people [have claimed] of the political way of life of the inhabitants of New Spain and Mexico: these, as I have already said, are regarded as the most human of all; their public institutions are lauded, as if it were a sufficient display of industry and humanity to have rationally constructed cities, to have elective rather than hereditary monarchies, and to conduct trade in the manner of human peoples. See how utterly they are deceived, and how much I dissent from their opinion: their public institutions are the greatest sign of their primitiveness, savagery, and innate servility. They are for the most part slavish and barbarous. For the fact that they have houses, some means of communal living, and trade, which natural necessity brings about, proves nothing but that they are not bears or monkeys, which totally lack reason.

---

[1] In ancient times, a nomadic people living in central Asia.

From "Of the Cannibals" (1580)
and "Of Coaches" (1588)

MICHEL EYQUEM DE MONTAIGNE (1533–92), the famous French essayist, was particularly influential in reviving the ancient philosophy of Pyrrhonism, which held that verifiable knowledge was impossible. Challenging the idea that Christianity was capable of rational demonstration, he argued that human reason was inevitably fallible. In his longest essay, "The Apologie of Raimond Sebond" (Book II, Essay xii), he argued that sensory information could not be verified and that customs varied so profoundly from culture to culture that it was impossible to assert the existence of universal moral values. Montaigne had a profound influence on the development of free thought: Oroonoko's French tutor is his intellectual heir. His cultural relativism and religious open-mindedness are evident in the way he compares European and American cultures, to the disadvantage of the former.

Influences on Montaigne include Las Casas and the French Huguenot writer Jean de Léry (1534–1613?), who had not only lived among Brazilian cannibals but also had experienced the horror of the French Wars of Religion (1562–98). The most famous atrocity committed in these wars was the Massacre of Saint Bartholomew in August 1572, but the catalogue of violence also included cannibalism, done both because of starvation (among Huguenots in the siege of Sancerre) and religious hatred: Some members of the St Bartholomew mob devoured the hearts and livers of their slain adversaries.[1] Léry's detailed description of the cannibals' ceremonies "both in killing and in eating" prisoners (122–33) amply demonstrates their cruelty

---

[1] Jean de Léry, *A History of a Voyage to the Land of Brazil*, trans. Janet Whatley (Berkeley: University of California Press, 1990), xvii–xviii, xxviii.

From *Essayes*, trans. John Florio (London, 1613), I, 366–75, III, 209–11.

and barbarity, but he concludes by suggesting that the recent cannibalism in France itself was even worse.

Under the influence of Las Casas, Montaigne deplores Spanish cruelty, but whereas the former stresses the Native Americans' receptiveness to Christianity and contrasts it with the un-Christian behavior of the Spanish soldiers, Montaigne gives more emphasis to the intrinsic virtues of the native culture. He was influential in promoting primitivism – the idealization of primitive cultures, imagined to be in closer proximity to natural law – and some of his idealized details influenced Behn; for example, his account of the Native Americans' ignorance of verbal falsehood. He also, however, documented their violence and cannibalism, but suggested that these acts were far less cruel and culpable than the religious violence that had recently engulfed France; it is better, he said, to eat men dead than torture them alive. His essay inspired a long-standing tendency to portray Native American rulers as rationalistic critics of European suspicion and fanaticism.

In both essays, Montaigne stresses the absence of advanced systems of measurement and counting in the New World. This is far truer of the Caribs than the Aztecs, but Europeans in this period were fascinated by the mathematical otherness of the New World and tended to emphasize mathematical backwardness at the expense of the mathematical achievements of the Aztecs and Maya. In *Oroonoko*, Behn differentiates the Carib and European capacities for mathematical symbolism, emphasizing the Native Americans' inability to think in abstract numbers.

"Of the Cannibals"

I find, that there is nothing Barbarous and Savage in this Nation, by any thing that I can gather, excepting, That every one gives the Title of Barbarity to every thing that is not in use in his own Country: As indeed we have no other level° of Truth and Reason, than the Example and Idea of the Opinions and Customs of the place wherein we Live. There is always the true Religion, there the perfect Government, and the most exact and accomplish'd Usance of all things. They are Savages at the same rate, that we say Fruits are wild,[1] which Nature produces of her self, and by her own ordinary

level: standard
New Spain: Spanish possessions in North and Central America and the Philippines.

---

[1] The French word *sauvage* means both "savage" and "wild" (of plants, etc.), and Montaigne uses it in both contexts.

progress; whereas in truth, we ought rather to call those wild, whose Natures we have chang'd by our Artifice, and diverted from the common Order. In those, the Genuine, most useful and natural Vertues and Properties, are Vigorous and Spritely, which we have help'd to Degenerate in these, by accomodating them to the pleasure of our own Corrupted Palate. And yet for all this, our Taste confesses a flavor and delicacy, excellent even to Emulation of the best of ours, in several Fruits those Countries abound with, without Art or Culture; neither is it reasonable, that Art should gain the Preheminence of our great and powerful Mother Nature. We have so express'd her with the additional Ornaments and Graces, we have added to the Beauty and Riches of her own Works, by our Inventions, that we have almost Smother'd and Choak'd her; and yet in other places, where she shines in her own purity, and proper lustre, she strangely baffles and disgraces all our vain and frivolous Attempts.

> *Et veniunt hederæ sponte suæ melius,*
> *Surgit, & in solis formosior arbutus antris.*
> *Et volucres nulla dulcius arte canunt.*[2]

The Ivie best spontaneously does thrive,
Th' Arbutus best in shady Caves does live,
And Birds in their wild Notes, their Throats do streach,
With greater Art, than Art it self can teach.

Our utmost endeavours cannot arrive at so much as to imitate the Nest of the least of Birds, its Contexture, Quaintness and Convenience: Not so much as the Web of a Contemptible Spider. All things, says *Plato*, are produc'd either by Nature, by Fortune, or by Art;[3] the greatest and most beautiful by the one, or the other of the former, the least and the most imperfect by the last. These Nations then seem to me to be so far Barbarous; as having receiv'd but very little form and fashion from Art and Humane Invention, and consequently, not much remote from their Original Simplicity. The Laws of Nature however govern them still, not as yet much vitiated with any mixture of ours: But in such Purity, that I am sometimes troubled we were no sooner acquainted with these People, and that they were not discovered in those better times, when there were Men much more able to judg of them, than we are. I am sorry that *Lycurgus* and

---

[2] Propertius, *Elegies* 1.2.10–11, 14, slightly altered.
[3] See, e.g., Plato, *Laws* 10.888–90.

Plato[4] had no knowledg of them; for to my apprehension, what we now see in those Natives, does not only surpass all the Images with which the Poets have adorn'd the Golden Age,[5] and all their Inventions in feigning a Happy Estate of Man; but moreover, the Fancy, and even the Wish and Desire of Philosophy it self; so Native, and so pure a Simplicity, as we by Experience see to be in them, could never enter into their Imagination, nor could they ever believe that Humane Society could have been maintained with so little Artifice; should I tell *Plato*, that it is a Nation wherein there is no manner of Traffick, no knowledg of Letters, no Science of Numbers, no name of Magistrate, nor Politick Superiority; no use of Service, Riches or Poverty, no Contracts, no Successions, no Dividents, no Proprieties, no Employments, but those of Leisure, no respect of Kindred, but common, no Cloathing, no Agriculture, no Mettal, no use of Corn or Wine, and where so much as the very words that signifie, Lying, Treachery, Dissimulation, Avarice, Envy, Detraction and Pardon, were never heard of: How much would he find his Imaginary Republick short of his Perfection?

> *Hos Natura modos primum dedit.*
> These were the Manners first by Nature taught.[6]

As to the rest, they Live in a Country, beautiful and pleasant to Miracle, and so Temperate withal, as my intelligence informs me, that 'tis very rare to hear of a sick Person, and they moreover assure me, that they never saw any of the Natives, either Paralitick, Blear-eyed, Toothless, or Crooked with Age.... They have continual War with the Nations that Live further within the main Land, beyond their Mountains, to which they go Naked, and without other Arms, than their Bows, and Wooden-Swords, fashion'd at one end like the head of a Javelin. The Obstinacy of their Battels is wonderful, and never end without great effusion of Blood: For as to running away, they know not what it is. Every one for a Trophy brings home the head of an Enemy he has Kill'd, which he fixes over the Door of his House.

---

[4] Plato described an ideal state in *The Republic* and *The Laws*. Lycurgus is the perhaps legendary author of the constitution of Sparta.

[5] In classical myth, the Golden Age was the earliest period of human history, when men observed righteousness without legal compulsion and food grew spontaneously without the need for cultivation. There was no war and no navigation. (See, e.g., Ovid, *Metamorphoses*, 1.89–112.) The Golden Age provided a model for idealizing the pre-civilized state. Behn wrote a poem entitled "The Golden Age," portraying it as an age of sexual freedom, and praised Thomas Tryon's *The Way to Health, Long Life, and Happiness* (London, 1683) for restoring "that blest golden Age" (*Works of Aphra Behn*, I, 30–35, 179).

[6] Virgil, *Georgics* 2.20.

After having a long time treated their Prisoners very well, and given them all the Regalia's they can think of, he to whom the Prisoner belongs, invites a great Assembly of his Kindred, and Friends, who being come, he ties a Rope to one of the Arms of the Prisoner, of which, at a distance, out of his reach, he holds the one end himself, and gives to the Friend he Loves best, the other Arm to hold after the same manner; which being done, they two in the presence of all the Assembly, dispatch him with their Swords. After that, they Roast him, Eat him amongst them, and send some Chops to their absent Friends, which nevertheless they do not do, as some think, for Nourishment, as the *Scythians* anciently did,[7] but as a representation of an extream Revenge; as will appear by this, That having observ'd the *Portugals*, who were in League with their Enemies, to inflict another fort of Death upon any of them they took Prisoners: Which was, to set them up to the Girdle in the Earth, to shoot at the remaining part till it was stuck full of Arrows, and then to hang them: They that thought those People of the other World, (as those who had sown the knowledg of a great many Vices amongst their Neighbours, and who were much greater Masters in all sorts of Mischief than they,) did not exercise this sort of Revenge without Mystery,° and that it must needs be more painful than theirs; and so began to leave their old way, and to follow this. I am not sorry that we should here take notice of the Barbarous Horrour of so Cruel an Action, but that seeing so clearly into their faults, we should be so blind in our own: For I conceive, there is more Barbarity in Eating a Man Alive, than when he is Dead; in tearing a Body Limb from Limb, by Wracks and Torments, that is yet in perfect Sense, in Roasting it by degrees, causing it to be bit and worried by Dogs and Swine, (as we have not only read, but lately seen; not amongst inveterate and mortal Enemies, but Neighbours, and fellow Citizens, and which is worse, under colour of Piety and Religion,) than to Roast, and Eat him after he is Dead.

'Of Coaches'

Our World has lately discover'd another, (and who will assure us that it is the last of his Brothers, since the *Demons*, the *Sybils*,[8] and we our selves have been ignorant of this till now?) as large, well peopled, and fruitfull, as this whereon we live; and yet so raw and childish, that we yet teach it its

---

Mystery: secret reason.

[7] In ancient times, a nomadic people living in central Asia.
[8] Ancient prophetesses in Greco-Roman legend.

A B C: 'tis not above fifty years since it knew neither *Letters, Weights, Measures, Vestments, Corn,* nor *Vines.* It was then quite naked in the Mothers lap, and only liv'd upon what she gave it. If we rightly conclude of our end, and this Poet[9] of the youthfulness of that Age of his; that other World will only enter into the Light when this of ours shall make its *Exit.* The Universe will be Paralitick, one Member will be useless, another in vigour. I am very much afraid that we have very much precipitated its declension and ruine by our contagion; and that we have sold it our Opinions and our Arts at a very dear rate. It was an infant World, and yet we have not whipt, and subjected it to our discipline, by the advantage of our Valour and natural Forces; neither have we won it by our Justice and Goodness, nor subdu'd it by our Magnanimity. Most of their Answers, and the Negotiations we have had with them, witness, that they were nothing behind us in Pertinency, and clearness of natural Understanding. The astonishing magnificence of the Cities of *Cusco* and *Mexico,* and amongst many other such like things, the Garden of this King, where all the *Trees, Fruits* and *Plants,* according to the order and stature they are in a Garden, were excellently form'd in Gold; as in his Cabinet were all the Animals bred upon the Earth, and in the Seas of his Dominions; and the beauty of their Manufactures, in *Jewels, Feathers, Cotton,* and *Painting,* gave ample proof that they were as little inferiour to us in industry. But as to what concerns *Devotion, observance* of the *Laws, Bounty, Liberality, Loyalty,* and plain dealing, it was of Use to us, that we had not so much as they; for they have lost, sold, and betray'd themselves by this advantage. As to *boldness* and *courage, stability, constancy* against Pain, Hunger, and Death, I should not fear to oppose the Examples I find amongst them, to the most famous Examples of elder times, that we find in our *Records* on this side of the World. For, as to those who have subdu'd them, take but away the Slights and Artifices they practis'd to deceive them, and the just astonishment it was to those Nations, . . . and you take away all the occasion of so many Victories.

---

[9] Montaigne had previously referred to the Roman poet Lucretius' opinion that the world was still new (*De Rerum Natura* 5.330-34).

From *On Spreading the Gospel Among the Savages; or, on Securing the Salvation of the Indians* (1589)

J OSÉ DE ACOSTA (1539–1600) was a Jesuit who served as a missionary in Peru from 1571 to 1587. His *Historia natural y moral de las Indias* (1590) was an extremely influential description of the history, geography, and ethnography of the New World and was translated into English by Edward Grimstone in 1604. Like Las Casas, he opposed the oppression and over-taxation of the Native Americans and had several audiences with King Philip II, who favored his views over those of Sepúlveda.

❧

That the incapacity of the Indians proceeds not from nature but from upbringing and custom

I shall add something that I think of the highest importance. In every respect, the Indians' slowness of mind and savagery are not caused by factors of birth, origin, or native climate but by their daily upbringing, and by habits not greatly dissimilar from the life of beasts. I have indeed been convinced of this for a long time, and am now unshakeably assured by hard facts. If one considers the matter soundly, upbringing generally plays a far larger part in human intelligence than birth. Ancestry and country admittedly have considerable force: corroborating the poet Epimenides, the Apostle Paul wrote, "The Cretians are alway liars, evil beasts, slow bellies" (Titus 1:12), as though nationality contributed much to perversity of customs. The observation of another poet, however, is also widely known:

From José de Acosta, *De Natura Novi Orbis libri Libri II, et de promulgatione Evangelii apud barbaros, sive de procuranda Indorum salute, libri VI* (Cologne, 1596), 149–51. [Two Books on the Nature of the New World, and Six on Spreading the Gospel among the Savages; or, on Securing the Salvation of the Indians]. My translation.

"You would think him a Boeotian, born where the air is dense" (Horace, *Epistles* 2.1.244).[1]

In innumerable respects, however, upbringing is uppermost: the power of examples which have entered our unformed, tender minds through the senses and been engraved on them from earliest childhood. These are the forms which animate the human mind. Imbued with these it moves with its peculiar, private tendency to appetite, action, and aversion, even as a certain natural instinct works alongside the form implanted in it. Therefore all philosophers agree that what we are accustomed to causes pleasure not pain, and that the force of custom is another nature.[2] As our Wise Man said, "Train up a child in the way he should go: and when he is old, he will not depart from it" (Proverbs 22:6). In fact, no nation is so barbarous or brainless that, if it were brought up from birth carefully and nobly, it would not acquire civilization and refinement and leave its barbarity. We see, even in our very own Spain, men born in certain villages, who are held to be ridiculous and stupid if they remain among their own people. If the same people are transferred to schools, or the court, or populous cities, they will excel in intellect and wonderful cleverness. Take the very children of the Negroes, than whom nothing appears more absurd. If they are brought up in a palace, you will find them so quick in intelligence, and equipped for anything, that – if you were to remove their colour – you would take them for one of us.

---

[1] Boeotia was the central region in ancient Greece, whose principal city was Thebes. Its inhabitants were proverbially stupid.
[2] Aristotle, *Ethics 8.*

From *The English-American his Travail by Sea and Land* (1648)

T HOMAS GAGE (d. 1656) was a member of a prominent Catholic family. Against the wishes of his father, who wanted him to become a Jesuit, Thomas joined the Dominican order in Spain and set off for missionary work in the Philippines. Pausing en route in Mexico, he became disillusioned with the corruption of the Catholic church and made a cliff-hanging escape back to England. He was convinced that the Native Americans would welcome the English as liberators from Spanish oppression and was instrumental in encouraging Cromwell's largely unsuccessful Caribbean campaign of 1655. He served as chaplain on the expedition and died in Jamaica. Gage's work draws parallels between the cruel idolatry of the Aztecs and the practices of the Catholic church and interestingly shows how corrupt priests mingled Christianity and pagan superstition in order to extract money from the Native Americans. In a slight anticipation of *Oroonoko*, he describes the bravery of slaves in fighting with wild bulls and wrestling with alligators in rivers (129).

The charitable motives of Gage's dedication are somewhat contradicted by the ensuing commendatory poem by Thomas Chaloner (one of the signatories of Charles I's death sentence). It compares the colonial enterprise with Richard I's Crusade, and boasts

> Now shall the tawnie *Indians* quake for fear,
> Their direfull march to beat when they doe hear. (sig. [A5])

Gage, however, drew a more idealistic vindication of colonialism from the Quaker William Loddington (1626–1711), who stressed the missionary aspect of English expansion. He brusquely dismisses moral objections to

From *The English-American his Travail by Sea and Land* (London, 1648), Dedication.

the occupation of Native American land: Are not the English descended from Danish and Saxon invaders of Britain, and do not the Native Americans themselves invade and occupy each other's territory? He invokes Gage's "Travels in the Western Land" to promise the Indians that

> A People comes, not for the Silver Mines.
> More precious treasure draws their Love to thee:
> Poor Man! Thou hast a Soul as well as we.

(*Plantation Work the Work of this Generation* [London, 1682]. pp. 4, 13)

✵

To His Excellency

Sr. THOMAS FAIRFAX Knight,

Lord FAIRFAX

O F

CAMERON,[1]

CAPTAIN-GENERALL
of the Parliaments Army;

And of all their Forces in ENGLAND, and the Dominion
of WALES.

May it plese your
EXCELLENCY,

THE Divine Providence hath hitherto so ordered my life, that for the greatest part thereof, I have lived (as it were) in exile from my native Countrey: which happened, partly, by reason of my education in the Romish Religion, and that in forraign Universities; and partly, by my entrance into Monasticall orders. For twelve years space of which time, I was wholly disposed of in that part of *America* called *New-Spain*, and the parts adjacent. My difficult going thither, being not permitted to any, but to those of the Spanish Nation; my long stay there; and lastly my returning home, not onely to my Country, but to the true knowledge and free-profession of the Gospels purity, gave me reason to conceive, That

---

[1] Thomas Fairfax, third Baron Fairfax of Cameron (1612–71), commander-in-chief of the Parliamentary forces.

these great mercies were not appointed me by the heavenly Powers, to the end I should bury my Talent in the earth, or hide my light under abushell, but that I should impart what I there saw and knew to the use and benefit of my English Country-men; And which the rather I held my self obliged unto, because in a manner nothing hath been written of these Parts for these hundred years last past, which is almost ever since the first Conquest thereof by the *Spaniards*, who are contented to lose the honour of that wealth and felicity they have there since purchased by their great endevours, so they may enjoy the safety of retaining what they have formerly gotten in peace and security. In doing whereof, I shall offer no Collections,° but such as shall arise from mine own observations, which will as much differ from what formerly hath been hereupon written, as the picture of a person grown to man's estate, from that which was taken of him when he was but a Childe; or the last hand of the Painter, to the first or rough draught of the picture. I am told by others, that this may prove a most acceptable work; but I doe tell my self, that it will prove both lame and imperfect, and therefore had need to shelter my self under the shadow of some high protection, which I humbly pray your Excellency to afford me; nothing doubting, but as God hath lately made your Excellency the happy instrument, not onely of saving my self, but of many numbers of godly and well affected people in this County of *Kent*, (where now I reside by the favour of the Parliament) from the imminent ruine and destruction plotted against them by their most implacable enemies; so the same God who hath led your Excellency through so many difficulties towards the settlement of the peace of this Kingdom, and reduction of *Ireland*,[2] will, after the perfecting thereof (which God of his mercy hasten) direct your Noble thoughts to employ the Souldiery of this Kingdom upon such just and honourable designes in those parts of *America*, as their want of action at home may neither be a burden to themselves nor the Kingdome. To your Excellency therefore I offer a *New-World*, to be the subject of your future pains, valour, and piety, beseeching your acceptance of this plain but faithfull relation of mine, wherein your Excellency, and by you the English Nation shall see what wealth and honor they have lost by one of their narrow hearted Princes,[3] who living in peace and abounding in riches, did

---

Collections: conclusions

---

[2] After an uprising in 1641, Ireland was brutally reconquered in 1649–52 under Cromwell's generalship.

[3] Via his brother Bartholomew, Columbus had unsuccessfully sought backing from Henry VII of England.

notwithstanding reject the offer of being first discoverer of *America*; and left it unto *Ferdinando* of *Arragon*, who at the same time was wholly taken up by the Warrs, in gaining of the City and Kingdome of *Granada* from the *Moores*; being so impoverished thereby, that he was compelled to borrow with some difficulty a few Crowns of a very mean man, to set forth *Columbus* upon so glorious an expedition. And yet, if time were closely followed at the heels, we are not so farr behinde, but me might yet take him by the fore-top. To which purpose, our Plantations of the *Barbadoes, St. Christophers, Mevis*,[4] and the rest of the *Caribe-Islands*, have not onely advanced our journey the better part of the way; but so inured our people to the Clime of the *Indies*, as they are the more inabled thereby to undertake any enterprise upon the firm Land with greater facility. Neither is the difficulty of the attempt so great, as some may imagine; for I dare be bold to affirm it knowingly, That with the same pains and charge which they have been at in planting one of those pettie Islands, they might have conquer'd so many great Cities, and large Territories on the main Continent, as might very well merit the title of a Kingdome. Our Neighbors the *Hollanders* may be our example in this case; who whilst we have been driving a private Trade from Port to Port, of which we are likely now to be deprived, have conquered so much Land in the *East* and *West-Indies*, that it may be said of them, as of the *Spaniards, That the Sunn never sets upon their Dominions.* And to meet with that objection by the way, *That the Spaniard being intituled to those Countries, it were both unlawfull and against all conscience to dispossess him thereof.* I answer, that (the Popes donation excepted) I know no title he hath but force, which by the same title, and by a greater force may be repelled. And to bring in the title of *First-discovery*, to me it seems as little reason, that the sailing of a *Spanish* Ship upon the coast of *India*, should intitle the King of *Spain* to that Countrey, as the sayling of an *Indian* or *English* Ship upon the coast of *Spain*, should intitle either the *Indians* or *English* unto the Dominion thereof. No question but the just right or title to those Countries appertains to the Natives themselves; who, if they shall willingly and freely invite the *English* to their protection, what title soever they have in them, no doubt but they may legally transferr it or communicate it to others. And to say, That the inhumane butchery which the *Indians* did formerly commit in sacrificing of so many reasonable Creatures to their wicked Idols, was a sufficient warrant for the *Spaniards* to divest them of their Country; The same argument may by much better reason be inforced against the *Spaniards* themselves, who have sacrificed so many millions of

---

[4] A common seventeenth-century spelling of Nevis.

Indians to the Idol of their barbarous cruelty, that many populous Islands and large Territories upon the main Continent, are thereby at this day utterly uninhabited, as *Bartholomeo de las Casas*, the *Spanish* Bishop of *Guaxaca* in *New-Spain*, hath by his Writings in Print sufficiently testified. But to end all disputes of this nature; since that God hath given the earth to the sons of Men to inhabite; and that there are many vast Countries in those parts, not yet inhabited either by *Spaniard* or *Indian*, why should my Country-men the *English* be debarred from making use of that, which God from all beginning no question did ordain for the benefit of mankinde?

But I will not molest your Excellency with any further argument here-upon; rather offering my self, and all my weak endevours (such as they are) to be employed herein for the good of my Country; I beseech Almighty God to prosper your Excellency, Who am

The most devoted and humblest
of your Excellencies servants,

THO. GAGE.

RICHARD LIGON

From *A True and Exact History of the Island of Barbados* (1657)

RICHARD LIGON WENT TO BARBADOS IN 1647, where he had bought a half-share in a sugar plantation. His business failed, and he wrote his book in a London debtor's prison in 1653. His viewpoint is that of a paternalistic slave owner who believes that his slaves are easily made happy (44). He does not question the institution of slavery and indeed provides detailed and to our eyes chilling financial breakdowns of the costs of clothing and feeding the various categories of workers: Slaves "shall be allowed yearly but three pair of Canvas drawers a piece, which at 2s a pair, is 6 s."; their subordinate overseers, by contrast, are allowed six pairs. Servants are fed on beef and pork, slaves on turtles and fish. Although Ligon on the whole has a low opinion of the characters of black Africans, there is "no rule so general but hath his acception [*sic*]" (53), and he praises the honesty and decency of some slaves while believing that "the most of them are as near beast as may be, setting their souls aside". He deplores the cruelty of some masters and is indignant that an intelligent, good-natured slave (Sambo) should have been denied baptism. Yet he approves of the measures with which his friend Colonel Walrond discouraged a suicide epidemic among slaves, who believed that by dying they would return to their countries of origin: Walrond disproved this theory by displaying the heads of the suicides on poles.[1]

Ligon has no anxiety about miscegenation. He praises the black mistress of the Governor of Santiago, who outdid Queen Anne (the queen of James I) "in Majesty, and gracefulness," and writes with clumsy courtliness about the attractions of the young female slaves, "of such shapes, as would have

---

[1] Colonel Humphrey Walrond (?1600–?1670), deputy governor of Barbados (under Lord Willoughby) in the early 1650s and again after the Restoration.

From *A True and Exact History of the Island of Barbados* (London, 1673), 43–47.

puzzel'd *Albert Durer*, the great Master of Proportion, but to have imitated" (15). Ligon is the source of the story of Yarico, a young Native American woman who fell in love with and saved the life of a young Englishman, only to be sold into slavery by him. The story was retold by Steele in "On Inkle and Yarico" (*Spectator* 11) and dramatized by George Colman the Younger as *Inkle and Yarico* (1787), in which the villainous Englishman repents and marries his victim. The historical Yarico's end seems to have been less romantic: We last see her extracting parasites from the soles of Ligon's feet, his indignation at her condition obviously having its limits.

Toward the end of the narrative, there is an ironic reversal of roles between savage and European of a kind that Behn deliberately exploited in *Oroonoko*, but that is here inert and inadvertent. On the way back to England, the ship is becalmed and the white, European crew members threaten to turn cannibal and eat the passengers. Ligon is only saved from the cooking pot because "a little Virgin" uses her skill in needlework to repair the sails. The work ends with Ligon's prayer to be delivered from "this uncircumcised Philistine, the *Upper Bench*" (p. 122).[2]

⁂

The Iland is divided into three sorts of men, *viz.* Masters, Servants, and slaves. The slaves and their posterity, being subject to their Masters for ever, are kept and preserv'd with greater care then the servants, who are theirs but for five yeers, according to the law of the Iland. So that for the time, the servants have the worser lives, for they are put to very hard labour, ill lodging, and their dyet very sleight. When we came first on the Iland, some Planters themselves did not eate bone meat, above twice a weeke: the rest of the seven dayes, Potatoes, Loblolly,° and Bonavist,° But the servants no bone meat at all, unlesse an Oxe dyed: and then they were feasted, as long as that lasted, And till they had planted good store of Plantines, the *Negroes* were fed with this kind of food; but most of it Bonavist, and Loblolly, with some eares of Mayes° roasted, which food (especially Loblolly,) gave them much discontent: But when they had Plantines° enough to serve them, they were heard no more to complaine; for 'tis a food they take great delight in, and their manner of dressing and eating it, is this: 'tis gathered for them

Loblolly: maize gruel	**Bonavist:** a kind of bean
Mayes: maize	**Plantines:** plantains

[2] The Upper Bench was a prison.

(somewhat before it be ripe, for so they desire to have it,) upon Saturday, by the keeper of the Plantine grove; who is an able *Negro*, and knowes well the number of those that are to be fed with this fruite; and as he gathers, layes them all together, till they fetch them away, which is about five a clock in the after noon, for that day they breake off worke sooner by an houre: partly for this purpose, and partly for that the fire in the furnaces is to be put out, and the Ingenio° and the roomes made cleane; besides they are to wash, shave and trim themselves against Sunday. But 'tis a lovely sight to see a hundred handsome *Negroes*, men and women, with every one a grasse-green bunch of these fruits on their heads, every bunch twice as big as their heads, all comming in a train one after another, the black and green so well becomming one another. Having brought this fruit home to their own houses, and pilling off the skin of so much as they will use, they boyl it in water, making it into balls, and so they eat it. One bunch a week is a *Negres* allowance. To this, no bread nor drink, but water. Their lodging at night a board, with nothing under, nor any thing a top of them. They are happy people, whom so little contents. Very good servants, if they be not spoyled by the English. But more of them hereafter.

As for the usage of the Servants, it is much as the Master is, mercifull or cruell; Those that are mercifull, treat their Servants well, both in their meat, drink, and lodging, and give them such work, as is not unfit for Christians to do. But if the Masters be cruell, the Servants have very wearisome and miserable lives. Upon the arrivall of any ship, that brings servants to the Iland, the Planters go aboard; and having bought such of them as they like, send them with a guide to his Plantation; and being come, commands them instantly to make their Cabins, which they not knowing how to do, are to be advised by other of their servants, that are their seniors; but, if they be churlish, and will not shew them, or if materialls be wanting, to make them Cabins, then they are to lie on the ground that night. These Cabins are to be made of sticks, withs,° and Plantine leaves, under some little shade that may keep the rain off; Their suppers being a few Potatoes for meat, and water or Mobbie[3] for drink. The next day they are rung out with a Bell to work, at six a clock in the morning, with a severe Overseer to command them, till the Bell ring again, which is at eleven a clock; and then they return, and are set to dinner, either with a messe of Lob-lollie, Bonavist, or

---

Ingenio: sugar works					**withs:** flexible branches

---

[3] A liquor distilled from sweet potatoes. For a description of its manufacture, see Samuel Clarke, *A True and Faithful Account of the Four Chiefest Plantations of the English in America* (London, 1670), 62–63; Biet, 356.

Potatoes. At one a clock, they are rung out again to the field, there to work till six, and then home again, to a supper of the same. And if it chance to rain, and wet them through, they have no shift, but must lie so all night. If they put off their cloths, the cold of the night will strike into them; and if they be not strong men, this ill lodging will put them into a sicknesse; if they complain, they are beaten by the Overseer; if they resist, their time is doubled. I have seen an Overseer beat a Servant with a cane about the head, till the blood has followed, for a fault that is not worth the speaking of; and yet he must have patience, or worse will follow. Truly, I have seen such cruelty there done to Servants, as I did not think one Christian could have done to another. But, as discreeter and better natur'd men have come to rule there, the servants lives have been much bettered; for now, most of the servants lie in Hamocks, and in warm rooms, and when they come in wet, have shift of shirts and drawers, which is all the cloths they were, and are fed with *bone meat* twice or thrice a week. Collonell *Walrond* seeing his servants when they came home, toyled with their labour, and wet through with their sweating, thought that shifting of their linnen not sufficient refreshing, nor warmth for their bodies, their pores being much opened by their sweating; land therefore resolved to send into *England* for rug Gownes, such as poor people wear in Hospitalls, that so when they had shifted themselves, they might put on those Gowns, and lie down and rest them in their Hamocks: For the Hamocks being but thin, and they having nothing on but shirts and drawers, when they awak'd out of their sleeps, they found themselves very cold; and a cold taken there, is harder to be recovered, than in *England*, by how much the body is infeebled by the great toyle, and the Sun's heat, which cannot but very much exhaust the spirits of bodies unaccustomed to it. But this care and charity of Collonell *Walrond*'s, lost him nothing in the conclusion; for, he got such love of his servants, as they thought all too little they could do for him; and the love of the servants there, is of much concernment to the Masters, not only in their diligent and painfull labour, but in fore seeing and preventing mischiefes that often happen, by the carelessnesse and slothfulnesse of retchlesse servants; sometimes by laying fire so negligently, as whole lands of Canes and Houses too, are burnt down and consumed, to the utter ruine and undoing of their Masters: For, the materialls there being all combustible, and apt to take fire, a little oversight, as the fire of a Tobacco-pipe, being knockt out against a drie stump of a tree, has set it on fire, and the wind fanning that fire, if a land of Canes be but neer, and they once take fire, all that are down the winde will be burnt up. Water there is none to quench it, or if it were, a hundred *Negres* with buckets were not able to do it; so violent and spreading a fire this is, and such a noise it makes, as if two Armies, with a thousand shot of either side, were continually giving fire, every knot of every Cane, giving as great a report as a Pistoll. So that there is no way to stop the going on of this flame, but by cutting down and removing all the Canes that grow before it, for the breadth of twenty or thirty foot down the winde, and there the *Negres* to stand and beat out the fire, as it creeps upon the ground, where the Canes are cut down. And I have seen some *Negres* so earnest to stop this fire, as with their naked feet to tread, and with their naked bodies to tumble, and roll upon it; so little they regard their own smart or safety, in respect of their Masters benefit. The year before I came away, there were two eminent Planters in the Iland, that with such an accident as this, lost at least 10000l. sterling, in the value of the Canes that were burnt; the one, Mr. *James Holduppe*, the other, Mr. *Constantine Silvester*: And the latter had not only his Canes, but his house burnt down to the ground. This, and much more mischiefe has been done, by the negligence and willfulnesse of servants. And yet some cruell Masters will provoke their Servants so, by extream ill usage, and often and cruell beating them, as they grow desperate, and so joyne together to revenge themselves upon them.

A little before I came from thence, there was such a combination amongst them, as the like was never seen there before. Their sufferings being grown to a great height, & their daily complainings to one another (of the intol-erable burdens they labour'd under) being spread thoroughout the Iland; at the last, some amongst them, whose spirits were not able to endure such slavery, resolved to break through it, or die in the act; and so conspired with some others of their acquaintance, whose sufferings were equall, if not above theirs; and their spirits no way inferiour, resolved to draw as many of the discontented party into this plot, as possibly they could; and those of this perswasion, were the greatest numbers of servants in the Iland. So that a day was appointed to fall upon their Masters, and cut all their throats, and by that means, to make themselves not only freemen, but Masters of the Iland. And so closely was this plot carried, as no discovery was made, till the day before they were to put it in act: And then one of them, either by the failing of his courage, or some new obligation from the love of his Master, revealed this long plotted conspiracy; and so by this timely advertisment, the Masters were saved: Justice *Hethersall* (whose servant this was) sending Letters to all his friends, and they to theirs, and so one to another, till they were all secured; and, by examination, found out the greatest part of them; whereof eighteen of the principall men in the conspiracy, and they the first leaders and contrivers of the plot, were put to death, for example to the rest. And the reason why they made examples of so many, was, they found these so haughty in their resolutions, and so incorrigible, as they were like enough to become actors in a second plot; and so they thought good to secure them; and for the rest, to have a speciall eye over them.

It has been accounted a strange thing, that the Negres, being more then double the numbers of the Christians that are there, and they accounted a bloody people, where they think they have power or advantages; and the more bloody, by how much they are more fearfull than others: that these should not commit some horrid massacre upon the Christians, thereby to enfranchise themselves, and become Masters of the Iland. But there are three reasons that take a way this wonder; the one is, They are not suffered to touch or handle any weapons: The other, That they are held in such awe and slavery, as they are fearfull to appear in any during act; and seeing the mustering of our men, and hearing their Gun-shot, (than which nothing is more terrible to them) their spirits are subjugated to so so low a condition, as they dare not look up to any bold attempt. Besides these, there is a third reason, which stops all designes of that kind, and that is, They are fetch'd from severall parts of *Africa*, who speake severall languages, and by that means, one of them understands not another: For, some of them are fetch'd from *Guinny* and *Binny*, some from *Cutchew*, some from *Angola*, and some from the River of *Gambia*. And in some of these places where petty Kingdomes are, they sell their Subjects, and such as they take in Battle, whom they make slaves; and some mean men sell their Servants, their Children, and sometimes their Wives; and think all good traffick, for such commodities as our Merchants sends them.

Negres.

When they are brought to us, the Planters buy them out of the Ship, where they find them stark naked, and therefore cannot be deceived in any outward infirmity. They choose them as they do Horses in a Market; the strongest, youthfullest, and most beautifull, yield the greatest prices. Thirty pound sterling is a price for the best man Negre; and twenty five, twenty six, or twenty seven pound for a Woman; the Children are at easier rates. And we buy them so, as the sexes may be equall; for, if they have more men then women, the men who are unmarried will come to their Masters, and complain, that they cannot live without Wives, and desire him, they may have Wives. And he tells them, that the next ship that comes, he will buy them Wives, which satisfies them for the present; and so they expect the good time: which the Master performing with them, the bravest fellow is to choose first, and so in order, as they are in place; and every one of them knowes his better, and gives him the precedence, as Cowes do one another, in passing through a narrow gate; for, the most of them are as neer beasts as may be, setting their souls aside. Religion they know none; yet most of them acknowledge a God, as appears by their motions and gestures: For, if one of them do another wrong, and he cannot revenge himselfe, he looks up to Heaven for vengeance, and holds up both his hands, as if the power must come from thence, that must do him right. Chast they are as any people under the Sun; for, when the men and women are together naked, they never cast their eyes towards the parts that ought to be covered; and those amongst us, that have Breeches and Petticoats, I never saw so much as a knife, or embrace, or a wanton glance with their eyes between them. Jealous they are of their Wives, and hold it for a great injury and scorn, if another man make the least courtship to his Wife. And if any of their Wives have two Children at a birth, they conclude her false to his Bed, and so no more adoe, but hang her. We had an excellent Negre in the Plantation, whose name was *Macow*, and was our chiefe Musitian; a very valiant man, and was keeper of our Plantine-groave. This Negres Wife was brought to bed of two Children, and her Husband, as their manner is, had provided a cord to hang her. But the Overseer finding what he was about to do, enformed the Master of it, who sent for *Macow*, to disswade him from this cruell act, of murdering his Wife, and used all perswasions that possibly he could, to let him see, that such double births are in Nature, and that divers presidents were to be found amongst us of the like; so that we rather praised our Wives, for their fertility, than blamed them for their falsenesse. But this prevailed little with him, upon whom custome had taken so deep an impression; but resolved, the next thing he did, should be to hang her. Which when the Master perceived, and that the ignorance of the man, should take away the life of the woman, who was innocent of the crime her Husband condemned her for, told him plainly, that if he hang'd her, he himselfe should be hang'd by her, upon the same bough; and therefore wish'd him to consider what he did. This threatning wrought more with him, then all the reasons of Philosophy that could be given him; and so let her alone; but he never car'd much for her afterward, but chose another which he lik'd better. For the Planters there deny not a slave, that is a brave fellow, and one that has extraordinary qualities, two or three Wives, and above that number they seldome go: But no woman is allowed above one Husband.

SIR WILLIAM DAVENANT

From *The History of Sir Francis Drake* (1658)

S IR WILLIAM DAVENANT (1606–68) began his career as a playwright
in 1629 and provided masques (that is, ceremonial theatrical entertainments) for Charles I's court, succeeding Ben Jonson as poet laureate
in 1637. In that year, he wrote a poem supporting an abortive scheme to
establish a colony in Madagascar, in which the King's cousin Prince Rupert
was involved.

Davenant acted as a royalist soldier and agent during the Civil War and
in 1650 was captured by Parliamentary forces while sailing to Virginia. For
a while he was in serious danger of execution. He came to terms with the
Puritan regime and a few years later circumvented the ban on theatrical
performances by staging pieces of musical theater, which included *The
History of Sir Francis Drake* and *The Cruelty of the Spaniards in Peru* (both in
1658, and later included in his entertainment, *The Playhouse to be Let* [1663]).
These works portray the New World as groaning under Spanish oppression
and ready for liberation by the magnanimous British. Although both plays
capitalize on Cromwell's recent colonial adventure in the Caribbean, *The
Cruelty of the Spaniards* also glances at events in Britain, portraying Peru as
a nation in which civil war leads to the murder of the king. Much of the
play, however, concerns European fantasies of the New World, as a place
in which the Golden Age is still a living memory. Like *Oroonoko*, it is both
about Britain and not about Britain.

In this extract, Drake allies himself with some escaped African slaves
("Symerons" or Cimaroons), who have formed a community under their
king. (The fantasy of such a community is to play a role in Oroonoko's
escape plans.) While allied with Drake, they abduct a bride from her

From *The Play-house to be Let*, in *The Works of Sr William Davenant Kt* (London, 1673),
90–100.

wedding feast during an attack on a Spanish settlement. This incident, however, reveals no sinister prejudice about the sexual morals of the black African. The bride is unravished, and in abducting her the Africans are merely imitating the habits of the Spanish; they are quite receptive to the different cultural norms of the English.

Historically, Drake did ally himself with escaped African slaves in order to plunder Spanish mule-trains bearing treasure. The raid on Venta Cruz was in fact a fiasco, though a later raid brought rich booty.

Davenant was the founder of the Duke's Company, the more successful of the two Restoration theater companies, for which Behn was to write plays after his death.

❧❧

The Second ENTRY.

A Symphony variously humour'd prepares the change of the *Scene*.

The SCENE *is chang'd.*

> *In which is discern'd a Rockie Country of the* Symerons, *who were a Moorish People, brought formerly to* Peru *by the* Spaniards, *as their slaves, to dig in Mines; and having lately revolted from them, did live under the government of a King of their own Election. A Sea is discover'd, and ships at distance, with Boats rowing to the shore, and* Symerons *upon the Rocks....*

> *Enter the King of the* Symerons, Drake *senior*, Pedro, *and* Page.

King.   Great Wand'rer of the Sea,
        Thy walks still pathless be.
        The Races thou dost run,
        Are known but to the Sun.
        And as the walk above,
        Where he does yearly move,
  We only guess, though him we know,
        By great effects below.
  So, though thy courses traceless are,
  As if conducted by a wandring Star,
  Yet by thy deeds all Climes acknowledge thee;
  And thou art known and felt as much as he.

Drake Senior. So narrow is my merit wrought,
　That when such breadth you thus allow my fame,
　　　I stand corrected and am taught
　To hide my story, and to shew my shame.
　King.　As tireless as thy body is thy mind:
　No adverse current can thy progress stop.
　Thy forward courage leaves all doubts behind.
　And when thy Anchor's lost, thou keep'st thy Hope.
　　　Welcom! and in my Land be free,
　　　And pow'rful as thou art at Sea.
Drake Senior. Monarch of much! and still deserving more
　Than I have coasted on the Western shore!
　Slave to my Queen! to whom thy vertue shows,
　How low thou canst to vertue be;
　And, since declar'd a Foe to all her Foes,
　Thou mak'st the lower bow to thee.
King.　Instruct me how my *Symerons* and I
　　May help thee to afflict the Enemy.
Drake Senior. Afford me Guides to lead my bold
　　　Victorious Sea-men to their Gold:
　　　For nothing can afflict them more,
　　　Than to deprive them of that store
　　With which from hence they furnisht are
　　T'afflict the peaceful world with war.
King.　　Here from my bosom *Pedro* take,
　　　And him thy chief Conductor make.
　Who once was an unhappy slave to them;
　But now is free by my deserv'd esteem.
　　　He is as watchful as the Eye
　　　Of Age still wak'd with jealousie;
　　And like experienc'd Lovers wisely true
　　　Who after long suspicion find,
　　　They had no cause to be unkind,
　And then with second vows their loves renew.
Drake Senior. He is, since so deservingly exprest,
　Remov'd but from thy bosom to my breast.
King.　All other ayds requir'd to thy design,
　Chuse and receive, for all my strengths are thine.　　*Exeunt.*

　　Enter Four Symerons, *who dance a* Morisco *for joy of the arrival
　of Sir* Francis Drake, *and depart.*

The Scene *is suddenly changed into the former prospect of the rising of the Morning, and* Venta Cruz;[1] *but about the Middle, it is vary'd with the discov'ry of a Beautiful Lady ty'd to a Tree, adorn'd with the Ornaments of a Bride, with her hair dishevel'd, and complaining, with her hands towards Heaven: About her are likewise discern'd the* Symerons *who took her prisoner.*

Drake Senior. What dismal beauty does amaze my sight,
 Which from black sorrow breaks like Morn from Night?
   And though it sweetest beauty be
   Does seem more terrible to me
 Than all the sudden and the various forms
 Which Death does wear in Battels and in storms.
Rouse. A party of your *Symerons* (whose eyes
 Pierce through that darkness which does night disguise
   Whom weary toyls might sleepy make,
   But that revenge keeps them awake)
   Did e're the early dawning rise,
   And close by *Venta-Cruz* surprise
 A Bride and Bridegroom at their Nuptial Feast,
   To whom the *Sym'rons* now
   Much more than fury show;
  For they have all those cruelties exprest
 That *Spanish* pride could e're provoke from them
 Or *Moorish* Malice can revenge esteem.
Drake Senior. Arm! Arm! the honour of my Nation turns
   To shame, when an afflicted Beauty mourns.
 Though here these cruel *Symerons* exceed
 Our number, yet they are too few to bleed
   When Honour must revengeful be
   For this affront to Love and me.
Drake Junior. Our Forces of the Land,
   Brave Chief, let me command.
Drake Senior. March on! whilst with my Seamen I advance,
   Let none, before the Dice are cast, despair;
 Nor after they are thrown, dislike the chance;
   For Honour throws at all, and still plays fair.

---

[1] A small village in Central America.

Rouse.   In beauties noble cause no Seamen doubt,
     If Poets may authentick be.
For Sea-born *Venus*[2] sake let them march out:
     She leads them both at Land and Sea.
Drake Senior. Long yet e're night
      I shall in fight
     Their stormy courage prove:
Each Seaman hath his *Mermaid* too;
     And by instinct must love,
Though he were never taught to woo.
        Enter Pedro.[3]
Pedro.   Stay! stay! successful Chief! my heart as low
 As the foundation where thou tread'st does bow:
     But 'tis not for my own offence;
       For if I should offend
       My King, in thee his friend,
     I would not with my self dispence.
     Thy mercy shall our pattern be,
     Behold th'afflicted Bride is free.

   The Scene is suddenly chang'd again, where the Lady is vanisht, and
   nothing appears but that Prospect which was in the beginning of the
   Entry.

     She is as free and as unblemisht too
     As if she had a Pris'ner been to you.
Drake Senior. What are they who disguis'd in nights dark shade,
       Unlicens'd, from our Camp this sally made?
       Strait to the stroke of Justice bring me those!
Pedro.   They thought their duties was to take their foes.
     Be merciful, and censure the offence
     To be but their mistaken diligence.
Drake Junior. Suspect not *Pedro* in this crime, who still
       Has shewn exact obedience to thy will.
Pedro.   And noble Chief, the cruelties which they
     Have often felt beneath the *Spaniards* sway
     (Who midst the triumphs of our Nuptial feasts

---

[2] In Greek myth, Venus (Aphrodite) was born from the foam of the sea (*aphros* was the Greek for foam).
[3] One of the escaped slaves.

Have forc'd our Brides, and slaughter'd all our guests)
May some excuse even from your reason draw:
Revenge does all the fetters break of Law.
Drake Senior. The future guidance and the care
Of their demeanour in this war,
Is strictly, *Pedro,* left to thee:
The gentle Sex must still be free.
No length of study'd torments shall suffice
To punish all unmanly cruelties.
March on! they may e're night redeem
By vertuous Valour my esteem.   *Exeunt* Drake *senior,*
Drake *junior,* Rouse, *and* Page.
Pedro.   Ho! ho! the Pris'ners straight unbind,
And let the Bride all homage find;
The Father and the Bridegroom, hither bring.
E're yet our Van shall far advance,
Know *Diegos*° you must dance.
Strike up, strike up, in honour of my King.

*Enter the Father of the Bride, and her Bridegroom; the Bridegroom
dancing with* Castanietos, *to express the joy he receives for his liberty, whilst the Father moves to his measures, denoting the fright he
had receiv'd from the* Symerons, *when he was surpriz'd at his nuptial
Entertainment.*

Diegos: Spaniards

From *Voyage de la France Equinoxiale en l'Isle de Cayenne* (1664)

A NTOINE BIET (b. c. 1620) was a French Jesuit missionary who, after the fall of the French colony of Cayenne, visited Surinam and Barbados. He writes warmly about the hospitality and trustworthiness of William Byam. Though appalled by the cruel treatment of slaves, he was (as this passage reveals) not opposed to slavery.

***

Their greatest wealth is their slaves, and there is not one who does not make his master more than a hundred crowns profit per annum. The maintenance of each slave does not cost them more than four crowns in expenditure per annum, and they go completely naked, except for Sundays, when they put on some wretched cotton shorts, and a shirt. The little negroes and negresses go always completely naked, up to the age of fourteen or fifteen. As for their food, there is no nation which feeds them so badly as the English, since for every dish and every form of meat they have only potato, which serves them for bread, meat, fish, and for everything. They keep some poultry for the eggs, which they give to their little children. They are given meat only one time in the entire year, namely on Christmas day, which is the only feast day observed in this island. The English and French indentured servants are scarcely better treated. They are indentured for seven years, and also have nothing but potato. The English are obliged to maintain them, but God knows how they are maintained. Both groups are treated extremely badly. When they work, they constantly have overseers near them, like so many taskmasters in the galleys; these have sticks with

From Antoine Biet, *Voyage de la France Equinoxiale en l'Isle de Cayenne* (Paris, 1664), 290–91. My translation.

which they frequently rouse them, when they do not work as quickly as they wish. What I found strange, was that they had sent suspected Royalists from England, who had been taken prisoner in the battle which the King had lost.[1] Especially when recognized as Catholics, they were sold, the husband in one place, the wife in another, and the children in yet another, so that they could not console each other.

They treat their Negro slaves with great harshness. If some of them on a Sunday leave the limits of their plantation, they receive a beating of fifty strokes, with which they are sometimes completely broken. If they commit some other slight fault, they beat them excessively, to the point of applying firebrands to several parts of their body. This makes them cry in desperation. Thus I have seen a poor Negro woman, perhaps thirty-five or forty years old, whose body was full of wounds which she nursed,[2] caused by her master's application of firebrands. Since these poor wretches are very badly fed, they sometimes break out during the night and go to steal a pig or something similar from a neighbouring plantation. But if they are discovered, there is no pardon for them. I went one day to visit my Irish friend. There one of those poor Negroes, who had stolen a pig, was in irons. The overseer had him beaten every day with scourges by other Negroes, with his hands constantly manacled, until he was covered in blood. After having him treated like this for seven or eight days, the overseer cut his ear off, had it roasted, and forced him to eat it. He wanted to do the same with the other ear, as well as with his nose. I interceded for this poor wretch, and urged the overseer so well that he was delivered from his punishment. With tears in his eyes, he came to throw himself at my feet to thank me. That is a truly miserable state of affairs: to treat so cruelly creatures for whom Jesus Christ has shed his blood. It is true that one has to keep these sorts of people in obedience, but it is inhuman to treat them with such harshness.

---

[1] Probably the Battle of Worcester (1651), in which Charles II unsuccessfully tried to regain his throne. Political prisoners were sold into servitude, normally for terms of four to seven years. So were criminals and religious dissenters. See Smith, *Colonists in Bondage*, pp. 152–203. For a larger discussion of the enslavement of Europeans, see Colley, *Captives*.

[2] The French word is *pensoit*, an archaic form of *pansait*. The translation of Jerome S. Handler, used in Joanna Lipking's edition, mistranslates "claimed" (*Oroonoko*, ed. Joanna Lipking [New York: Norton, 1997], 106). I am grateful to Ms Virginia Perin for help on this matter.

WILLIAM BYAM

From *An Exact Relation of the Most Execrable Attempts of John Allin, Committed on the Person of His Excellency Francis Lord Willoughby of Parham* (1665)

S URINAM WAS FACTION-RIDDEN, though it is difficult from the surviving records to reconstruct the nature of the power struggles. In
1663, the Baptist Henry Adis wrote to Lord Willoughby, complaining of
"drunkenness and so much debauchery" in the "rude rabble," and of "many
bitter Oaths, horrid Execrations, and lascivious Abominations."[1] Byam
appears as an honorable and trustworthy figure in the accounts of Biet and
Warren, and as the voice of Christian morality in the following document.
Yet he was the villain of the piece in an account by Lt. Col. Robert Sanford, a
member of the colony's council, who accused Byam of bypassing democratic
process in the aftermath of the Restoration and seeking absolute authority.
Each side accused the other of drunkenness. It is clear that there was considerable unrest, and Sanford prides himself on not misusing a force that
he was to lead against the Indians. Confusingly, George Marten – Byam's
exemplary antagonist in *Oroonoko* – is in Sanford's account his unscrupulous
accomplice, of "violent counsels," and "offering himself the Hangman of
any at the Governours single command."[2] The present document, written
by William Byam, documents an assault on Lord Willoughby.

There are some details in Byam's account of Allin's crime that may
have impressed Behn: the protagonist's self-destructiveness, his taste for
romance and biographies of the Romans, and the treatment of his body.

✴✴✴

[1] *A Letter Sent from Syrranam, to his Excellency, the Lord Willoughby of Parham* (London,
1664), 5.
[2] Robert Sanford, *Surinam Justice* (London, 1662), 11.

From William Byam. *An Exact Relation of the Most Execrable Attempts of John Allin, Committed on the Person of His Excellency Francis Lord Willoughby of Parham.* (London, 1665.)

THIS ABOMINABLE VILLAIN (as the sequel of this story will demonstrate him) was born in *London*, traded some years in *Barbadoes*, from whence he ran off, and on the 10. of *April, Anno 57*. arrived in this Colony.

Here he settled with an active industry, but much addicted to Swearing. Cursing, and Drunkenness; and on the 15. of *February Anno 59*. was accused and tried for horrid Blasphemy, cursing the most blessed Redeemer of the world, with expressions unfit to be named but by Devils; at the instant recital of which in his Penance and Recantation enjoyned him by the Court, the very Foundation of the house wherein they fate (I being then an Auricular witness) gave a fearful crack, to the terrible amazement of all the trembling Auditours. This dreadful signal of Divine displeasure wrought no remorse in this vile Blasphemer, who disregarding Scripture, and scoffing at Piety, entertained his hours of leisure with Romances, and the Lives of some bold *Romans* and daring Valiant ones, which bred in him an admiration (which he often uttered in his discourse) how any man, endued with the least reason or courage, would on any account suffer torment or publick ignominious death, when his own hands with a stab or poison could give him ease and remedy. Besides, he would often plead that children in misery might justly curse and stab their parents who begat them to beggery. He had good natural parts, but low education, which (had he had Grace) he might have improved. His principles Atheistical; on some subjects he would discourse very rationally, especially on Planting, in which time and experience had tutoured him. By his knowledge in this he advanced his humble fortune, which increasing, heightened strange apprehensions in him, at length more adapting him for Errantry than Planting; he would often say, that if he thought his labour and industry would not present him with more horses in his Coach than the Emperour, he would never toil; and gave out, that as soon as his Estate enabled him, he would buy a ship, sail to *Constantinople*, and kill the Great Turk. That he scorned contests with private men, for he was born to blow up Parliaments, destroy Kingdoms, &c. and these and such like swelling Vapours would often arise from the frothy brain of this *Desperado*.

On the 4. of *November Anno* 63. He was exercising his sarcastical wit to the prejudice of Captain *John Parker*, who retorting grated on *Allins* former blasphemy: this begat a peek° which ended in a Duel, and Captain *Parker* being wounded, *Allin* retires, expecting the issue; hearing no danger, appears, and was bound over to Sessions. Captain *Parker* afterwards recovering, *Allin* declared, that had he miscarried, he would have erected a large pile of wood by his *Negroes*, and when throughly kindled,

peek: pique

would have stabbed himself, and run into its consuming flames to prevent anignominious death.

On the 18. of *November* last His Excellency arrived in this River, to the unexpressible joy of all the Inhabitants, His Excellency under God being the foundation and essence of this Colony. *Allin* was advised that His Excellency was informed in *Barbadoes* of his Blasphemy and Duelling, and that strict inquisition was made what punishment he had undergone for such an accursed crime, and whether since his penance and recantation he had expressed any remorse and amendment, what life he had led, and how he came to be chosen a Representative, and possesse some Offices of eminency in the Colony, it being a deserved scandal unto it, that such a known Blasphemer should be intrusted with places of Dignity in it. *Allin* wrongfully conjectured that this intelligence was blown into His Excellency's ears by Captain *Parker*, whereupon he writes a very civil Letter to His Excellency in vindication of himself, utterly denying that he ever uttered those accursed expressions, that the accusations were malicious, and as he pretended, by reason he had formerly committed one for drinking the Kings health, and that Captain *Parker* continuing his animosities against him, had kindled his prejudice and disesteems.

At Christmas all the Gentlemen near his Excellencies Plantation were invited, *Allin* (though not called) intrudes, and on the morrow after Christmas day His Excellency sends for *Allin* privately into his chamber, tells him he had received his Letter whereby he had perceived his parts, and on that was very fit for the service of the Country, and should be sorry that this business, which he had said he durst not name, should be proved against him; that he sent for him, to let him know, he was not prejudicated, but must do justice; several people had complained against the lewdness of this Country, and not only Captain *Parker*, but several others told him of the business; that he never could perceive Captain *Parker* had any prejudice to the Country (as *Allin* had alleged) and for Duelling he must and would be severe according to the Laws, it preserved mens lives, &c. But that he had no design on his Person or his Estate; *Allin* replyed, that malicious times produced strange effects, &c. and as he was going away he asked His Excellency whether his stay was any thing offensive; His Excellency replyed, he would not thrust any person out of his house, but was no ways desirous of his company, till the business was cleared. This private conference in his Excellencies chamber was immediately penned by *Allin*, and found amongst his papers. Immediately after this, *Allin* informs several of his acquaintance of what had past, retires, and was shy of exposing himself to the publick view; they all assured him that His Excellency had no design neither on his person nor estate, for if he had he would have secured him. Notwithstanding all their good advice *Allins* obstinate suspicion falsly concluded, that His Excellency had a design upon his Vineyard (as he called it) and therefore would put him to death that it might be forfeited. This groundless apprehension made him desperately mad, and guided by an Atheistical Tenet, designed a most murderous inveterated revenge on his innocent Excellency, and his own death. And that his designed malice might have opportunity to effect his intentions, on the second of *January*, after he had made a short stiff Cutlash, exceeding sharp, he commanded five Negroes and a Christian servant to put some provision into his Boat with some Axes and Bills, and then called another Christian servant, and told him, that if he heard he were dead, he should take what he could get, and that he gave him his freedom. This done, he directs his course to the upper end of *Parham* Plantation, and near the open ground, not far from a path leads to *Noetia*, of an old saw-pit, he commanded his Negroes to build a Hut, and sent some of them to observe whether any approched that place, and that they might be unsuspected, ordered them to carry wood on their shoulders, as if they had belonged to a Plantation near unto His Excellency's Plantation, where he sometimes walkt with very slender attendance. These recreations of His Excellencies gave *Allin* encouragement for his desir'd conveniency, but divine providence still steered His Excellency from that part, where this murderer expected him. On Monday the second of *January* His Excellency visiting a Neighbours Plantation, came home late at the landing place, *Allin* lay undiscovered to murder him at his arrival, but a light, and attendance suddenly coming down to receive him, *Allin* at that time was disappointed. The day following His Excellency honoured a Neighbour with a visit, about two leagues from *Parham*, during his absence *Allin* sent a Letter by the hands of a Negroe Boy, but 'twas not left for, nor delivered to His Excellency that day, for it was late before his Bark returned. That night *Allin* called for victuals, and said, come lets eat a little before I die; his servant replied, I hope not so Master, I hope there is no cause or fear of death; I cannot tell answered *Allin*.

The next morning being the fourth day, *Allin* sent a letter very early, by the very same Negroe Boy, and charged him most strictly to deliver it with his own hand; the I'd most confidently goes to His Excellencies chamber, presents the Letter which was wrapped up in a leaf, and unsealed, and so departs; His Excellency (because that *Allin* stood on his justification, and pleaded guiltless, to the Blasphemy[3] for which he was accused) had sent for the papers out of the Records which concerned his tryal, and this morning about the time of the delivery of *Allins* Letter, received them, where

---

[3] Emended from "that *Allin* . . . to the Blasphemy".

he found three positive Depositions, his Indictments, and the Penance enjoyned him by the Court for his blasphemy: After this His Excellency shewed my self, and Major *Banister* (as he was walking in his Plantation) none attending him besides our selves, *Allins* Letter, with what impudency penned, the inserted Copy will evidence, and discoursing of him, His Excellency averred, he need not have any suspicion of him, for he intended him no injury, but he was bound for to take cognizance of his fearful Blasphemy, and to search what judicial proceedings there had been about it, for such a business as this, being of a most dreadful nature, ought not to be slubbered over; and withall informed us, that for his satisfaction he had sent for, and that morning received all papers relating thereunto. And as for his Duelling which *Allin* so much feared to be punished for, he intended not to question him upon the late strict Act, being it was never published nor known here, &c.

His Excellency had summoned the Council here to attend him this evening at *Parham*. At which time as he intended to walk to his Wind · mill, near the place where *Allin* lurked, arrives some Gentlemen of his Council which prevented him. Had he gone, *Allin* had at the place attempted to murther him. The usual hour for evening Prayers being come, all went to divine service in an upper dining Room, where my self, Council, and several Gentlemen of the *Colony*, besides Domestick Servants, attended His Excellency. And as his Chaplain was reading the first Lesson, being the 3. of the 2. *Samuel*, and the 27 verse, *And Joab smate Abner under the fifth rib, &c. Allin* enters the room with a ghastly and direful countenance, at first unknown to any present, and going towards His Excellency with his left hand somewhat extended, as if he intended some civil address, and his right hand aloof behind his right thigh, with his sharp Cutlace in it, and as soon as within reach smote his Excellencies head with all his fury, and seconded his blow before I, who was one of his nearest, could enterpose; immediately other Gentlemen rushed on him: at the instant in which I seized him, *Allin* stabs himself with his short Cutlace in his right side, and down he fell; all were surprized with amazement and horrour, and had I not with a passion- ate earnestness most strictly commanded them to forbear, that he might be reserved for the hand of Justice, several would have slain him; and he hearing them cry out, Kill the Dog, replyed, I came here to dye, to kill my Lord, and then my self. After I had secured him with a Guard, I waited on His Excellency, whom I found through Gods mercy far better than I expected, wounded in the Forehead with a slanting blow, but his worst hurt was in his left hand, with holding it up after he had received the first

By Letters since from *Surinam*, we understand that the Lord *Willoughby's* wounds were so dangerous, that his braines were seen to beat.

blow, had his forefinger and middle finger cut off, and had lost a child had not a large Ring which he wore thereon defended it.'

This night he lay in torment, with the anguish of his wound, which caused a violent Feaver. He repented for nothing but that he had not killed His Excellency; and cursed the Coat which he wore (which was one of his Negroes, that he might be the less known) that dulled his sword from entring deep enough into his body. His Excellencies Chaplain giving him some spiritual advice, he bid him talk to the rabble, and not to him.

He gloried in the action he had committed, but grieved it was unsuccesful; and being by an intimate acquaintance interrogated of his Complices; he answered, He scorned any man should share with him in so noble an action. Being demanded whether he desir'd any thing to dispatch himself, he answered, He could do that at any time: and about 12 at night, the Marshal being gone out of the room, he drew forth a Pistol (which was supposed to be tyed to his thigh) charged up to the Muzzel, clapt it to his Brest, struck fire but 'twould not go off; he then called to a Centinel to spare him a stick of fire to light his Pipe, which observed, he clapt the burning cole to the Pan, but all would not discharge the Pistol, which then discovered, was taken from him.

Being deprived of his Instrument to murther himself, he in vain sollicited the Marshal privately for another, still continuing obstinately unrelenting, and grieved at nothing but that he had not murthered His Excellency and butchered himself.

On the sixth day he was sent down to the Gaol with a strong Guard, and seemed chearful when he was put into the Boat, but had not gone above two Leagues, when feeling death approching, but undiscernably to the Marshal and Guard, he discoursed a little, and was immediately seized with internal tortures, and in a short time became senseless and expired. His carcase was delivered to the common Gaol, where I commanded several Chirurgeons to dissect him, and narrowly observe whether he had taken any poison in his Maw. They found a Pill of *Landocum*[4] undigested, some digested, and some that had passed into his Intestines. This was privately given him by one *Serjeant* the Chirurgeon that dressed him, enticed thereunto by a Diamond-ring and some small presents, who now in durance too late bewails his folly.

The Jury of Inquest found *Allin Felo de se*;° and because such an unheard attempt merited an unusual punishment, his naked carkase was ordered

---

Felo de se: suicide (lit. a criminal towards himself)

[4] Perhaps a misprint for laudanum. I am grateful to Professor John Baird for pointing out that this would be an easy typographical mistake to make.

to be dragged from the Gaol by the common Hangman, and Negroes, to the Pillory at the Town of *Toorarica*, where a barbicue was erected; his Members cut off, and slung in his face, they and his Bowels burnt under the Barbicue, with a seditious paper which he had left to be published after his death, his Head to be cut off, and his Body to be quartered, and when dry-barbicued or dry roasted, after the *Indian* manner, his Head to be stuck on a pole at *Parham*, and his Quarters to be put up at the most eminent places of the Colony.

The Pole to be of the most durable wood, to the future terrour and cursed example of such incorrigible Villains.

Thus died this perverse Atheist, unparallel'd in History, whose pride and passion, and overweening judgment of his cursed Tenet, hurried him to this ignominious end, which his folly fansied should never seize him.

A most remarkable Example to be seriously considered by all that slight the Omnipotent God, his Word and Service, blaspheme the most holy Saviour of the world, value their own vanities, and deny their ears to good advice.

> *It is my duty, and it hath been my care, to inform the World aright of all the passages of this vile Assassinate and matchless Miscreant, wherein I have been exceeding cautious that only Truth should direct my pen.*

Jan. 11.64.

WILLIAM BYAM.

FINIS.

CHARLES DE ROCHEFORT

From *The History of the Caribby-Islands* (1658)

C HARLES DE ROCHEFORT (d. 1690) was a French Huguenot resident
of Holland. His work is criticized by the Catholic missionary writer
Du Tertre, who accuses him of plagiarism and of mocking the church. Du
Tertre, for instance, disputes Rochefort's account of a noble Carib who
converted to Christianity in Paris and reverted to his old ways on returning
home.[1] Certainly, Rochefort's viewpoint is more secular than that of Du
Tertre or Biet. He claims that he wants *"to make a certain parallel between
the Morality of our* Caribians, *and that of divers other yet Barbarous Nations"*
(sig. [A4]), and there is a great deal of cultural relativism in the work,
refusing the Caribs the simple status of Other. For example, Rochefort
discusses the differing cultural norms of beauty and differing cultural attitudes toward nakedness. After deploring the cannibalism of the Native
Americans, he points out that they are, relatively speaking, restrained in
their use of the practice. He does not, in fact, confine himself to com-
paring the Caribs with other *"Barbarous Nations,"* but occasionally brings
European cultural or religious norms into question; indeed, he claims that
the Caribs have been corrupted by the example of the Europeans, who
break promises, burn and pillage their houses, and ravish their wives and
daughters (270). In the Caribbean (as in Europe) women stay at home and
do the housework, but this was not the practice in Peru or ancient Egypt
(295). Commenting on the custom of presenting the head of an enemy to
the king in order to gain permission to marry, Rochefort draws his parallel
not from other primitive cultures but from the Bible: "And who knows not
that King *Saul* demanded of *David* the lives of an hundred *Philistines*, for

[1] Rochefort, 286; Du Tertre II, 416.
From *The History of the Caribby-Islands.* 1658. Trans. John Davies of Kidwelly (London,
1666), 199–203.

the dower of his Daughter, before he gave her him in Marriage?" (334).[2] (The narrative to which Rochefort alludes is rather more graphic: David delivers a hundred Philistine foreskins).

Rochefort notes with disapproval the English practice of entertaining Native Americans on board ship, getting them drunk, and then enslaving them (p. 323). In an interesting testimony to the universality of slavery, he reveals that the Native Americans had captive black Africans as slaves (p. 295). He also provides a striking instance of the French encouragement of intermarriage with the Native Americans: "Nay, there are some handsom Maids and Women amongst the Savage *Caribbians*, witness *Madamoiselle de Roßelan*, wife to the Governour of *Saintalousia* [St Lucia]" (252).[3]

⁂

Of the more honourable Employments of the European *Inhabitants of the* Caribbies; *their Slaves; and their Government.*

And whereas all persons of Quality, whereof there is a considerable number in those Islands, have Servants and Slaves who are employ'd about the works before-mentioned, and that in most parts of *Europe* they do not make use of Slaves, there being only the *Spaniards* and the *Portuguez* who go and buy them up at the places of their birth, such as are *Angola, Cap-vert,*° and *Guinny*, it will be but requisite that we here give a short account of them: But we shall in the first place speak of those who are hired Servants, and to continue such only for a certain time.

As for the *French* who are carried over out of *France* into *America*, to serve there, they commonly deliver obligatory acts to their Masters, which is done before publick Notaries; by which writings they oblige themselves to serve them during the space of three years, conditionally to receive from them so many pounds of Tobacco, according to the agreement they have made during that term. These *French Servants*, by reason of the three years service they are engag'd to, are commonly called the *Thirty-six-months-men*, according to the Language of the Islands. There are some so Simple as to imagine, that if they be not oblig'd to their Masters in writing before their departure out of *France*, they are so much the less oblig'd when they

---

Cap-vert: Cape Verde.

---

[2] Samuel I 18:25.

[3] Louis de Kerengoan, sieur de Rosselan, who took possession of St Lucia in 1650 and governed it peacefully until his death in 1654.

are brought into the Islands, but they are extremely mistaken; for when they are brought before a Governour to complain that they were carried aboard against their wills, or to plead that they are not oblig'd by writing, they are condemn'd for the space of three years to serve either him who hath paid for their passage, or such other as it shall please the Master to appoint. If the Master hath promis'd his Servant no more then the ordinary recompence of the Islands, he is oblig'd to give him for his three years service but three hundred weight of Tobacco, which is no great matter to find himself in linnen and cloaths; for the Master is not engag'd to supply him with any thing but food; But he who before his departure out of *France* promises to give three hundred weight of Tobacco to him whom he receives into his service, is oblig'd exactly to pay it, nay though he had promis'd him a thousand: It is therefore the Servants best course to make his bargain sure before he comes out of his Country.

As concerning the Slaves, and such as are to be perpetual Servants, who are commonly employ'd in these Islands, they are originally *Africans*, and they are brought over thither from the Country about *Cap-vert*, the Kingdom of *Angola*, and other Sea-ports which are on the Coasts of that part of the world; where they are bought and sold after the same manner as Cattle in other places.

Of these, some are reduc'd to a necessity of selling themselves, and entring into a perpetual slavery, they and their children, to avoid starving; for in the years of sterility, which happen very frequently, especially when the Grasshoppers, which like clouds spread themselves over the whole Country, have consum'd all the fruits of the earth, they are brought to such a remediless extremity, that they will submit to the most rigorous conditions in the world, provided they may be kept from starving. When they are reduc'd to those exigencies, the Father makes no difficulty to sell his children for bread; and the children forsake Father and Mother with out any regret.

Another sort of them are sold after they have been taken Prisoners in War by some petty neighbouring Prince; for it is the custom of the Princes of those Parts to make frequent incursions into the Territories of their Neigh-bours, purposely for the taking of Prisoners, whom they afterwards sell to the *Portuguez*, and other Nations with whom they drive that barbarous Trade: They receive in exchange for them Iron (which is as precious with them as Gold), Wine, *Aqua-vitae*,° Brandy, or some poor Clothing: They make Slaves of the women as well as the men, and they are sold one with another, at a higher or lower rate, according to their youth, age, strength,

---

Aqua-vitae: distilled spirits

or weakness, handsomness, or deformity of body. They who bring them over to the Islands make a second sale of them, at fifteen or sixteen hundred weight of Tobacco every head, more or less, as the parties concern'd can agree.

If these poor Slaves chance to fall into the hands of a good Master, one who will not treat them with too much severity, they prefer their present slavery before their former liberty, the loss whereof they never afterwards regret: And if they are permitted to marry, they multiply extremely in those hot Countries.

They are all Negroes, and those who are of the brightest black are accounted the fairest: Most of them are flat-nos'd, and have thick lips, which goes among them for beauty; nay there are some affirm, that in their Country the Midwives do purposely crush down their noses, that they may be flat, as soon as they come into the world: The hair of their heads is all frizl'd, so that they can hardly make use of Combs; but to prevent the breeding of vermine, they rub their heads with the oil of that shrub which is called *Palma-Christi*:° They are very strong and hardy, but withal so fearful and unwieldy in the handling of Arms, that they are easily reduc'd under subjection.

They are naturally susceptible of all impressions, and the first that are deriv'd into them among the Christians, after they have renounc'd their Supersitions and Idolatry, they pertinaciously adhere unto; wherein they differ much from the *Indians* of *America*, who are as unconstant as Cameleons. Among the *French* Inhabitants of the *Caribbies* there are some Negroes who punctually observe abstinence all the time of Lent, and all the other Fasting-days appointed by the Church, without any remission of their ordinary and continual labour.

They are commonly proud and insolent; and whereas the *Indians* are desirous to be gently treated, and are apt to dye out of pure grief, if they be put to more then ordinary hardship, these on the contrary are to be kept in awe by threats and blows; for if a man grow too familiar with them, they are presently apt to make their advantages of it, and to abuse that familiarity; but if they be chastiz'd with moderation when they have done amiss, they become better, more submissive, and more compliant, nay will commend and think the better of their Masters: But on the other side, if they be treated with excessive severity, they will run away, and get into the Mountains and Forests, where they live like so many Beasts; then they are call'd *Marons*, that is to say, Savages: or haply they will grow so desperate as to be their own Executioners. It is therefore requisite, that in the conduct

Palma-Christi: castor oil

of them there should be a mean observ'd between extream severity and too much indulgence, by those who would keep them in awe, and make the best advantage of them.

They are passionate Lovers one of another; and though they are born in different Countries, and sometimes, when at home, Enemies one to another, yet when occasion requires they mutually support and assist one another, as if they were all Brethren: And when their Masters give them the liberty to recreate themselves, they reciprocally visit one the other, and pass away whole nights in playing, dancing, and other pastimes and divertisments; nay, sometimes they have some little Entertainments, every one sparing what he can to contribute to the common repast.

They are great Lovers of Musick, and much pleas'd with such Instruments as make a certain delightful noise, and a kind of harmony, which they accompany with their voices. They had heretofore in the Island of S.*Christophers* a certain Rendezvouz in the midst of the Woods, where they met on Sundays and Holidays after Divine Service, to give some relaxation to their wearied bodies: There they sometimes spent the remainder of that day, and the night following, in dancing and pleasant discourses, without any prejudice to the ordinary labours impos'd upon them by their Masters: nay, it was commonly observ'd, that after they had so diverted themselves, they went through their work with greater courage and chearfulness, without expressing any weariness, and did all things better than if they had rested all night long in their huts. But it being found, that the better to enjoy themselves in these publick Meetings, they many times stole the Poultry and Fruits of their Neighbours, and sometimes those of their Masters, the *French* General thought fit to forbid these nocturnal assemblies: So that now if they are desirous to divert themselves, they are enjoyn'd to do it within their own Neighbourhoods, with the permission of their Masters, who are willing enough to allow them convenient liberty.

As to the Advantages accrewing from the labours of these Slaves, he who is Master of a dozen of them may be accounted a rich man: For besides that these are the People who cultivate the ground in order to its production of all necessary provisions for the subsistence of their Masters and themselves; being well order'd and carefully look'd after, they promote the making of several other Commodities, as Tobacco, Sugar, Ginger, Indico, and others, which bring in great profit. Add to this, that their service being perpetual, their number increases from time to time by the Children that are born of them, which have no other Inheritance than that of the slavery and subjection of their Parents.

From *Histoire Generale des Antilles Habitées par les François* (1667–71)

J EAN-BAPTISTE DU TERTRE (1610–87) was a Dominican missionary. Although he describes the violence and idolatry of the Native Americans (Behn used him for her description of priestly frauds), he also regards their existence as paradisal (I, 357). He movingly documents the miseries of slaves, asserts their common humanity with their owners, and denounces the sexual coercion of women slaves, noting with approval that the French oblige fathers of half-breed children to maintain them until the age of twelve and that such children are treated as European. He also gives an interesting account of the half-Indian son of the Englishman Thomas Warner, who was made governor of Dominica. Yet, du Tertre does not condemn slavery: "I do not claim here to act in the capacity of a legal authority, and to examine the nature of servitude, and of the dominion which man acquires over his like by purchase, birth, or the right of war." He will, he says, simply defend France against the charge that it enslaves Christians (I, 483). He also concedes that harsh punishment of slaves is a practical necessity, but nevertheless stresses St Ambrose's statement that those who are slaves by condition are our brothers in divine grace.

Whereas Antoine Biet warmly describes English hospitality, du Tertre had been captured en route from France to the West Indies and briefly imprisoned at Plymouth. He repeatedly stresses the villainy of Lord Willoughby, whom he accuses of wishing to exterminate all the French settlers in the islands (III, 286). The hurricane in which he died "aborted all his detestable designs" (IV, 102).

From Jean-Baptiste Du Tertre, *Histoire générale des Antilles habitées par les François*. 4 vols. (Paris, 1667–71), II, 493–505.

Of Negro Slaves, commonly called Moors, in France

It is truly in the person of the Negroes that we deplore the fearful miseries that accompany slavery. The Brazilians and Arawaks[1] that the French inhabitants buy to serve them are truly slaves, since they have lost their liberty, and their masters can dispose of them as they please, but they suffer almost nothing of the fatigue and labour of this distressing condition; the Negroes alone bear all the suffering. And as if the blackness of their bodies were the symbol of their misfortune, one treats them as slaves, feeds them as one wishes, drives them work like beasts, and one way or another extracts from them all the service of which they are capable.

Of the Country of the Negroes, the manner in which they are bought there, and in which they come to the West Indies.

The Negroes all originate in Africa, and are taken from the coasts of Guinea, Angola, Senegal, or Cape Verde.

French, Spanish, English, and Dutch traders go there to exchange other merchandise for them. When a ship arrives at these coasts, the trader who owns the vessel applies to the princeling or the governor of the province where he lands, and they sell them these poor, miserable men, women, and children of all ages for bars of iron, grindstones, pieces of silver, brandy, cloth, and for other commodities of which they have most need in these countries.

Normally, they expose three sorts of people for sale. Firstly, enemy prisoners of war. Secondly, those who have merited death for some crime, from whom they prefer to make profit rather than take their lives in the supreme penalty. In third place are those who have been caught red-handed in some theft; the judge treating as equivalent to banishment their loss of liberty among the strangers who buy them.

There are some quite unjust traders, who abducted innocents along with criminals, even robbing of their liberty the very people who sold them these captives, or people who had come on board for dinner. I was told that a certain captain had attracted several people onto his ship with drink and gifts. While these poor people thought of nothing but pleasant entertainment, the pilot raised the anchor, and as soon as the ship was under sail

---

[1] A major grouping of native Americans in the Caribbean, distinguished from the Caribs. In practice, Europeans would class friendly native Americans as Arawaks and hostile ones as Caribs.

they are seized, loaded with chains, and taken to the West Indies, where they were sold as slaves.

I do not know what this nation has done, but it is enough to be black to be captured, sold, and enlisted into a grievous, lifelong slavery. . . . .

Among these slaves there are sometimes those who were of great quality in their own country, but we have never been able to find out what rank among them had been held by the first Negro that we bought at Guadeloupe, nor the manner in which she had been captured in war. She had the demeanour of a queen, and a mind so raised above the misery of her condition, that one saw perfectly well that she had lost nothing of her dignity in her disgrace. All the other Negroes of her country, both men and women, paid respects to her as to a princess. When they saw her in church or on the road, they stopped abruptly in front of her, put both hands on the ground, struck their thighs with them, and held them for a moment raised above their heads, which is the manner in which they pay homage to their rulers. . . .

[Du Tertre stresses the loyalty of slaves to masters who treat them well.]

In the attack on the gloomy De Riflet at Martinique, in which the escaped Negroes combined with the Caribs in the year 1657, the Negroes of the Prince of Orange fought bravely against the rebels, who wanted to corrupt them. They alone, with cutlass in hand and shield on arm, prevented these madmen from burning down the house, and ravaging the dwelling of their good master (who was absent), while those of his neighbours were completely in flames. I could produce a thousand other examples of their fidelity to masters who treat them gently and – as Seneca says – like little friends, not like slaves: "Are they slaves? Rather intimate companions. Are they slaves? Rather humble friends."[2]

If Negroes are very sensitive to kindnesses, they are equally so to injuries; for they preserve a secret hatred towards those who mistreat them, and only the inability to exact vengeance will stifle any part of their resentment. It is to these slaves reduced to despair that we should refer that saying which Seneca – once again – mentions: "you have as many enemies, as you have slaves."[3] Martinique witnessed a dreadful example of this during the attack that I have just mentioned, in the persons of the Lord and Lady de la Planche, who were among the wealthiest inhabitants of the Island. For these slaves, seeing themselves excessively ill treated, had fled, and taking the opportunity provided by the Caribs to take vengeance on their master

[2] Lucius Annaeus Seneca (d. 65 CE), Roman philosopher, *Epistle* XLVII.
[3] *Epistle* XLVII.

and mistress, they came shamelessly in full daylight, entered the house, and having denounced them for the ill treatment they had received from them, split the heads of both with billhooks. After this cruel murder, these madmen started to shout that they had no further fear of death, since they had avenged the cruelties which had been visited on them. . . .

There was a case at Guadeloupe of a young Negress, so convinced of the misery of her condition that her master could never make her agree to marry the Negro whom he offered to her. This master, at first believing that she loved someone else, asked one of our priests to discover his identity, and to promise her that he would buy him, whatever the price. But she never made any other reply than that she had absolutely no wish to marry. Mocking her resolution, her master led her one Sunday to our church to marry the Negro he wished to give her. She offered no resistance, but waited until the priest asked her whether she wanted such a person for her husband; for she then replied with a firmness that astonished us: "No, my Father: I wish neither this man nor even anyone else. It is enough for me to be miserable as an individual, without bringing children into the world, who would perhaps be more unhappy than I, and whose pains would touch me more intensely than my own." She always remained just as constantly in her maiden state, and she was commonly known as the Virgin of the Isles.

From *An Impartial Description of Surinam* (1667)

T HIS PAMPHLET contains a number of details that recur in *Oroonoko*, and for which it is sometimes the direct source: for example, the descriptions of armadillos and "cusharees" and the Caribs' inability to count in large numbers. Like Antoine Biet but unlike Behn, Warren has a high opinion of William Byam. Nothing further is known of the author.

᯽

I'le but name a third, which, for the strangeness of its Nature, deserves a more particular Description, 'Tis the *Torpedo* or *Num-Eele*, which, being alive, and touching any other Living Creature, strikes such a deadness into all the parts, as for a while renders them wholly useless, and insensible, which, is believ'd, has occasioned the Drowning of several persons who have been unhappily so taken, as they were Swiming in the River: It produces the like Effect if but touch'd with the end of a long Pole, or one man immediately laying hold of another so benumm'd: The Truth of this was experienced, One of them being taken and thrown upon the Bank, where a Dog spying it stir, catches it in his Mouth, and presently falls down, which the Master observing, and going to pull him off becomes motionless himself; another standing by, and endevouring to remove him, follows the same fortune; the *Eele* getting loose they Return quickly to themselves.

Plantations are setled Thirty Leagues up the River, higher than which, 'tis not probable, the Limits of that New Colony can extend, by reason of Cataracts or Falls of Water, that descend from ledges of Rocks, from one side of the River to the other, rendring any passage by Water (the best means of Conveying necessaries) altogether impossible; nor is it only one,

From George Warren. *An Impartial Description of Surinam* (London, 1667).

for which, in time, perhaps some Remedy might be invented, but they are observed to be within five or six Leagues one of another, for ought is known, up to the very head: There was once an occasion to go up those Falls in Chase of some *Indians*, who had been down, and kill'd an *English*-Woman, and robb'd the house wherein she was: This Expedition was undertaken by a good number of men well provided, who, after they had with most grievous labour hall'd their Boats by Land above seven or eight of those Falls, were at last, compell'd to return without desired Success, not having so much as seen an *Indian*, and adventuring as they came back to shoot those Precipices in their Boats, were some of them dash'd to pieces in the Descent, and the rest hardly escaped with their Lives: These Cataracts are in most of the Rivers upon the Coast, and are the only Let to the more perfect discovery of that rich Continent. . . .

The Land next the Rivers mouth, is low, woody, and full of *Swampes*:[1] One, but about thirty Leagues up, high, and mountainous, having plain Fields of a vast Extent, here and there beautified with small Groves, like Islands in a Green Sea; amongst whose still flourishing Trees, 'tis incomparably pleasant to consider the delightful Handy-works of Nature, express'd in the variety of those pretty Creatures, which, with Ridiculous Antick Gestures, disport themselves upon the Branches. There is a constant Spring and Fall, some leaves Dropping, and others succeeding in their Places: But the Trees are never quite divested of their Summer Livery; Some, have always Blossoms, and the several degrees of Fruit at once: The Sense of Smelling may, at any time, enjoy a full delight amongst the Woods, which disperse their Aromatick Odours a good distance from the Land, to the no little Pleasure of the Sea tired Passenger.

The various productions of Insects from the heat and moisture, is admirable in that Country. I have observed a white Speck, at first, no bigger than a Pins Head upon a new sprung soft Excrescency from the Root of a Great Tree, which, by degrees in two or three-dayes; has grown to a kind of *Butter-flye*, with fair painted black and Saffron-Coloured Wings. I have found others not quite perfect sticking upon the Bodies of Trees, as it were incorporated into the Wood it self. There is another, called a *Cammel-Flye*, from its long neck, how Generated I know not, which has its Wings like small Leaves, and, having lived a while, at length lights upon the ground, takes Root, and is transformed into a Plant. This I relate, not from any certain Knowledge of my own, but I was encouraged to insert it, from the

---

[1] The word was originally used "only in the N. American colonies, where it denoted a tract of rich soil having a growth of trees and other vegetation, but too moist for cultivation" (*OED*).

Information of the Honourable *William Byam*, Lord General of *Guiana*, and Governour of *Surinam*, who, I am sure is too much a Gentleman to be the Author of a Lye. Many more Observations of this Nature no doubt I might have made, if the vanity of my years would have suffered me to mind it.

The Government is Monarchical, an Imitation of ours, by a Governour, Council, and Assembly; the Laws of *England* are also theirs, to which are added some by Constitutions, no less oblieging, proper to the Conveniencies of that Country. . . .

The Inhabitants of the Trees are *Baboons, Quottoes*;° *Monkeys, Marmazetts, Cusharees,*° *Sloths,* and many more, I have forgotten. The *Deer* are much like our ordinary ones in *England.* The *Hares* more resemble a *pig,* than any other Creature that I know, they are Brown, Smooth-haired, Spotted with white, and are far bigger than an *English*-Hare, which, beside the mouth, they have no part like: They are excellent good meat, much better than any Four-footed Game in *England.* The *Conies* are red, not so good meat, and less than the *Hares,* but not differing in Shape. The *Armadillaes* are of two kinds, great, and little; of the greater, I saw one weighed Eighty Pounds. They are short Legg'd, have three Clawes upon their feet, are Headed like a *Hog,* have no Teeth, and but very little Mouths, they are defended all over, save the Head and Belly, with an Armour as it were plated, scarce penetrable by a Launce, unless it happen in a Joint, they Burrow in the ground, and had they not quite so strong a Smell of *Musk,* would be no Contemptible meat. . . .

Of the *Tigers* there are three kinds, Black, Spotted, and Red,[2] The first is accounted fiercest, but he very seldome appears amongst the Dwellings. The Spotted, which I think are miscall'd, being rather *Leopards,* than *Tigers,* do no little hurt to Plantations, by destroying the Cattle, and Poultry. They are of so vast a strength, that one of them will make nothing to leap over a five or six foot Rail, with a *Hog* in his Mouth. There was once one came into a Plantation, kill'd a *Bull* of two years old, and dragged him above a quarter of a Mile into the Woods. Unless they be wounded, or very hungry, they will hardly assault a man in the day time. I never heard of above two or three they have killed one way or other, since the setling of the Colony: one of them (who was a Huntsman and a lusty Fellow) was often heard to with he could meet with a *Tyger,* and made it a great Complaint in all his Searches through the Woods, it was never his good fortune; at length, one

Quottoes: coaitas; red-faced spider monkeys
Cusharees: lion tamarin monkeys

---

[2] Black jaguars, jaguars, and cougars.

night, lying in his Hamacko, in an open House, a *Tyger* comes, takes him up, and carries him two miles into the Woods, in vain Crying for help, which was heard by an *English-woman* in a Close House hard by, who had so much Courage (more than is usual in her Sexe) to fire a Musquet from the Window; but those who have had to do with them know, it is not noise only can scare a *Tyger* from his Prey: the Man was found next day with his Head and Shoulders eaten off; they are observed to be not so numerous now as formerly, partly retireing further into the Woods, and a great many having been taken by the Hunters. There is one *John Millar*, who has killed no fewer than a dozen or fourteen, singly with his Gun and Launce, from some miraculously escaping with his Life, and having been dangerously hurt by others. There are not many of the Red, and those not so fierce as either of the former. . . .

Monkeys, and *Baboons*, are so familiarly known in *England*, they need not a particular Description here; though one thing of the *Baboons*, wherein, I think, they differ from all others, I cannot omit inserting, which is, that at certain hours both of the night and day, they send so horrid a Roreing from their hollow Throats, that, to those un-wonted to such noises, nothing can seem at first more strange, and terrible, being easily to be heard above two miles off. The *Marmazet* is a very pretty Creature of a greenish yellow Colour, and, though far less than a *Monkey*, is Commander of all those lofty Dwellers, riding them from Tree to Tree at his pleasure, they not being able to shake him off, and in stead of Spurs, to provoke their speed, he bites them by the Ears. The *Quotto* is black, something bigger than a *Monkey*, having a very long tail, with which he swings himself from Bough to Bough, his Face is Red, with hair hanging a little over his Forehead, and his Aspect is almost like an old *Indian*-Womans, his Cry is shrill, and very loud. The *Cusharee* is black, less than a *Marmazet*, and shap'd every way perfectly like a *Lyon*. . . .³

※

Of the Negroes or Slaves

WHo are most brought out of *Guiny* in *Africa* to those parts, where they are sold like *Dogs*, and no better esteem'd but for their Work

---

³ The description of the cusharee is recalled in Behn, *Oroonoko*, 124. According to Biet, "There are male and female monkeys of different kinds. Some, called tamarins, are tiny and wonderfully pretty. They are no bigger than squirrels, and have a head and face like a lion, and little, ivory-white teeth, the same size as the teeth of a medium-sized watch, and just as well arranged" (341).

sake, which they perform all the Week with the severest usages for the slightest fault, till *Saturday* after noon, when, they are allowed to dress their own Gardens or Plantations, having nothing but what they can produce from thence to live upon; unless perhaps once or twice a year, their Masters vouchsafe them, as a great favour, a little rotten Salt-fish: Or if a *Cow* or *Horse* die of itself, they get Roast-meat: Their Lodging is a hard Board, and their black Skins their Covering. These wretched miseries not seldome drive them to desperate attempts for the Recovery of their Liberty, endevouring to escape, and, if like to be re-taken, some-times lay violent hands upon themselves; or if the hope of Pardon bring them again alive into their Masters power, they'l manifest their fortitude, or rather obstinacy in suffering the most exquisite tortures can be inflicted upon them, for a terrour and example to others without shrinking. They are there a mixture of several Nations, which are always Clashing with one another, so that no Conspiracy can be hatching, but 'tis presently detected by some party amongst themselves disaffected to the Plot, because their Enemies have a share in't: They are naturally treacherous and bloody, and practice no Religion there, though many of them are Circumcis'd: But they believe the Ancient *Pythagorean* Errour of the Soul's Transmigration out of one body into another,[4] that when they dye, they shall return into their own Countries and be Regenerated, so live in the World by a Constant Revolution; which Conceit makes many of them over-fondly wooe their Deaths, not otherwise hoping to be freed from that indeed un-equall'd Slavery.

Of the Indians

WHo are a People Cowardly and Treacherous, qualities inseparable: there are several Nations which Trade and familiarly Converse with the People of the Colony, but those they live amongst are the *Charibes*, or *Caniballs*, who are more numerous than any of the rest, and are setled upon all the Islands, & in most of the Rivers, from the famous one of *Amazones*, to that of *Oronoque:* They go wholly naked, save a Flap for Modesty, which the Women, after having had a Child or two, throw off. Their Skins are of an Orange Tawny Colour, and their Hair black, without Curles: A happy people as to this World, if they were sensible of their own hap: Nature with little toyl providing all things which may serve her own necessities. The Women are generally lascivious, and some so truly handsom, as to Features and

---

[4] The Greek philosopher Pythagoras (6th century BCE) believed in reincarnation.

Proportion, that if the most Curious Symetrian had been there, he could not but subscribe to my opinion: and their pretty Bashfulness (especially while Virgins) in the presence of a Stranger, adds such a Charming grace to their perfections (too nakedly expos'd to every wanton Eye) that who ever lives amongst them had need be owner of no less than *Joseph's* Continency, not at least to Covet their embraces: They have been yet so unfortunately ignorant, not to enrich their amorous Caresses with that innocent and warm delight of Kissing, but Conversing so frequently with Christians, and being naturally docile and ingenious we have Reason to believe, they will in time be taught it. Their Houses for the night, are low thatch'd Cottages, with the Eves close to the ground; for the day, they have higher, and open on every side, to defend them from the violence of the Sun's Raies, yet letting in the grateful Coolness of the Air. Their Houshold Utensils are curiously painted Earthen Pots and Platters, and their Napery is the Leaves of Trees. Their Beds or Hamackoes (which are also used amongst the *English*) are made of *Cotton*, square like a Blanket, and so ordered with strings at each end, that being tyed a Convenient distance from one another, it opens the full breadth. For Bread and Drink, they plant Gardens of *Cassader*,[5] and the Woods and Rivers are their constant Suppeditories° of Flesh and Fish. For ornament they Colour themselves all over into neat works, with a red Paint called *Anotta*,° which grows in Cods° upon small Trees, and the Juice of certain Weeds; they bore holes also through their Noses, Lips, and Ears, whereat they hang glass Pendants, Peices of Brass, or any such like Bawbles their Service can procure from the *English*; they Load their Legs, Necks, and Arms too, with Beads, Shels of Fishes, & almost any trumpery they can get; they have no Law nor Government but Oeconomical,° living like the Patriarchs of old, the whole Kindred in a Family, where the eldest Son always succeeds his Father as the greatest; yet they have some more than ordinary persons, who are their Captains, and lead them out to Wars, whose Courage they first prove, by sharply Whipping them with Rods, which if they endure bravely without Crying, or any considerable motion, they are acknowledg'd gallant fellows and honour'd by the less hardy. These Chiefs or Heads of Families, have commonly three or four Wives a piece, others but one, who may indeed more properly be termd their Vassals than Companions, being no less subjected to their Husbands than the meanest

Suppeditories: supplies	**Anotta:** an orange dye
Cods: pods	**Oeconomical:** household

[5] Cassava, manioc. Its "fleshy tuberous roots . . . 'yield the greatest portion of the daily food of the natives of tropical America'" (*OED*).

Servants amongst us are to their Masters, the Men rarely oppress their Shoulders with a Burthen, the Women carry all, and are so very humble and observant in their Houses, that at Meals, they alwayes wait upon their Husbands, and never eat till they have done; when a Woman is delivered of her first Child, she presently goes about her business as before, and the Husband fains himself distemper'd, and is hang'd up to the Ridge of the House in his Homacko,° where he continues certain dayes dieted with the Bread and Water of Affliction, then, being taken down is stung with *Ants* (a punishment they usually inflict upon their Women, Dogs, or Children, when they are foolish for that's the term they usually put upon any misdemeanours) and a lusty drinking Bout is made at the Conclusion of the Ceremony. Their Language sounds well in the expression, but is not very easie to be learn'd, because many single Words admit of divers Senses, to be distinguish'd only by the tone or alteration of the voice. When any Martial Expedition is resolv'd upon, the General, or chief Captain, summons the Towns and Families to Assemble by a Stick with so many Notches in't, as he intends days before he sets out, which when they have received, they cut out every day one, till all are gone, and by that only they know the expiration of the time, for their Numbers exceed not twenty, which they want Names for too, but express them by their Fingers and Toes, which they will sometimes double, and treble, but their Arithmetick's quickly at a loss, and then they Cry out *Ounsa awara* that is, like the Hair of ones Head, innumerable.[6] They go to Sea in *Canoa's* or Boats bravely painted, made of one entire piece, being Trees cut hollow like a Trough, and some so large, that they'l carry five or six Tons of Goods at once. Their Arms are Bowes, with poysoned Arrowes, and short Clubs of Speckle-wood, some, for Defence, carry Shields made of light wood, handsomly painted and engraved. They observe no Order in their Fighting, nor, unless upon very great advantages, enterprize any thing but by night. The men they take Prisoners, they put to Death with the most barbarous Cruelties a Coward can invent for an Enemy in his power. Women and Children they preserve for Slaves, and fell them for Trifles to the *English*. They did once Cut off some *French* in *Surinam*, and made several Attempts upon the *English* at their first Setling, which were always frustrated, and they soundly smarted for their folly: now the Colony is grown potent they dare not but be humble. They are highly sensible of an Injury amongst themselves, and will, if

Homacko: hammock

---

[6] The mathematical limitations of the Caribs were often mentioned. See Behn, *Oroonoko*, 170 and n. 70.

possible have Revenge at one time or other, which they alwayes effect by treachery and dare never Assault a Man to his Face. They have no Religion amongst them that ever I could perceive, though they'd talk of a Captain of the Skies, but neither worship him nor any other. They have some knowledge of the Divel, whom they call *Tarakin*, and their Impostors, or, as they call them *Pecies*,[7] make them believe they frequently Converse with him, whether they do so really or no, I know not, however, it serves to scare the rest, and makes think, Death, or any Misfortune proceeds immediately from him. They have also a glimpse of an after Life, in which shall be Rewards and Punishments for the good and bad, but are wiser than to pretend to any certain knowledge of what, or where. The belief of the *Peeies* familiarity with the Divel, and skill in Herbs, to which also they pretend, causes them to be employ'd by others as Physicians, though they need not be over fond of the Profession, for one of them being sent for to a Sick Person, and, that, notwithstanding his Charms and Fooleries the Patient dye, the surviving friends, if he be not the more wary, will give the poor Doctor Death also for his Fee. They burn the Dead Body, and with it, all the Goods he was Master of in the World, which are combustible, and what is not, (is Iron-work) they'l destroy by some other means, that no necessaries may be wanting in the other life: and, if he had any Slaves they are kill'd also, to attend him there. They solemnise the Funeral with a drunken Feast and confused Dancing (in which they are frequent and excessive) while some Woman of neerest kin to the deceased sits by, and in a doleful howling tune, lamentably deplores the loss of her Relation.

Hast, and an unfaithful Memory, made me omit an Observation, in my opinion, very remarkable, and for which, I want a greater reason than my own, to give me satisfaction. I have said the Warmth and Moisture causes a constant Verdancy and Flourishing of Plants in *Surinam*, holding true not only in all Trees natural to that Country, but also in Transplanted Vines which bear there twice a year; yet this Exception I observed in an *European* Apple-Tree, which, notwithstanding the equality of Seasons, always shed its Leaves, and continu'd bare after the usual manner in its Native Soil all our Winter Months, and grew green again in Spring: But how it comes to pass, that the Heat and Moisture of that Climate should not Cause in that Tree an Assimilation with the rest (aswel those transplanted as natural to that Country, since they say the spirit of Nature is universally diffusive) I leave the *Virtuosi* to dispute.

FINIS.

---

[7] Native American priests. See Behn, *Oroonoko*, 171, and n. 75.

From *Great Newes from the Barbadoes* (1676)

T HIS ACCOUNT OF THE ABORTIVE Barbados slave revolt of 1674 begins by celebrating the increased prosperity of Barbados since the time of Richard Ligon and briefly listing its fruits and herbs, with emphasis on "newly introduced Fruits," such as the orange (7). After describing the conviction and execution of the rebel slaves, the author returns to praising the island's "admirable Pork, Poultry &c. Their Wood Pidgeons, Turtle-Doves of several kinds, wild Fowls, Plovers, Thrushes, Crabs, Lobsters, Prawns, and all other necessary and pleasant Provisions in abundance, both Fish and Flesh" (13). As Thomas Tryon was to do, this author juxtaposes the resources of the landscape with the institution of slavery, but their purposes contrast. Tryon presents European cruelty as a violation of a potential Eden; the present work portrays the slave revolt as a threat to an economic dream. In *Oroonoko*, Behn was ironically to explore both the paradisal and commercial aspects of the Surinam landscape.

❊❊❊

GREAT

N E W E S

FROM THE

Barbadoes.

OR,

A True and Faithful ACCOUNT

OF THE

Grand Conspiracy

OF

The *Negroes* against the *English.*

AND

The Happy Discovery of the same.

WITH

The number of those that were burned alive, Beheaded, and otherwise
Executed for their Horrid Crimes.

With a short Discription of that PLANTATION.

𝖂ith 𝖆llowance.

London, Printed for *L. Curtis* in *Goat-Court* upon
Ludgate · Hill, 1676

THE

RELATION of a CONSPIRACY in the *BARBADOES.*

T His *Conspiracy* first broke out and was hatched by the *Cormantee* or
Gold-Cost Negro's about Three years since, and afterwards Cuningly
and Clandestinely carried, and kept secret, even from the knowledge of
their own Wifes.

Their grand design was to choose them a King, one *Coffee* an Ancient
Gold-Cost *Negro,* who should have been Crowned the 12th of *June* last past
in a Chair of State exquisitely wrought and Carved after their Mode; with
Bowes and Arrowes to be likewise carried in State before his Majesty their
intended King: Trumpets to be made of Elephants Teeth and Gourdes to be
sounded on several Hills, to give Notice of their general Rising, with a full
intention to fire the Sugar-Canes, and so run in and Cut their Masters the
Planters Throats in their respective Plantations whereunto they did belong.

From *Great Newes from the Barbadoes* (London, 1676).

Some affirm, they intended to spare the lives of the Fairest and Handsomest Women (their Mistresses and their Daughters) to be Converted to their own use. But some others affirm the contrary; and I am induced to believe they intended to Murther all the White People there, as well Men as Women: for *Anna* a house Negro Woman belonging to Justice *Hall*, overhearing a Young[1] *Cormantee Negro* about 18 years of age, and also belonging to Justice *Hall*, as he was working near the Garden, and discoursing with another *Cormantee Negro* working with him, told him boldly and plainly, *He would have no hand in killing the* Baccararoes[2] *or White Folks; And that he would tell his Master.* All which the aforesaid *Negro* Woman (being then accidentally in the Garden) over-heard, and called to him the aforesaid Young *Negro* Man over the Pales, and enquired and asked of him *What it was they so earnestly were talking about?* He answered and told her freely, *That it was a general Design amongst them the* Cormantee Negro's, *to kill all the* Baccararoes *or White People in the Island within a fortnight.* Which she no sooner understood, but went immediately to her Master and Mistris, and discovered the whole truth of what she heard, saying withal, *That it was great Pity so good people as her Master an Mistriss were, should be destroyed.* Which was the first discovery that I can learn came to the knowledge of the worthy Inhabitants of that Noble and most flourishing Island.

Afterwards the Discreet and Prudent Justice sent presently for the young *Negro* Man, who discovered and impeached several, as well his own Master's *Negro's* as others belonging to the adjacent Plantations who hand a hand in this Plot.

Of all which the said Justice sending the true Information to that Noble Person (now Governour there) Sir *Jonathan Atkins*, he with his Life-Guard presently came to the house of the aforesaid Justice *Hall*, and granted him and others Commissions to apprehend the guilty and impeached *Negroes*, with the Ring-leaders of this fatal Conspiracy; which in pursuance was put in Execution with much Celerity and Secrecy, that the Heads and Chief of these ungrateful wretches (who I have often heard confess to live better in Servitude there, then at Liberty in their own Native Country) were apprehended and brought to Tryal at a Court of *Oyer* and *Terminer*[3] granted

---

[1] From Kormantin, the slaving fort in present-day Ghana, which Behn transforms into a kingdom.

[2] Backearary in Behn's *Oroonoko* (155, and n. 40).

[3] A commission empowering officials to hear (*oyer*) and determine (*terminer*) indictments on offenses, "special commissions being granted on occasions of extraordinary disturbance" (*OED*).

by the aforesaid Governour to a Dozen or more of the Colonels and Field-Officers as Judges of that Island; Who after strict and due Examination of the matter of Fact of their Conspiracy, at first Seventeen were found guilty and Executed, (*viz.*) Six burnt alive, and Eleven beheaded, their dead bodies being dragged through the Streets, at *Spikes* a pleasant Port-Town in that Island, and were afterwards burnt with those that were burned alive.

One of those that were burned alive being chained at the stake, was perswaded by that honest Gentleman Mr. *George Hannow*, the Deputy Provost-Marshall, *That since he was going to suffer death, Ingeniously to Confess the depth of their design.* The *Negro* calling for water to drink (which is a Custome they use before they tell or discover any thing) he just then going to speak and confess the truth of what he knew in this Matter; The next *Negro* Man chained to him (one *Tony*, a sturdy Rogue, a *Jew's*[4] *Negro*) jogged him, and was heard to Chide him in these words, *Thou Fool, are there not enough of our Country-men killed already? Art thou minded to kill them all?* Then the aforesaid *Negro* that was a going to make Confession, would not speak one word more.

Which the spectators observing, cryed out to *Tony, Sirrah, we shall see you fry bravely by and by.* Who answered undauntedly, *If you Roast me to day, you cannot Roast me tomorrow*: (all those *Negro's* having an opinion that after their death they go into their own Countrey). Five and Twenty more have been since Executed. The particulars of whose due Punishment are not yet come to my hands.

Five impeached Hanged themselves, because they would not stand Tryal.

Threescore and odd more are in Custody at the *Hole*, a fine Haven and small Town in the said Island, and are not as yet brought to Tryal.

Thus escaped from Eminent dangers, this flourishing and Fertile Island, or to say more properly Spacious and profitable Garden, one of the chiefest of his Majesties Nurseries for Sea-men.

This little Spot imploying every year above 100 good Merchants Ships, to carry off its product, *viz.* Sugar, Ginger, Cotton, and Indigo; of which I have heard it affirmed, That that Earth and Rich soyl being so thinly placed on most part of the said Island, as not exceeding above half a foot in depth, the said product since its first manuring carried off in several years, much exceeds in bulk and weight the surface of the Island, it being only a Rock. So leaving to others the giving an account of the great plenty of fresh Fish there, though of different shapes and names from ours, which

---

[4] There was a large settlement of Portuguese Jews in Brazil, as well as a substantial Jewish presence in Surinam, Barbados and other Caribbean territories. Barbadian Jews were granted freedom of worship in 1670.

it exceeds in pleasantness and nourishment, especially the Turtles there caught; their admirable Pork, Poultry &c. Their Wood Pidgeons, Turtle-Doves of several kinds, wild Fowls, Plovers, Thrushes, Crabs, Lobsters, Prawns, and all other necessary and pleasant Provisions in abundance, both Fish and Flesh. But above all, admirable (considering it is so small an Island) is the Populousness thereof; for I have seen at a General Rendezvous in *Hethersals* Pasture 12000 well Armed fighting men, Horse and Foot, of the Train-Bands, besides *Negro's* that waited on their Masters: And I have lately seen a list taken by Authority that amounts to above 80000 Souls. 'Tis fortified (besides the stone Wall all along the places of most danger for Landing, near the Sea-side) with several strong uniform Forts Alla Modern, well mounted with store of great Guns; so as considering the strength, Riches, Pleasant situation, Populousness and good Hospitality of those Noble Gentlemen there now inhabiting, I conclude it to be the finest and worthiest Island in the World.

FINIS.

From *The Negro's and Indians Advocate* (1680)

ODWYN WAS A MEMBER of a distinguished British ecclesiastical family. He graduated from Christ Church, Oxford, in 1665, served briefly as a vicar in Wendover, Bucks, and then traveled to Virginia and subsequently Barbados. His work is particularly interesting in that it records the intellectual bases on which slave owners were attempting to deny human status to black Africans. Prominent among these beliefs is the use of the pre-Adamite heresy (the belief that there were men before Adam) to deny that Europeans and black Africans had a common ancestor in Adam. Godwyn insists that black Africans have the same bodily constitution and intellectual faculties as Europeans and that differences between them are not innate, but rather the products of culture and education. He is, however, promoting the conversion and humane treatment of slaves, not their liberation, and he argues that a Christian slave is more docile than a heathen one.[1]

And the *Spaniards* question (which the same *Taverneir*[2] also mentions) touching the Brutality of the *Americans*, (and, which I have heard was held in the *Affirmative* in one of the *Universities of Spain*)[3] serving not a little to make my report more credible; and to acquit me of all *fictitious Romancing*

---

[1] An account of Godwyn's life and writings is given in Alden T. Vaughan, *Roots of American Racism: Essays on the Colonial Experience* (New York: Oxford University Press, 1995), 55–81. For the origins of racism in America, see Vaughan, 136–74, and Winthrop Jordan, *White over Black: American Attitudes Toward the Negro, 1550–1812* (Chapel Hill: University of North Carolina Press, 1968).

[2] Jean Baptiste Tavernier, baron d'Aubonne (1605–89), a celebrated travel writer.

[3] Presumably an allusion to Sepúlveda's debate with Las Casas.

From Morgan Godwyn. *The Negro's and Indians Advocate* (London, 1680), 12–41, 114–20.

herein. Wherefore it being granted for possible that such wild Opinions, by the inducement and instigation of our Planters chief Deity, *Profit*, may have lodged themselves in the Brains of some of us; I shall not fear to betake my self to the refuting of this one which I have spoken of.

For the effecting of which, me-thinks, the consideration of the shape and figure of our *Negro's* Bodies, their Limbs and Members; their Voice and Countenance, in all things according with other Mens; together with their *Risibility* and *Discourse*[5] (Man's *peculiar* Faculties) should be a sufficient Conviction. How should they otherwise be capable of *Trades*, and other no less Manly imployments; as also of *Reading and Writing*; or shew so much Discretion in management of Business; eminent in divers of them; but wherein (we know) that many of our own People are *deficient*, were they not truly Men? These being the most clear *emanations* and results of *Reason*, and therefore the most genuine and perfect characters of *Homoniety*,[6] if I may so speak. Or why should they be tormented and whipt almost (and sometimes quite) to death, upon any, whether *small or great* Miscarriages, it is not material, were they (like Brutes) naturally destitute of *Capacities* equal to such undertakings? Or why should their *Owners*, Men of Reason no doubt, conceive them fit to exercise the place of Governours and *Overseers* to their *fellow Slaves*, which is frequently done, if they were but meer Brutes? Since nothing beneath the *Capacity* of a Man might rationally be presumed proper for those Duties and Functions, wherein so much of understanding, and a more than *ordinary* Apprehension is required. It would certainly be a pretty kind of *Comical* Frenzie, to imploy Cattel about Business, and to constitute them *Lieutenants, Overseers*, and *Governours*, like as *Domitian*[7] is said to have made his Horse a *Consul*.

2. Their Objections against this, are poor and trivial; yet because with a great many here, seeming to carry no little weight, (for otherwise they

Since my return to England, *the Reverend* D. *of* H.[4] *told me, that an Inhabitant of* B[arbados] *being by himself urged to get his* Attendant Negro's *Baptized, made the like Objections, with those which he found recited in the Papers I shewed him, which were no other than a part of this Book. And tho such Practices may seem strange to People in* England, *yet the same Persons going thither are suddenly changed, so that they make nothing of it.*

---

[4] Probably the Dean of Hereford, where Godwyn's father had been canon and his grandfather bishop. The Dean of Hereford from 1672 until his death in 1692 was George Benson, a particularly trusted friend of the then bishop, Herbert Croft.

[5] Capacities for laughter and reason.   [6] Sameness.

[7] Domitian was emperor of Rome from 81 to 96 CE. This doubtless apocryphal story is, however, actually told of the emperor Caligula. See Suetonius, *Gaius* 55.3; Dio Cassius, *Roman History* 59.14.7.

could never both argue and act so absurdly, as they do); And because found serviceable to their great *End*, which I have before spoken of, not rejected by the Wiser; they must not, *silly and idle as they be*, for these Reasons be slighted. They are of divers sorts. The first whereof are certain impertinent and blasphemous *distortions of Scripture*, out of which they would fain bribe four places, to wit, in *Genesis* 1. 27, 28. and 2. 7. and 4. 15. and lastly, 9. 25, 26. to give in *evidence* for them. Now in the two first of these they strain hard to derive our *Negro's* from a stock *different* from *Adam's*: but by the third, they bespeak them as descendents from *Cain*, and to carry his *Mark*: And yet by the last, as if *condemned* to contradictions, they make them the Posterity of that unhappy Son of *Noah*, who, they say, was, together with his whole *Family* and Race, *cursed* by his *Father*. Of which *Curse* 'tis worth the observing what *blessed use* they to themselves do make, and what variety of advantages they thereby reap. For from thence, as occasion shall offer, they'll infer their *Negro's Brutality*; justifie their reduction of them under Bondage; disable them from all *Right and Claims*, even to *Religion* it self; pronounce them *Reprobates*, and upon a sudden (with greater speed and cunning than either the nimblest Jugler, or which) *transmute* them into whatsoever substance the *exigence* of their wild reasonings shall drive them to.

3. I confess, as for the third of these, which is *Cain's Mark*, they insist not much upon it, because thwarting their *Pre-Adamitism*,[8] of which they are extreamly fond, tho many times 'tis by their less skilful Disputants *prest to the Service*. But the *Pre-Adamites* whimsey, which is preferred above the *Curse* (because so exceeding useful to undermine the *Bible* and *Religion*, unto both which they have vowed never to be *reconciled*) they believe invincible; tho upon but a very superficial trial, found (as will instantly appear) to be in some things *false*, in other, *empty* and *silly*; but in nothing, of any considerable *weight* or moment. For the fuller proof whereof, I shall crave leave to refer the *Reader* to that no less *Learned* than *Judicious* Person, *Judge Hales*, in his Book lately published concerning the *Origination of Man*, wherein the whole *Mystery* of that foul *Heresie* is unravelled, and most strongly refuted. . . . [9]

12. I shall begin with the first [argument for the Negro's inhumanity], and that is their *Complexion*, which being most obvious to the sight, by which the *Notion* of things doth seem to be most certainly conveyed to the Understanding, is apt to make no *slight* impressions upon rude Minds, already prepared to admit of any thing for *Truth* which shall make for

[8] The claim that Adam was not the first man was advanced in Isaac de La Peyrère's *Prae-Adamitae* (1655), translated as *Men Before Adam* (London, 1656).

[9] Sir Matthew Hale (1609–76), Lord Chief Justice, author of *The Primitive Origination of Mankind* (London, 1677); see especially 184–87.

Interest,° especially if supported with but the least *shadow of Argument*. And therefore it may not be so improbable (as I have (elsewhere) heard affirmed) that from so poor a *Medium*, our *Negro's* Brutality should be inferred, by such whose affection to so *gainful* a Doctrine, cannot but make the Way smooth and easie to their Conviction. Such People in these Cases being not apt to reflect, (*and, probably not caring*) how derogatory to the Goodness and *Justice* of God it is, to represent him thus idly Propitious to empty *Shadows*, and even to White and Red, that so out of his infinite regard thereto, he should throw off all *respect to the Work of his Hand*, and to unman and unsoul so great a part of the Creation. Nor yet, (which is more strange, because their own immediate concern) that the Argument may come one Day to be turned against themselves, and improved to chastise their *Brutishness*, who from thence did as first so maliciously infer that *absurd* Conclusion to the prejudice of so numerous and vast a People.

13. For it is well known, that the *Negro's in their Native Country*, and perhaps here also, if they durst speak their inward *Sentiments*, do entertain as high thoughts of themselves and of their *Complexion*, as our *Europeans* do; and at the same time holding the contrary in an equal disdain, (the like whereof is affirmed of the *Natives of Japan*, as to their own, and the Fashions and Manners of all Strangers, as Mr. *Bloom* in his *Geography* witnesseth):[10] Whereby the *Missionaries of the Roman Church*, (who to facilitate their Conversion, do condescend to humour them in divers things) are said to represent our Blessed Saviour in the *Negro's Complexion*; themselves also describing the *evil Spirit* in ours. Now if Fancy and Opinion against *Reason* must carry it, there is no doubt but they will not spare for that, even to vie with the best of us; and then for number, 'tis certain they can out-muster us. So that without a recourse to Force, the Contest on our part will be managed upon very *unequal terms*, and in no case is like to succeed but to our disadvantage. And for *Force*, I shall in due place shew, how little it can avail in things of this Nature.

14. But the determination of this Point will much depend upon the right understanding and knowledge of *Real Beauty*, a true standard whereof the Nations have not yet pitcht upon. That being Deformity with others, which amongst us is the only *perfect and compleat Figure*. As a certain Author in a *Treatise* upon this Subject, by infinite Collections and Instances in the practice and behaviour of more distant Nations, hath abundantly shewn. So that if the other part of the World should once come to agree upon this

---

Interest: self-interest

[10] Richard Blome, *A Geographical Description of the Four Parts of the World* (London, 1670), 97.

particular, without consulting us here (which 'tis possible, when ever they go about it, they may omit), and *like unto us*, maliciously determine the Matter in favour of themselves, they only may be the *Men*, and our selves but *Beasts*. . . .

The cause of their Ignorance [is] the want of Converse and Education, which may also befal other Nations, and even the Inhabitants of our *Mother Country*. It being certain, that *Africa* was once famous for both Arts and Arms; that *Carthage*[11] did rival with *Rome* for the Worl'd Empire, and had well nigh gotten it, tho now become an *Aceldama*[12] of Barbarism; even to the degree of rendring its Inhabitants suspected for Brutes, as we here find and see. And it is also evident, that all our own People do not exceed these either for *Knowledg*, or *Piety*; nor yet always for *Civility*, whatsoever Brutishness is by some proudly objected to them. And without a provision for Schools (of which the scattering way of living in these *Colonies* is scarce capable) together with a stricter Care taken to suppress Debauchery (hardly to be outdone (therein) by *Sodom*, were it standing) may at last end in the like Barbarity. . . .

Nor to speak truth, without that *prôton pseudos*° of their *Negro*'s brutality, do I see how those other *Inhumanities*, as their Emasculating and Beheading them, their *croping off their Ears* (which they usually cause the Wretches to broyl, and then compel to eat them themselves); their *Amputations of Legs*, and even Dissecting them alive; (this last I cannot say was ever practised, but has been certainly affirmed by some of them, as no less allowable than to a Beast, of which they did not in the least doubt but it was justifiable). Add to this their *scant allowance* for Clothes, as well as Diet, and (which is often the calamity of the *most Innocent and Labourious*) their no less working than starving them to Death; all which could never otherwise be so glibly swallowed by them, but upon a *persuasion* of this, or of the former worse Principle. Both without doubt contrived in Hell, receiving their first impressions in no other than the *Devil's Mint*, purposely designed for the *murthering* of Souls; Invented only *to defeat the Mercies of God in their blessed Redeemer*, and to render void and ineffectual his precious Blood shed upon the *Cross*, for the saving of the World. And thus much shall suffice for proof of the *Antecedent* of my second Proposition, deduced from my first general *Assertion*.

prôton pseudos: first falsehood (Greek)

---

[11] Carthage was a state in North Africa and a dominant Mediterranean power from about 600 BCE until its destruction by Rome in 146 BCE. Its inhabitants were, however, not African, but Phoenician colonists from the Middle East.

[12] "The field of blood" in which Judas Iscariot died (Acts 1:18–19).

THOMAS TRYON

From *Friendly Advice to the Gentlemen Planters of the East and West Indies* (1684)

THOMAS TRYON (1634–1703) wrote on a variety of moral, dietary, and other topics, including the virtues of vegetarianism and the nature of dreams. He was a hatter by trade and visited Barbados in connection with his business. Behn published a poem in praise of his *The Way to Health, Long Life, and Happiness* (1683), which appeared in *Miscellany* (1685) and, in the same year, in Tryon's *The Way to Make All People Rich*. In the poem, she praises Tryon for restoring the "Golden Age" and the life of "the Noble Savage."[1]

Friendly Advice is divided into three parts. Like George Warren and the author of *Good Newes*, Tryon discusses the plants and fruits of the West Indies, with descriptions of pineapples, plantains, bananas, and other fruit. There follows "The Complaints of the Negro-Slaves against the hard Usages and barbarous Cruelties inflicted upon them," from which the following extract is taken, and "A Discourse in way of Dialogue between an *Ethiopean* or *Negro-Slave*, and a *Christian* that was his Master in *America*." One example of cruelty is of a woman who burned a slave alive for running away.

Whereas the other authors, such as Behn in *Oroonoko*, describe vegetation with an eye to its commercial potential, Tryon's emphasis is medicinal and moral. Chiefly, he portrays the West Indies as a place where strenuous labour is unnecessary because of the natural fertility of the land. It is, however, unhealthy because of its hot climate. The toil of the slave violates the Edenic nature of the New World and exceeds the duty of labor imposed

---

[1] "On the Author of that Excellent Book Intituled The Way to Health, Long Life, and Happiness," ll. 3, 6 (*Works of Aphra Behn*, I, 179).

From Thomas Tryon, *Friendly Advice to the Gentlemen Planters of the East and West Indies* ([London], 1684), 114–20.

at the Fall, and Tryon allusively identifies the suffering Negro with the murdered Abel, whose blood cried to Cain from the ground (Genesis 4:10) (182, 207). One of the points emphasized in the final dialogue is that the Christians are more irrational and barbaric than the Africans. In the end, the master is persuaded by his slave's arguments and promises him an easier life in the future.

In addition to giving voice to the oppressed slave, Tryon in *The Way to Health* gives voice to animals oppressed by people in the chapter entitled "The *Voice of the Dumb*, or the Complaints of the *Creatures*, expostulating with Man, touching the cruel Usages they suffer from him" (495–515).

※

But perhaps you will say, That not by virtue of your Religion, but by some super-excellent or higher Dignity of Nature above us, you claim a Right to make us your Slaves and Vassals. But pray, have you this Prerogative from your Descent or Pedigree? Or from some different Fabrick of your Bodies? Or from your extraordinary *Endowments* of Mind? As for the first, do not the Oracles of your Religion oblige you to believe, that the great God created the Man whom you call *Adam*, and that from him came all the People that ever since were, or are in the World? And if so, are we not of as good Parentage, as ancient a Family, as noble a Descent as the best of you? Ought you not then to love us as your Brethren, descended from the same common Father? or at least respect us as your Kinsmen, and of the same Lineage.

Are not our *Bodies* of as proportionable a Frame, and as well furnisht with useful *Limbs?* Are not all our *Senses* as good and quick as yours? Nay, are we not naturally obnoxious[2] to fewer Diseases than you, though now indeed by your harsh usage our Days are often shortned, and our Health impaired; but this is not the fault of our Constitutions, but of your Severities, which bring upon us those Weaknesses and Disorders, which we were never before acquainted with: For any Exercises of Running, Leaping, Swimming, and the like, which of you can equal us? As for the *blackness* of our Skins, we find no reason to be ashamed of it, 'tis the *Livery* which our great Lord and Maker hath thought fit we should wear; Do not you amongst Furs, prize pure *Sables* as much as *Ermins?* Is *Jett* or *Ebony* despised for its Colour? Can we help it, if the Sun by too close and fervent Kisses, and the nature

---

[2] Liable. This is the original sense; the meaning of "offensive" arises from confusion with *noxious*.

of the Climate and Soil where we were Born, hath tinctur'd us with a dark Complexion? Have not you variety of Complexions amongst your selves; some very *White* and *Fair*, others *Brown*, many *Swarthy*, and several *Cole-black*? And would it be reasonable that each sort of these should quarrel with the other, and a man be made *a Slave* forever, meerly because his Beard is *Red*, or his Eyebrows *Black*? In a word, if our *Hue* be the only difference, since *White* is as contrary to *Black*, as *Black* is to *White*, there is as much reason that *you* should be our *Slaves*, as we yours.

Lastly, as to our 𝕾ouls, you dare not deny but they are *Immortal* as well as yours, consequently capable of as much Bliss and Happiness, being as well as yours, created in the Image of God, and of an heavenly Original: Have we not the same Faculties, Understanding, Memory and Will? Are we not endued with a reflex Power, whereby to condemn or approve our own Actions as they are either good or evil? Are we not, if we had the advantages of Education, altogether as docible,° and apt to learn Arts and Soiences as any of you? witness *Averoes*, *Avieenna*,[3] and others of our Country-men, who were famous *Physitians, Philosophers, Astrologians*, and the like. For in us as well as you, are contained the true Natures of all Elements, the Seeds of all Sciences, and an hidden Epitom of the four Worlds, *Intellectual, Rational, Elemental* and *Sensitive*.

'Tis true, we are not so ready at Words, nor so nimble to express our Conceptions, but we can more than guess at what is Just, and Fit, and Honest, and Seemly, and know what is agreeable to the dignity of humane Nature, and what not, though the *Christians* despise us by the Name of *Heathens*; we must acknowledge that we are not so well acquainted with the wordy and notional matters of Religion, nor do talk so much of it, nor keep so much ado about it, as many of the *Christians* do, for we do not Wrangle, nor Fight, nor Backbite or Hate one another for, or touching the Worship of God: Nor do we Kill, Burn or Imprison any for not agreeing with us, or being of our Intellectual Complexions, because God in his Wisdom has made all things to differ; many there are whose Eyes are open see into the truth of these things.

As for our Faith, touching God and Eternity, we have not much to say, neither do we ever use many Words; For we have only one Book, *viz.* 𝕯ur felbes, in which is contained the true Nature and Property of all things,

---

docible: teachable

---

[3] Averroës (Abul Walid Mohammed ben Ahmed ibn Roshd, 1126–98), a Moslem doctor and commentator on Aristotle, born at Cordoba. Avicenna (Abu ibn Sina, 980–1036), a Persian physician, philosopher, and commentator on Aristotle.

both Internally and Externally, and happy is he that can read but the *Christ Cross-Row*[4] in his own Book, it is more profitable to him than a multitude of Books, cry'd up and admired by the World: And this we do know and acknowledge, that there is a good and an evil Spirit or Principle within us, one which prompts, and invites, and leads us to Good and the other drawing us to Evil; and by the light of the good Principle, we distinguish between what is Right, and the contrary; and whensoever we do Evil, we are convinced and reproved for it by this good Genius, whereby we are sensible that Lying, Swearing, Adultery, Idleness, Disobedience to our Masters, Burning of Houses, Murther, and the like, are Sins against God; and when at any time we commit any such things, we are accused and condemned for the same in our Hearts, though our Masters, nor any Creature else know thereof.

In short, the main Differences between the *Christians* and us, seem to be no more than these, that they are *White*, and we *Black*, because they are born in one Climate, and we in another; they have *Learning*, as Reading, Writing, speaking of various Languages, and we have none of those Ornamental Advantages; but they may please to remember that the more Paint Glass has upon it, the more it keeps out the Light; They are educated under certain *Rights* and *Forms*, and taught divers *Notions of Religion*, which we are not skill'd in: But the grand point of Religion, *To do as we would be done by*, we understand as well as they, and are sure they practise it less than we. What then do they talk so much of *the Leaves*, when we can see *no Fruits*? let us *feel* their *Christianity*, and *see* it, as well as *hear of it*, and no doubt then we shall be more in love with it.

---

[4] Or criss-cross-row: the alphabet, so called from the figure of a cross prefixed to it in horn-books (*OED*).

Discussions of Colonialism

T HOMAS THOROWGOOD (d. circa 1669) was a Norfolk clergyman. He
supported John Eliot, the proselytizer of the Native Americans, and
corresponded with the Jewish scholar Manasseh ben Israel. *Iewes in America* propounds the tenacious theory that the Native Americans were the lost
tribes of Israel, a theory that had been advanced by early Spanish writers,
such as Diego Durán, and by Jewish scholars, such as Antonio Monterinos
and ben Israel (and persisting in the beliefs of the Mormons). Thorowgood documents and deplores Spanish atrocities in the New World, citing
Las Casas and other authorities, though he uses the atrocities as evidence
that the Native Americans bear the curse placed upon the Jews. His primary aim is to argue that the Native Americans are ready for conversion
to Christianity, though in the process he writes about the ethics of colonization. His pamphlet was answered by Hamon L'Estrange (1605–1660),
brother of the royalist polemicist Roger L'Estrange. L'Estrange documents
the fancifulness of Thorowgood's parallels between Native American and
Jewish customs and stresses the diversity of Native American culture. He
also argues that it is immoral to take land from native peoples.

The third passage, from Thomas Hobbes's *Leviathan* (1651), expresses
a quite different viewpoint and takes the discussion of colonialism outside
the religious framework in which we have so far predominantly seen it.
Hobbes (1588–1679) was perhaps rightly reputed to be an atheist; he saw
man as a purely material being driven by egocentric desires, which meant
that his natural relationship to other men was one of war. In the pre-social
state of nature, there were no valid moral principles, for there was no power
to enforce them: All had right to all. By bonding into political societies,
men surrendered their natural rights in return for protection and security,
the most secure form of government being an absolute monarchy. Hobbes's
view of the state of nature as a horrifying state of war is the opposite of

the primitivistic idealization of the savage found in Montaigne. Restoration writers (including Behn) were fascinated by Hobbes's interpretation of human nature and often exploit an interplay between idealizing and Hobbesian views of primitive life (as to some extent Behn does in *Oroonoko*). Here, Hobbes sees colonialism in characteristically hard-headed terms of competition and the management of people, and his account is dominated by the language of power: "strong," "forced," "constrain." Colonization is a way of coping with over-population: with surplus strength, which is to be expressed in labour. Yet, if over-population becomes global, we are returned to the imperative of the original state of nature, which is war.

Hobbes's work attracted many answers, including one by Edward Hyde, Earl of Clarendon (1607–74), who had been made Lord Chancellor after the Restoration, was forced into exile in 1667, and completed his answer to *Leviathan* in Montpellier in 1670. Clarendon takes a less dark view of human nature than Hobbes and also a more limited view of kingly authority. The right to property is for him the founding principle of society. The instinct for property caused the evolution of culture and society, and we would revert to barbarism were it to be frustrated. His concern for property rights extends to those of colonized natives, and he attacks Hobbes for wishing to violate them. His remarks are of particular interest in that he himself had colonial interests, as one of the original Lords Proprietor to whom Charles II granted the territory of Carolina.

The final passage is from another figure closely associated with the founding of Carolina: the philosopher John Locke (1632–1704), who was secretary to Anthony Ashley Cooper, later Earl of Shaftesbury, another of the Lords Proprietor. Locke drew up *The Fundamental Constitutions of Carolina* (1670). The section specifying religious toleration urges that the Native Americans' heathenism "gives us no right to expel, or use them ill"; more chillingly, while guaranteeing Negro slaves freedom of religion, it asserts that "Every *Freeman* of *Carolina* shall have absolute Power and Authority over his *Negro Slaves*, of what Opinion or Religion soever."

Shaftesbury was leader of the party that, in 1679–81, unsuccessfully attempted to exclude Charles II's Catholic brother, James, from the succession. Locke's *Two Treatises of Government* were written in the context of these attempts (known as the Exclusion Crisis), but were not published until after the revolution that deposed James. The first rebuts the absolutist theories of monarchy advanced by Sir Robert Filmer (1588–1653), which had been revived by supporters of James and which deny man any natural freedom; the second advances Locke's own theory of government. The essential purpose of government, he argues, is the protection of property. Monarchy is not a naturally inevitable form of government, and governors may be deposed if they break the contract with the people on which their authority rests; that is, if they no longer fulfill their essential function of protecting property.

The second treatise is notable for its advance in the theory of surplus value, arguing that objects acquire extra value from the labor invested in producing them. (Behn had considered the topic of surplus value in her play *The Luckey Chance*, in which a circulating sum of money mysteriously increases in value.) In primitive times – and in a primitive country like America – there was more than enough land for all: "in the beginning all the World was *America,* and more so than that is now." Initially, men had merely produced enough for their immediate needs, for there was no point in hoarding perishable foodstuffs. The introduction of money, which was imperishable, however, changed the dynamics and scale of production. Land in England is scarce, heavily exploited, and valuable in its produce. Land in America is under-exploited and under-populated. Europeans can exploit it without dispossessing the natives.

One of the few works of Restoration imaginative literature recorded in Locke's library is Behn's *Oroonoko.* It, and the *Two Treatises,* both emerge from the crises of kingship that had racked England throughout the authors' lifetime. They emerge on opposite sides of the debate: Locke's theory that rulers may be deposed for breaking their contract with the people was too extreme even for the framers of the post-revolutionary settlement, and he had far more influence on the framing of the American constitution nearly a century later. Locke is forging a new world; Behn (like Southerne) is lamenting the dissolution of an old one. The dispensability of kings is a tragedy in Behn; in Locke, it is an imperative. Both Behn and Southerne lament the decay of aristocratic virtues of faith and the word before the amoral demands of commerce, whereas for Locke the invention of money makes possible the transition from small-scale subsistence to a complex and diversified civilization. Money is one of the villains of *Oroonoko,* as it is of Behn's mature plays; in Locke's vision, it is a major constructive force. In previous extracts, colonialism has largely been viewed in terms of religious or nationalistic purposes; here, it is viewed as the evolution of permanent economic laws.

From *Iewes in America; or, Probabilities that the Americans are of that Race* (1650)

WHEN THE BISHOP *De las Casas* had set forth his tract of the Spanish cruelties committed in the Indies, some guilty persons he supposeth suborned Doctor *Sepulveda*, the Emperours Historian, to undertake their patronage, which he did in an elegant and rhetoricall discourse, endeavouring to prove, that the Spanish wars against the Indians were just and lawfull, and that they were bound to submit unto the Spaniards, as Ideots to the more prudent; but he could not obtaine leave to print a booke so irrationall and unchristian.

Their more plausible plea is, that *Columbus* was first employed by them to discover some of those parts; but the same offer was before tendred to this our Nation, and the King thereof; yea and the English were as early in that very designe as the Portingales, for our Chronicles shew that *Sebastian Gobat* or *Cabot*,[1] borne at *Bristol*, was employed by King *Henry* the seventh, and he with some *London* Merchants, adventured three or foure ships into those New-found lands, *Anno* one thousand foure hundred ninety eight; and it cannot be doubted, but they had made some former sufficient experiments, before that their so confident engagement: [Thorowgood cites further alleged evidence of Britain's prior claim to the New World]. But yet more particularly, Dr *Donne*[2] allowes that as a justifiable reason of mens removall from one place to another, publique benefit; *Interest Reipublice ut re sua quis bene utatur*, every one must use his private for the common good: and if a State may take order that every man improve what

---

[1] Sebastian Cabot was in fact born in Venice, probably around 1484. He was thus only in his early teens in 1498; Newfoundland was discovered by his father, John.

[2] John Donne, *A Sermon . . . Preached to the Honourable Company of the Virginian Plantation*, in Donne (1625), 26–27 (separate pagination).

From Thomas Thorowgood, *Iewes in America, or, Probabilities that the Americans are of That Race* (London, 1650), 55–58.

he hath for the benefit of the Nation where he lives, then, *interest mundo*,°
all mankinde may every where, as farre as it is able, advance the good of
mankinde in generall, which not being done by the Natives there, others
are bound, at least have liberty to interpose their endeavours, especially,
when by divine providence one land swells with inhabitants, and another
is disempeopled by mutuall broiles, infectious diseases, or the cruelty of
Invaders, all which have helped to sweepe away the Americans, while the
English in the meanetime did multiply in such manner and measure, as they
could scarcely dwell one by another; and because man is commanded more
than once to *bring forth, multiply, and fill the earth*, Gen. 1. 28.9. 1. he may
well therefore, and justly looke abroad, and if he finde convenient and quiet
habitation, he may call the name of that land *Rehoboth, because the Lord hath
made him roome*, Gen. 22. 26. . . . Againe, the Territories of strangers may
be possessed upon the donation and fore-gift of the naturall Inhabitants,
as *Abimelech* said to *Abraham, behold the land is before thee, dwell where it
pleaseth thee*, Gen. 20. 15. and *Pharaoh said to Ioseph, in the land of Goshen let
shy father and brethren dwell*, Gen. 47. 5, 6. So in *Virginia* King *Powhatan*[3]
desired the English to come from *Iames* Town, a place unwholsome, and
take possession of another whole Kingdome, which he gave them; thus the
surviving Indians were glad of the comming of the English to preserve them
from the oppression of the next borderers; and surely divine providence
making way, the care of emprovement, the purchase from the Natives, their
invitation and gift, some, or all these, may satisfie the most scrupulous in
their undertaking, or else what will such our inquisitors say to maintaine
the right of their owne inheritances? The English invaded the Britons the
ancient inhabitants of this Island, and crowded them into the nooke of
Wales, themselves in the meane time taking possession of the fat of this
Land, by what right, or by what wrong I dispute not, saith *Crantzius*;[4] but
such in those daies were the frequent emigrations of people to seeke out
new habitations.

---

interest mundo: it is in the interest of the world

---

[3] Died 1618, Native American chief, and father of Pocahontas.
[4] Albrecht (or Albert) Crantz (?1448–1517), German theologian and historian. I am grateful
to Dr Robert Cummings for information about Crantz.

From *Americans no Iewes; or, Improbabilities that the Americans are of that Race* (1651)

I N PAG. 55. the Author gives a little touch upon the *jus*° and right of entring into, and setling in anothers land or dominion, wherein *Acosta* hath learnedly and elaborately handled that question, and *Barthol. de las Casas*, and sundry Civilians° have travailed excellently herein; but I fear there is ever more of an inordinate desire of enlargement of wealth and dominion, than any warrant of Law or Religion to attain, and consequently offorce to maintain a possession, and to that end *qui minor est armis*° is the *ratio ultima*,° the ever finall result and resolution, and the *ergo*° of the Syllogisme.

I know there are many Meanders and windings in this question of Plantation, and setling in anothers land; and if the Commandement *Exod.* 22.v.21. *Thou shalt not oppresse a stranger*, much lesse shalt thou (being a stranger) presume to oppresse another at his own home; and the counsell of not removing a Land-mark be well considered,[5] we may find argument to help us; I doe but now peepe into this question, and may happily hereafter adventure to tread the maze of it; in the mean time we are not to forget what we have sometimes suffered by the natives in the *West-Indies*, for our invasion and usurpation upon them, and we are now become staffeholders of a first precarious interest, and begin to prescribe in intrusion,° and an unprovoked conquest. . . .

jus: right	**Civilians:** civil lawyers
qui minor est armis: the weaker in arms	**ratio ultima:** final argument
ergo: therefore	
prescribe in intrusion: legislate, though intruders	

5 "Thou shalt not remove thy neighbor's landmark" (Deuteronomy 19:14).

From Hamon l'Estrange. *Americans no Iewes, or Imporbabilities that the Americans are of that Race* (London, 1651), II, 71–72.

The cautions and directions which the Author gives for setling and securing Plantations, are especially worthy of embracement and approbation; to which *I* adde, *breviter per exemplum*,° example is the shortest and surest master.

> — *non sic inflectere sensus*
> *Humanos edicta valent quam vita regentis.*
> Laws and Edicts we do find
>   do not bind,
> Nor doe bow the hearts of man,
> As the great ones lives we see
>   powerfull be,
> And their good example can.[6]

I wish an increase of all happiness to the successesses mentioned in the tenth Chapter, if the foundation be layd upon pious principles, I may promise more in the building and progresse; but I fear too much of *Boltons*[7] *white devil of spirituall pride*, and the sacred hunger of Gold[8] (which the Americans call the *Christians God*) and too much *meum* and *tuum*° have over-leavened the whole lump, and been the prime authors and actors in our plantations.

About 40 years since I adventured for the discovery of the North-west passage, to contract our travailes and returns to, and from the *East Indies*; and I confess that I embrace the innocence of such action to the fair advantage of trading, or to a plantation in an unhabited land, with better thoughts than to invade or exterminate natives, and by means (too commonly coarse and cruell) to get and to keep dominion.

---

breviter per exemplum: briefly, as an example
meum and tuum: mine and yours; questions of property

---

[6] Claudian, "Panegyric on the Fourth Consulate of Honorius Augustus": the example of a ruler's life impresses the human senses more than his edicts.

[7] Robert Bolton (1572–1631), Puritan writer. *Some Generall Directions for a Comfortable Walking with God* (London, 1626), 88, 340, 347, 348.

[8] An allusion to Virgil, *Aeneid* 3.56–57: "to what will you not compel human breasts, accursed [*sacer*] hunger for gold?"

THOMAS HOBBES

From *Leviathan* (1651)

AND WHEREAS MANY MEN, by accident unevitable, become unable to maintain themselves by their labour; they ought not to be left to the Charity of private persons; but to be provided for, (as far-forth as the necessities of Nature require,) by the Laws of the Commonwealth. For as it is Uncharitableness in any man, to neglect the impotent; so it is in the Soveraign of the Common-wealth, to expose them to the hazard of such uncertain Charity.

But for such as have strong bodies, the case is otherwise: they are to be forced to work; and to avoyd the excuse of not finding empolyment, there ought to be such Laws, as may encourage all manner of Arts; as Navigation, Agriculture, Fishing, and all manner of Manifacture that requires labour. The multitude of poor, and yet strong people still encreasing, they are to be transplanted into Countries not sufficiently inhabited: where nevertheless, they are not to exterminate those they find there; but constrain them to inhabit closer together, and not to range a great deal of ground, to snatch what they find; but to court each little Plot with art and labour, to give them their sustenance in due season. And when all the world is overcharged with Inhabitants, then the last remedy of all is War; which provideth for every man, by Victory, or Death.

From Thomas Hobbes. *Leviathan, or, The Matter, Form, and Power of a Commonwealth Ecclesiastical and Civil* (London, 1651), 181 (Part 2, Chap. 10).

EDWARD HYDE, EARL OF CLARENDON

From *A Brief View and Survey of the Dangerous and Pernicious Errors to Church and State, in Mr. Hobbes's Book, entitled 'Leviathan'* (1676)

L ASTLY, since he reckons the sending out Colonies, and erecting Plantations, the encouraging all manner of Arts, as Navigation, Agriculture, Fishing, and all manner of Manufactures, to be of the Policy and Office of a Sovereign, it will not be in his power to deny, that his Soveraign is obliged to perform all those promises, and to make good all those concessions and priviledges which he hath made and granted, to those who have bin thereby induc'd to expose their Fortunes and their Industry to those Adventures, as hath bin formerly enlarg'd upon in the case of Merchants and Corporations, and which is directly contrary to his Conclusions and Determinations. And I cannot but here observe the great vigilance and caution, which Mr. *Hobbes* (who hath an excellent faculty of employing very soft words, for the bringing the most hard and cruel things to pass) uses out of his abstracted love of Justice, towards the regulating and well ordering his poor and strong people, whom he transplants into other Countries for the ease of his own; whom he will by no means suffer to exterminate those they find there, but only to constrain them to inhabit closer together, and not to range a great deal of ground; that is in more significant words, which the tenderness of his nature would not give him leave to utter, to take from them the abundance they possess, and reduce them to such an assignation,° that they may be compell'd, if they will not be perswaded, (pag. 181.) *to court each little plot with art and labor to give them their sustenance in due season.* And if all this good Husbandry will not serve the turn, but that they are still over-charg'd with Inhabitants, he hath

assignation: apportionment of property

From Edward Hyde, Earl of Clarendon. *A Brief View and Survey of the Dangerous and Pernicious Errors to Church and State, in Mr. Hobbes's Book, Entitled Leviathan* (Oxford, 1676), 183–84.

out of his deep meditation prescrib'd them a sure remedy for that too, (pag. 181.) *War*, which he saies *will provide; for every man by victory, or death*; that is, they must cut the throats of all men who are troublesom to them, which without doubt must be the natural and final period of all his Prescriptions in Policy and Government.

From *An Essay concerning the True Original, Extent, and End of Civil Government*, in *Two Treatises of Government* (1694)

THOUGH THE EARTH, and all inferior Creatures be common to all Men, yet every Man has a *Property* in his own *Person*. This no Body has any Right to but himself. The *Labour* of his Body, and the *Work* of his Hands, we may say, are properly his. Whatsoever then he removes out of the State that Nature hath provided, and left it in, he hath mixed his Labour with it, and joyned to it something that is his own, and thereby makes it his Property. It being by him removed from the common state Nature placed it in, it hath by this labour something annexed to it, that excludes the common right of other Men. For this *labour* being the unquestionable Property of the labourer, no Man but he can have a right to what that is once joyned to, at least where there is enough, and as good left in common for others. . . .

Thus this Law of reason makes the Deer, that *Indians* who hath killed it; 'tis allowed to be his goods who hath bestowed his labour upon it, though before, it was the common right of every one. And amongst those who are counted the Civiliz'd part of Mankind, who have made and multiplied positive Laws to determine Property, this original Law of Nature for the beginning of Property, in what was before common, still takes place; and by vertue thereof, what Fish any one catches in the Ocean, that great and still remaining Common of Mankind; or what Ambergriese any one takes up here, is by the labour that removes it out of that common state Nature left it in, made his Property who takes that pains about it. And even amongst us the Hare that any one is Hunting, is thought his who pursues her during the Chase. For being a Beast that is still looked upon as common, and no Man's private Possession; whoever has imploy'd so much labour about any of that kind, as to find and pursue her, has thereby removed

From John Locke. *Two Treatises of Government* (London, 1694), 185–201.

her from the state of Nature wherein she was common, and hath begun a Property.

But the chief matter of Property being now not the Fruits of the Earth, and the Beasts that subsist on it, but the Earth it self; as that which takes in and carries with it all the rest: I think it is plain, that Property in that too is acquired as the former. As much Land as a Man Tills, Plants, Improves, Cultivates, and can use the Product of, so much is his Property. He by his Labour does, as it were, inclose it from the Common. Nor will it invalidate his right to say, Every body else has an equal Title to it; and therefore he cannot appropriate, he cannot inclose, without the Consent of all his Fellow-Commoners, all Mankind. God, when he gave the World in common to all Mankind, commanded Man also to labour, and the penury of his Condition required it of him. God and his Reason commanded him to subdue the Earth, *i.e.* improve it for the benefit of Life, and therein lay out something upon it that was his own, his labour. He that in Obedience to this Command of God, subdued, tilled and sowed any part of it, thereby annexed to it something that was his Property, which another had no Title to, nor could without injury take from him. . . .

Nor was this appropriation of any parcel of Land, by improving it, any prejudice to any other Man, since there was still enough, and as good left; and more than the yet unprovided could use. So that in effect, there was never the less left for others because of his inclosure for himself. For he that leaves as much as another can make use of, does as good as take nothing at all. No Body could think himself injur'd by the drinking of another Man, though he took a good Draught, who had a whole River of the same Water left him to quench his thirst. And the Case of Land and Water, where there is enough of both, is perfectly the same.

'Tis true, in Land that is common in *England*, or any other Country, where there is Plenty of People under Government, who have Money and Commerce, no one can inclose or appropriate any part, without the consent of all his Fellow-Commoners: Because this is left common by Compact, *i.e.* by the Law of the Land; which is not to be violated. And though it be Common, in respect of some Men, it is not so to all Mankind; but is the joint propriety of this Country, or this Parish. Besides, the remainder, after such inclosure, would not be as good to the rest of the Commoners as the whole was, when they could all make use of the whole; whereas in the beginning and first peopling of the great Common of the World, it was quite otherwise. The Law Man was under, was rather for appropriating. God Commanded, and his Wants forced him to labour. That was his Property which could not be taken from him where-ever he had fixed it.

And hence subduing or cultivating the Earth, and having Dominion, we see are joined together. The one gave Title to the other. So that God, by commanding to subdue, gave Authority so far to appropriate. And the Condition of Human Life, which requires Labour and Materials to work on. necessarily introduce private Possessions. . . .

For supposing a Man, or Family, in the state they were at first peopling of the World by the Children of *Adam*, or *Noah*; let him plant in some in-land, vacant places of *America*, we shall find that the Possessions he could make himself, upon the measures we have given, would not be very large, nor, even to this day, prejudice the rest of Mankind, or give them reason to complain, or think themselves injured by this Man's Incroachment, though the Race of Men have now spread themselves to all the corners of the World, and do infinitely exceed the small number was at the beginning. . . . For 'tis labour indeed that puts the difference of value on every thing; and let any one consider, what the difference is between an Acre of Land planted with Tobacco, or Sugar, sown with Wheat or Barley; and an Acre of the same Land lying in common, without any Husbandry upon it; and he will find, that the improvement of labour makes the far greater part of the value. I think it will be but a very modest Computation to say, that of the Products of the Earth useful to the Life of Man $\frac{9}{10}$ are the effects of labour: nay, if we will rightly estimate things as they come to our use, and cast up the several expences about them, what in them is purely owing to Nature, and what to labour, we shall find, that in most of them $\frac{99}{100}$ are wholly to be put on the account of labour.

There cannot be a clearer demonstration of any thing, than several Nations of the *Americans* are of this, who are rich in Land, and poor in all the Comforts of Life; whom Nature having furnished as liberally as any other people, with the materials of Plenty, *i.e.* a fruitful Soil, apt to produce in abundance, what might serve for food, rayment, and delight; yet for want of improving it by labour, have not $\frac{1}{100}$ part of the Conveniencies we enjoy. And a King of a large and fruitful Territory there feeds, lodges, and is clad worse than a day Labourer in *England.* . . .

An Acre of Land that bears here Twenty Bushels of Wheat, and another in *America*, which, with the same Husbandry, would do the like, are, without doubt, of the same natural, intrinsick Value. But yet the Benefit Mankind receives from one in a Year is worth 5 *l.* and the other possibly not worth a Penny; if all the Profit an *Indian* received from it were to be valued, and sold here; at least, I may truly say, not $\frac{1}{1000}$. 'Tis Labour then which puts the greatest part of Value upon Land, without which it would scarcely be worth any thing; 'tis to that we owe the greatest part of all its useful Products; for all that the Straw, Bran, Bread, of that Acre of Wheat, is more worth than the Product of an Acre of as good Land, which lies wast, is all the Effect of Labour....

The greatest part of things really useful to the Life of Man, and such as the necessity of subsisting made the first Commoners of the World look after, as it doth the *Americans* now, are generally things of short duration, such as, if they are not consumed by use, will decay and perish of themselves. Gold, Silver, and Diamonds, are things that Fancy or Agreement hath put the Value on, more than real Use, and the necessary Support of Life: Now of those good things which Nature hath provided in common, every one hath a Right (as hath been said) to as much as he could use, and had a Property in all he could effect with his Labour; all that his Industry could extend to, to alter from the State Nature had put it in, was his. He that gathered a Hundred Bushels of Acorns or Apples, had thereby a Property in them, they were his Goods as soon as gathered. He was only to look that he used them before they spoiled, else he took more than his share, and robb'd others. And indeed it was a foolish thing, as well as dishonest, to hoard up more than he could make use of....

And thus came in the use of Money, some lasting thing that Men might keep without spoiling, and that by mutual consent Men would take in exchange for the truly useful, but perishable supports of Life.

And as different degrees of Industry were apt to give Men Possessions in different Proportions, so this Invention of Money gave them the opportunity to continue and enlarge them. For supposing an Island, separate from all possible Commerce with the rest of the World, wherein there were but a hundred Families, but there were Sheep, Horses and Cows, with other useful Animals, wholsome Fruits, and Land enough for Corn for a hundred thousand times as many, but nothing in the Island, either because of its Commonness, or perishableness, fit to supply the place of Money: What reason could any one have there to enlarge his Possessions beyond the use of his Family, and a plentiful supply to its Consumption, either in what their own Industry produced, or they could barter for like perishable, useful Commodities, with others? Where there is not something both lasting and scarce, and so valuable to be hoarded up, there Men will not be apt to enlarge their Possessions of Land, were it never so rich, never so free for them to take. For I ask, What would a Man value Ten thousand, or an Hundred thousand Acres of excellent Land, ready cultivated, and well stocked too with Cattle, in the middle of the in-land Parts of *America*, where he had no hopes of Commerce with other parts of the World, to draw Money to him by the Sale of the Product. It would not be worth the inclosing, and we should see him give up again to the wild Common of Nature whatever was more than would supply the Conveniencies of Life to be had there for him and his Family.

Thus in the beginning all the World was *America*, and more so than that is now; for no such thing as Money was any where known.

The Germantown Protest (1688)

T HE GERMANTOWN PROTEST was drawn up by four German immigrants to Pennsylvania, mostly Quakers, in 1688, the year of Behn's *Oroonoko*, and was the first public protest against American slavery. It lay forgotten until its rediscovery in 1844.

❧

THIS IS TO YE MONTHLY MEETING HELD AT RICHARD WORRELL'S.

These are the reasons why we are against the traffick of men-body, as followeth. Is there any that would be done or handled at this manner? viz., to be sold or made a slave for all the time of his life? How fearful and faint-hearted are many on sea, when they see a strange vessel, – being afraid it should be a Turk, and they should be taken, and sold for slaves into Turkey. Now what is this better done, as Turks doe? Yea, rather is it worse for them, which say they are Christians; for we hear that ^{ye} most part of such negers are brought hither against their will and consent, and that many of them are stolen. Now, ^{tho} they are black, we can not conceive there is more liberty to have them slaves, as it is to have other white ones. There is a saying, that we shall doe to all men like as we will be done ourselves; making no difference of what generation, descent or colour they are. And those who steal or robb men, and those who buy or purchase them, are they not all alike? Here is liberty of conscience, ^{wch} is right and reasonable; here ought to be likewise liberty of ^{ye} body, except of evil-doers, ^{wch} is an other

The Germantown Friends' Protest against Slavery, 1688. Philadelphia [1879].

case. But to bring men hither, or to rob and sell them against their will, we stand against. In Europe there are many oppressed for conscience sake; and here there are those oppressed ^{wh} are of a black colour. And we who know that men must not comitt adultery, – some do commit adultery, in others, separating wives from their husbands and giving them to others; and some sell the children of these poor creatures to other men. Ah! doe consider well this thing, you who doe it, if you would be done at this manner? and if it is done according to Christianity? You surpass Holland and Germany in this thing. This makes an ill report in all those countries of Europe. where they hear off, that ^{ye} Quakers doe here handel men as they handel there ^{ye} cattle. And for that reason some have no mind or inclination to come hither. And who shall maintain this your cause, or pleid for it? Truly we can not do so, except you shall inform us better hereof, viz, that Christians have liberty to practise these things. Pray, what thing in the world can be done worse towards us, than if men should rob or steal us away, and sell us for slaves to strange countries; separating housbands from their wives and children. Being now this is not done in the manner we would be done at therefore we contradict and are against this traffic of men-body. And we who profess that it is not lawful to steal, must, likewise, avoid to purchase such things as are stolen, but rather help to stop this robbing and stealing if possible. And such men ought to be delivered out of ^{ye} hands of ^{ye} robbers, and set free as well as in Europe. Then is Pennsylvania to have a good report, instead it hath now a bad one for this sake in other countries. Especially whereas ^{ye} Europeans are desirous to know in what manner ^{ye} Quakers doe rule in their province; – and most of them doe look upon us with an envious eye. But if this is done well, what shall we say is done evil?

If once these slaves (^{wch} they say are so wicked and stubbern men) should joint themselves, – fight for their freedom. – and handel their masters and mastrisses as they did handel them before; will these masters and mastrisses take the sword at hand and warr against these poor slaves, licke, we are able to believe, some will not refuse to doe; or have these negers not as much right to fight for their freedom, as you have to keep them slaves?

Now consider well this thing, if it is good or bad? And in case you find it to be good to handel these blacks at that manner, we desire and require you hereby lovingly, that you may inform us herein, which at this time never was done, viz., that Christians have such a liberty to do so. To the end we shall be satisfied in this point, and satisfie likewise our good friends and acquaintances in our natif country, to whose it is a terror, or fairful thing, that men should be handeld so in Pennsylvania.

This is from our meeting at Germantown, held ^{ye} 18 of the 2 month, 1688, to be delivered to the Monthly Meeting at Richard Worrel's.

> Garret henderich
> derick up de graeff
> Francis daniell Pastorius
> Abraham up Den graef.

At our Monthly Meeting at Dublin, ^{ye} 30–2 mo., 1688, we having inspected ye matter, above mentioned, and considered of it, we find it so weighty that we think it not expedient for us to meddle with it here, but do rather commit it to ^{ye} consideration of ^{ye} Quarterly Meeting; ^{ye} tenor of it being nearly related to ^{ye} Truth.

> On behalf of ^{ye} Monthly Meeting,
> Signed,   P.   Jo. Hart.

This, above mentioned, was read in our Quarterly Meeting at Philadelphia, the 4 of ^{ye} 4th mo. '88, and was from thence recommended to the Yearly Meeting, and the above said Derick, and the other two mentioned therein, to present the same to ^{ye} above said meeting, it being a thing of too great a weight for this meeting to determine.

> Signed by order of ^{ye} meeting,
> Anthony Morris.

Yearly Meeting Minute on the above Protest.

At a Yearly Meeting held at Burlington the 5th day of the 7th month, 1688.

A Paper being here presented by some German Friends Concerning the Lawfulness and Unlawfulness of Buying and keeping Negroes, It was adjudged not to be so proper for this Meeting to give a Positive Judgment in the Case, It having so General a Relation to many other Parts, and therefore at present they forbear It.

Bibliography

PRIMARY TEXTS

An Abridgement of the Laws in Force and Use in Her Majesty's Plantations (London, 1704).

Acosta, José de, *De Natura Novi Orbis Libri II, et de promulgatione Evangelii apud barbaros, sive de procuranda Indorum salute, libri VI* (Cologne, 1596). [*Two Books on the Nature of the New World, and Six on Spreading the Gospel among the Savages; or, on Obtaining the Salvation of the Indians.*]

The Acts of Assembly Now in Force, in the Colony of Virginia (Williamsburg, 1752).

Adis, Henry, *A Letter Sent from Syrranam, to his Excellency, the Lord Willoughby of Parham* (London, 1664).

Bandele, 'Biyi, *Aphra Behn's "Oroonoko"* (Charlbury: Amber Lane Press, 1999).

Behn, Aphra , *Oroonoko*, ed. Janet Todd (Harmondsworth: Penguin, 2003).

——— *Oroonoko*, ed. Joanna Lipking (New York: Norton, 1997).

——— *The Works of Aphra Behn*, ed. Janet Todd, 7 vols. (London: Pickering & Chatto, 1992–96).

Biet, Antoine, *Voyage de la France équinoxiale en l'Isle Cayenne* (Paris, 1664).

[Blome, Richard], *The Present State of His Majesties Isles and Territories in America* (London, 1687).

Blount, Charles, [Charles] Gildon, et al., *The Oracles of Reason* (London, 1693).

Breton, Raymond, *Dictionnaire caraïbe-français* (Auxerre, 1665).

Bruce, Susan, ed., *Three Early Modern Utopias: Thomas More, "Utopia," Francis Bacon, "New Atlantis," Henry Neville, "The Isle of Pines"* (Oxford: Oxford University Press, 1999).

Byam, William, *An Exact Relation of the Most Execrable Attempts of John Allin* (1665).

Clarke, Samuel, *A True and Faithful Account of the Four Chiefest Plantations of the English in America* (London, 1670).

A Compleat Collection of the Laws of Maryland (Annapolis, 1727).

Davenant, William, *The History of Sir Francis Drake*.

Dekker, Thomas, *The Dramatic Works of Thomas Dekker*, ed. Fredson Bowers, 4 vols. (Cambridge: Cambridge University Press, 1953–61).

Donne, John, *Foure Sermons upon Special Occasions* (London, 1625).

Dryden, John, *The Works of John Dryden*, ed. Edward Niles Hooker et al., 20 vols. (Berkeley, Los Angeles, and London: University of California Press, 1956–2000).

Du Tertre, Jean-Baptiste, *Histoire générale des Antilles habitées par les François*, 4 vols. (Paris, 1667–71).

Frazer, Sir James George, *The Golden Bough*, abridged and ed. Robert Fraser (Oxford and New York: Oxford University Press, 1994).

Gage, Thomas, *The English-American his Travail by Sea and Land* (London, 1648).

Godwyn, Morgan, *The Negro's & Indians Advocate* (London, 1680).

Great Newes from the Barbadoes (London, 1676).

Harcourt, Robert, *A Relation of a Voyage to Guiana* (London, 1613).

Hariot, Thomas, *A Brief and True Report of the New Found Land of Virginia*, 2nd ed. (Frankfurt am Main, 1590).

La Borde, Sieur de, *Relation de l'Origine, Moeurs, Coustumes, Religion, Guerres et Voyages des Caraibes* (n.p., 1684).

La Calprenède, Gauthier de Costes, Sieur de, *Cassandra*, trans. Sir Charles Cotterell (London, 1661).

—— *Hymen's Præludia*, trans. Robert Loveday (London, 1674). (Translation of *Cléopâtre*, 1647–58).

Las Casas, Bartolemé de, *The Tears of the Ladies*, trans. John Phillips (London, 1656).

Léry, Jean de, *A History of a Voyage to the Land of Brazil*, trans. Janet Whatley (Berkeley, Los Angeles, Oxford: University of California Press, 1990).

Ligon, Richard, *A True and Exact History of the Island of Barbados* (London, 1673).

Locke, John, *An Essay Concerning Human Understanding*, ed. Peter H. Nidditch (Oxford: Clarendon Press, 1979).

—— *The Fundamental Constitutions of Carolina* (London, 1670).

Loddington, William, *Plantation Work the Work of this Generation* (London, 1682).

Middleton, Thomas, *Anything for a Quiet Life* (London, 1662).

Milton, John, *Paradise Lost*, ed. Alastair Fowler (London: Longman, 1971).

Montaigne, Michel Eyquem de, *Essays*, trans. John Florio (London, 1613).

Neville, Henry, *The Isle of Pines* (London, 1668).

Ogilby, John, *Africa* (London, 1670).

—— *America* (London, 1671).

P., J., *A Complete Collection of All the Laws of Virginia now in Force* (London, 1684).

Penn, William, *A Letter from William Penn... To the Committee of the Free Society of Traders of that Province, residing in London* (London, 1683).

Raleigh, Sir Walter, *Discoverie of the Large, Rich, and Bewtifull Empire of Guiana* (London, 1596).

Rochefort, Charles de, *The History of the Caribby-Islands*, trans. John Davies of Kidwelly (London, 1666).

Sanford, Robert, *Surinam Justice* (London, 1662).

Sepúlveda, Juan Ginés de, *Democrates Secundus*, in Juan Ginés de Sepúlveda, *Obras completas*, ed. E. Rodríguez Peregrina and B. Cuart Moner, III (Pozoblanco, 1995–).

Shadwell, Thomas, *The Virtuoso*, ed. Marjorie Hope Nicolson and David Rodes, Regents Restoration Drama Series (Lincoln: University of Nebraska Press, 1966).

Shakespeare, William, *The Norton Shakespeare*, ed. Stephen Greenblatt et al. (New York and London: Norton, 1997).

Southerne, Thomas, *Oroonoko*, ed. Maximillian E. Novak and David Stuart Rodes (Lincoln: University of Nebraska Press, 1976).

—— *The Works of Thomas Southerne*, ed. Robert Jordan and Harold Love, 2 vols. (Oxford: Clarendon Press, 1988).

Tavernier, Jean Baptiste, *A New Relation of the Inner-Part of the Grand Seignior's Seraglio* [1675] (London, 1684).

Trott, Nicholas, ed., *The Laws of the Province of South-Carolina*, 2 vols. (Charles-Town, 1736).

Tryon, Thomas, *Friendly Advice to the Gentlemen Planters of the East and West Indies* (London, 1684).

—— *The Way to Health, Long Life, and Happiness* (London, 1683).

Villault, Nicolas, Sieur de Bellefond, *A Relation of the Coasts of Africk Called Guinee* (London, 1670).

Warren, George, *An Impartial Description of Surinam* (London, 1667).

SECONDARY WORKS

Armitage, David, *The Ideological Origins of the British Empire*, Ideas in Context, 59 (Cambridge: Cambridge University Press, 2000).

Ballaster, Ros, "New Hystericism: Aphra Behn's *Oroonoko*: The Body, the Text and the Feminist Critic," in *New Feminist Discourses: Critical Essays on Theories and Texts*, ed. Isobel Armstrong (London: Routledge, 1992), 283–95.

Beach, Adam R., "Anti-Colonist Discourse, Tragicomedy, and the 'American' Behn," *Comparative Drama* 38 (2004), 213–33.

Beckles, Hilary McD., *White Servitude and Black Slavery in Barbados, 1627–1715* (Knoxville: University of Tennessee Press, 1989).

Brown, Laura, "The Romance of Empire: *Oroonoko* and the Trade in Slaves," in *The New 18th Century*, ed. Felicity Nussbaum and Laura Brown (New York: Methuen, 1987), 41–61, reprinted in Laura Brown, *Ends of Empire: Women and Ideology in Early Eighteenth-Century English Literature* (Ithaca and London: Cornell University Press, 1993), 23–63, and Janet Todd, ed., *Aphra Behn* (Basingstoke: Macmillan, 1999), 180–208.

Canny, Nicholas, and Anthony Pagden, eds, *Colonial Identity in the Atlantic World: 1500–1800* (Princeton; Guildford: Princeton University Press, 1987).

Chernaik, Warren, "Captains and Slaves: Aphra Behn and the Rhetoric of Republicanism," *Seventeenth Century* 17 (2002), 97–107.

Chibka, Robert L., "'Oh! Do Not Fear a Woman's Invention': Truth, Falsehood, and Fiction in Aphra Behn's *Oroonoko*," *Texas Studies in Literature and Language* 30 (1988), 510–37.

Colley, Linda, *Captives* (London: Jonathan Cape, 2002).

Crump, Thomas, *The Anthropology of Numbers* (Cambridge: Cambridge University Press, 1990).

Cuder-Dominguez, Pilar, "Of Spain, Moors, and Women: The Tragedies of Aphra Behn and Mary Pix," in *Re-Shaping the Genres: Restoration Women Writers*, ed. Zenón Luis-Martínez and Jorge Figueroa-Dorrego (Bern: Peter Lang, 2003), 157–73.

Dhuicq, Bernard, "Further Evidence of Aphra Behn's Stay in Surinam," *Notes and Queries* 26 (1979), 524–26.

——— "New Evidence on Aphra Behn's Stay in Surinam," *Notes and Queries* 42 (1995), 40–41.

Dunn, Richard S., *Sugar and Slaves: The Rise of the Planter Class in the English West Indies, 1624–1713* (London: Cape, 1973).

Elliott, J. H., *The Old World and the New, 1492–1650* (Cambridge: University Press, 1970).

Ferguson, Margaret W., *Dido's Daughters: Literacy, Gender, and Empire in Early Modern England and France* (Chicago: University of Chicago Press, 2003).

——— "Juggling the Categories of Race, Class, and Gender: Aphra Behn's *Oroonoko*," *Women's Studies* 19 (1991), 159–81, reprinted in Margo Hendricks and Patricia Parker, eds., *Women, "Race," and Writing in the Early Modern Period* (London: Routledge, 1994), 209–24, and in Janet Todd, ed., *Aphra Behn* (Basingstoke: MacMillan, 1999), 209–33.

——— "News from the New World: Miscegenous Romance in Aphra Behn's *Oroonoko* and *The Widow Ranter*," in *The Production of English Renaissance Culture*, ed. David Lee Miller, Sharon O'Dair, and Harold Weber (Ithaca: Cornell University Press, 1994), 151–89.

——— "Transmuting *Othello*: Aphra Behn's *Oroonoko*," in *Cross-Cultural Performances: Differences in Women's Re-Visions of Shakespeare*, ed. Marianne Novy and Peter Erickson (Urbana: University of Illinois Press, 1993), 15–49.

Ferguson, Moira, "*Oroonoko*: Birth of a Paradigm," *New Literary History* 23 (1992), 339–59.

Finch, G. J., "Hawkesworth's Adaptation of Southerne's *Oroonoko*," *Restoration and 18th Century Theatre Research* 16 (1977), 41–43.

Ford, Worthington Chauncey, ed., *The Isle of Pines, 1668. An Essay in Bibliography* (Boston: Club of Odd Volumes, 1920).

Frohock, Richard, "Violence and Awe: The Foundations of Government in Aphra Behn's New World Settings," *Eighteenth-Century Fiction* 8 (1996), 437–52, reprinted in *Women at Sea: Travel Writing and the Margins of Caribbean*

Discourse, ed. Lizabeth Paravisini-Gebert and Ivette Romero-Cesareo (New York: Palgrave; 2001), 41–58.

Galenson, David W., *White Servitude in Colonial America: An Economic Analysis* (Cambridge: Cambridge University Press, 1981).

Gallagher, Catherine, "Oroonoko's Blackness," in *Aphra Behn Studies*, ed. Janet Todd (Cambridge: Cambridge University Press), 235–58, reprinted in *Nobody's Story: The Vanishing Acts of Women Writers in the Marketplace, 1670–1820* (Oxford: Oxford University Press, 1994), 49–87.

Grafton, Anthony, *New Worlds, Ancient Texts: The Power of Tradition and the Shock of Discovery* (Cambridge, MA: Harvard University Press, 1992).

Greenblatt, Stephen, *Marvellous Possessions: The Wonder of the New World* (Chicago: University of Chicago Press, 1991).

Hoegberg, David E., "Caesar's Toils: Allusion and Rebellion in *Oroonoko*," *Eighteenth-Century Fiction*, 7 (1995), 239–58, reprinted in *The Eighteenth-Century English Novel*, ed. Harold Bloom (Philadelphia: Chelsea House; 2004), 329–46.

Holmesland, Oddvar, "Aphra Behn's *Oroonoko*: Cultural Dialectics and the Novel," *ELH* 68 (2001), 57–79.

Hudson, Nicholas. "From 'Nation' to 'Race,'" *Eighteenth-Century Studies* 29 (1996), 247–66.

Hughes, Derek, "Race, Gender, and Scholarly Practice: Aphra Behn's *Oroonoko*," *Essays in Criticism* 52 (2002), 1–22.

——— *The Theatre of Aphra Behn* (Basingstoke and New York: Palgrave, 2001).

Hughes, Derek, and Janet Todd, eds., *The Cambridge Companion to Aphra Behn* (Cambridge: Cambridge University Press, 2004).

Hulme, Peter, *Colonial Encounters: Europe and the Native Caribbean, 1492–1797* (London: Methuen, 1986).

Hulme, Peter, and Neil L. Whitehead, eds., *Wild Majesty: Encounters with Caribs from Columbus to the Present Day* (Oxford: Oxford University Press, 1992).

Hutner, Heidi, ed., *Rereading Aphra Behn: History, Theory, and Criticism* (Charlottesville: University Press of Virginia, 1993).

Ifrah, Georges. *The Universal History of Numbers: From Prehistory to the Invention of the Computer*, trans. David Bellos et al. (London: Harvill Press, 1998).

Iwanisziw, Susan B., "Behn's Novel Investment in *Oroonoko*: Kingship, Slavery and Tobacco in English Colonialism," *South Atlantic Review* 63 (1998), 75–98.

Jones, Jane, "New Light on the Background and Early Life of Aphra Behn," *Notes and Queries* 37 (1990), 288–93.

Jordan, Winthrop, *White over Black: American Attitudes Toward the Negro, 1550–1812* (Chapel Hill: University of North Carolina Press, 1968).

Kaul, Suvir, "Reading Literary Symptoms: Colonial Pathologies and the *Oroonoko* Fictions of Behn, Southerne, and Hawkesworth," *Eighteenth-Century Life* 18 (1994), 80–96.

Klein, Herbert S., *African Slavery in Latin America and the Caribbean* (New York: Oxford University Press, 1986).

——— *The Atlantic Slave Trade* (Cambridge: Cambridge University Press, 1999).

———— *The Middle Passage: Comparative Studies in the Atlantic Slave Trade* (Princeton: Princeton University Press, 1978).

Kroll, Richard, "'Tales of Love and Gallantry': The Politics of *Oroonoko*," *Huntington Library Quarterly* 67 (2004), 573–605.

Kupperman, Karen Ordahl, ed., *America in European Consciousness, 1493–1750* (Chapel Hill and London: University of North Carolina Press, 1995)

———— *Indians and English: Facing Off in Early America* (Ithaca, N.Y.; London: Cornell University Press, 2000).

Lestringant, Frank, *Mapping the Renaissance World: The Geographical Imagination in the Age of Discovery*, trans. David Fausett (Los Angeles: University of California Press, 1994).

Lipking, Joanna, "Confusing Matters: Searching the Backgrounds of *Oroonoko*," in *Aphra Behn Studies*, ed. Janet Todd (Cambridge: Cambridge University Press), 259–81.

———— "'Others', Slaves, and Colonists in *Oroonoko*," in *The Cambridge Companion to Aphra Behn*, ed. Derek Hughes and Janet Todd (Cambridge: Cambridge University Press, 2004), 166–87.

Louis, William Roger, ed., *The Oxford History of the British Empire*, 5 vols. (Oxford: Oxford University Press, 1998–99).

MacDonald, Joyce Green, "The Disappearing African Woman: Imoinda in *Oroonoko* after Behn," *ELH* 66 (1999), 71–86.

———— "Gender, Family, and Race in Aphra Behn's *Abdelazer*," in *Aphra Behn (1640–1689), Identity, Alterity, Ambiguity*, ed. Mary Ann O'Donnell, Bernard Dhuicq, and Guyonne Leduc (Paris: Harmattan, 2000), 67–73.

———— "Race, Women, and the Sentimental in Thomas Southerne's *Oroonoko*," *Criticism* 40 (1998), 555–70.

Manning, Patrick, ed., *Slave Trades, 1500–1800: Globalization of Forced Labour* (Aldershot and Brookfield: Variorum, 1996).

Mignolo, Walter D., *The Darker Side of the Renaissance: Literacy, Territoriality, and Colonization*, 2nd ed. (Ann Arbor: University of Michigan Press, 1995).

Munns, Jessica, "Reviving *Oroonoko* 'in the Scene': From Thomas Southerne to 'Biyi Bandele," in *Troping "Oroonoko" from Behn to Bandele*, ed. Susan B. Iwanisziw (Aldershot and Burlington: Ashgate, 2004), 174–97.

Nash, Gary B. "The Hidden History of Mestizo America," in *Sex, Love, Race: Crossing Boundaries in North American History*, ed. Martha Hodes (New York and London: New York University Press, 1999), 10–32.

O'Donnell, Mary Ann, *Aphra Behn: An Annotated Bibliography of Primary and Secondary Sources* (New York: Garland, 1986).

Pacheco, Anita, "Royalism and Honor in Aphra Behn's *Oroonoko*," *Studies in English Literature, 1500–1900* 34 (1994), 491–506.

Pagden, Anthony, *European Encounters with the New World: From Renaissance to Romanticism* (New Haven: Yale University Press, 1993).

———— *The Fall of Natural Man: The American Indian and the Origins of Comparative Ethnology* (Cambridge: Cambridge University Press, 1982).

Quint, David, *Epic and Empire: Politics and Generic Form from Virgil to Milton* (Princeton: Princeton University Press, 1992).

Rinaldo, Peter M., *Marrying the Natives: Love and Interracial Marriage* (Briarcliff Manor, NY: Dorpete Press, 1996).

Rivero, Albert J., "Aphra Behn's *Oroonoko* and the 'Blank Spaces' of Colonial Fictions," *Studies in English Literature, 1500–1900* 39 (1999), 443–62.

Rosenthal, Laura J., "*Oroonoko*: Reception, Ideology, and Narrative Strategy," in *The Cambridge Companion to Aphra Behn*, ed. Derek Hughes and Janet Todd (Cambridge: Cambridge University Press, 2004), 151–65.

——— "Owning Oroonoko: Behn, Southerne, and the Contingencies of Property," *Renaissance Drama* 23 (1992), 25–38.

Rubik, Margarete, "Estranging the Familiar, Familiarizing the Strange: Self and Other in *Oroonoko* and *The Widdow Ranter*," in *Aphra Behn (1640–1689), Identity, Alterity, Ambiguity*, ed. Mary Ann O'Donnell, Bernard Dhuicq, and Guyonne Leduc (Paris: Harmattan, 2000), 33–41.

Sandiford, Keith A., *The Cultural Politics of Sugar: Caribbean Slavery and Narratives of Colonialism* (Cambridge: Cambridge University Press, 2000).

Schwartz, Stuart B., ed., *Implicit Understandings: Observing, Reporting, and Reflecting on the Encounters Between Europeans and Other Peoples in the Early Modern Era* (Cambridge and New York: Cambridge University Press, 1994).

Smith, Abbot Emmerson, *Colonists in Bondage: White Servitude and Convict Labor in America, 1607–1776* (Chapel Hill: University of North Carolina Press, 1947).

Steele, Ian K., *The English Atlantic 1675–1740: An Exploration of Communication and Community* (New York and Oxford: Oxford University Press, 1986).

Sussman, Charlotte, "The Other Problem with Women: Reproduction and Slave Culture in Aphra Behn's *Oroonoko*," in *Rereading Aphra Behn: History, Theory, and Criticism*, ed. Heidi Hutner (Charlottesville: University Press of Virginia, 1993), 212–33.

Thomas, Susie, "This Thing of Darkness I Acknowledge Mine: Aphra Behn's *Abdelazer, or, The Moor's Revenge*," *Restoration* 22 (1998), 18–39.

Todd, Janet, ed., *Aphra Behn* (Basingstroke: Macmillan, 1999).

——— ed., *Aphra Behn Studies* (Cambridge: Cambridge University Press, 1996).

——— *The Secret Life of Aphra Behn*, revised ed. (London, New York, and Sydney: Pandora, 2000).

——— "Spectacular Deaths: History and Story in Aphra Behn's *Love Letters*, *Oroonoko* and *The Widow Ranter*," in *Gender, Art, and Death*, ed. Janet Todd (Cambridge: Polity Press, 1993), 32–62.

Vaughan, Alden T., *Roots of American Racism: Essays on the Colonial Experience* (New York and Oxford: Oxford University Press, 1995).

Visconsi, Elliott, "A Degenerate Race: English Barbarism in Aphra Behn's *Oroonoko* and *The Widow Ranter*," *ELH*, 69 (2002), 673–701.

Wallace, Elizabeth Kowaleski, "Transnationalism and Performance in 'Biyi Bandele's Oroonoko," *PMLA* 119 (2004), 265–81.

Index